THE MAGIC OF

1817

HARPER & ROW, PUBLISHERS, New York
Cambridge, Philadelphia, San Francisco
London, Mexico City, São Paulo, Sydney

OBELISKS

PETER TOMPKINS

FIRST EDITION

Designer: Gayle Jaeger

Library of Congress Cataloging in Publication Data

Tompkins, Peter.
  The magic of obelisks.
  Bibliography: p.
  Includes index.
    1. Obelisks—Egypt—Miscellanea. 2. Occult sciences—Egypt—
Miscellanea. 3. Egyptian language—Writing, Hieroglyphic—Miscellanea.
I. Title.
DT62.02T65   932   81-47239
ISBN 0-06-014899-3   AACR2

81 82 83 84 85 10 9 8 7 6 5 4 3 2 1

CONTENTS

PICTURE CREDITS

For photographic reproduction and organization, I am much indebted to Nicholas Vreeland, Ptolemy Tompkins, Edward O. Mitchell, Bert Stamler, Eddie Becker, and in particular to Lizabeth Loughran, Musa Train, Rebecca Myers, and Dolores Martin.

For permission to reproduce illustrations, I am indebted to:

Manly P. Hall of the Philosophical Research Society of Los Angeles, California, for the portrait of Francis Bacon, page 85, which shows his identity with the Canonical Shakespeare, and the illustration, page 150, from his reprint of *La très sainte trisonophie.*

Iowa State Archaeologist for the drawings from *The Davenport Conspiracy* by Marshall Baseford McKusic, pages 341, 342, 344.

New York Times Books, New York, for the illustration from *America B.C.* by Barry Fell, page 348.

Epigraphic Society, San Diego, California, for the illustration from *Occasional Papers* by Barry Fell, page 353 (bottom).

Tryckbaren, Lund, Sweden, for drawings from *Ritual Lovemaking and Punishment in Egyptian Myths* by Oscar Reutersvard, pages 361, 449.

Turnstone Press, Wellingborough, England, for illustrations from *Needles of Stone* by Tom Graves © copyright 1978 by Tom Graves, pages 373 (top), 374, 375 (bottom), 382, 383 (bottom), 386.

Thames & Hudson, London, for the drawing in *Ley Hunter's Companion* by Paul Devereux, page 378.

Noonday Press, New York, for the drawing adapted by Tom Graves in *Selected Writings* by Wilhelm Reich, page 383 (top).

Miss Lucie Lamy for illustrations from *Le Temple de l'homme* by R. A. Schwaller de Lubicz (Dervy Livres, Paris) and from *Her-Bak* by Isha Schwaller de Lubicz (Inner Tradition International, Ltd., New York), pages 422, 424, 425, 427.

Ithell Colquhoun, for illustration from *Sword of Wisdom* (Putnam, New York), page 416.

ACKNOWLEDGMENTS

A long list of those who have helped this book to life would be a sorry substitute for the thanks I owe them. Each cheerful donor knows the invaluable measure of his contribution, and what it did for the work. If ever an effort was joint, this is it. But the Inquisition is not dead, and I would not wish for them to be tarred for a heresy the responsibility for which is solely mine. But I can without scruple thank my publisher, and all those who so willingly labored there without prejudice, and I can thank the Librarian of Congress—without whom this book would not be—in the hope that he and his successors will reconstitute in this our New Atlantis a library wherein the ashes of Pergamum and Alexandria may, like our emblematic bird, live again, and from whose stacks no book shall evermore be burned or branded as heretical.

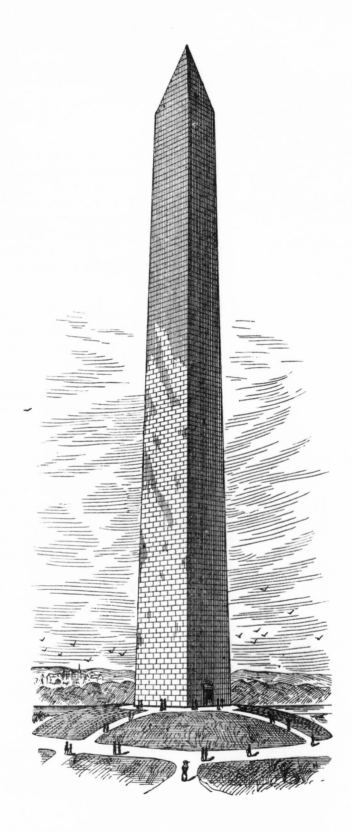

Washington National Monument

1. HISTORICAL BACKGROUND

The most stunning and prestigious monument in the capital of the United States is an enormous obelisk, named for the founder of the country, George Washington, a thirty-third-degree Mason. It is the tallest such monument in the world, 555 feet high, though not truly an obelisk, because it is not quarried from a single piece but put together from 36,000 separate blocks of granite faced with marble.

New York has a true obelisk, brought there from Egypt in 1880 at the substantial cost at that time of $100,000 to stand in Central Park near the Metropolitan Museum of Art. European capitals such as London, Paris, Rome, and Constantinople have their obelisks, also brought from Egypt, the apparent source of the fashion at least five thousand years ago, though where the Egyptians got the notion is a matter of conjecture.

In ancient Egypt there were a great many obelisks. The pharaoh Seti I, son of Ramses I and father of Ramses II, who reigned in the second half of the second millennium B.C., boasted that he alone fairly "filled Heliopolis with obelisks." This city of the sun, as it was called by the Greeks—the On of the Old Testament and the modern El Mataria, near Cairo—must have been an extraordinary sight standing on a rocky plateau in Lower Egypt, with its forest of slender gilded obelisks reflecting sunlight into the bright clear air of the wide Nile Delta.

Obelisks had already been raised at Memphis and Thebes by Thothmes III, named after Thoth, the Egyptian god of learning and science. Thothmes, whose reign is dated from the beginning of the sixteenth century B.C., is considered by many Egyptologists to have been the greatest pharaoh in the country's history. One of his more beautiful obelisks is now in New York. Another is in London. Thothmes brought the tallest standing obelisk in Egypt, 106 feet high, to Karnak, which already had at least thirteen such monoliths. It now stands in the square of Saint John Lateran in Rome. Thothmes's stepmother, Queen Hatshepsut, who was also his rival, raised four more (slightly smaller) obelisks in Karnak.

The next great name in Egyptian conquerors and obelisk raisers was Ramses II. This Nineteenth Dynasty king, who is said to have reigned for most of the thirteenth century B.C., is credited with having raised fourteen obelisks at

1

Obelisk reraised in Constantinople by the emperor Theodosius In A.D. 390. Originally more than 100 feet tall, it was reduced to half that size in transit from Egypt, where it had been originally raised in Karnak by Thothmes III.

Two of Queen Hatshepsut's obelisks being floated down to Thebes from Aswan. Pliny tells how Ptolemy Philadelphus later brought Nectabis' obelisk to Alexandria. From the Nile he dug a canal to where the monolith lay. He then filled two flat-bottomed barges with granite blocks equalling twice the weight of the obelisk, and floated the barges under the needle. As the barges were unloaded they rose to accept the obelisk and float it away.

Tanis alone; but his most renowned examples are the two he placed outside the Temple of Luxor in Thebes, one of which is now in Paris's Place de la Concorde.

The Roman historian Pliny the Elder, who died in the eruption of Vesuvius in A.D. 79, tells how Ramses, with the help of 100,000 workers, brought down to Heliopolis a great obelisk, all of 162 feet high. To prevent the workers from being careless with the dangerous machinery needed to raise such a monster, he had his son tied to the top of the obelisk. To save the one, workers must save the other—and thus their heads. Not that Ramses II ran much risk of losing an only heir: he is reputed to have fathered several dozen sons. The task was successfully accomplished; though what became of the obelisk, nobody knows.

Three of the most eminent historians of the ancient world, Herodotus, Diodorus Siculus, and Pliny, all tell the story of another pharaoh who raised two great obelisks at On. While crossing the Nile, this monarch is said to have been caught in a terrible storm, so menacing that the turbulent waters became a threat to his life. Outraged, the pharaoh is described as having seized a lance and hurled it into the seething river. The Nile, so the story goes, was offended, and struck the pharaoh blind. Nor could anyone cure him, though he tried a variety of doctors. Then an oracle informed the king of a remedy: he must bathe his eyes in the urine of a married woman who had slept *only* with her husband. With the help of his beautiful queen, the pharaoh daily bathed his eyes in the manner prescribed; but he still remained blind. In despair, he experimented with several more women until at last he found one who cured him. Those who had failed, he collected into a city called Zolla Rossa, and had them burned—women and city. The faithful lady with the successful remedy, he married. And so happy was this monarch, say the historians, that he raised all kinds of monuments in Egypt, including two huge obelisks, each reputedly 100 cubits

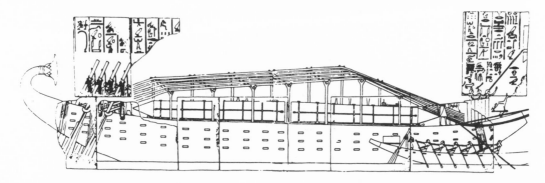

Dragging Constantine's obelisk to be raised in the Byzantine Hippodrome

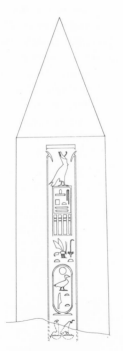

The obelisk of Teti, the earliest known true obelisk

high—which would be 165 feet—dedicated to the sanctuary of the sun. What happened to these, nobody knows; and if one had to rely on "classical" Greek and Roman authors to find out how such great obelisks were raised or what their real purpose may have been, one would be left ill informed.

There are other records—some more, some less plausible—of very ancient obelisks farther up the Nile, as far as Philae and Elephantine, by the first cataract, and even as far south as Soleb in Nubia. Available records of obelisks extend back to the Old Kingdom, with its first four dynasties, dated by Egyptologists to the third millenium B.C., whose pharaohs are credited with having built the Great Pyramids on the Giza plateau. But no obelisk of this era is known to exist. The records tell that Sahure, and other pharaohs of the Fifth Dynasty, built magnificent temples, such as the Temple of Neurine at Absia, adorned with obelisks, only parts of which survived. The earliest example of a complete needle appears to be that of King Senusret I of the Twelfth Dynasty, found at Heliopolis.

Fragments of earlier obelisks, attributed to King Entef of the Eleventh Dynasty, date back to the end of the third millennium B.C. Though broken, their hieroglyphs have been well preserved, thanks to the protective coating of sand under which they were buried. Only no one yet knows what these particular hieroglyphs mean. Recent excavations show that these obelisks differ from later, more familiar ones, being shorter and squatter, and having taller masonry bases, sometimes as long as one-third of their shaft. According to Egyptologists, the longer bases were re-

3

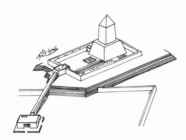

Pharaohs of the Fifth Dynasty added to their pyramid complexes vast solar temples built around a huge benben. But these early needles, rather than true monoliths, were obeliscoid structures composed of separate blocks raised high on a truncated pyramid.

quired to raise these sacred "pryamidions," or *benben* as the Egyptians called them, nearer to the sun. In fact, there may have been other reasons, both occult and scientific.

Of the hundreds of obelisks that once stood in Egypt, only nine still stand; ten more lie broken, victims of infuriated conquerors, or of the religious fanaticism of competing cults. The rest are buried or have been carried away to foreign lands to dwell in dumb mimicry of Egyptian grandeur.

The first conquerer to remove an Egyptian obelisk was the Assyrian monarch Assurbanipal, better known by his Greek name of Sardanapalus, who ravaged Thebes in 664 B.C. and carried away two obelisks to his palace at Nineveh, presumably floating them down the Red Sea, across the Indian Ocean, up the Persian Gulf to the Tigris, and thence to Nineveh, some 1,600 miles away.

Sardanapalus in his harem

The next foreign conqueror, seeking to undo humiliation suffered at the hands of both Thothmes III and Ramses II, was the Persian leader Cambyses (or Kembathet), who defeated the Egyptian pharaoh Psametic III near Pelusium in a battle in which the Persians killed fifty thousand Egyptians. With the help of the battle fleet of the Phoenicians, who had also suffered repeatedly at the hands of pharaohs, the Persians swept the Egyptian navy from the seas, and made themselves masters of Egypt. Marching his army through the delta, Cambyses desolated the land with fire and sword till he came to the great city of On, which he took by storm and set on fire. In the holocaust that followed, the great Temple of the Sun was destroyed. Obelisks were dragged to the ground and mutilated, the

4

Constantine I, known as the Great (A.D. 280–337), bastard son of emperor Constantius I, became the first Christian emperor after defeating Maxentius at the gates of Rome.

most hated specimens being those that bore the inscriptions of the cruel deeds Thothmes III and Ramses II had performed against the Persians. Only when fire reached the base of one magnificent obelisk over 100 feet tall, did Cambyses, apparently out of admiration for its size (or so we are told by Pliny), relent and make his followers extinguish the flames.

Later conquerors of Egypt removed one or more obelisks as souvenirs. After the Macedonian generals of Alexander the Great had subdued Egypt and established a Ptolemaic line of Egyptianized Greek pharaohs, who ruled for three centuries, the Romans in 30 B.C. reduced the once proud kingdom to a province of Imperial Rome. It was their turn to loot Egypt of its obelisks. But first, in commemoration of their conquest, they built in Alexandria a great temple known as the Caesarium, or Palace of the Caesars. Started by Cleopatra after the birth of Cesarion, her son by Julius Caesar, the palace grew into the tallest and most impressive building in the city, surrounded by a sacred grove, embellished by porticoes, complete with library and works of art. As sentinels to guard its grand water-gate entrance, Julius Caesar's adoptive son Augustus, as Rome's first emperor, brought from Heliopolis, where they had stood for a millennium and a half, two great obelisks which came to be known as Cleopatra's needles. One is now in London, the other in New York.

Transporting and raising obelisks was no easy task, even for such expert engineers as the Romans. Although the records of Roman operations with obelisks are almost as incomplete as those of the Egyptians, Vitruvius, architect and military engineer to Augustus—claimed by modern Freemasons as one of their own—writes that the motive power for raising such enormous weights came from men working in a squirrel cage, thereby gaining a wheel-and-axle mechanical advantage. Vitruvius also describes a large two-legged shears for supporting tackle with which to raise an obelisk and set it on its base. But just how the job was really done remains a mystery.

Somehow, the Egyptians had developed a means of placing these huge blocks of granite directly onto a cubical pedestal which had to be absolutely level in order to have the apex of the obelisk truly vertical over its base—no easy task. The Romans, either because they could not match this expertise or because their obelisks had been injured at the base—by Persians or in transport—came up with a system of wedging astragals, or metal footings, to a column, between the base of the obelisk and the top of the pedestal. For this purpose the

5

The standing obelisk at Heliopolis is the oldest known surviving needle in Egypt. Twenty meters high, it weighs 121 tons. From the inscription on it, Egyptologists have deduced it was raised on the jubilee of pharaoh Sesostris I in 1942 B.C. Heliopolis, with its Temple to the Sun, "its 13,000 priests chanting before a huge mirror of burnished gold, the sacred hawk in the golden cage, the pyramidal ben-ben, and the sacred calf Mnevis on its purple bed," was the greatest theological center in ancient Egypt. There the pyramid texts, the largest single collection of religious compositions yet recovered from early Egypt, were mostly composed by Heliopolitan priests. Of the ancient city, with its scores of obelisks, nothing remains but this lone example.

Reconstruction of an Egyptian
temple with its standing obelisks

Romans cast bronze crabs, each about 16 inches in
diameter, with shanks made to fit downward into the
pedestal and upward into the shaft of the obelisk. As
each monolith was settled onto its four crabs, hot lead
was poured around dovetailed shanks so that future
vandals could not so easily remove them—though they
did, repeatedly. Crabs are said to have been chosen by
the Romans as appropriate symbols to sustain obelisks
dedicated to the Egyptian sun god because the Romans
somehow considered the crab a symbol for their own sun
god, Apollo.

Not content with moving two obelisks within Egypt,
Augustus decided to transport another great needle all the
way to Rome to be raised along the spine of the chariot-
racing course of the oldest Roman circus, the Maximus,
which had been laid out by Tarquin between the Palatine
and Aventine hills. Augustus had no trouble choosing his
obelisk. According to Pliny, the 75-foot porphyry needle
he selected had been carved with hieroglyphs on order of
the pharaoh whom Pliny calls Psemetnepserphreo and
modern Egyptologists call Psammetikos, ''during whose
reign Pythagoras went to Egypt.'' This would have been in
the sixth century B.C., though it is clear that the obelisk
had been quarried many centuries earlier.

The main difficulty in transporting an obelisk consisted
in being able to build a ship large enough to carry the
enormous weight of 200 tons or more. To accommodate
his obelisk, Augustus ordered a ship to be built at least
100 feet long. When the journey was successfully completed, the emperor exhibited the vessel in the naval yard
of Pozzuoli, outside Naples, so that it could be admired by
the people. After the obelisk was raised in the Circus

7

Painting in the Vatican of a Roman ship designed to bear an Egyptian obelisk to Rome. One such vessel could accommodate 1,200 passengers besides a cargo of niter, papyrus, and 400,000 bushels of wheat.

The emperor Gaius (A.D. 12–41), generally known as Caligula. A slave to his wild compulsions, he eventually went insane.

Maximus, Augustus decided he liked it so much he had another one brought from Egypt to be erected in the Campus Martius, or Field of Mars, where the Roman armies had once exercised, and where the censor G. Flaminius had built a circus in 220 B.C. This second obelisk was 9 feet shorter than the first but was covered with beautifully carved hieroglyphs, incomprehensible to the natives, though Pliny, with his intuitive ear for worthwhile lore, reported the glyphs to be "interpretations of natural phenomena according to the philosophy of the Egyptians."

The next Roman emperor to bring an obelisk to Rome was Caligula, contemptuously described by the historian Suetonius as a singer, dancer, gladiator, and chariot driver—a job normally reserved for slaves—who brought an even taller one to adorn the Vatican Circus, which he built to entertain himself with chariot racing. To import his obelisk, along with the five enormous pieces of numidian

Roman chariot race around a central obelisk. These races date from the founding of Rome in the eighth century B.C. and were dedicated to the seasonal revitalizing of nature by the sun—symbolized by the central obelisk, pillar of life, and axis of the solar system. The race-course was likened to the path of the planets around the ecliptic, with altars to each planet along the spine. Smaller obelisks marked the equinoctial and solstitial limits of the course. The charioteers bore different colors attributed to the various planets. Such festivals were worldwide. In Nineveh chariots with planetary colors raced around the city's crenellated walls; and in Yucatán the ballcourts similarly represent the concourse of planets wheeling around the vivifying sun in a narrow circuit of 7° north and south of the celestial equator.

Towered docks at Rome's harbor, built by the emperor Claudius

granite designed to sustain it, Caligula constructed an even longer ship than Augustus's. The obelisk, taken from Heliopolis, had no inscriptions on its faces, and its ancient history could not be easily determined. It is believed to have been cut at Syene, the Arab Aswan, far up the Nile near the Tropic of Cancer, in the thirteenth century B.C. According to Pliny this may have been the obelisk set up by the pharaoh he calls Noncoreo, who raised it in gratitude for his restored eyesight. What is certain, says Pliny, is that nothing like the ship which bore it, with its three hundred oarsmen, had ever been seen before. To bolster the obelisk, and keep it from moving when the ship rolled, more than 1,000 tons of lentils in sacks were stuffed around its shaft. If the obelisk weighed 330 tons, as reported by Pliny, the base 174 tons, and the lentils 1,000 tons, the ship would have sailed with a minimum displacement of more than 1,500 tons, no small undertaking for those days.

Once the obelisk was safely at the mouth of the Tiber, Caligula ordered the ship tied up in Ostia harbor as a museum piece. In A.D. 40, just before Caligula was murdered, the obelisk was set in place in his Vatican Circus by means of a heavy framework of timber. Claudius, who succeeded Caligula, had the ship filled with the ubiquitous Roman mortar, *pozzulana*, and sunk to make a bigger harbor, with three docks "as tall as towers." During recent excavations for Rome's international airport at Fiumicino, the outlines of Caligula's ship were found, and it was seen to have been all of 240 feet long.

Nero, who succeeded Claudius, and, like Caligula, enjoyed driving a *quadriga*, or four-horse chariot, had the Vatican Circus protected by a wall all around so he could practice without being seen (or laughed at) by the people. Once he considered himself sufficiently proficient, he had the plebes called in to "raise their applause to the skies."

The obelisk as it was raised on the Pincian Hill, in 1820

Giambattista Piranesi's etching of the Basilica of Santa Maria in Gerusalemme, where Hadrian's obelisk dedicated to Antinoüs was found. Its glyphs, honoring Hadrian, were carved in Rome, in imitation of Egyptian originals.

When Nero put the blame on the early Christians for burning Rome—orders for which he had given—many of them were martyred in the Vatican Circus, among them Simon, called Peter, who is supposed to have met his death somewhere near the foot of the great obelisk.

The emperor Hadrian, pained by the drowning in the Nile of his favorite boyfriend, the beautiful Antinoüs, decreed the building of a city on the banks of that river, to be called after him, and ordered an obelisk raised in Rome as a monument on which they said was writ in hieroglyphs the sad tale of the sacrifice made by this youth to serve his master. For many centuries no one knew quite where this obelisk had been raised. It was believed the self-castrated emperor Heliogabolus had taken it as a phallic ornament for his own small circus, but eventually it turned up near the present Basilica of Santa Croce in Gerusalemme in 1770 and was reraised in the Villa Borghese by Pious VII fifty years later.

The only non-emperor in ancient Rome to have had an obelisk on his property was Julius Caesar's friend Caius

Veduta della Facciata della Basilica di S. Croce in Gerusalemme

The supposed crucifixion of Saint Peter beside Caligula's obelisk in Nero's Vatican Circus, from a thirteenth-century fresco reproduced by Cesare d'Onofrio

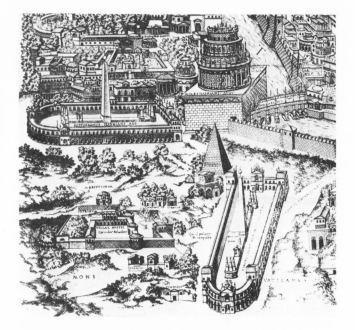

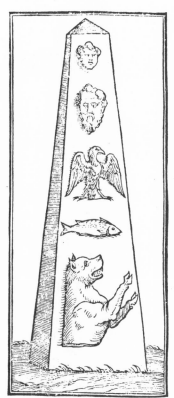

Sallustius Crispus, who managed to accumulate such a fortune in Africa—without too much scruple—that he could afford to have a palace with baths, forum, tribune, and obelisk on a large estate that ran between the Quirinal Hill and the Pincio (and part of which is now the French Academy in the Villa Medici). Though this obelisk came from Egypt, its hieroglyphs were carved in Rome, copied from the obelisk of Augustus in the Circus Maximus. The work was so poorly done that some of the glyphs are backwards.

At the beginning of the fourth century A.D., when the Roman Empire began to split, and the emperor Constantine founded a new capital in Constantinople, he too had to have an obelisk. For "New Rome" on the Bosporus, he chose the tallest obelisk yet tackled by any Roman emperor, the great monolith which Thothmes III had brought from Syene to the Temple of Amon at Karnak before he died, and which his grandson Thothmes IV had raised some years later. Augustus had seen this colossus, and had thought of bringing it to Rome, but had not dared to do so because it was dedicated to Amon, of whom he stood in awe. Constantine, with fewer qualms, had the monolith dragged and floated to Alexandria in 330. But there it lay prostrate, as Constantine lay dying. In the ensuing insurrections, the Caesarium, with its extraordinary remnants of the great Library of Alexandria—wherein may have lain an explanation of the purpose of the great obelisks—also suffered its first destruction.

11

The Karnak obelisk of Queen Hatshepsut. "First of noble women," so named at the age of 13 after a mysterous ceremony, this queen is described as a sensuous, mystical creature who considered herself an incarnate goddess (born by theogamy) divinely ordained to rule Egypt. She was depicted wearing the traditional artificial beard of a pharaoh, and was referred to as "he." The daughter of Thothmes I, she married her half brother Thothmes II and ruled jointly with him. Her father, as third king of the Eighteenth Dynasty, was responsible for erecting the first pair of red granite obelisks at Thebes, each weighing close to 150 tons, for which he had a boat 180 feet long and 60 feet wide built to transport to Karnak. One of the obelisks still stands between the third and fourth pylons. Each face bears his name, but Ramses IV added his own, as did Ramses VI. Hatshepsut raised four other obelisks at Karnak, one of which still stands. Another lies broken beside it. On the occasion of her jubilee, she had another pair of obelisks quarried by the Aswan cataract and floated to Thebes, where they were raised in the Temple of Amon-Ra at Karnak. They were a hundred feet tall and weighed 232 tons, and their pyramidions were sheathed with electrum to reflect the sun. A text of thirty-two lines on the base describes the events. One of Hatshepsut's engineer-architects, Senenmut, is reputed to have controlled the clergy, as a state within the state, a secret society of architects and masons, devoted to the mother

When Constantine's son and successor, Constantius, traveled to Old Rome, then governed by his brother Constans, he was so impressed by the grandeur of its monuments he decided to tie his own name to the eternal city by having the tallest of all known obelisks brought there from Alexandria. It took another enormous ship with three hundred oarsmen to ferry the red granite monolith, carved from the hills of Aswan, safely to the port of Ostia. From there it was floated up the Tiber on a huge raft as far as the Ostiense docks, where it was thrown into a side street, because the tyrant Magnentius had just slain Constantius's brother and occupied Rome.

Only when Magnentius conveniently committed suicide in Lyons in 353 was Constantius able to resume the job of dragging the obelisk along the present Aventine avenue to the center of the Circus Maximus. Ammianus Marcellinus, the Greek historian who wrote about Rome and was alive at the time, says that to raise it in the year 357 thousands of men were employed to pull on huge ropes, and that so many timbers were required the circus looked like a forest. He adds that as the needle finally stood erect, many more thousands of spectators were dumbfounded to see that it dwarfed the obelisk of Augustus, about 50

goddess, spread among the temples to survey "strict observance" of the rule. After her death, the images and names on Hatshepsut's monuments were removed. Her successor, Thothmes III, raised seven obelisks in Karnak and Heliopolis.

meters away, which had dominated the area for 367 years.

Meanwhile the inhabitants of Constantinople obtained another obelisk from Karnak, one believed to have been raised there by the pharaoh Menkherra-sonb. It too had been dragged to Alexandria on orders of Constantine, but had lain neglected since his death. Constantius's cousin, Julian, who succeeded him as emperor, got it moving again by urging the people of Alexandria to forward the old shaft to New Rome, in return for a colossal statue of himself. The ship which bore the obelisk from Alexandria was driven ashore in a storm near Athens, whence the shaft was at last brought to Constantinople by Theodosius I, who came to the throne twenty years after Julian.

Along with the fifteen authentic Egyptian obelisks which the Romans ferried across the inland sea to adorn their streets, forums, and circuses, they also raised a forest of imitations, many with hieroglyphs carved in the style of the Egyptian originals, which no one could any longer read or understand. Decay was at hand. Within a few centuries of the decline and fall of Rome came the decline and fall of its obelisks. With but one exception, all were knocked down and badly damaged by fire, especially around the bases, as if with the deliberate intent that they never be raised again.

The circus at Constantinople, with its obelisks along the spine, where the ancient festivals gradually lost their meaning in the course of the decadent Byzantine millennium

For a long time this vandalizing was attributed to the various barbarous invaders who succeeded each other in waves. Later writers, beginning in the Renaissance, concluded that the obelisks had been disposed of not by barbarians, envious of such imposing monuments, but by bigoted Christians who hated or feared all that was pagan. Rodolfo Lanciani, the Italian-born historian and antiquarian, pointed out at the turn of the century that obelisks were not the only pagan monuments to be destroyed, desecrated, and broken up to make new buildings. In his *The Ruins and Excavations of Ancient Rome* he flatly absolves the barbarians: "We can discard the current opinion that attributes to barbarians the disappearance of Rome's monuments." According to Lanciani, whereas the scourge of invaders passed over the massive constructions of the Roman Republic and the Roman Empire, leaving what he calls hardly a trace of damage, the real harm was done by Christianized Romans of the Middle Ages and of the early Renaissance. "Can one," Lanciani asks, "really see the barbarians pulverizing the 65 kilometers of marble around the Circus Maximus?"

Ruins of ancient Rome with a fallen obelisk—and incomprehensible glyphs—depicted by Piranesi

The demolition and retrogression perpetrated by Christians lasted for a thousand years. As the great city slowly decayed, grass grew in the marketplaces and the forums; carefully laid stones were toppled, one after the other, till wolves roamed the empty spaces. Of the great obelisks, with one exception—that brought by Caligula—not a trace was left. They were buried, lost, forgotten. Even the sole standing example was up to its navel in refuse and dirt, its pedestal and bronze astragals completely buried. It still stood only because of the Christian basilica of Saint Peter, founded by Constantine, whose walls it almost touched. Any attempt to knock down the obelisk would have risked destroying this most holy of Christian churches, deliberately built on the spot in Caligula's Vatican Circus where Saint Peter was said to have been martyred.

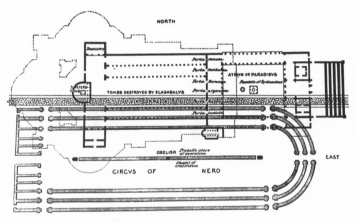

Plan of Saint Peter's Basilica as it was built over the remains of Nero's circus beside Caligula's still-standing obelisk

If the Goths and Vandals had been interested in destroying obelisks, they would hardly have spared this example for that reason. More likely, the early pontiffs, exponents of an antipagan religion, wished to supplant once and for all these erect symbols of a pantheistic way of life and, as they did in the case of so many ancient pagan sites, turn this sole remaining obelisk into a Christianized place of worship, granting indulgences to pilgrims who would crawl about its base, praying to Saint Peter.

But such is the karmic wheel of life that it was to be the succeeding pontiffs in later rounds of history who would do their damnedest to raise again the old obelisks to their former grandeur, like so many phoenixes rising from their ashes to proclaim the very wisdom which the Church had wished to silence.

Obeliscus Caesaris in uia olim Triumphali ad Vaticani
radices erectus, prope sacrarium Basilicae nunc
Sancti Petri

34

2. RESURRECTION OF THE OBELISKS

Ball atop Caligula's obelisk, close by the Vatican Basilica, said to contain the ashes of Julius Caesar. From a sixteenth-century print reproduced by Cesare d'Onofrio

An English prelate who traveled to Rome at the beginning of the fourteenth century, Master Gregorius, found the last obelisk still standing up against the walls of Saint Peter's Basilica, in a dark alley flanked by crumbling old houses. As its shaft was covered with dirt and weeds, well above the sign of any base, Master Gregorius had no way of telling the length of the obelisk, and conjectured it might be as long as 250 feet. More interested in the pagan antiquities of Rome than its Christian churches, Gregorius was captivated by the tradition that the bronze ball on top of the obelisk contained the ashes of Julius Caesar. In letters to his English parishioners, in which he cheerfully admitted that "he read much but understood little," Gregorius passed on the story that the obelisk had been raised on the exact spot where Caesar, on the way to the Capitol, had been accosted by an astrologer who warned him he would be killed on the ides of March.

The assassination of Julius Caesar

The antiquarian and historian Cesare d'Onofrio, in his *Gli Obelischi di Roma,* attributes the belief partly to the fact that the words *Julius* and *Caesar* appear four times in the Latin inscription below the obelisk, and partly to a misunderstood passage in Suetonius, "one of those cases of false etymology," says d'Onofrio, "so common among the learned when they try to explain away something they cannot understand." Suetonius, in his *Lives of the Caesars,* relates that right after the dictator's remains were

Nicholas V replaced the anti-pope Felix V, a duke of Savoy—not even a priest—elected when the Council of Basel in 1439 deposed Eugenius IV as a heretic.

With the end of the schism of the Church, Nicholas V reestablished Rome as the seat of the papacy, and to celebrate this triumph proclaimed a jubilee whose participants he milked to embellish Rome.

Antonio Sangallo

burned, the populace erected in the Forum a solid column of numidian stone, 20 feet high, dedicated to the Father of His Country.

The first serious attention paid to this last of the standing obelisks came in the Renaissance from Tommaso Parentucelli, Pope Nicholas V (1447–55), a humanist of considerable erudition, of whom his secretary—later Pope Pius II—reported that "what he does not know is outside the range of human knowledge." Part of Nicholas's grandiose scheme of rebuilding Rome into a stunning capital of Christendom was to have Caligula's Vatican obelisk moved from its dark hiding place to the center of Saint Peter's Square, there to be raised on four life-sized bronze statues of the Evangelists. By placing atop the obelisk a huge bronze Jesus with a golden cross in his hand, Nicholas declared, his wish was "to strengthen the weak faith of the people by the greatness of that which it sees." The night before the job was to be assigned to his favorite architect, a Bolognese engineer named Ridolfo Fioravante degli Alberti, better known by the nickname of "Aristotle," the old pope died, reputedly of a broken heart because Constantinople had fallen to the Turks.

Fifteen years later, when the Franciscan general Francesco della Rovere, who had spent his life as a mendicant friar, came to the papacy as Sixtus IV (1471–84), his secretary was to say of him "he was so exempt from avarice he could not endure the sight of money." Result: he depleted the papal treasury, waging war against the Florentines, the Venetians, and the Neapolitans, sending a battle fleet to its doom against the Turks, and spending a great deal of money beautifying Rome with such lavish constructions as the Sistine Chapel. Among his grander projects was a revival of the idea of moving Caligula's obelisk. But the project failed; this time because his architect, the same Aristotle whom Nicholas V had befriended, was caught minting his own coin and was locked up in Castel Sant'Angelo, from where he defected to Russia to build churches in the Kremlin.

A generation later, after Antonio da Sangallo had presented plans for a basilica of Saint Peter's in which Michelangelo was to become involved, Pope Paul III (Alessandro Farnese, 1534–49) became determined to have Caligula's obelisk raised in Saint Peter's Square. On several occasions he discussed the matter with Michelangelo, whom he knew had invented special equipment for raising heavy stones, but Michelangelo would not go along with the idea. When asked by friends why he, who was such an ingenious fellow, and had invented such good

18

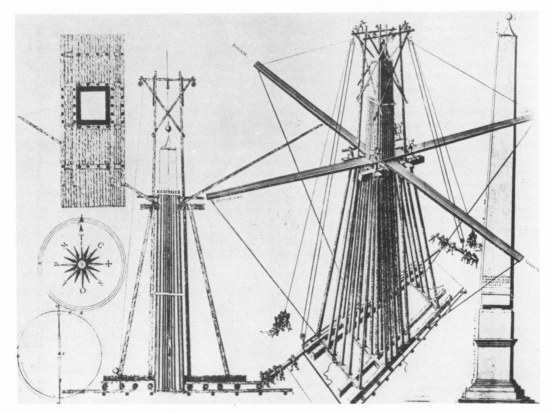

Paul III, a great lover of luxury and a phenomenal nepotist, by means of which he alienated great fiefs of papal land to his bastard children. This pope introduced the Inquisition into Italy in 1542. He also approved the foundation of the Society of Jesus as an army to combat heresy. And it was he who established rigorous censorship and an index of forbidden books.

equipment, would not give the pope the pleasure of moving the obelisk, Michelangelo is reported to have replied: "What if it breaks?" More likely, Michelangelo disagreed with the motive behind the scheme—the raising of a mighty symbol to reinforce the suppression of heresy—and when commissioned by Paul III to paint the Last Judgment in the Sistine Chapel, made a point of painting a pope in hell.

It remained for a poor swineherd from the Adriatic coast near Ancona, another mendicant Franciscan friar, who came to the papal throne as Sixtus V (1585–90), to raise sufficient money to fell and reerect the obelisk. Born in poverty as Felice Peretti, the son of a chambermaid and a farmhand, this new pope turned out to be even more extravagant in his expenditures of public funds than had been Sixtus IV. But unlike his predecessor, Peretti managed rapidly to accumulate an enormous fortune through the imposition of heavy taxes and the sale of offices. Romans quipped that the only remaining commodity untaxed by Sixtus was the heat of the sun. In the short five years during which he was pope, Sixtus V got the reputation of having "built five bridges, watered five fountains, erected five obelisks, and left five millions in the treasury."

Sixtus V (1585–1590). Crafty and malignant, this new pope announced: "I come not to bring peace but the sword!" In all parts of the Papal States stakes were erected, on each of which stood the head of an "outlaw." With the sale of offices Sixtus refilled the papal coffers, raising the price for becoming treasurer from 15,000 to 50,000 scudi. He then placed a heavy burden on the poor by taxing such indispensable articles as firewood. With the vast wealth he accumulated in Castel Sant'Angelo, Sixtus created a battle fleet to fight the Ottomans and was the first to draft an army of his own people in the hope of seizing the Kingdom of Naples from Philip II of Spain. A compulsive "moralist," Sixtus ordered courtesans whipped naked for trafficking with married men, and was dissuaded by the governor of Rome from confining all the prostitutes in a ghetto only because there were too many. The ancient ruins of Rome Sixtus considered "festering sores" of an ugly pagan civilization riddled by superstition, to be obliterated; and the destruction of the Colosseum was only avoided by his sudden death, accredited by *vox populi* to a dose of poison administered by the Jesuits.

Domenico Fontana

Most of this was accomplished with the help of a Swiss-Italian architect from Lugano in the Ticino, Domenico Fontana, whom Peretti had hired when he was still Cardinal di Montalto, to construct for him several imposing edifices, including the mausoleum for Pope Nicholas IV. At that time, the incumbent pope, Gregory XIII, disapproving of such ostentatious shows of magnificence from a mere cardinal, had suspended Montalto's income. But Fontana, at his own expense, had kept right on architecting his patron's extravagant projects, a gesture which was to pay off handsomely two years later when Peretti became Pope. Not only was Fontana reimbursed from the papal treasury, he was given the job of completing the construction of the dome of Saint Peter's, which Michelangelo had left unfinished on his death twenty years earlier in 1564.

Three months later, he was given an even bigger task, one which would make his fame and fortune.

A tough reactionary, whom later historians were to dub "the Fascist Pope," Sixtus quickly cleaned up the papal states with a ferocious campaign against "outlaws and bandits," so as to be able to concentrate his efforts against all forms of heresy, of which Protestantism was the most rampant. More severed heads appeared on pikes outside the gates of Castel Sant'Angelo "than melons for sale in the market at Campo de' Fiori." Blasphemers had a hole burned in their tongues. Bandits had their guts ripped out and their quartered limbs hung on spikes. Death was meted out for adultery; and mothers who prostituted their daughters were condemned to the gibbet while the daughters were obliged to witness the execution. Pederasts were burned alive, as was a baker, for baking inferior bread. When several cardinals begged Sixtus to reprieve an innocent teen-ager, condemned for some peccadillo, the pope replied he would ennoble the boy's death by witnessing the execution.

While still a cardinal, Montalto had been inquisitor general for the extirpation of heresy in Venice, but he had been so high-handed in the conduct of his duties that he was forced to leave that island republic. So intransigent was he considered that on his election to the papacy one Roman wit seen leaving the city in a hurry explained he didn't believe Sixtus would even forgive Jesus His sins. With the excuse that he wished to "quench the detestable memories of idolatry" and "extirpate the idols exalted by pagans, such as pyramids, obelisks, and columns," Sixtus V decided to move Caligula's obelisk, and raise above it a Christian symbol to "enhance the spirit of the Counter-Reformation" and "exalt the mysteries of the Catholic religion."

On August 24, 1585, Sixtus V appointed a special commission to study the problem and to make a recommendation for the transport of the obelisk. Among those chosen were four cardinals, a bishop, a senator from Rome, and three conservators. But, as d'Onofrio notes, not a single technician was included. Having endowed the commission with sufficient funds and authority to ensure results, the pope specified that the learned gentlemen define the precise spot where the obelisk could be reerected, as a symbol of the conquest of Church over paganism and Protestantism. More important, they were to determine how such a fragile shaft of granite weighing 334 tons was to be dismantled, transported over a distance of almost 300 yards, and reerected without being broken.

21

Various models were designed to move the Vatican obelisk. Fontana measured the height of the monolith as 83 feet on a base of 9 feet 2 inches, narrowing to a little less than 6 feet at the beginning of the 4-foot-high pyramidion. He estimated its weight to be 681,222 pounds. Forty capstans—truncated cones of timber around which the ropes were wound—would be needed to raise 90 percent of the obelisk's weight. Each rope had to be 3 inches in diameter, and 1,000 feet long. In determining the diameter and tensile strength of the rope, Fontana based his calculation on the premise that the steady pulling force of a horse would average 100 pounds. Two horses to a capstan with a nine-to-one ratio gave him a pull of 1,800 pounds per capstan. And when the ropes were passed through pulleys or blocks with a two-to-one ratio attached to four points of the obelisk's length, Fontana obtained an increase of motive power of $2 \times 4 \times 1,800$, or 14,400 pounds per capstan. For the additional 10 percent lifting power, Fontana relied on the leverage of the long timbers by which the capstans would be turned.

Unanimously the commission invited anyone with a suggestion, no matter how farfetched, to step forward. Within less than a month, five hundred candidates presented themselves from all over Italy and from as far afield as Rhodes and Greece, including several engineers and a smattering of adventurous monks. Each came with his own suggestions and specially devised equipment. Most of the applicants brought plans, sketches, or models. The majority considered it essential that the obelisk be transported upright, believing it to be too difficult a task to lower and then raise it again. Others grandly proposed carrying both obelisk and base simultaneously in an upright position. Still others suggested carrying the obelisk at an angle of 45°. One architect, Francesco Masini, wanted to build a canal and float the obelisk to its new location.

Fontana, more conservative, brought a model in wood of a mechanism designed to handle the job, with ropes and pulleys all to scale, and a 2-foot obelisk made of lead. To the assembled congregation he demonstrated with words and motions how he could lower, transport, and reraise the full-scale obelisk without any problem. The commission appeared impressed by the plan, model, and presentation, as well as the fact that Fontana was the pope's protégé. Nevertheless, the commission hesitated to give such responsibility to a man of only forty-two. As a compromise, they appointed Fontana engineer-in-chief, placing over him, as supervisor, the seventy-four-year-old Florentine mannerist architect and sculptor, Bartolommeo Ammanati, who contributed nothing to the job, was ignored by Fontana, and is remembered mostly for having designed the Pitti Palace in Florence.

Sixtus V expressed his desires very precisely to Fontana: "Eradicate the memory of the superstitions of antiquity by raising the greatest footing ever for the Holy Cross."

On October 5, 1585, the pope, bypassing his own committee, ordered an edict of authority issued to Fontana for as long as it took to move the obelisk, granting him blanket license to impress men, draft animals, requisition timber, equipment, and subsistence of any sort, and even create a right of way in the city—which meant he could tear down any private house that got in his way. The decree also freed Fontana from the threat of litigation due to possible damage incurred in the operation. Everyone in the Holy See was given strict orders not to interfere in any way with the architect's actions or requirements. They were enjoined, on the contrary, to obey him, favor him, and help him.

Fontana's first problem was to create a solid base around the obelisk where the soil was soft and wet. For this he used pile drivers to pound oak beams 20 feet long and 9 inches in diameter deep into the ground, capping them with a layer of peeled, rot-resisting chestnut beams. On top of these he poured an aggregate of finely crushed basalt, flint, stone, and broken brick, mixed with a mortar of lime and clay, which set very hard. As a religious observance, appropriate to the occasion, votive bronze medals of the patron pope were laid in the concrete.

Fontana next had to create in real life the machine he had modeled for raising the obelisk. It meant building a *castello,* or huge scaffold of tall timber beams, high

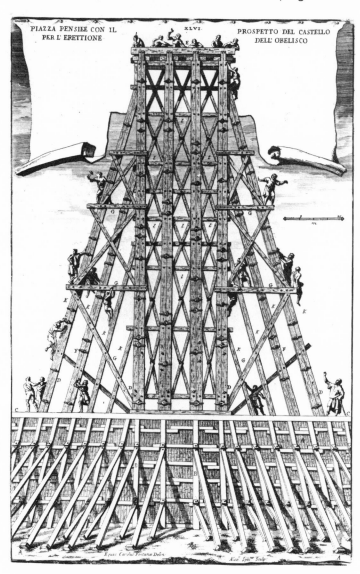

Fontana tried to break one of the ropes with a pull of 50,000 pounds, but failed; so he concluded that this margin of safety would cover not only variations in the rope manufacture but also the peaks of tension imposed on any one capstan when other capstans might run slack. The blocks were made of wrought iron 5 feet long, with six metal sheaves, or grooved wheels, set in layers of three each. When the ropes were laid out on the ground, they passed over rollers to keep the thousands of feet from fouling.

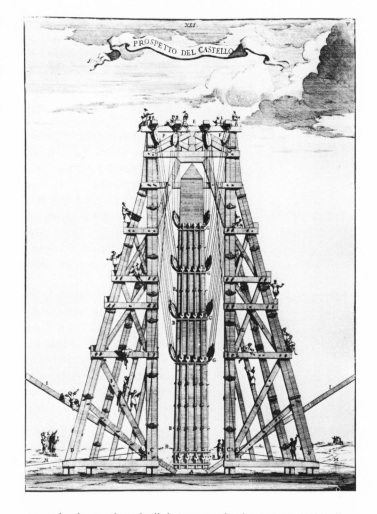

enough above the obelisk to sustain the ropes and pulleys by means of which he planned to lift it, and strong enough to withstand a weight of almost 350 tons. Each sustaining member of this *castello* had to be built up of four columns of timber, 92 feet tall, each 11 feet square, bound together by iron hoops. To obtain the requisite 20-by-20-inch oak beams, 30 feet long, Fontana had to scour afield halfway to Naples. Each beam was then dragged to Rome from Campomorto, Santa Severa, or Terracina by teams of fourteen oxen. Iron bands and huge iron bolts with which to weld together the beams were obtained from ironsmiths in Ronciglione and Subiaco.

As soon as the *castello* was ready, Fontana had the obelisk protected by a double layer of reed matting over which was placed a layer of 2-inch planking, the whole held together by the great iron hoops. The long ropes were attached, leading to massive capstans, or wooden winches, like truncated cones, which could be revolved with levers to tighten the ropes. Realizing how vital the ropes were to success, Fontana personally occupied himself with their manufacture, going to the picturesque Umbrian town of Foligno near Assisi, where thousands of feet of rope were handwoven from endless strands of hemp.

All of these complex preparations took seven months of febrile work. By the end of April 1586, all was in order. Fontana set April 30 as the date for lowering the obelisk. A last preparatory task was the removal of the ancient metal ball still atop the obelisk, placed there fifteen centuries earlier by Romans in the belief it contained the ashes of Julius Caesar. When the ball was taken off, no ashes were found, and the myth was gently dispelled. Only no one bothered to ask what purpose the ball might have served.

On April 30, two hours before dawn, two masses were said in the small church of Santa Martinella, an annex of the Palazzo del Priorato, right off Saint Peter's Square. All around the great piazza, the access roads were blocked off with barricades and wooden palisades, making of it a closed *serraglio,* where a ban forbade anyone, on pain of death, from entering on the day the obelisk was to be moved, with the exception of those assigned to the job.

Crowding Saint Peter's Square

When all these hardy fellows had communed and made their prayers, they went into the *serraglio* just before break of day.

People were at the windows, on the balconies, and on the roofs of all the surrounding houses, even on the cornices of Saint Peter's Basilica, and on the drum of Michelangelo's still unfinished cupola. Among the spectators were the pope's sister, Camilla, the majority of the college of cardinals, and virtually all the religious and lay authorities of Rome, as well as many foreigners who had appeared from all over Italy and Europe to witness so extraordinary and marvelous a spectacle.

The city police, under the local sheriff, reinforced by Swiss Guards and a special detachment of cavalry, kept the swarming populace in order, administering summary punishment to anyone who misbehaved. No one was allowed to speak, spit, or make a noise of any sort during the course of the operations; and in anticipation of possible executions, a gibbet had been raised on the spot.

By each of the forty capstans, around which the great hawsers had been wound, stood two horses and twenty workers, all together seventy-six horses and eight hundred men, most of whom had their heads protected with metal helmets. The success of the enterprise depended on the uniform distribution of the great weight over the many ropes holding the obelisk, with no rope straining more than any other. To ensure that all the capstans turned synchronously, and to prevent some of the ropes from stretching harder than others, Fontana arranged for a trumpet to be blown every time he gave the order (from a high spot visible to all), and everyone was to make his wheel turn. The moment a bell was rung, this time from atop the *castello,* everyone was to stop. Two foremen were assigned to each capstan and twenty extra men were assigned to emergency calls; their task was to quickly bring rope, blocks, or replacement parts when failure threatened. Twenty more horses and drivers were placed in reserve, ready to move toward any point of need. Additional men with sledges and mauls clambered through the *castello* and around the obelisk, driving wedges to tighten the binding members and stiffen the system.

When all was ready, and Fontana had reminded those present that the work was being performed for the glory of God, everyone knelt and followed him in prayer. As soon as they had recited a *Pater Noster* and an *Ave Maria,* Fontana gave the signal for the trumpet to be blown. Nine

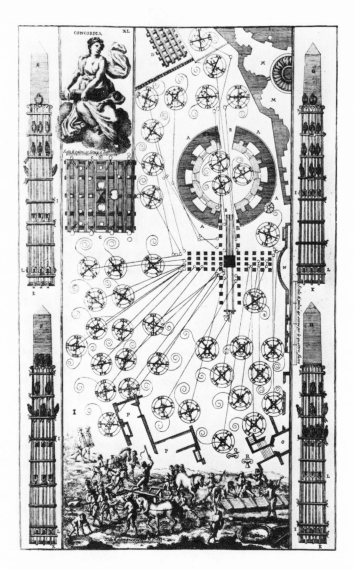

hundred and seven men and seventy-six horses pulled on the forty capstans. The ropes tightened to the breaking point. As Fontana described the scene, the earth appeared to tremble and the *castello* gave forth a terrible and agonizing screech. Those who had competed against Fontana in the competition now jeered at his plan, proclaiming that the ropes would fail because of unequal stress.

After the terrible creaking, when nothing seemed to have given way, and no man seemed to have suffered, Fontana gave the signal for the bell. Foremen ran to examine the equipment. It was noticed that one of the horizontal bands, closest to the top, had broken. All the other metal bands had also suffered, either having slid

28

from their original positions or been twisted and nearly broken. Their radial component of tension had evidently been underestimated. But as all the rope bindings had held, Fontana decreed that the metal bands be replaced by ropes.

Repairs were made and power was once more exerted on the capstans to raise the obelisk. Up it went, millimeter by millimeter, till it had been lifted about a palm and the sun stood almost directly above it. Not wanting the work to be interrupted, Fontana had lunch brought to the workers on the spot in large baskets, the menu being bread, sausage, cheese, and smoked ham. All together two full barrels of wine were consumed. When work was

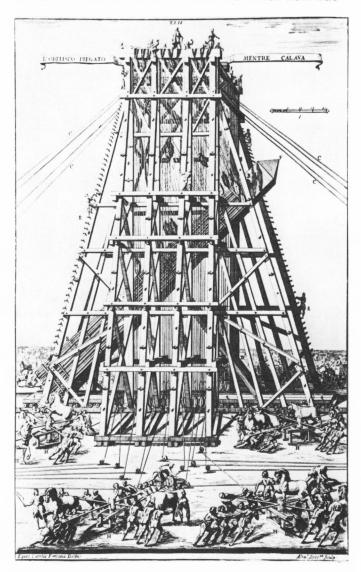

Lowering the obelisk

29

resumed, the obelisk was raised in further short increments until it reached a height of 2¾ palms, or 61 centimeters, above its base, the amount necessary to insert a dolly of beams on rollers. This was to facilitate lowering the obelisk from its vertical to a horizontal position.

By ten o'clock that evening, the obelisk rested upright on its dolly. The quitting signal was sounded. Success for this first part of the operation was celebrated by the firing of a signal gun, which was answered by a burst of artillery from the city's batteries, and by a great show of joy from the multitude.

The obelisk now had to be lowered from its vertical position and gently laid on a huge wooden cradle which

The obelisk safely on its cradle

was to move it on rollers to its new location. Room had to be made for its butt to swing out, so the shaft could be laid flat. This meant demolishing the walls of the sacristy of Saint Peter's Basilica, then rebuilding them. The great granite base also had to be unearthed and moved to its new position. And the four bronze crabs had to be removed to be replaced by recumbent bronze lions. Above all, the great *castello* had to be demolished and reassembled in its new location.

These operations took longer than expected. To dig out the pedestal, fifteen hundred years of accumulated earth and debris had to be removed from around the base. The solid bronze astragal crabs turned out to weigh 600 pounds apiece. Using hot lead the ancient Romans had so cunningly inserted them that masons could not pry them loose. Finally they had to chip them out. The main granite base was found to be a cube, 8½ feet on a side, weighing 55 tons. Beneath it, a rougher base weighed 63 tons. Farther down, as a footing, was a solid white marble slab. All of these, weighing a total of 140 tons, had to be raised and transported to the new site. When reassembled, they would reach a height of 27 feet.

As the obelisk itself had to be dragged 115 canes (256.4 meters) to a spot 40 palms lower on the hill, and Fontana wished to avoid having to go almost 9 meters downhill with the obelisk and then having to raise it again that much, he had a great causeway built of earth dug ιιom the Vatican Hill and held in place by a shored timber crib which maintained the level.

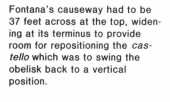

Fontana's causeway had to be 37 feet across at the top, widening at its terminus to provide room for repositioning the *castello* which was to swing the obelisk back to a vertical position.

31

By May 7 the obelisk was laid on its dolly, intact, without having caused harm to a single person. The pope was overjoyed, and the crowd accompanied Fontana to his home to the sound of drums and trumpets.

Preparations for resetting the obelisk dragged on through June and July. The *castello*'s timbers had to be moved one by one to the new site and carefully reerected on the broadened causeway. Despite the heat of summer, the work continued without pause. The pope declared he would not move to his summer residence until the obelisk was safely emplaced, which meant work had to continue all through August. But the heat became intolerable. Work

Fontana's rendition of the great square of Saint Peter's with his teams of 140 horses and 800 men ready to attempt to hoist the obelisk to its new position on the morning of September 10, 1586

DISPOSITIONE E VEDVTA GENERALE DELLE MACHINE CHE SERVIRONO PER ALZARE L'OBELISCO VATICANO.

was suspended so that the ropes would not catch fire. On August 30 the whole piazza was closed off with high palisades to prevent onlookers from seeing what was going on.

Sixtus hoped to be able to inaugurate the raised obelisk on September 14, the Feast of the Exaltation of the Cross. And to meet that deadline work was resumed. In order to superintend and to keep things on the go, the pope took his meals in rooms overlooking the piazza. On September 10, a Wednesday, everything appeared to be ready, despite a heat which still threatened the ropes. Again two masses were said before daybreak, this time in the Church of Santo Spirito, at the end of the piazza, toward the south. When the ceremony ended, each took up his allotted place. This time, because of the heavier strain in raising the obelisk, the number of horses had to be increased to 140. At dawn the forty capstans were ready and fully manned.

It was the crucial test. According to one source, the pope blessed Fontana and warned him to be most careful in what he was about to do that day, because he would have to pay for any error with his head. At the same time, says this source, Sixtus V, in his ambivalent love for Fontana, ordered that at all four gates of the borough horses be readied, so that if anything sinister should occur, Fontana would have a chance to escape the pope's ire. Other sources, less romantic, attribute to Fontana the preparation of the horses.

As the trumpet blew, 140 beasts and 800 men turned their capstans, tightening the ropes, and the obelisk slowly rose from its bed. By noon it had reached the critical halfway mark of 45°, at which point it was firmly trussed, and everyone broke for lunch. When work was resumed, the heat was tremendous and the tension on the ropes at its highest. The story goes that at one crucial point the strain became so great the ropes were again on the verge of catching fire. Despite the ban, on pain of death, of uttering a word, a boy is said to have shattered the silence of the great piazza with the cry of "Moisten the lines," which being done, the obelisk was saved from crashing down. The pope, so the story goes, instead of punishing the bold youth, rewarded him and his descendants in perpetuity, with the lucrative concession of bringing palms to the Palm Sunday festivities. The story, not substantiated by any contemporary sources or the research of Cesare d'Onofrio, is illustrated by a later fresco in the Vatican which depicts the boy being apprehended by papal guards.

Fresco in the Vatican showing the arrest of the boy for calling out, "Moisten the lines"

33

Most spectators, not to miss a single move, remained at their places throughout the day without even going home at mealtimes. Hawkers, selling food, made a fortune. By evening, as the French ambassador, the duke of Luxembourg, came to render his first obedience to the pope, he stopped to watch two separate heaves of the obelisk. At the end of fifty-two pulls and pauses, the obelisk was firmly vertical above its dolly.

The pope, on his way back from Pietro da Monte Cavallo to give a public consistory for the French ambassador, was advised that the obelisk was erect, and declared himself happy. It was September 14. Mortars were fired to inform Castel Sant'Angelo, from which many pieces of artillery resounded. Once more, the whole city rejoiced, running to Fontana's house with the usual noisy hosannahs.

Fireworks at Castel Sant'Angelo

On September 16 the dolly was removed, and the obelisk rested squarely on its base, held in place no longer by the astragal crabs of the ancient Romans but by four gilded lions of modern Rome. Created by the sculptor Prospero Bresciano, the lions were an architectural anomaly in that each lion had one head and two half-bodies, split down the middle like a hotdog bun so as to show a flank from any direction, of which d'Onofrio remarked, "I do not think there is any more monstrous invention around and about the streets of Rome." The allegorical significance of these lions, apart from the fact that they were the heraldic symbols on the Peretti coat of arms, was in demonstrating that just as the lions had been yoked by the weight of the obelisk, so the ferocity and arrogance of gentiles had been suppressed by true religion. Now all that was needed was to uncover the structure, embellish it with finishing touches, and bring the great square back to an even level.

By the twenty-seventh the obelisk stood in its pristine glory. The pope, admiring it from the windows of the Vatican Palace, ordered a procession to consecrate it with a golden cross and to purge it of its pagan past.

The first Friday after the erection, a bishop celebrated a most solemn Mass of the Holy Cross. When the procession reached the obelisk, the bishop blessed a great iron cross which was to be placed atop its pyramidion. With various exorcisms he proceeded to purge the obelisk, dousing it the while with holy water, and scratching crosses on its sides. The great iron cross was then hoisted by a rope, while a subdeacon climbed a ladder to hold the metal in place until it could be fastened to the top of the obelisk.

The obelisk standing before Saint Peter's Basilica, still bereft of Michelangelo's cupola, and of Bernini's colonnade

35

The event was celebrated by reading the poems of
forty-five poets, including the Jesuit-educated Torquato
Tasso, who, though he suffered from delusions of heresy,
correctly noted that the Egyptians considered their obelisks symbols of the rays of the sun and named their
pharaohs sons of the sun. Music followed the poets, and
at the sound of trumpets the crowd all knelt. A public
indulgence of fifteen years was conceded by His Holiness
to all present, and to all who, passing the cross, should
honor it. Artillery was fired from the battlements of Castel
Sant'Angelo and the bishop cried out: "I exorcise you;
creature of stone, in the name of omnipotent God, that you
may become an exorcised stone worthy of supporting the
Holy Cross, and be freed from any vestige of impurity or

The new alphabet of ornamental "Christian" letters designed by Sixtus's protégé, Luca Orfeo of Fanok, to adorn Christian monuments instead of the pagan inscriptions of ancient Rome

shred of paganism and from any assault of spiritual impurity.''

But this was not enough for the pope. He considered the exorcism insufficient, and had the formula immortalized in large "Christian" letters (to differentiate them from pagan Roman letters) on the eastern and western sides of the base, just below the bodies of the four bronze lions.

Fontana's work had lasted exactly thirteen months, and had cost the Reverend Household 37,975 scudi, though Fontana in his bid for the competition had estimated only 16,000. To protect himself against this obvious eventuality, Fontana had all the while wisely maintained a regular public-relations office issuing bulletins and magnificent prints to illustrate the progress of the work, drawn mostly by Giovanni Guerra and etched by Natale Bonifacio, with ample captions by Fontana. They not only informed the world of the progress of the work, but were to form the basis for Fontana's own book on the subject, *Della trasportatione dell'obelisco vaticano,* printed in 1590, which left to posterity one of the most complete and handsome records, in format, type, and engraving, of what was considered by contemporary Europeans one of the greatest engineering feats ever performed. The pope was only too happy to pay Fontana in full.

On October 1, 1586, Sixtus V announced he had given his architect a chain of 80 gold scudi to support a gold medallion bearing the image of His Beatitude, along with a yearly pension of 2,000 scudi, of which 800 could be left to his heirs. Fontana was also made a citizen of Rome, a Knight of the Golden Spur, and a Palatine count with an escutcheon bearing a golden obelisk on an azure field. He received gratis all the lumber and equipment left over from the moving of the obelisk; and architectural commissions were thrust upon him. The pope, with a ghastly pun, had Fontana kneel as he dubbed him *"te nobelisco eterna-mente."*

Scathingly, d'Onofrio remarks that Pope Sixtus V, hated by his people, managed to spend 80,000 scudi of their money in what amounted to a singular affirmation of his own personal power. By placing his name carved in beautiful letters on the base of the obelisk, says d'Onofrio, Sixtus V compared himself in greatness to the pharaohs who had first raised the obelisks and to the deified Roman emperors, such as Augustus, who had moved them to Rome. As d'Onofrio points out, not everyone in Rome was happy with the exploit, paid for by insufferable taxes wrung from the people. In a fierce lampoon of December 16, 1586, it was suggested that the

37

architect transfer Saint Peter's *"guglia,"* or prick, to a
more honorable and more decent place for such a tool: his
own backside.

Unperturbed by such negative reactions, Sixtus V continued in the grip of his compulsion to erect great
obelisks, starting a vogue which was to become the
standard Freudian fantasy of a whole succession of
Roman pontiffs up to the present. So ingrained is the
Roman taste for anal and phallic jokes that as late as
1948, on the occasion of the Holy Year, or Anno Santo,
when a great avenue of phoney obelisks was erected by
Pius XII along the hideous via della Conciliazione (which

38

Augustus's mausoleum, built in the second decade B.C. on the confines of the Campus Martius, surrounded by sacred groves. Two obelisks, raised in the Alexandrine style, stood by the entrance until the fourth century A.D. One can be seen lying broken in the side street; the other is presumably buried.

runs straight from the Tiber to Saint Peter's Square, entirely destroying the former stunning shock of coming suddenly on Bernini's great colonnade), Romans were quick to dub the row of obelisks *supposte dell'Ano Santo,* suppositories for the Holy Anus.

As early as September 1586, while the scaffolding was being demolished in Saint Peter's Square, Sixtus summoned Fontana and ordered him to raise another obelisk. The only one left unburied in Rome lay in three fragments near Augustus's mausoleum, where it had been dug up during the reign of Leo X (1513–21). Fontana studied the possibility of putting the pieces of this relic together, but finally concurred with Leo's great military architects, Baldassare Peruzzi and Antonio da Sangallo, who had both declared it unsalvageable.

Instead, Fontana pursued the century-old rumor that a barber in the Campus Martius area, digging for a latrine in his tiny kitchen garden, had knocked against the base of an ancient obelisk, buried hard by the Church of San Lorenzo in Lucina. Almost a century earlier the antiquarians of Pope Julius II had viewed this relic and recognized it as a piece of one of the obelisks brought from Egypt by Augustus, and had urged the pope to re-erect it where it once stood in the Campus Martius. Julius II, occupied with his many wars, could not be persuaded, so the barber had reburied the obelisk. Now Fontana took picks and shovels to the site and began to dig, finding an obelisk that was broken into five pieces. In order for Sixtus V conveniently to observe these half-buried fragments, a wall was specially knocked down, but when the pope saw that the obelisk was in even worse condition than the one by Augustus's mausoleum and that several houses would

Luxurious summer villa of Sixtus V, known as Casa Peretti, on the Esquiline Hill, surrounded by its vast acreage of gardens

have to be destroyed in order to remove it, he decided to have the fragments reburied where they lay.

Yet Sixtus remained determined to have an obelisk to embellish the entrance to his private villa, recently completed by Fontana, on the Esquiline Hill near the Basilica of Santa Maria Maggiore. There, surrounded by vast gardens, his sister, Camilla, who had given up her job as washerwoman to take care of him, held sway over Sixtus's nieces and nephews, judiciously marrying them one by one into the nobility of Rome, where they produced for the Peretti family a succession of Roman princes both secular and churchly.

Sixtus's only alternative for an obelisk was to revive the possibility of putting together the three pieces of Augustus's other relic, which still lay near his mausoleum by the Church of San Rocco along the via Ripetta, a hazard to passersby and to traffic on its way to Piazza del Popolo. This time Fontana agreed; but perhaps because he doubted the outcome of the venture, he gave the delicate job of moving the fragments to his brother Marsilio, aided by his nephew, Carlo Moderno. To everyone's amazement the three pieces reached the piazza in front of Santa Maria Maggiore without mishap. There Fontana raised one above the other to hold firm on the spot where they still stand, a grand entrance to the gates of the papal villa, which, in the meantime, has given way to Mussolini's atrocious Terminus railway station.

Encouraged by this second success, and still prone to more erections, Sixtus summoned his historian, Monsignor Michele Mercati, to collect for him from the Vatican Library all the data he could find from classical authors on the subject of obelisks. Such a study might indicate where

Veduta della Facciata di dietro della Basilica di S. Maria Maggiore

The third obelisk of Sixtus V, raised at the back of the Basilica of Santa Maria Maggiore so as to face the entrance to his summer villa. To make way for the pedestal, Sixtus had several houses and old Roman ruins demolished. The inscription tries to link Augustus with the birth of Christ. The papal emblem and the cross atop the obelisk disguise the fact that its pyramidion had been destroyed sometime before it was buried. The etching is by Piranesi.

more obelisks lay buried in Rome. Mercati, who was later to put the fruit of this research to his own use in the first authoritative book on the subject of obelisks (*De gli obelischi di Roma,* 1589), came running to the pope, texts in hand, to inform him that there had once been two great obelisks in the Circus Maximus, the one raised by Augustus and another by Constantius. As no one, Mercati argued, could have lifted them, they must still be there, either whole or in pieces, somewhere under the vast expanse of vineyards and vegetable gardens of the friars of Santa Maria in Cosmedin, which now covered what had once been the great circus. This meant several acres would have to be probed. But no one knew exactly where to look, or how deep, and dowsing for needles was as yet an underdeveloped art. So the pope offered a prize to whoever could first locate a missing obelisk.

Spurred by the offer, an enterprising fellow named Matteo Bartalani da Castello fashioned for himself a 6-meter rod, with a sharp point for easier penetration and a ring handle for easier withdrawal, to probe the area. A few months later, in February 1587, while poking in a cabbage patch, Bartalani came across something hard at a depth of 5 meters. Digging a larger hole, he saw that he had struck the side of an obelisk, which turned out, after more digging, to be part of the great 106-foot-high obelisk brought to Rome by Constantius, the largest ever moved

41

across the sea, and which now lay broken in three large pieces.

Four days later, some thirty paces away, in the direction of the old Baths of Caracalla, Bartalani struck a second obelisk, smaller than the first. From the account of Diodorus Siculus, it was clear to Monsignor Mercati that the obelisk must be the one Augustus had brought from Heliopolis to raise in his circus.

Hole dug by Carlo Moderno in the Circus Maximus, overshadowed by the ancient Baths of Caracalla

42

For his efforts, Bartalani received from the pope the relatively enormous prize of 600 scudi, "a munificence," says Cesare d'Onofrio, "quite incomprehensible in Sixtus V, were it not for the fact that these labors had been performed by Bartalani under the aegis of his favorite, Fontana, who had obtained from the pope the new concession for his nephew Carlo Moderno of digging up the obelisks."

To bring to the surface the two monoliths from where they lay buried in the mud, more than 20 feet below the surface of the kitchen garden, was an enormous task, mostly because of the great amount of water that continually seeped through the ground from springs on the nearby Palatine Hill. Five hundred men were needed to work at the job, three hundred of whom were kept busy day and night drawing off water by various means. By May, both obelisks had been cleared of earth and laboriously raised to the surface under the guidance of Fontana's nephew.

Yet the hardest part was still to come. The three pieces of Constantius's obelisk had to be dragged to the spot where Sixtus V intended to raise them as a single obelisk in the square outside Saint John Lateran, a distance of over 3 kilometers, through narrow streets and up the

Constantius's Circus Maximus obelisks—reraised by Sixtus V in the Lateran Square before the new winter palace built for him by Fontana—had originally been raised in Karnak by Thothmes IV, in 1492 B.C. Spared by Cambyses, in 521 B.C. (when he tripped on his gown and pierced himself with his dagger), the needle, though reduced 3 feet by Fontana to 105 feet, is still the tallest monolithic obelisk standing in the world. Further to destroy pagan Rome, Sixtus ordered the perfectly preserved Arch of Janus demolished to build a base for the obelisk. Fortunately contemporary Roman conservationists raised such a protest, the arch still stands. The obelisk lying in the foreground belonged to Sallustius, and was eventually raised in the Pincio.

The Madonna del Popolo church, at the main entrance to Rome, was deliberately built to lay to rest the ghost of Nero, who was believed to haunt the area. After a cross was placed atop the exorcised obelisk, the spot was used as the starting point for horseracing up the Corso, and as an ideal setting for public executions.

The obelisk, originally quarried by Seti I, second pharaoh of the Ninth Dynasty, was raised by his son Ramses II in Heliopolis about 1300 B.C. Removed to Rome by Augustus it was set up along the spine of the Circus Maximus in 10 B.C. and overturned and buried in the Middle Ages. The original dedicatory inscription of Augustus was replaced on a new pedestal, along with the pious words of Sixtus V.

steep climb to the top of Monte Celio, which required the construction of a massive sloping roadway.

Working fast, Fontana was able to place the first piece on its base a year later, on July 5, 1588. By the twentieth, with the aid of the reconstructed and lengthened *castello* brought piece by piece from Saint Peter's Square, the second fragment had been securely placed above the first. By August 10, another great cross was raised above the pyramidion of the tallest obelisk in Rome. A fresh inscription specially carved into the base told obelisk-weary Romans of the apocryphal tradition that in that same piazza, a few feet from the raised obelisk, Constantine had been baptized the first Christian emperor of Rome.

Further to exalt the cross and demonstrate how "true religion had subjugated idolatry," Sixtus had Fontana drag the second obelisk, the one brought from Alexandria by Augustus, to the Piazza del Popolo, there to be raised, in

The message Sixtus V wished to convey *urbi et orbi* with the re-erection of his obelisks was the ultimate triumph of the church militant against the demons of paganism. Each of his three obelisks in its new Christian surroundings became, in the words of Erik Iversen, "a monumental emblem on a gigantic scale, a sacred allegory and a subtle hieroglyphic enigma of the fashion of the period, to be expounded by the initiated and deciphered by the erudite."

The reraising of Sixtus's obelisks was considered an epoch-making technical achievement. It marked, says Iversen, the end of the Renaissance and the birth of the new orthodoxy of the baroque and the Counterreformation. Everywhere obelisks began to appear on cornices, pinnacles, roofs, buttresses, or as detached monuments in parks and squares. Yet these Catholic symbols were to be taken over almost *in toto* as the Freemasons' symbols of liberty.

the words of Mercati, "as the spoils of war won from paganism by triumphant religion." As the base of this obelisk was in very bad shape, almost 3 palms (76 centimeters) had to sliced away, leaving the obelisk only 23.9 meters long. Thus truncated to a mere 78 feet, Augustus's 235-ton obelisk was raised by Fontana and consecrated on March 25, 1589, with a gilded bronze cross above a star and some mountains to symbolize the reigning pontiff.

The advantage of placing Augustus's obelisk in the Piazza del Popolo was that it could be seen from the end of four of Rome's main streets: the Corso, the Babuino, and the Ripetta, as well as entering Rome from the Flaminias. The disadvantage to Romans in achieving these grand vistas was the destruction of whole neighborhoods of popular hostelries and wineshops. Also destroyed, to provide a new base for the obelisk, was one of the most beautiful of ancient Roman travertine buildings, the Septizodium of Septimus Severus.

Sixtus V—who considered it his duty to destroy as much of pagan Rome as possible—had his name and the date chiseled on one side of the base in bold "Christian" letters. On another side, Cardinal Antoniani, the papal secretary of state, placed a fatuously punning inscription which read as if it were the obelisk speaking: "More august and happier I rise before the sacred temple of her from whose virginal bosom [Santa Maria del Popolo] the sun of justice [Jesus] was born during the empire of Augustus."

3. SYMBOLS OF HERESY

Hermes, known as Trismegistus, or thrice great (as philosopher, priest, and king), is the reputed author of innumerable books, and revealer to mankind of the science of medicine, chemistry, law, art, astrology, music, rhetoric, philosophy, geography, mathematics, anatomy, oratory, and—magic. He is also considered the author of Masonic initiatory rituals, for "nearly all the Masonic symbols are Hermetic in character." Forty-two of the most important of the scientific books attributed to Hermes are believed to have been destroyed in the burning of Alexandria; says Manly P. Hall, "the Romans— and later the Christians—realized that until these books were eliminated they could never bring the Egyptians into subjugation." Hermes' *The Pymander* contains an exposition of Hermetic cosmogony, and the secret sciences of the Egyptians regarding the unfoldment of the human soul, the key to which is the phrase "He who realizes that the body is the tomb of his soul, rises to immortality."

What might have given Sixtus a clue to the original purpose of his newly raised obelisk were the inscriptions on its four sides beautifully carved in hieroglyphs. But these were a mystery to one and all. What little was known about the enigmatic writing of the ancient Egyptians had been painstakingly gleaned from Greek and Roman authors, none of whom, as the Danish historian Erik Iversen puts it, "knew what they were writing about."

Diodorus, who traveled extensively in Egypt in the first century B.C., explained the hieroglyphs as "metaphysical and symbolic." He said that when the Egyptians drew a hawk they meant by it to signify anything that moved swiftly—a concept which they transferred to all swift things. For evil, said Diodorus, the Egyptians used as their symbol a crocodile.

How far the Sicilian was off the mark may be judged by recent discoveries that the crocodile was used by the Egyptians as a symbol for the benevolent dragon in the polar constellation of Draco (the plumed serpent of the Mexicans, and the celestial dragon of the Chinese), and it was also used to express the natatory power of the sun god Horus, who, as a crocodile, could traverse the waters of the deep from equinox to equinox, from Virgo in the fall to Pisces in the spring. Even more esoterically, the crocodile was the symbol of the initiate to the "mysteries" because it could see in the water even with its eyelids closed.

More sensible among the classical authors was Plutarch, the Greek biographer of the first century A.D., who said he was an initiate into the secret mysteries, and considered the hieroglyphs to be rebuslike pictorial expressions of divine ideas and sacred knowledge. The only treatises on hieroglyphs known to have existed were attributed to one of Plutarch's contemporaries, the Alexandrine scholar Chairemon, who was also a tutor to Nero. These had been lost, but fragments quoted from them describe nine hieroglyphs, one of which, a weeping figure, was largely understood to convey the concept of misfortune. Clearly, the classical visitors to Egypt had understood no more of the glyphs than modern tourists, although most of the Greeks and Romans, as Iversen, the most lucid modern scholar on the subject, cuttingly notes,

As the Egyptians likened humanity to a flock of sheep of whom the Supreme Being was the Shepherd, Hermes was depicted as the shepherd's dog. According to Manly P. Hall, the name Hermes is derived from "Herm," a form of Chiram, the personified universal life principle, generally represented by fire. The Greeks equated Hermes with the Egyptian god Thoth.

Hermes, regarded as the embodiment of the human mind, explained how mortal man came to his plight. The Father, the Supreme Mind, says Hermes, being Light and Life, fashioned a glorious universal Man in its own image, not an earthly man but a heavenly Man dwelling in the Light of God. But the Man beheld a shadow upon the earth and a likeness mirrored in the waters, which shadow and likeness were a reflection of Himself. The Man fell in love with His own shadow and desired to descend into it. Nature, beholding the descent, wrapped herself around the man she loved, and the two were mingled. For this reason earthly man is composite. Within him is the Sky Man, immortal and beautiful, without is Nature, mortal and destructible. Thus, suffering is the result of the Immortal Man's falling in love with His shadow and giving up Reality to dwell in the darkness of illusion. . . ."

"tried to cover their ignorance with the pompous cloak of a learned 'philosophical terminology.'"

By the time the Egyptians had become Christianized *en masse* in the second-century reign of the emperor Justinian, the hieroglyphs had been reduced to sinful pagan symbols, no longer to be read, discussed, or understood. Wherever possible they were to be disfigured or destroyed. With the burning of the great library of Alexandria a further quietus was laid on the subject which was to last a thousand years. Having burned the libraries and defaced the inscriptions, says Manly P. Hall, "Christians invented a ridiculous conglomeration of puerility which for several hundred years was palmed off upon a comparatively illiterate world under the name of Egyptology." And so it wasn't until the fifteenth century that any new light could be shed on the significance of the mysterious glyphs.

What the bright young minds of the Renaissance were to learn about their meaning was based largely on three manuscripts, fortuitously recovered, from late classical authors. One of these was found in 1414 in a monastery in Germany by the Florentine Poggio Bracciolini, later chancellor of the Florentine Republic. It consisted of the last eighteen books of the history of Rome written in the fourth century A.D. by Rome's last major historian, Ammianus Marcellinus. In Florence, the manuscript was given to Niccolò de Nicolli, then the greatest authority on classical bibliography, who had it copied and circulated in humanistic circles. Book seventeen contained a history of the obelisk of Constantius, and included a short general digression on obelisks and on Egyptian writing; there Ammianus said the Egyptians did not write with letters "as we do," but with signs expressing whole words or concepts. As an example he used the honeybee to represent a king, "for kings must exercise their rule with sweetness and also possess a sting."

Ammianus gave an extensive translation into Greek of the inscription on Augustus's Circus Maximus obelisk, which he said was quoted from the work of Hermapion, about whose person or work little or nothing was, or is, known, other than that he is presumed to have been a Hellenistic scholar living in Rome about the time of Augustus.

From Ammianus's manuscript the Florentines learned that the obelisk Augustus had raised in the Circus Maximus had once stood in Heliopolis, where it had been erected by the pharaoh Seti I, presumably about 1300 B.C.; also, that Seti had died before the inscription could be completed, a job carried on by his son Ramses II. As

Glyphs on Augustus's obelisk. In the Renaissance, says William R. Heckscher, obelisks were considered "the most powerful witnesses of a primordial religiosity and spirituality" and were accordingly interpreted as links between earth and heaven, "for if one looked at them from base to apex they would seem to suggest by their evanescence the transition from things terrestrial to incorporeal Divinity itself." To this Heckscher adds that, more importantly, if seen conversely, the obelisks, by their pyramidal shape, might be compared to the pencil of rays issuing from the center of the sun. Thus the "Egyptologists" of the Renaissance deduced from the classical authors of Greece and Rome that "through their obelisks the Egyptians imitated the rays of the sun whom they themselves worshipped."

to which of the enigmatic symbols represented what words or letters in Latin, Greek, or in any other language, the mystery remained, only slightly illuminated by a second document which surfaced five years later, in 1419.

This was a manuscript found on the Greek island of Andros by another Florentine traveler, Cristoforo Buondelmonte, who brought it back to Florence in 1422. Entitled *Hieroglyphica,* it purported to be a sixth-century A.D. translation into Greek of an original treatise on hieroglyphs written by one Horapollo of Nilopolis—an obvious pseudonym concocted from the gods Horus and Apollo—believed to have been an Egyptian scribe who had lived a couple of centuries earlier than the translator. Though the Greek was considered inferior, and the meaning of the glyphs had evidently already been lost by the time the original work was composed, it still constituted the only major treatise on hieroglyphs to have survived from classical times. As such, if only because of its uniqueness, it was, as Iversen points out, one of the first manuscripts to be set in print, in 1505, along with Aesop's fables, becoming for a while the canonical authority on all hieroglyphical questions.

The work is divided into two books, similar but possibly from different sources. Each of a total of 189 paragraphs deals with a separate hieroglyph, and its purported meaning.

To denote impudence, said Horapollo, the Egyptians represented a housefly, because "though perpetually driven away, it nevertheless returns." The ant, according to the *Hieroglyphica,* was the Egyptian glyph for knowledge, "For whatever a man may carefully conceal, this creature obtains a knowledge of." More discerning is his Egyptian glyph for discernment: a mouse. "When many different sorts of bread lie before him, the mouse selects the purest from among them, and eats it. Hence the baker's selection is guided by mice."

The number 16 was used by the Egyptians, according to Horapollo, to indicate voluptuousness, the explanation being that sixteen is the age "when men begin to hold commerce with women and to procreate children." Sexual intercourse was depicted by two 16s; and in Cory's English translation of the Greek, the explanation is discreetly left in Latin: *"Cum enim sedecim voluptatem esse disimus: congressus autem, duplici constet, maris ac foeminae, voluptate, proptera alia sedici adscribunt"*; which simply means that as intercourse requires voluptuousness from both male and female, another 16 must be added. Some of the Horapollion aphorisms were drawn

Thoth, self-produced divine intelligence, at the creation, uttered
the words which formed the material world, is depicted as a
man with the head of an ibis. He
was known as the "Scribe of the
company of Gods," and was the
author of the secret *Book of
Thoth,* since lost, which was said
to contain the arcana of the mysteries. Filled with hieroglyphics,
the book was purported to give
those acquainted with its use
unlimited power over the spirits
of the air and over subterranean
divinities. From the older Egyptians, the Ptolomaic priests
learned that Thoth bore the head
of an ibis because the bird
sleeping with its head beneath
its wing assumes the shape of a
heart—seat of life and true intelligence. The footstep or pace of
the ibis was said to measure
exactly 1 cubit a unit considered
sacred and which, according to
initiates, was given by Thoth,
and appears mathematically in
all the measures of the universe.
The ibis's intestines were said to
be exactly 96 cubits, or 144
feet, long.

from folklore. The beaver was to symbolize a man with
self-inflicted injuries. "For the beaver," says Horapollo
"tears out his own testicles, and casts them as spoil to
his pursuer." Other bits of wisdom verge on magic,
similiar to that of the Hawaiian Huna, who, according to
Harvard's modern epigrapher, Barry Fell, may be descendants of the same Egyptians. To symbolize a woman who
miscarries, notes Horapollo, the Egyptians depicted a
mare kicking a wolf: "Not only by kicking a wolf does a
mare miscarry, but it immediately miscarries if it should
merely tread on the footstep of a wolf." Despite such
farfetched homilies, there remain in the paragraphs of
Horapollo strains of the perennial wisdom of the ancients,
as is evident when he uses the grasshopper as a symbol
for mystic man, a notion which survived through the
Platonic philosopher Apuleius to Collodi in Pinocchio's
talking cricket, who, in Horapollo's words, "does not utter
sounds through his mouth, but chirping by means of his
spine sings a sweet melody." And although only a dozen
of the seven-score glyphs or symbols described by Horapollo turned out to be even closely related to their
meaning in Egyptian, as deciphered by modern Egyptologists, publication of the book launched a vast quest into
their secret meaning.

The best clue was to come from the most extraordinary
of the three documents that surfaced in the fifteenth
century, one which was to have a powerful revolutionary
effect on political minds to this day, a Greek manuscript in
seventeen books brought from Macedonia to Cosimo de'
Medici. It was said to contain the secret wisdom of Thoth,
the Egyptian sage whom the Greeks called Hermes Trismegistus, or the Thrice Great Hermes. Translated into
Latin by Marsilio Ficino in 1471, it came to be known as
the *Corpus Hermeticum,* a source for all the various and
powerfully effective Hermetic philosophies that followed.
According to Ficino, a quiet, scholarly philosopher with
strong leanings toward paganism, Thoth, or Hermes, considered a contemporary or predecessor of Moses, had
attained to gnosis, or the knowledge of God, by a sort of
union with the godhead. Hermes was thus considered the
first great teacher of the gnosis. After his death, he
became a god, "as anyone who attains to gnosis becomes a god after death."

Man, according to Hermes, had taken on a mortal body
merely to commune with nature, but at heart remained a
spirit, a divine, creative, and immortal essence. Living
beings did not die, but, being composite, dissolved the
bond in order to reunite and re-form. Nothing dies; it only

Marsilio Ficino (1433–1499), Florentine philosopher patronized by Cosimo de' Medici, was the guiding spirit of Florence's Platonic Academy, which he wished to make into a spiritual community. He revived the Neoplatonic doctrine of a world-soul and identified demons with the Christian hierarchy of angels, "supercelestial" and "elemental," with souls and etheric bodies according to their status, of a like nature to human spirits. Ficino believed that the Egyptians with their magic could bring down spiritual entities into their statues of gods and maintain communication with them.

Giovanni Pico della Mirandola (1463–1494)

dissolves and transforms. The gnosis consisted in re-becoming a god.

To keep this explosive knowledge secret from those who might profane it, yet have it available to the initiate, it was, said Ficino, originally recorded in the Hermetic language of glyphs. As an explanation, he adduced that "the Egyptian priests, when they wished to signify divine things, did not use letters, but whole figures. . . ." This he followed with the Goethian notion that "God doubtless has a knowledge of things which is not complex discursive thought about its subject, but is, the simple steadfast form of it."

To Ficino the hieroglyphs were Platonic ideas about the universe and its spiritual realms, made visible, and through his translations into Latin of the works of Plato and of the Neoplatonist Plotinus, Ficino brought to the Renaissance an entirely new concept of Egypt as the source of the cosmic wisdom of both Plato and Pythagoras.

From Plotinus, the Florentines learned that the hieroglyphs were not images of the things they represented but Hermetic symbols devised by Hermes and endowed with qualities by means of which the symbols could recall to the initiate an insight into the very essence and substance of reality. Functioning not through rationalization, but by divine inspiration or illumination, they were to reveal the world of the soul, leading to an ultimate understanding of the true nature of the cosmos; this to be made possible by an immediate contact between the human intellect and divine ideas. Compared with the pedestrian tenets of Aristotle and Aquinas, these were flighty concepts. But because Plotinus was born in Egypt, and because Clement of Alexandria was also from Egypt, the men of the Renaissance were willing to go along with this interpretation of the hieroglyphs.

Convinced by such sensitive minds as that of Ficino's brilliant pupil, Giovanni Pico della Mirandola, who had mastered Hebrew, Chaldee, and Arabic as well as Latin and Greek, that profound religious doctrine was best expressed in enigmas, Renaissance scholars realized that the mysterious hieroglyphs which appeared on the obelisks could be explained as symbols by means of which it might be possible to express the innermost secrets of life, and open a window onto the world of magic. Magic, as practiced by the Renaissance magus, or master of esoteric wisdom, was designed to enable the "magus-man" to regain powers which were virtually godlike, there being, they believed, no latent force in heaven or on earth which could not be released by an initiate through proper

51

When Savonarola raised his voice in the pulpit against the gangster methods and the gross corruption of the Church, prophesying a holocaust if the pope did not reform, he was offered a cardinal's hat to desist. When he replied, "No hat will I wear but that of a martyr reddened by my own blood," he was seized and obliged of his request. For forty days he was tortured to elicit a false confession, then hung on a cross with two of his accomplices and burned alive before a howling mob.

EGO SV̄ PAPA

Cartoon deriding Alexander VI as venal and corrupt. A Spaniard by birth, known as the "infamous Roderic Borgia, greedy for gold and lustful for women," he owed his cardinal's hat to the nepotism of an uncle, Pope Calixtus III, and his papal crown to the vast sums of money he spent

inducements: a conceit, in the eyes of the Church, which bordered on heresy.

By blending the wisdom of the Jewish Cabala with the gnostic-Neoplatonist tradition to create the foundations of his higher magic, Pico found in meditative trances the technique for escaping from his body to explore higher realms of consciousness. And here came the rub. Both Ficino and Pico stressed the essentially sexual essence of their magic. Both provided justification for sexual magic as an ecstatic reconciliation of opposites in which a higher state could be attained.

An early forerunner of the political martyr Wilhelm Reich, Ficino regarded sexual desire as a current of energy responsible for the cohesion of the entire universe. To Florentine sensitives, erotic love could thus be a method of absorption into, or magical mastery of, the world of the divine. Ficino even went so far as to commend the pagan revels of Bacchus (or Pan) as a way of escaping from normal human limitations into an ecstasy in which the soul was miraculously transformed into the beloved god himself. To the churchmen of Rome, who officially condemned sex as satanic and evil, though they were personally clandestinely happy to indulge, this was heresy, to be dealt with by torture and the stake.

Because of the heretical nature of Pico's pronouncements, and especially because of his surprising thesis that no science gave a better confirmation of the divinity of Christ than "magia and the Kabbalah," he was arrested by the self-appointed vicar of Christ, Pope Innocent VIII (1484–92), a supposed celibate who openly subsidized a litter of bastards at the Church's expense (funded from the sale of indulgences to those guilty of killing innocent heretics) and who had launched his reign by issuing a bull ordering a holy war for the extermination of all witches and magicians. Only by making a public apology was Pico able to avoid being burned at the stake. Influenced by his friend, the reforming monk Girolamo Savonarola—who *was* burned, for constantly inveighing against the infamously corrupt rule of Innocent and accurately prophesying his imminent death—Pico, a tall, handsome young man, much loved by the ladies, chose to abandon the gay life of a Renaissance nobleman with his princely patrimony, to wander barefoot through the world preaching the simple Christianity of Jesus of Nazareth. Though somewhat vindicated by Innocent's successor, Alexander VI, Pico, to avoid further persecution, judiciously translated himself to another dimension at the early age of thirty-one, depriving the world of one of its brightest minds and its sweetest

52

bribing other cardinals to obtain their vote. Once in office, Borgia lavished several fortunes on a score of illegitimate children provided by a variety of mistresses. His son Caesar, named archbishop of Valencia at 16, was made a cardinal at 18, along with his nephew Giovanni. Another son became duke of Gandia, owner of a vast personal fiefdom carved out of Church property. For himself, Borgia indulged in a life of extraordinary luxury, enlivened—as pornographically described in his secretary's memoirs—with dancing, stage plays, and sexual orgies. Only when the corpse of the duke of Gandia was washed up by the Tiber did Alexander shut himself up in Castel Sant'Angelo, overcome with grief, and promise to reform the Church. But this too proved an idle promise when suspicion of the murder fell on his son Caesar, then the most powerful cardinal in Rome. Alexander rewarded the suspect with the confiscated property of another noble, and allowed him to become a general to launch a series of military campaigns designed to refill the papal coffers. Cardinal Michaeli was cynically poisoned and his property seized. Any cardinal, nobleman, or official with money could be accused of an offense, imprisoned, tortured, and made to confess; murdered, he was deprived of his property. Anyone trying to oppose such action was seized by the pope's Spanish mercenaries and punished with death. When Alexander finally died at the age of 72, apparently by poison he intended for someone else, Caesar kept the news from the world long enough to seize the papal treasury. By the time the pope's death was announced, his body was so horribly decomposed it had to be quickly and forcibly stuffed into the first available coffin, too small for his rotting six-foot carcass.

souls. Ficino, determined to pursue the magical lore derived from the Egyptians, managed to avoid the stake only by taking holy orders.

What Pico had been guilty of was following two dangerously libertarian notions—as spelled out in Ficino's translation of Hermes's *The Pimander* and *The Asclepius*—which the Catholic Church, a political institution determined to defend by force its temporal power and financial benefits, could not tolerate. The first of the notions considered anathema by the Church, because it made superfluous the role of priest, bishop, or pope, consisted in the suggestion that "unless you make yourself equal to God, you cannot understand God; for like is not intelligible save to like. . . ." This was followed by the simple recipe for attaining to such a grand conceit: "make yourself grow to a greatness beyond measure; by a bound free yourself from the body; raise yourself above all time, become Eternity; then you will understand God." The divinity in question was, of course, neither the vindictive patriarch of Moses nor the caster-into-hellfire of the Roman Inquisitors, but the gnostic's wonderfully loving and all-pervasive One.

As the Church suspected that the revival of the Hermetic tradition—going back to the wisdom of the ancient Egyptian religion as symbolized by the great obelisks and their enigmatic hieroglyphs—posed a direct threat to its control, and that this "heretical" wisdom might be more truly a religion of love than their own debased and cruel version, popes and Inquisition began to exterminate on a grand scale followers of the gnosis wherever its proponents overtly displayed their beliefs.

As early as A.D. 321, when Constantine became the first Christian emperor, the Church of Rome set about suppressing all that was pagan, refusing to recognize the ancient mysteries. No longer teaching a universal religion, the Church pronounced the arts of ancient Egypt wicked and magical. Of these arts, hieroglyphic writing was considered the worst because it appeared to concentrate the secrets of them all.

At the Council of Nicea, presided over by Constantine—ostensibly to suppress the Arian heresy—the spiritual considerations of Christianity became once and for all subordinate to political control. Shortly after Constantine's death, to secure total temporal power, the Church produced what one historian has labeled perhaps the most shameless forgery in the history of false presences: the Donation of Constantine. "This document," says historian Michael Harrison, "purported to be the instrument by which the Emperor Constantine surrendered the imperial

Constantine defeating Maxentius
at the Milvian Bridge

insignia of sovereignty over the Western Empire to the
Pope of Rome"—applying to himself and his successors
forever the emperor's title of Pontifex Maximus. "Appeal
to this impudent forgery," says Harrison, "was made by
Pope after Pope for centuries until, indeed, with the
smashing of Rome's total power by the Reformation, the
Donation of Constantine might be denounced for the
swindle that men had long known it to be."

By the seventh century the Church had rewritten Catholic dogma to obliterate most of the original teachings of
Jesus, substituting for the gentle Christian Gospels the
narrow authoritarianism of Rome. Gone was the original
Christian doctrine of reincarnation in favor of what has
been called "a one-way trip to heaven or hell." This
limited view, coupled with the Church's unwillingness to
recognize the value of human sexuality, or the ancient
pagan rites of fertility, was to have a deadly effect on man
and nature, worsening as the centuries passed.

Then came the papal encyclical cynically laying perpetual sexual chastity on the priests of Rome. Unable to
contract a valid marriage and thus beget legitimate heirs,
priests and prelates could only will their property back to
a Church which could only grow richer; that is, all with the
exception of the cardinals and popes, who managed to
create an enduring "black" aristocracy with the property
they alienated from the Church to their "nephews." Being
a rule and not an option, priestly chastity had the effect of
unleashing on Christian women a pack of sex-starved
clerics who could only satisfy their lust illicitly, with a
sense of guilt to besmirch any tenderness or love, a shift
from the world of eros to that of porno, and the sadistic
persecution of happier, healthier mortals.

Blinding the archbishop of Ravenna

Piercing the eyes of an "heretical" bishop with a sharp iron

Using a hodgepodge of undigested mythology picked up from Egypt and the East, the Church set about scaring those who would not obey them (and pay them a 10-percent tax) with threats of eternal damnation in a fiery hell for sins or purported sins which only the Church could forgive, against payment of cash. Thanks to the sale of indulgences, crime without risk could be committed by payment in advance of the required sum: 7 pounds for perjury, 36 for incest, 1 ducat and 4 pounds for parricide, 11 ducats 6 pounds for poisoning a stranger.

But the system, further corrupted by simony, risked total collapse, and the Church, determined to survive, hit upon the only method it could envisage: the extermination of its enemies. For the dirty work, the pontiffs organized an SS Corps of investigating executioners: the Inquisition.

Anyone teaching a gospel closer to that of the ancient Egyptians—such as the Essene, the Therapeut, the gnostic, and the Manichee—was relentlessly persecuted, tortured, and painfully put to death.

Theodorus (642–649) started the vogue of dipping his pen into consecrated wine when signing the death warrants of heretics. The inhuman ordeal of torture by water was invented by Eugenius II (824–827). Gregory II (996–999) had the eyes of antipope John pierced and his nose and tongue cut out.

Among the first to be executed was Manes, originator of the Manichaean "heresy," which he had learned from the Egyptian philosopher and magician Terebinthus. Manes was crucified and flayed alive for having considered the philosophical system of the pagan sages superior to that of either Judaism or Christianity. The followers of Manes, known as the "Sons of the Widow" in memory of the widowed Isis and of the Osirian mysteries of Egypt, were accused of the crime of believing the spirit of God to be Light, radiant with the virtue of love, faith, fidelity, high-mindedness, wisdom, meekness, knowledge, understanding, mystery, and insight. Like the Essenes, the Manichaeans called themselves "Sons of the Light." Believing in metempsychosis and the ultimate salvation of all men, they held enlightened and purified love as the highest of human emotions, a love expressed through kindliness, friendliness, tolerance, and patience. In their opinion, only those who truly loved their fellow men and women and proved that affection through the defense of the rights of man were entitled to regard themselves as religious.

Gnostic sects, who found their primeval wisdom in the ancient mysteries of Egypt, and in the efficacy of numbers and hieroglyphs, were found guilty of searching for the

55

Gnostic symbols

At the end of World War II in the cave-riddled mountains of Jabal-al-Tarif in Upper Egypt, a discovery was made which threw light on the beliefs of the early Christian gnostics. Most of what had been known about them had come from their Catholic detractors who considered them heretics. In a cave, where they were hiding in the course of a blood feud, two Arabs (who had just murdered a rival, dismembered his body and eaten his heart) came upon a red earthen jar about a meter high. Inside were thirteen papyrus books bound in leather. Several were used to make fires, but in what remained scholars were to decipher fifty-two texts in Coptic dating from the early Christian era. They contained previously unknown gospels such as that of Thomas, of Philip, and of The Egyptians,

esoteric meaning in religion, and ritually massacred by the early followers of the Church. What the sexually tortured Fathers held against the gnostics was their love feasts, which the Fathers, without a glimmer of the philosophy entailed, characterized as grossly perverted orgies. Early Christian gnostics were accused of putting out the lamps in their churches at the end of evening services to indulge in indiscriminate sexual intercourse; also of practicing the Tantric ritual of offering human semen as a sacrament.

Even the Neoplatonic school of Alexandria was attacked; its beautiful and eloquent leader Hypatia, stripped naked by a mob of Catholic monks, was barbarously murdered with the complicity of Cyril, bishop of Alexandria. Yet from the Alexandrine school the ancient mysteries of the Egyptian gnostic-Christians were kept alive by the sect of Sufis, overtly Moslem, but with deeper philosophical roots. In Islam, Hermes became Idris, master of the Hermetic mystery, known only to the few. A Sufi heir to the mystery cults was Dhun-Nun, an Upper Nile Egyptian who derived his gnosis, or vision of unity, from a decipherment of hieroglyphs on the Egyptian temples. His ideal of an interreligious reconciliation was carried on by the sect of Ismaeli, who passed on to the Crusaders from the West, and especially to the Knights Templar, elements of Sufi esotericism and what came to be known as the Rosicrucian secrets.

Brought from the Levant to southern Europe, the Egyptian beliefs of gnostic, Manichee, and Sufi gave rise to the Bogomils, Cathars, Albigeois, Paulicians, Pataranes, Tisserands, and Waldensians. Secret assemblies of the Manichees and Cathars were dedicated to the liberation of human beings from the despotism and tyranny of the Roman Church, so that in the end all nations might dwell together in peace, governed by just laws and noble examples.

The Albigensians, with a stronghold in the south of France during the twelfth and thirteenth centuries, went even further. Heirs to a magical secret inherited from Egypt, known to gnostic and early Christian, they could help a soul painlessly across the threshold of death into what they termed "reunion with the Light." The Albigensian creed offered an escape from the endless wheel of reincarnation, an escape from the illusory prison of the body, with its seeming pleasures, and a "return within the compass of a single life into union with spirit." Here was an echo of the ancient Vedas, along with the message of the Buddha. Nirvana to the Albigensians was not an annihilation of consciousness but a participation in the

evidently translations made about 400 A.D. of more ancient Greek manuscripts, possibly earlier than the Canonical Gospels attributed to Mark, Matthew, Luke and John. The content of the gospels, condemned by "orthodox" Catholics some time after Constantine, ranged from descriptions of the origin of the universe to myths, magic and instruction in mystical practice. One of the reasons for condemning these "Gnostic Gospels," as they came to be known, is given by Elaine Pagels in her book by that title. From the Apocalypse of Peter, she quotes the risen Christ as explaining to Peter that those "who name themselves bishop and also deacon, as if they had received their authority from God, are in reality waterless canals" and although they "do not understand mystery, boast that the mystery of truth belongs to them alone." The author of this little known gospel accuses the orthodox of setting up an "imitation Church" in place of the true Christian "brotherhood."

Another reason for condemning these early Christian texts may be found in the Gospel of Mary Magdalene, which hints at an erotic relationship between Jesus and his lovable follower; though, as Pagels is quick to point out, mystics have constantly chosen sexual metaphors to describe mystical experiences. But the most obvious reason for condemning these gospels—which some dedicated soul took the trouble to secrete in a cave some sixteen hundred years ago—was clearly political. Whoever could claim to *know* through inner vision could claim that his or her authority equalled or even surpassed that of Peter and his bloodthirsty successors. The gnosis, offering the initiate a direct access to divinity—of which priests and bishops might even be ignorant—also offered a theological justification for refusing to obey either bishop or priest. So the moment the Catholic Church obtained political and military power, the subversive gospels were everywhere destroyed and their proponents butchered.

universal consciousness—a state of love bordering on the divine.

In the Roman Church, the Albigensians saw an institution ridden with superstition, lacking in philosophical depth, corrupt and cruel; it seemed to them that Satan himself must have been responsible for setting up the Churches of Christendom as a means of destroying human souls. Like the Cathars, they renounced not Satan and his works and pomp, but "the harlot Church."

To the Albigeois enforced marriage by the Church was odious; he recognized no other sanction for the union of man and woman than mutual attraction. Some went so far as to proclaim the sacraments useless, suggesting that women ought to be communalized on account of the vanity of the pleasure obtained from them. Yet an advanced Cathar would not commit adultery, nor homicide, nor lie, nor swear an oath, nor pick and steal, nor do unto another that which he would not have wished done unto himself. He was to pardon wrongdoers, love his enemies, pray for them that calumniated him, offer the other cheek to the smiter, give up his mantle to him that took his tunic, and neither judge nor condemn.

Dante is reputed to have been a secret member of the Albigensian Church and to have officiated as a pastor in various European cities. He was also a member of a group called Fedeli d'Amore, or Faithful in Love; and Roberto Cesare Ambesi in his *I rosa croce* mentions a ciphered Rosicrucian wisdom hidden in the lines of the *Divine Comedy,* obtained mystically and by initiation, which, says Ambesi, transcends the limits of the times in which Dante lived.

The gnostics' radiant cult of the spirit, which took possession of men, a cult without vast buildings, elaborate decorations, pontifical hierarchy, or rich vestments, was seen by the popes as a serious threat to their materialistic church. Once it became clear that perhaps a third of all nominal Christians were secretly practicing an heretical religion, Christian persuasion was replaced by the rack, the gibbet, and the stake. Declaring that anyone who attempted to construe a personal view of God which conflicted with the dogma of the Church of Rome must be burned without pity, Pope Innocent III decided on a crusade "to exterminate the impious," accusing the Cathars of being "lascivious sects, who, overflowing with libertine ardor, are but slaves to the pleasures of the flesh."

To the cold nobility of northern France he offered as a lure the conquest of temperate and independent Provence,

57

Burning a victim of religious persecution

with its beautiful châteaus, its luscious vineyards, olives, and fig trees. German mercenaries were enlisted on the promise of looting the rich southern towns and of raping their lovely women, renowned as lighthearted, hot-blooded, and perversely sensuous.

And so was inflicted on the south of France one of the most ferocious massacres in history. Bands of northern brigands pillaged and plundered. In the Cathedral of Saint-Nazaire twelve thousand "heretics" were killed when the roof collapsed. Those who tried to flee were cut down and butchered. Thousands more were burned at the stake. At Toulouse, Bishop Foulque put to death ten thousand people accused of heresy. At Beziers the entire population of more than twenty thousand was slaughtered. At Citeau, when asked how to distinguish Catholics from Catharists, the abbé replied with his famed cynicism: "Kill them all; God will know his own."

Thus it fell to the Knights Templar to act as custodians of the esoteric tradition descended from the Egyptian and Chaldean sages. Anomalously acting as "military apostles of the religion of love," they dedicated themselves to the restoration of the Church as they believed it to have existed in the time of the apostles, setting up a bulwark against the abuses of the theocratic regime in Rome, with its cruel and despotic Inquisitors. From their Moslem peers in the Orient the Templars had learned to acknowledge Jesus as a great and holy prophet, one who had been taken to Egypt to be initiated into the highest degrees of occult science, recognized by the priests of Osiris as the long-promised incarnation of Horus, eventually to be consecrated Sovereign Pontiff of a Universal Religion.

Along with a reverence for the doctrines of alchemy, astrology, magic, and cabalistic talismans, the Templars

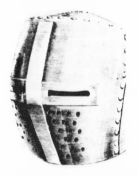

The torture and execution of Waldensian "heretics"

Grand Master of Templars

Templar uniforms and arms

appear to have brought to Europe from the East the secret teachings of the gnostics and the Sufis dealing with Tantric sex. According to the nineteenth-century German historian von Hammer-Purgstall the Templars secretly adopted a form of the rites of Gnosticism founded on phallic worship or reverence for the sexual principle in nature.

Formed in Palestine in 1118 by Hugues de Payen and Godefroy de Saint-Aumer, with seven other French knights, the Templars set up their order in the ruins of the Temple of Solomon; and the symbolic rebuilding of the temple was to become one of their spiritual goals: the temple of God being man. Digging in the foundations, they are said to have found a rare manuscript which traced for them the procedure employed by King Solomon in realizing the *Great Work,* the alchemical transmutation of the human soul back into light.

It was then that the Templars came into contact with the sect of the Johannite followers of Saint John the Apostle, whose secret objective was the restoration of the esoteric Egyptian tradition, to be achieved by the overthrow of the Bishops of Rome, in order to establish universal civil liberty, and thus reunite mankind under the one eternal religion of the world. This goal became the secret dream of the Templars: the formation of a civilization that would reconcile East and West, starting with a unique brotherhood of Christian and Moslem. But to achieve their goal they chose the same anomalous path as their opponents: they set about amassing great riches, becoming not only the greatest soldiers of the West, but its greatest bankers. They also became great builders of cathedrals, accomplished diplomatists, and the most reliable chamberlains at the courts of Europe.

59

Encounter between Christians
and Saracens at Mt. Hattin in
Palestine on July 4, 1187. Thirty
thousand Moslems and Jews
were massacred in Jerusalem by
Christian crusaders. To stop this
senseless slaughter, the Knights
Templar found means of communicating with their Moslem broth-
ers-in-arms as brothers in spirit.

Knights Templar entering their
fortified temple in Paris, built in
the thirteenth century opposite
the Louvre

Philip the Fair, king of France from 1285 to 1314

Baphomet, the Templar symbol of Gnostic rites based on phallic worship and the power of directed will. The androgynous figure with a goat's beard and cloven hooves is linked to the horned god of antiquity, the Goat of Mendes. The Tantric sexual symbolism of the figure is highlighted by the caduceus in place of the phallus. Modern exegesists see in the androgynous glyph the formula of sexual magic, symbolizing "the perfect fusion of Solar and Lunar energies in one organism."

The torture of de Molay

Then came disaster. King Philip the Fair of France developed a similar idea of making himself ruler of a vast Christian empire centered at Jerusalem. He also needed money. First he seized all the Jews in his kingdom and forced them to give up their fortunes by removing one of their eyes and threatening to remove the other. Then he so debased the value of the national currency he was obliged to take refuge from an angry populace in the Paris temple. There, among his protecting Templars, he coined the idea of seizing their riches.

On October 13, 1307, throughout France, some five thousand knights were arrested by officers of the king. Seized without warning, and kept in ignorance of their fellow knights, they were told that others had confessed and that their lives would be spared if they too confessed. But to what?

To have charged the Templars with planning an ecumenical world would have meant unveiling Philip's own scheme. So recourse was had to the easier charge of magic and heresy. Public indignation was aroused by further charges of sodomy and orgies with female demons. To these accusations were added denying Christ, spitting on the Cross, and worshiping the devil in the form of an idol called Baphomet.

Grand Master Jacques de Molay, with his bodyguard of sixty knights, was imprisoned in his own temple. Only a few hundred knights escaped. The rest were turned over for interrogation to Guillaume de Paris, Grand Inquisitor for France. Of the 140 Templars seized in Paris 36 soon died under torture; 54 more, in horrible torment, some being strung up by the testicles, confessed to whatever the Inquisitors asked, but repudiated their confessions as

Templar strung up by the testicles

Clement V (Pope, 1305-1314)—
Bertrand de Got, a Frenchman
and former archbishop of Bordeaux—had the seat of the papacy transferred from Rome to
Avignon by King Philippe le Bel.
He is accused by historians of
issuing "a series of bulls, perhaps the most disgraceful that
ever proceeded from a vice-
regent of God." Thirsting for the
Templar riches, he let himself be
bribed by the Knights of Saint
John to share the loot. In what is
described as "the most suggestive sale of indulgence on record," he offered Edward II of
England full remission of his sins
if he allowed reinstatement of
the use of torture by the Inquisition. A month after the burning of
de Molay, Clement died in agony
from the loathsome disease of
lupus.

soon as the torture was stopped. They were piled into
wagons and carried to the fields near the convent of
Saint-Antoine, where they were tortured to death by slow
fire. All refused offers of pardon if they recanted, manifesting instead a constancy which, as a contemporary
chronicler tells us, "placed their souls in great peril of
damnation, for it led people to believe they were
innocent."

Anyone who dared defend the knights was himself
accused of heresy and condemned to death. When the
pope, Clement V, tried to intervene on behalf of the
imprisoned Templars, he was thwarted by Philip. Being a
Frenchman who held court at Avignon, dependent on Philip
for his freedom, the pope quickly gave in. And he too had
his eye on the riches of the Templars.

De Molay, de Charney, de Peraud, and de Gonneville,
the top officers of the Temple, were kept in jail for seven
years, repeatedly tortured, until they confessed. Brought
to trial and condemned to perpetual imprisonment, de
Molay and de Charney, to everyone's amazement, arose
and declared themselves guilty not of the crimes imputed
to them, but of having basely betrayed the order to save
their lives under torture.

On the same day, by sunset, two stakes had been
erected on a small island near Notre Dame, the Island of
Jews, opposite the king's gardens, piled around with
burning charcoal to cause a slow death. When Grand
Master de Molay saw the fire he stripped and slowly
approached the patibulum, his body already so scarred
that the skin of his back, belly, and thighs hung in shreds.
It took all night and all day for him to die in a drawn-out,
deliberate agony.

With the Temple suppressed in France, Philip seized
what he could of its vast fortune. But the spirit of the

Templars was long to outlive him. In prison, de Molay is said to have secretly instituted four lodges of occult Masonry and to have designated a hiding place for much of the order's wealth. Some of the Templars who managed to escape from France took refuge in Scotland and England. In the latter the Temple survived in London's Inns of Court, keeping alive, underground, the ancient wisdom of Egypt passed on by Cathar, Manichee, gnostic, Sufi, Albigensian, and Free Mason.

With the suppression of the guilds on the Continent, the secret wisdom was no longer built into the stonework of the great cathedrals funded by the Templars. It was to survive instead in the veiled ritual of the lodge, and in the Hermetic language of the poet.

The same lawyer, de Nogaret, who prosecuted the Templars had previously seized and imprisoned Pope Boniface VIII, the shock of which so maddened the old pope he killed himself by beating his head against the walls of his room. Boniface had excommunicated Philip for contravening canon law by taxing French clergy to finance his war against England. After Boniface's death Philip, in order to have all his bulls annulled, especially *Unam sanctum* (which asserted the supremacy of the papacy over any temporal ruler), had his docile minion Clement V condemn Boniface posthumously for sodomy, murder, sorcery, and consulting with demons. Boniface was further accused by de Nogaret of murdering his predecessor, the weak-minded Pope Celestine V, by drilling a hole in the wall of his bedchamber and representing his voice as that of a messenger of God.

4. ELIZABETHAN WITS AND WIZARDS

What the Church most disliked about magic was the notion that individuals might commune directly with disembodied entities, especially to use them as intermediaries with higher or angelic realms. The priests of Rome wished to keep for themselves the sole right to deal with the beyond; and though they maintained they could invoke into their own churches a holy spirit, they considered anyone else who did anything similar worthy only of hell.

It was not that the Church did not believe in the existence of spirits that communed with mortals; the churchmen simply changed their nature from Greek δαενοηs—immaterial beings or departed souls believed to hold a middle ground between man and the deities of the pagans—into Latin demons, characterized by the Church as evil and satanic.

On the authority of Aquinas, any commerce with such demons, though it might bring instant reward, was believed in the end to serve only the demons who were considered deceptive, and even if apparently good, actually only lying in wait to delude those who sought them.

Jan Wierus, one of the best known physicians of the sixteenth century, considered an originator of modern psychiatry, and famous in his time for an outspoken opposition to the persecution and torture of witches, even took a census in which he counted 7,405,926 demons, divided into 72 companies, under a captain or a prince, all commanded by *the* Evil One, a fiend, who, in the eyes of the Church, bore a relentless hatred for the human race. That these devils of an airy substance could penetrate human beings, "could take possession of a human spirit, and give rise to spectral images," Wierus had no doubt. So *all* magic, black or white, with the exception of that perpetrated by the Church in its own rites and incantations, became taboo.

This trend against magic had been growing in the Roman Church since the reign of Pope John XXII (1316-49), who issued a bull *Super Illius Specula* against the use of magic, and ordered all books on the subject turned in for burning. Accusing his opponents of heresy, sorcery and demon worship, he condemned those accused of magic, and especially those who claimed to commune with spirits, to be tortured and burned alive—a profitable

According to Saint Augustine, two realms have existed since the beginning of the world, the City of God (which includes the angels and good people) and the City of the Devil, in which he included not only demons, but the whole pagan world with its cult of demons. By magic, says Augustine, people try to compel the assistance of demons, but the demons in the end seduce people into worshiping them as gods. The magicians maintained, to the contrary, that only the pure in heart could practice the art of magic and that the demons were commanded through the power of God.

In a bull dated 1478, Sixtus IV allowed Ferdinand and Isabella of Spain "to appoint and depose Inquisitors and to possess themselves of the property of the condemned for the royal treasury." This Inquisition developed into a secret association of spies, fanatics, and informers determined to destroy freethinkers, philosophers, scholars, mystics, and anyone not crassly subservient to the "authority" of Rome. Under the system anyone could be accused by anyone, anonymously or otherwise, of suspicion of heresy. The mere accusation removed the victim from the jurisdiction of the state to that of a special ecclesiastical court. Once in the hands of the Inquisition, all friends and family had to cease association with the victim. Any "sympathy" displayed for a "heretic" was considered tantamount to heresy. There was no recourse to the civil law, no *habeas corpus*. All regular police officers, magistrates, and public officials, including governors and viceroys, were obliged to assist the Inquisition on pain of being considered sympathetic to the heretic. No one, no matter how high his station, was immune from persecution. Anyone was a heretic who spoke disrespectfully of church services, read or lent books condemned by the Inquisition, ate meat on fast days, missed mass, disapproved of anything done by the Inquisition, denied any assertion made by an Inquisitor, believed that the adherent of any other form of religion could be saved, or that the Church itself might someday be reformed and primitive Christianity restored.

process, as the property of the condemned was split between Church and Inquisition, a system of revenue legalized by Sixtus IV with a papal bull in 1478.

Throughout Europe the slaughter grew out of bounds. The entire population of the Netherlands was declared heretical and condemned to death by the Catholic Inquisition. Whole cities were denuded of men, the women systematically raped. Recalcitrants were buried alive, strangled, beheaded or had their breasts ripped off with red hot pincers. In Germany a hundred thousand perished; many more died in agony in Switzerland, France, and Italy; altogether more than a quarter of a million souls. Protestants were no better; Calvin and Luther, bigoted, intolerant, heartless, determined to crush what to them was "heresy" or "unorthodoxy," by the same means of physical terror employed by the Catholics. Protestant Dutchmen were crueler still in the revenge against Catholics and nonconformists.

In England the butchery was not so widespread, but nonetheless fiendish. John Rogers, minister of the gospel in London, the first Protestant martyr in Catholic Mary Tudor's reign, was burned alive at the stake at Smithfield in February 1554 while his wife and nine children, one of them still at the breast, were obliged to watch. But the Spanish archbishop Caranza, who introduced the Inquisition to England, only managed to do away with three hundred victims before he was driven from the country. After Bloody Mary's death in 1558, Catholics suffered similar persecution. Dermid O'Hurley, Catholic archbishop of Cashel, was fastened to a tree, his boots filled with combustibles, and set on fire, a fire which was alternately

All over Europe Christians butchered one another in the cruelest ways in the name of God.

The burning of John Rogers

Dr. John Dee (1527–1608) was not only Elizabeth's occult adviser but acted as secret agent for the queen on frequent trips to Europe. Code-named 007, his adventures were even stranger than Bond's. A friend of Francis Bacon and Walter Raleigh, he was a member of the circle known as The School of Night, which met secretly at Raleigh's house in Dorset to discuss occult and scientific policy. A religious Hermeticist and practitioner of the religion of love and unity, Dee encouraged toleration to heal the breach in Christendom and establish a new Golden Age in which man could recover his intellectual capacity, his beauty, and his place beside God. Dee believed that through a mystical rapport with the world man could rediscover and regenerate the divine within. He was convinced that within man was an "astral" spirit, whose powers could be channeled to achieve more with science than did nature unaided. Aware, like Bruno, that all was ensouled, he believed man could do wonders with the effluvia from the stars, and that the main weapon of the magus was his own imagination. But Dee's theurgy, or invoking of spirits, got him in trouble with James I, who abhorred witchcraft, and once more he was nearly burned for sorcery.

quenched and relighted, prolonging his torture through four successive days.

But by this time the tune was changing at the court of Elizabeth. An Hermeticist follower of Pico and Ficino— very nearly burned for sorcery and treason by Mary Tudor when he cast her horoscope and that of her Catholic husband, Philip of Spain—was nevertheless convinced that Protestant and Catholic could yet be united through a return to the early Christian religion of universal love and to the more ancient Egyptian cult on which it was based. He was Dr. John Dee. Under Queen Elizabeth's protection, this venerable magus was able to propagate in England the Egyptian wisdom acquired in his prolonged and various travels in Europe, often as a secret agent of Elizabeth. Through his constant efforts, and his tutoring of the highborn nearest Elizabeth, Dee was to come close to fulfilling his dream of a united and spiritualized Christendom.

Avid for data on magic and how to perform it, Dee had gradually built up at his country house at Mortlake, 30 miles up the Thames from London, the greatest library in England, one far superior to those of either Oxford or Cambridge, with a special leaning toward the occult. On its shelves he accumulated all of Ficino's works, the greatest number of the manuscripts of Roger Bacon, the works of Paracelsus, Cardano, Agrippa, and as many of the other magicians whose treatises were available in manuscript or print. Still, he complained that no man and no book could give him the answers he required. To fill this void he "beseeched the giver of wisdom" to communicate to him what he sought through an angelic intermediary, as had been done with Abraham, and later with Ficino and Pico. Dee's plea was rewarded with the appearance of Edward Talbott, a strange sensitive who assumed the bogus name of Sir Edward Kelley, a scryer, or crystal-ball gazer, who could evoke what he called nonterrestrial entities in a black stone the size of a hat crown, specially polished and treated to catch the spectral forms of unearthly visitors.

As the operation is described by Dee, these forms would point to certain letters on various tablets and put together messages in what came to be called "Enochian," each message spelled backwards because "the words contained such potency that direct communication would have invoked forces disruptive of the whole work." Enochian, according to Dee, was a definite, though unknown, language, which he classified as "angelic." Through it, Dee developed nineteen calls, or keys, the first eighteen

With Kelly as his medium, Dee claimed he chiefly communicated with the archangels Michael, Gabriel, Raphael, and Uriel, who had instructed the Hebrew patriarch Enoch—hence Dee's use of that name for his angelic language. Enoch was said to have lived before the Flood, to have "walked with God," and been raised living into heaven after having engraved the primitive elements of religion and universal science on the two "columns of Enoch." The Book of Enoch purports to tell the story of the "sons of God" who came down from heaven to mate with the daughters of man—who then learned their secret magic. The civilizing force which the Hebrews personified in Enoch was the Trismegistus of the Egyptians, the Cadmus of the Greeks. Enoch-Hermes was said to have seen the living stones of Thebes rise up to the strains of Amphion's lyre.

By means of the "shew-stone" as a scrying instrument, Dee obtained his Enochian language from a number of charts divided into squares, each with a letter of the alphabet. Kelley would see visions of an angel pointing letter by letter as it spelled out a message.

The Enochian tablets consisted of 156 pyramids, each with over a hundred squares filled with letters, totalling 2401. Dee used one or more of these tables (as a rule 49 × 49), some full of letters, others only lettered on alternate squares. Kelley would gaze into the "shew-stone" and tell Dee the angel was pointing to a square, but not mention the letter.

being to summon various elements, the nineteenth enabling him to envisage thirty Aethyrs, or "spheres of the spirit world." So adept was Kelley at summoning spirits, he became scryer-in-residence at Mortlake at £50 a year, and the minutes of his seances, carefully noted by Dee over a period of eight years, cover several hundred pages now in the British Museum along with the original black "shew-stone."

One of the books produced by Dee on various scientific subjects, his *Steganographia,* gives details of the procedure required for summoning "angels who govern the various planets and various parts of the earth." Dee's magic was also designed to protect the soul during its upward journey through the various spirit realms toward the goal of Gnosis. And that is how Dee got in trouble with Pope Sixtus V, nearly at the cost of his life. In Prague, at the court of Rudolph II, Dee conjured spirits for a friend, Francesco Pucci, an Italian Catholic, also infused with the Hermetic ideals, who had abjured the Church. Apprised of

69

the magical seances, the papal nuncio in Prague sent word to Sixtus, who immediately ordered Rudolph to have Dee and Kelley delivered to Rome for interrogation, an order which Rudolph would have been bound to enforce had not Dee, forewarned, wisely left Prague and taken refuge with Kelley in a castle at Tribau. Pucci, who had decided to return to the Church to explain his ecumenical, Hermetic views to the religious authorities in Rome, foolhardily traveled under the nuncio's safe-conduct, only to be seized, condemned, and promptly beheaded as a heretic.

Had Sixtus known of Dee and Kelley's next adventures in the realm of angelic or demonic forces, he would, doubtless, have been even more outraged. Kelley, suspicious that the manifesting spirits might—as the papal nuncio had insisted—be demons, and that he might be lured to his destruction, wished to desist. Dee, considering himself a pious man and a devoted Christian, was determined to continue obeying the messages from what he considered angelic voices.

The ensuing situation turned into a limited agape, or early Christian sharing, with overtones of experiments in Tantric sex, when—as reported in chronicles of the time—Kelley "cast a lustful eye on Dee's shapely vivacious young wife." Speaking through Kelley, a spirit named Mandini told both men "they had their wives in such sort that they should use them in common." When Dee asked Mandini if that meant spiritual or carnal copulation, the answer was "both." At dinner the decision was conveyed to the ladies. Surprised or not, they were evidently willing to comply; and for several months the quartet enjoyed a joint relationship until Kelley went back to Prague to be knighted in return for the promise of producing for the Bohemian sovereign alchemical gold by means of a red dust Dee had found in the grave of a bishop at Glastonbury Abbey.

Back home at Mortlake, Dee found that a mob, accusing him of necromancy and of desecrating graves in order to have intercourse with spiritual essences, had ransacked and vandalized his great library, which caused him to compare the persecution he was suffering to the "raging slander of the Malicious Ignorant" endured by his young mentor Pico della Mirandola. But once more under Elizabeth's protection, Dee's house resumed its function as a meeting place for that distinguished cabal of English Hermeticists close to the Crown, such as Sir Francis Bacon, the Earl of Southampton, the Earl of Leicester and Sir Philip Sydney to whom Dee had been tutor. With great

Queen Elizabeth of England had a double agent at the Vatican, appropriately known as le Chevalier Carré, and the perfidy of Sixtus V is exemplified by his having kept Elizabeth informed by le Carré of every detail of the organization of the great Spanish Armada for the invasion of England. At the same time Sixtus cunningly offered Philip II of Spain a million gold scudi to be paid as soon as he had successfully landed on the territory of "the bastard heretic" in England, hoping so to weaken Philip by a "Bay of Pigs" landing that Sixtus could, unopposed, seize from him a plum he longed for: the Kingdom of Naples.

subtlety the group was using Shakespeare's plays as a means of political and religious pamphleteering for a return to the Hermetic values of Egypt, the secret wisdom of which they had been nurtured on by Dee, and by studying law in the old Temple, or the Inns of Court. As members of the Queen's Privy council, they too, if only to save their necks, wished to avoid the ghastly religious intolerance and religious warfare which was rending Europe.

To add his wisdom to this clandestine group of wits, there came from Italy perhaps the greatest philosopher of the sixteenth century, a fiery "heretic" who was to pay with his life for overtly challenging the Church of Rome whom he accused of having missed the secret message in the Egyptian glyphs adorning the obelisks and of having fallen from the path of the ancient wisdom.

Shortly before Sixtus V had come to the throne, Henry III of France, anxious for the hand of Elizabeth, had named as ambassador to the Court of Saint James's, Michel de Castelnau, marquis of Mauvissière, who, according to his peers, was a "remarkable and attractive man whose humanity transcended the religious cleavages of the times." Ten years earlier, Mauvissière had been sent by Henry's elder brother, Charles IX, equally interested in Elizabeth's hand, to try to pacify the outraged English queen after the ghastly Saint Bartholomew massacre, when a hundred thousand French Protestant men, women, and children had been cold-bloodedly ambushed and butchered by bigoted Catholics. This time, Mauvissière chose to take with him as a companion to the London of Shakespeare an Italian ex-monk, Giordano Bruno of Nola.

On the day of Saint Bartholomew, August 24, 1572, French Catholics ambushed and murdered all the French Protestants they could seize—men, women, and children—even ripping infants from the womb to prevent any survivors. As blood flowed in rivers and the streets were choked with corpses, the Catholic murderers went about the slaughter with white crosses on their hats and capes to be distinguished from their victims. In Rome the news was greeted with great feasts and gaieties.

Philosopher, poet, dramatist and intrepid supporter of intellectual freedom, Giordano Bruno obtained his doctorate in philosophy at Toulouse. With vast erudition, a vivid imagination, and originality of thought, Bruno lashed out with subtle irony and biting sarcasm against pedants in religion, science, philosophy or letters. In England, Sir Philip Sidney, who had studied jurisprudence at the University of Padua and was imbued with a love of Italian culture, may have financed the publication of Bruno's Italian works. Bruno dedicated to him his *Spaccio della bestia trionfante* and *De gli eroici furori*. Of Bruno's influence on contemporary drama, his biographer, Vincenzo Spampanato, points out that no less than ten of Molière's plots were influenced by Bruno's comedy, and he argues that half a dozen of Shakespeare's plays are strongly reminiscent of Bruno's work.

Bruno's reputation for dangerous views on matters spiritual had preceded him to England. Elizabeth's chief of intelligence, Sir Francis Walsingham, received a note from the British ambassador in Paris, Sir Henry Cobham, that "Dr. Jordano Bruno Nolano, a professor of philosophy, intendeth to pass into England whose religion I cannot commend." Indeed, in her *Bruno and the Hermetic Tradition,* Frances Yates—that remarkable historian of the Elizabethan age—suggests that the Italian was specifically brought to England on a secret political assignment of an obviously Hermetic or anti-Jesuit nature.

A small, thin man, with a meager dark beard, scornful of his attire—three buttons off his coat and hose pieced together from bits of his abandoned Dominican gown—Bruno seemed hardly presentable in society; yet this defrocked priest was to become such an intimate of the Hermetic conspiracy formed around the wits behind Shakespeare that he turned up in *Love's Labor's Lost* as the character Berowne. Charged with unorthodoxy for reading Erasmus in the toilet of his Dominican monastery in Naples, Bruno had escaped across the Alps to France to avoid being tried on a more serious count of heresy. What threatened to damn him was his conviction that a return to the Hermetic wisdom of the ancient Egyptians was the sole remedy against the fratricidal warfare ravaging Europe. An opinion identical with that of John Dee, who Peter J. French, in his biography of the old magus, suggests "was perhaps the only person in England who could have prepared the Sidney circle for that wild but brilliant ex-friar."

The England to which Bruno came was a haven for foreigners persecuted for their religious beliefs. Sensitive Elizabethans had been looking, since the guidance of Dee, to Renaissance Italy for the light of Hermeticism. Scores of distinguished Italians had taken refuge in London, including another ex-Dominican monk, Matteo Bandello, whose *Novelle* formed the basis of *Romeo and Juliet* and *Taming of the Shrew*. Bruno was quickly introduced by Mauvissière into the heart of the Shakespeare cabal, and was quickly patronized by Philip Sidney, by Walter Raleigh, who had been educated at Oxford with Sidney, and by Sidney's uncle, the queen's beloved Earl of Leicester, then chancellor of that stronghold of conservative Aristotelian study, Oxford University.

Bruno, who considered Aristotle *"stupidissimus omnium philosophorum,"* paralyzed his Oxonian audience with astonishment and indignation by expounding Hermetic conceits and by supporting what the ancient Egyptians

Nicolaus Copernicus (1473–1543), Polish astronomer, canon of the cathedral of Frauenburg, practiced medicine, giving his services free to the poor. His *De revolutionibus orbium coelestium*, dedicated to Paul III, described the sun as the center of a great system, with the earth as one of several planets revolving around it. But the first printed copy only reached him on his deathbed, saving him from the acrimonious debates of those who wished to refute a heliocentric system known to the Egyptians for several thousand years.

had known all along, Copernicus's proposition that the sun and not the earth was the center of the solar system, flatly contradicting Aristotle's notion of a finite universe constructed out of fixed geometric circles. Bruno insisted instead that the universe was infinite, that the sun was merely another star, and that stars were not fixed, but in reality suns, each with its own train of planets, cycling through the universe, "like great animals, animated by the divine life"—all of which had been standard to the ancient Egyptians, but denied and buried by the priests of the Catholic Church.

Following the Hermetic tradition, and the lead given by the magician Cornelius Agrippa, Bruno said he considered it unreasonable to suppose that the stars which give life and animation to all should themselves be without life and animation. Laying the Hermetic vision before his audience, the ex-monk allowed that he found it hard to believe any part of the universe could be without soul-life, without sensation, without organic structure. "From this infinite All, full of beauty and splendor, from the worlds which circle above us, to the sparkling dust of the stars beyond, the conclusion is drawn that there are an infinity of creatures, a vast multitude, which, each in its degree, mirrors forth the splendor, wisdom, and excellence of the divine beauty." Taking Copernicus's revalidation of the sun as the center of the solar system, Bruno used it to herald the dawn of a new age, the return of the Egyptian sun god Horus, and of the magical sun-worshiping religion of ancient Egypt, a true Aurora for philosophy after its burial in the dark ages of corrupted Christianity.

The Oxford academies received Bruno less than warmly. His lectures led to so much acrimony, he was forced to decamp in haste. For his part, the impression left on him by members of the university was that of a "pedantic pig-headedness fit to try the patience of Job." He accused the pedants of using empty words with which to mouth a sterile philosophy in language both trivial and superficial, without magical or incantatory power, instead of appealing to the magical hieroglyphic language of the Egyptians with its wisdom of the ages. As Bruno put it, by using the symbolic language of hieroglyphs, the Egyptians had managed to capture with marvelous skill the language of nature. "Later when letters of the kind we now use were invented by Thoth, or some other, it brought about a great rift both in memory and in the divine magical sciences." The most essential element in Bruno's outlook, says Fances Yates, was to find "these living 'voices,' signs, images, seals, to heal the rift in the means of communica-

In *Del'infinito universo et mondi* Bruno goes beyond Copernicus in his speculation about the nature of the universe, attacking the foundations of Aristotle's cosmology. And in *La cena de le ceneri* Bruno, expanding the Copernican theory, inveighs against contemporary English scholars, especially those at Oxford whose world he describes as "a constellation of the most pedantic, obstinate ignorance and presumption, mixed with a kind of rustic incivility, which would try the patience of Job." In his *Spaccio* Bruno reveals his strong attraction to Egyptian religion, condemning the hypocrisy of sixteenth-century princes who, with their sycophants, had created a "faithless, dissolute, irresponsible and indolent upper class." But for Queen Elizabeth, whom he visited frequently with Ambassador Castelnau, Bruno had great admiration because of her "judgement, wisdom, council and rule."

tion with divine nature which had been introduced by pedantry." In some trancelike experience, Bruno wished to unify through these "voices" the universe as reflected in the psyche "and thereby obtain the Magus' powers to live the life of the Egyptian priest in magical communion with nature."

And it is here that Frances Yates finds a link between Bruno and the Shakespeare texts where the English poet, rather than using the vacuous language of the pedants, searches for "significant" language with which, in Bruno's words, "to capture the voices of the gods." It warrants, she says, an entirely new approach to the relation between the two poets, both of whom subscribe to the same Hermetic philosophy championed by Dee.

In the works Bruno wrote in Italian during his stay in London, especially the *Cena delle ceneri* and the *Spaccio della bestia triumphante,* he preached a general reformation of the world based on a vision of nature achieved through Hermetic comtemplative exercises—a return to the magical metaphysical communion with other dimensions of consciousness, as practiced in Egypt. The basic theme of Bruno's *Spaccio* is the glorification of the magical religion of the ancient Egyptians, as described in Ficino's translation of the *Asclepius.* In his *De immenso,* Bruno attacked those who had destroyed this Egyptian religion, spreading instead cruelty, schism, evil customs, and contempt for the law. Like Ficino, Bruno picked up the gauntlet of the Renaissance magus in his stand for the dignity of man, for liberty, for toleration, for the right to say what he thought, irrespective of ideological censors.

Bruno upheld the value of both "heroic" and "profane" love, as opposed to what the pedants had made of Christianity. For Bruno, all religious persecution, all war in the name of religion, broke the law of love. Varying the Renaissance theme of Platonic love treatises, Bruno opposed to profane love heroic love, or "frenzy" as he called it, pointing out that heroic love, as the Gnostics practiced it, had a divine object and led the soul in a gradual ascent from the sense world through intelligible objects toward the divinity.

As Yates sums it up, Bruno's fundamental ideal was a God-informed, God-governed universe, a universe embodying power, wisdom, and love, a universe essentially accessible to the human consciousness, partially now and progressively more so with the development of that consciousness. In a cabalistic sense, Bruno saw love as the living virtue in all things, one which the magician could intercept to lead him up from lower-level love to the supercelestial reality of divine love.

As for sexual love, far from condemning it, Bruno believed that man should make use of *all* his faculties. In an address to Philip Sidney he wrote: "It is not for me to oppose the sacred order of nature . . . God forbid that such a thought should ever enter my head . . . I never had a desire to become a eunuch. On the contrary I should be ashamed if I agreed to yield on that score were it only a hair to any man worth his salt in order to serve nature and God." Admitting that he had not managed to possess quite as many women as King Solomon, Bruno added that it had not been for lack of trying. And he did not believe in being tied down. "For I am certain that all the laces and tags that all present and future dealers in laces and tags have ever been able, or will be able, to plait or knot, even though they were aided by death itself, would not suffice for that purpose."

When Bruno left England, to resume his wanderings through Europe, he preached, as Yates notes, a kind of Egyptian Counterreformation, prophesying a return to Egyptianism in which the religious difficulties of the age would be dispelled. There would follow a moral reform with an emphasis on social good works and an ethic of social utility. Breaking with the Christianity of all the Churches, Bruno favored, as had the Gnostics, the Cathars, and the Albigeois, a purer religion which he considered the very essence of original Christianity.

The trouble, says Yates, is that by his rejection of orthodox Christianity and his enthusiastic adoption of Hermetic Egyptianisms, Bruno moved toward a form of

75

Obelisk raised for Henri IV on the occasion of his triumphant entry into Rouen in 1596.

magic which went beyond the mild "Christian" variety of Ficino, designed to reunite the soul with the deity. Bruno aspired to what she calls "a more medieval necromancy," one in which he wished to expand Ficino's magic into a full restoration of the magical religion of Hermes's *Asclepius,* a return, in Yates's eyes, to an old-style, frankly "demonic" conjuring. Hence the rub, as it had been for Ficino and Pico, and for Dee. The very heart of this magic (considered deadly dangerous by the Church) was not only the summoning into manifestation of spiritual entities, but the raising of consciousness to an ecstatic vision by means of sexual arousal, awakening the dormant serpent of fire. Somewhere Bruno appeared to have learned the secrets of Tantric sex.

In his *Opera Latine conscripta* he makes an attempt to outline a technique for controlling all emotions which is explicitly based on sexual attraction. And in *De vinculis in genere* he discusses "linking" through love or sexual attraction. As Yates cautiously remarks: "the problem can be put in terms of Eros." In the *Pimander,* in the Hermetic account of the creation of the magus man, this half-divine being came down to earth because he loved beautiful nature and was united to her in a passionate embrace.

But the world was not ready for Bruno's Egyptian Renaissance with its pagan love of nature—a nature in which man could find the image of a loving deity. Catholic and Protestant both turned on Bruno in disgust. In Wittenberg he was warned to leave town. From Marburg he was obliged to escape the malevolence of the rector of the university. In Helmstedt he was excommunicated from the Reformed Church. Frankfurt refused to let him lodge in the town, and the prior of the Carmelite convent, who did give him hospice, scathingly described him as "writing all day or walking up and down filled with fantastic meditations."

By this time Bruno had developed his life-long study of the art of memory into a technique for training the imagination into acting as the instrument for obtaining the magical power with which to communicate with "angels, demons, the effigies of stars, and the inner 'statues' of gods and goddesses in contact with celestial things." Here the hieroglyphs on the obelisks of Egypt took on a function as magical keys to another dimension. To Bruno the glyphs were symbols which, when imprinted on the memory through an imaginative effort, enabled man to recover knowledge of his true self, remember past lives, his spiritual essence, and become again one with the universe. But his opponents continued to dog him until in Zurich he received the invitation from an apparent support-

76

Henry IV (1553–1610), King of France and of Navarre, reared as a Protestant, only saved himself from the Massacre of Saint Bartholomew by announcing himself a Catholic. Returning to his faith he was excluded from succeeding Henry III, until he abjured his Protestantism and entered Paris in 1594. Excommunicated by Gregory XIV, he was assassinated by a Catholic fanatic, François Ravaillac.

Gregory XIII (Pope, 1572–85) joyfully receiving the severed head of Protestant leader Gaspard de Coligny, first victim of the Massacre of Saint Bartholomew, which Gregory celebrated in Rome with a festival of public thanksgiving

er, a young Venetian nobleman (Zuane, or Juan, or Giovanni Mocenigo), to visit Venice and there teach him the art of memory as well as any other magical tricks he might be able to impart, presumably Tantric and sexual.

Somewhat foolhardily Bruno agreed to return to Catholic Venice in 1591. Sixtus V, the city's old Inquisitor, had been dead a year, and the atmosphere appeared to have softened sufficiently for Francesco Patrizi's *Nova de universalis philosophia* to be published, containing a new edition of the Hermetica along with a dedication to the new pope, Gregory XIV (Nicolò Sfondrati, 1590–91), in which Patrizi urged the pontiff to have taught everywhere and especially in the schools of the Jesuits this peace-loving Hermetic religious philosophy. But Gregory, subservient to Philip II of Spain, was not that liberal, and replied by excommunicating the one sovereign in whom Bruno had put his faith as a potential Hermeticist, Henry IV of Navarre, who had projected a unified Christian Europe. Only Henry's eventual murder by an aspirant Jesuit was to put the quietus on another Nolan dream.

In Mocenigo's Venetian house, Bruno found his host's behavior peculiar. As impatient with ignorance as he was scornful of prejudice, Bruno argued with his pupil, and decided to return to Frankfurt, where his extraordinary work *De triplici minimo* had just been published, and where he wished to have more manuscripts put into print. Mocenigo, jealous that Bruno might impart his secret knowledge to others, threatened to have the ex-monk detained by the Holy Office—no idle threat, as Mocenigo had once been attached to the Venetian Inquisition.

That Mocenigo was looking for a way to trap his teacher is clear from the fact that he had collected from Bruno's works and conversations a mass of testimony bearing on his heretical beliefs, which he turned over to the Father Inquisitor of Venice. When Bruno continued to insist on leaving, Mocenigo had a band of toughs rouse him from sleep on May 23, 1592, and drag him to a Holy Office dungeon. Though he did not know it, for Bruno it was to be the end of freedom.

The Venetian procurator, Federico Contarini, explained to the doge that Bruno's crimes of heresy were most serious, "though he is otherwise one of the most excellent and rare talents that can be desired, and of exquisite doctrine and knowledge."

Brought before the Inquisition, Bruno made a confession of faith: "I presuppose an infinite universe, a work of infinite Divine Power, because I consider it unworthy of the Divine Power and Goodness to produce only this world when it could have created infinitely many worlds similar to our earth, which I understand along with Pythagoras, to be an orb similar to the moon, and the other planets and stars, inhabited worlds, the immesurable number of which, in infinite space, forms an endless universe." This statement alone, in direct contradiction to the concepts of Aristotle and Ptolemy, was considered by the officials of the Inquisition "altogether the most absurd of horrors" (*horrenda prosus absurdissima*), and was enough to condemn the prisoner as heretical.

Cardinal Santaseverina, the Supreme Inquisitor of Rome, who had declared the massacre of St. Bartholomew "a glorious day, exceedingly agreeable to Catholics," ordered Bruno conveyed to the Holy See to stand trial before the supreme tribunal of the Inquisition, accused formally of heresy and of having composed various books in which he praised the queen of England and other heretical persons. Convinced that if he could reach the font of authority at the Holy See, he would eventually not only be understood, but even honored, and his writings accepted, Bruno seems to have welcomed the transfer to Rome.

In February 1593 he passed through the dungeons of the Roman Inquisition, where he was visited by his judges, the lord cardinals who cross-examined the prisoner on his heresies and interrogated him concerning his necessities. As a result, he was provided with a cloak, a pillow, and a copy of the *Summa* of Saint Thomas Aquinas. With no pen or paper on which to compose his defense or make use of his talent for writing, Bruno was left to rot, his verbal

The papal fortress of Sant'Angelo in which prisoners were tortured and interrogated. If required, their bodies could be dumped down secret chutes directly into the Tiber.

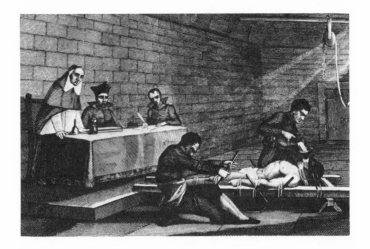

A victim being broken on the rack while being interrogated by Inquisitors

A victim's arms being dislocated by jerks on a pulley

petitions unheeded. Four slow years went by before the prisoner was again visited by the cardinals, in 1597. After another cross-examination and probable torture, they told him he would have to relinquish "his vanities concerning diverse worlds." On January 14, 1599, eight heretical propositions were extracted from Bruno's works and read aloud to him in prison. He was given six days in which to recant. When faced with a decision, Bruno said simply: "I ought not to recant; therefore I will not."

He agreed, however, to accept the personal decision of the pope as to whether his system of thought was or was not heretical; but he insisted on being allowed to defend his views in writing. Pen and paper were provided. In his "Memorial to the Pope," Bruno claimed that his opinions had been unadroitly excerpted from context by ministers of the Holy Office, that he was prepared to give an account of all his writings and defend them against any

79

Clement VIII (Pope 1592–1605), renowned for his piety, declared that it was sinful to accept the smallest degree of venereal pleasure, and that anyone should be denounced to the Inquisition who maintained that kissing, touching, and embracing for the sake of sexual pleasure were not grievous sins. The sexual act had already been declared sinful in itself by Saint Augustine, as "the essence of original sin was the concupiscence which accompanied the act of generation." Priests were given explicit instructions on how to punish sexual infractions of all imaginable sorts. A raped girl could douche herself only during the first ten hours, or risk Hell. Once conception had taken place, she could do nothing. A man was not to masturbate even to produce sperm for a doctor; both would be commiting a deadly sin.

Francesco Romolo Bellarmino (1542–1621) entered the Society of Jesus in 1560 and was made a cardinal in 1599. As a consultant to the Holy Office (or Inquisition) he took a prominent part in the first examination of Galileo's "heretical" writings. A strong supporter of the Jesuits at the Vatican, Bellarmino came to be considered the greatest Roman Catholic controversialist of his day.

theologian. However, he would only abide by the opinion of the pope concerning things said or written by him, or by sacred canons if it should be proved there was anything in his writings or sayings contrary to them. Bruno further declared that if the Apostolic See and His Holiness definitely declared his eight propositions to be heretical, if His Holiness knew them to be so, or by the power of the Holy Spirit declared them to be so, then he was disposed to retract.

Along with the memorial went a long written defense of his position addressed to the new Pope, Clement VIII (Ippolito Aldobrandini, 1592–1605), who had succeeded Gregory XIV and had just ordered the beheading of Beatrice Cenci. But Clement, who has been described by the French author R. Gagey as "more audacious than Boniface VIII, more dominating than Sixtus V, and more perfidious than Alexander VI," was not even going to see Bruno's paper. On January 20, 1600, Bruno's "Memorial to the Pope" was opened by the Inquisition, but was apparently not passed on to the pontiff.

On February 4, Clement decreed before a full Congregation of Cardinals that if Bruno recognized his propositions as heretical, well and good; if not, he was to be condemned after forty days "to the treatment usual for impenitent and pertinacious persons." At his final trial, Bruno was pathetically certain that if only he could make his judges understand what he had to say, they would welcome his philosophy. In the great hall of the consistory with its baroque gilding and its damask hangings, Bruno knelt, pale, thin, while the judges remained obdurate and negative, especially Cardinal Bellarmine, who for twenty years embodied the Curia's opposition to science, and now did his best to secure a condemnation. After a short delay, the inquisitional notary pronounced sentence of death upon Bruno, ordering him turned over to the civil authorities for execution. Bruno heard the fatal words, unflinchingly, then rose and in a clear voice replied: "It may be that you fear more to deliver this judgement, than do I to hear it."

On February 8, the condemned man was subjected to the demeaning ritual of deconsecration of a former monk, and transferred from the ecclesiastical to the secular arm of the law with the cynical request that he be punished "as mercifully as possible and without shedding of blood"—the Church's sophistical formula for being burned alive at the stake. Locked in the Tor di Nona jail, near Sixtus's new bridge across the Tiber, Bruno awaited execution. As Rome at that time was full of Catholic

pilgrims from all countries, the Inquisition prepared a
monstrous spectacle for the occasion. Faggots were
stacked around a stake in front of Pompey's theater in the
Campo dei Fiori.

Early on the morning of February 17, Bruno was made to
attend mass in the prison chapel and then fed a frugal
breakfast of sweetmeats and wine from Ischia, so as not
to faint on the way to the scaffold. At last the ghastly
procession started from the prison of the Inquisition, as
Bruno was led out through a jeering, leering crowd of
Catholics come to see a "Lutheran" heretic meet his
deserved doom. Accompanying the victim were the hood-
ed Brothers of the Holy Sepulcher, chanting a lugubrious
litany, and sardonically carrying green candles to symbolize the three theological virtues: the wick for faith; the
wax for hope; the flame for charity.

Rome's Campo dei Fiori, or Field of Flowers, where Bruno met his death

Bruno given to the flames

With a firm step Bruno mounted the *patibolum,* consoling himself no doubt with his own gnostic dictum: "He who still fears for his life has not yet made himself one with the godhead." An eyewitness described the victim being bound to the stake, around which wood was piled. As the fires were lit, the "mystical poet, whose love encompassed the entire universe," turned his head from the proffered consolation of a crucifix and delivered his final words: "I die a martyr, willingly."

Bruno's body was burned and his ashes scattered to the winds so that not a trace be left on earth of any of his corporeal shell. But, judged from his own words, death to Bruno was only a slightly greater change than takes place every day in our bodies, in no way a diminution of life, but an exaltation of it: "We suffer a perpetual transmutation, whereby we receive a perpetual flow of fresh atoms, while those that we have received are leaving us." In his *Cabala del Cavallo Pegaseo* Bruno had openly accepted the reality of reincarnation, a tenet condemned by the Church since the Council of Nicea.

The Church, not satisfied with killing its victim, set about ruining his reputation, both as a thinker and as a man. All of Bruno's works were placed on the Index of forbidden reading; as many as possible were burned. For two hundred years Bruno's reputation for atheism, impiety, and misconduct was such that his writings were complete-

82

ly taboo, not only among Catholics, but even among Protestants. As late as 1830 they were forbidden to be shown in the public library of Dresden. Many were lost or remained unknown in archives of the Inquisition. Of those known to exist, no complete or reasonably accurate edition was published for more than two centuries. Yet the Hermetic tradition continued, and sensitive souls became aware of the magnitude of Bruno's contribution to philosophy. Through his intuition and vision he had anticipated a number of ideas which others in later centuries were to adopt and develop on the basis of more solid evidence.

The doctrine of evolution, the progressive development of nature, an idea unknown to classical philosophy, was first pronounced by Bruno, not vaguely or partially: he extended its laws to the inorganic as well as the organic world, maintaining that unbroken line of evolution from matter to man which only modern science later began to recognize.

In a number of ways Bruno's cosmology anticipated the conception of the universe as it was to be developed by modern physics and astronomy. In her recent thesis on Bruno, Dr. Ksenija Atanasijevic says: "Bruno's contribution to the development of subsequent philosophy and modern astronomy is beyond proper evaluation not only in terms of his conception of the infinity of the universe; with his comprehensively conceived and elaborately argued doctrine of the triple minimum he is also one of the leading forerunners of later monadology, atomism and the teachings about the discontinuity of space, time, motion, and geometrical bodies. . . . Bruno laid the firm foundations upon which was to rise, in the course of time, the magnificent edifice of new atomic science."

And she concludes: "By pointing out the complexity and non-uniformity of the ultimate parts of substance, Bruno revealed not only the unfailing correctness of his intuition but also the whole depth of his philosophical mind and thus became the illuminated precurser of later atomists and monadologists as well as the founder of geometrical finitism."

Philosophically, what Bruno died for was the belief that man could stand again "under the faithful guidance of the eye of the divine intelligence," and, with the powers within him, by the gnostic ascent, recover his knowledge of an infinite god in an infinite universe, a divinity, as Bruno reminded his audience, not far distant, but within us, its center everywhere, its circumference nowhere.

Holy Mountain of Initiation

5. SUB ROSA CRUCIS

Francis Bacon, Baron Verulam, and Viscount St. Albans (1561–1626?). Philosopher and statesman, lord chancellor of England, formulated and proclaimed the inductive method of modern science in opposition to the *a priori* method of scholasticism, the official philosophy of the Roman Catholic Church.

Johann Valentin Andreae

With the death of Elizabeth of England in 1603, there was no monarch left to guarantee an original or outspoken thinker or follower of the Hermetic Egyptian wisdom preached by Bruno; so it went underground to be pursued *sub rosa*. Francis Bacon and John Dee ran into trouble with Elizabeth's successor James I, and in Bohemia, Rudolph II was forced by the Jesuit spearhead of the Counter Reformation to flee his ideal Hermetic court at Prague, leaving his library and laboratory to be sacked and destroyed. As Yates points out, the Egyptian philosophy, freely debated in the fifteenth century, struggling for supremacy in the sixteenth, was relegated, in the seventeenth, to the care of a minority of hidden initiates: the Rosicrucians.

To perpetuate the Egyptian heritage as outlined by Ficino, Pico, Dee, and Bruno, there sprang up in the German states, or was revived there, a restricted society of conspirators announcing themselves to the world as the Brothers of the Rosy Cross. Pamphlets detailing their tenets appeared from secret presses, known as the *Fama Fraternitatis,* the *Confessio Fraternitas,* and *The Chemical Wedding of Christian Rosenkreutz.* Considering themselves good Christians, the brothers addressed the intelligentsia, warning against egotism and materialist covetousness, suggesting that it is man, not the Creator, who causes the bloodshed which ravages the world.

Some occultists would have it that Francis Bacon, as the reincarnation of Christian Rosenkreutz, reconstituted the fraternity in England whence he took it to Germany after a faked death, to reappear as Johann Valentin Andreae, presumed author of the three Rosicrucian manifestos. What actually happened has not been resolved historically. It is certain, though, that Bacon was involved with the brotherhood, which aimed to revive and spread throughout Europe and the world the wisdom of Hermes Trismegistus. Overtly in his *Advancement of Learning,* written shortly after Elizabeth's death, and in *Novum Organum* fifteen years later, Bacon professes the ideal of a reconstruction of science. In his "posthumous" *New Atlantis,* he sets forth the dream of an equally ideal religion and scientific society, and promises more, cryptically hinting on the title page that *"Tempora patet occulta veritas,"* or "with time, the hidden truth will out."

Christian Rosenkreutz, legendary founder of the Brotherhood of the Rosy Cross, is said to have traveled to Damascus, city of 300 mosques, to read the sacred books of the Sufis and acquire the wisdom of a mystic and cabalist. In Fez, with its 600 fountains, he went to learn magic from a school of astrologers, and how to communicate with elementals so as to govern the hidden forces of nature and open access to the realm of angels. Back in Germany with the mysterious book of *"M,"* he is reputed to have founded a brotherhood, originally inspired by Thothmes III, to give to European society the light and knowledge of the mysteries of Egypt, and so spread the doctrine of tolerance and the brotherhood of man. The Brothers' tenet that through love it was possible to be reabsorbed into the divine essence begat such virulent opposition it obliged the Brothers to go underground, communicating thereafter through allegory and cipher. The *Chemical Wedding of Christian Rosenkreutz,* an Hermetic fantasy, suggested that real alchemy deals not with the transmutation of base metals into gold, but with regenerating the human soul. Its attribution to Johann Valentin Andreae is contested on the grounds that he would have been a mere boy at the time of its appearance; a more likely author is believed by occultists to be Francis Bacon. The *Fama fraternitatis* recounts in allegory the rediscovery of an ancient philosophy, related to medicine and healing, the revelation of which would bring about a general reformation and advancement of learning leading man to an understanding of his true nobility and worth. In terms similar to those of Dee, Bruno, Ficino, and their antecedents, the Brothers of the Rosy Cross called upon the learned and the great of Europe to support them in a quest for a deeper understanding of nature, urging the world to desert the false philosophical teachings of Aristotle and the popes, and abandon the false medicine of Galen. The objective of the Brothers is de-

The Rosicrucian program was to reconcile Christianity with science, a program to be carried out by an elite of the wise, leading to a regeneration of religion and society. The intent was to revive what they considered to have been original Christianity, along with the healing talents of the therapeut and the Egyptian magical communion with spirits, plus the technique of the alchemist, in whose philosopher's stone they saw tne human heart, transmutable into a golden light. In nature, the Rosicrucian saw all around him the hieroglyphic symbols of divinity, crying out to be deciphered—the same nature, extolled by Bruno, in which he preached that all that there is to be known can be read.

But the Counter Reformation, spearheaded by the Jesuits, was in full swing. Reaction from Rome was violent: the Hapsburg-Jesuit alliance was on the point of achieving a universal victory of Catholicism over the Reformed Churches, loosing a fresh wave of persecution across Europe. As Catholics gained the upper hand, sorcerers and magicians were again burned by the thousand. Libraries of rare books and manuscripts were pillaged and given to the flames. It got so bad that the Rosicrucian Brothers issued a poster announcing they were leaving the fray to retire to Tibet. Whether they did or not, the Hermetic wisdom of Egypt disappeared from sight to find temporary succor with the strangest of foster mothers: the very organization devoted to its destruction: Ignatius Loyola's Society of Jesus.

Just as the French Jesuit François Garasse was accusing the Rosicrucians in 1623 of being wicked sorcerers, dangerous to religion and the state, "witch-like characters belonging to a diabolical secret society who should be broken on the wheel or hanged on the gallows," a twenty-year-old postulant Jesuit, Athanasius Kircher, unaccountably found himself holding the torch of Hermes. Asked to find a book in the library of the German Jesuit college in which he was a probationer, Kircher accidentally put his hand to Hans Georg Hörwarth von Hohenburg's *Thesaurus* with its illustrations of the hieroglyphs on the obelisks erected in Rome by Sixtus V. The magic of the obelisks had its instant effect. "My curiosity," said Kircher, "was aroused, and I began to speculate on the meaning of these mysterious glyphs."

But another flare-up of religious intolerance—the Thirty Years' War—cut short his speculations. As a Jesuit, Kircher found himself pursued by angry Protestants. Forced to flee Germany, he swam across the icy Rhine, nearly getting himself hanged by a Protestant patrol, but

scribed as the liberation of humanity from ignorance, disease, and poverty. Their hope was to bring about a spiritual awakening of society, to extend human faculties beyond the physical plane into what would later be described as the "etheric, astral and spiritual worlds," reaching up to a transcendental plane of illumination.

Father Athanasius Kircher, S.J.

Nicholas Claude de Peiresc

eventually managing to find refuge in the papal city of Avignon, where he was able to continue his passion for obelisks and hieroglyphs by teaching mathematics and biblical languages in the local Jesuit college, cuckooing the wisdom of Hermes into the very organization designed to destroy it.

In those days, material on ancient Egypt was almost nonexistent; but fate propelled Kircher to a remarkable source in the nearby city of Aix-en-Provence, in the house of one of the most erudite and wealthy of antiquarian collectors, Nicholas Claude Fabri de Peiresc, a humanist and amateur scientist, a friend and correspondent of Galileo, who had found and brought back from his travels in Egypt a long roll of papyrus, discovered in a box at the foot of a mummy, whose hieroglyphs he hoped Kircher might help him decipher. Also in Peiresc's collection were several manuscripts never before seen in Europe, written in Coptic, the language of the Christian descendants of the Ptolemaic Egyptians, mostly biblical translations and lives of the saints. Spelled with an ordinary Greek alphabet—supplemented by seven special characters—the Coptic language had become virtually extinct since the Arab conquest of Egypt in the sixth century, except for its use in Upper Egypt in liturgical ceremonies. But Kircher was convinced that a study of this late-Egyptian language might give him a lead to the decipherment of the Egyptian hieroglyphs.

Kircher also found a rare manuscript attributed to the Arab author Rabbi Brachis Apenephius, which purported to give a method for interpreting the glyphs. But just as the young Jesuit was progressing in his study of Coptic, he

87

Cavalier Bernini

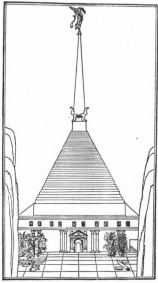

A Rosicrucian clue to Tantra, in which Poliphilo, in his dream of love, is led by a nymph to an agape, or orgy of love, and thence to witness an ancient rite dedicated to the phallic god Priapus, said to be the son of Hermes. Poliphilo also attends the nuptial rites of two ancient androgynous Roman deities, Vertunno and Pomona, indicating, according to Cesare Ambesi, the marriage of cosmic and telluric forces which, together, bring forth life on the planet, a mechanism admirably detailed by the modern Rosicrucian Rudolf Steiner. To Ambesi, Colonna's extraordinary poem links all the

received orders from Rome to replace Johann Keppler as mathematician to the anti-Protestant Holy Roman Emperor Ferdinand II at the court of Vienna. It was an unwelcome assignment; it meant giving up his Egyptological studies. Fortunately for Kircher, Peiresc was on good enough terms with Urban VIII (Matteo Barberini), to have the pope countermand the order—which turned out to be welcome news also to the pope's nephew, Cardinal Francesco Barberini, who had just brought to his palace gardens an obelisk which had been found in the vineyard of certain Saccoccia brothers outside the Porta Maggiore in what had once been Heliogabalus's old circus. The cardinal was anxious to have Kircher come to Rome to see if he could fathom its hieroglyphs, and help him raise the 12-meter obelisk on a stone elephant as designed by his favorite baroque architect, Giovanni Lorenzo Bernini.

According to historian Cesare d'Onofrio, what may have suggested the idea of the elephant was nothing more hermetic than the recent arrival in Rome of a pachyderm for a sideshow to entertain curious Romans who had not seen such an animal since the king of Portugal had sent one as a present to Pope Leo X almost a century earlier. But New York's art historian William S. Heckscher in a fascinatingly erudite article on *Bernini's Elephant and Obelisk* in The Art Bulletin, of June 1973, thinks Bernini got the idea from a sketch which appeared in Francesco Colonna's *Hypnerotomachia Poliphili*, or *The Strife of Love on a Dreame*, originally published in Venice in 1499, translated into Elizabethan English in 1598, and into French in 1600. If so, both Bernini and Kircher were dealing with the subtlest of Rosicrucian symbolism. As analyzed by Alberto Cesare Ambesi in *I Rosa Croce*, Colonna's work "marks the true birth of the Rosy Cross, but in code," or what Italian philosopher Benedetto Croce calls "a language which intentionally suggests and underlines another more effective one." Like Dante's *Divine Comedy*, the tale starts with the hero lost in the woods. Asleep in a valley Poliphilo dreams of an elephant with an obelisk on his back and of another taller obelisk rising from a stepped pyramid, surmounted by a winged nymph. Into this obelisk Poliphilo is led by Cupid for initiation into the mysteries of love and life.

Bernini made several *bozzetti* for an obelisk atop an elephant, but for reasons that are unclear the project was dropped by the cardinal who set Kircher to transcribing the hieroglyphs from the broken pieces of obelisk lying in the garden of his palace in the hope that a translation might divulge their hidden meaning.

previous esoteric literature of the Middle Ages, including that of the Templars and Dante's *Faithful in Love,* to the future texts of the Rosicrucians, marking the true beginning of the fraternity. In the poem, Eros is the love force which moves the sun and the stars; and lovemaking between humans is associated with the power that makes for the growth of crystals, and the levitating force of trees toward the sun. The depicted obelisks represent access to superhuman states of consciousness, and the cornucopia held by the winged creature atop the obelisk is a symbol of the abundance that flows from the conquest of angelic states, leading to deeper esoteric levels of Sufi wisdom, the seven inner levels that must be conquered to become one with an occult sun.

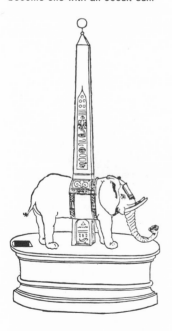

Of assistance to Kircher in this puzzling assignment was a Roman patrician, Pietro della Valle, who had acquired in Egypt a unique manuscript in the form of a Coptic-Arabic dictionary. Kircher, with his knowledge of Arabic, soon found that Coptic differed decidedly from Hebrew, Chaldean, Syrian, Ethiopian, Armenian, and Samaritan, which further encouraged him to believe he was on the track of the enigmatic language of the ancient Egyptians.

At the Collegio Romano, a model university where the Jesuits trained their most talented scholars, Kircher was given the chair of mathematics, vacated by Father Christoforo Schein, who had been sent to Vienna in his stead. But it was a sad time for science: Lucilio Vanini, a brilliant young free-thinking teacher, who claimed that nature should be worshiped as the source of all things, was condemned for atheism. On his way to the scaffold to be burned he said: "Let us go joyfully to die, as becomes a philosopher." His tongue was forced from his mouth and severed by the executioner's knife. The ex-Dominican philosopher Tommaso Campanella, author of the splendid *City of the Sun,* with its ideal society, reflective of Bruno's admiration for the ancient Egyptians, had been kept in prison twenty-seven years, and frequently tortured—despite his having performed salutary magic for Urban VIII— and only escaped execution by pretending to be mad. Peiresc's friend Galileo had just been condemned by the Inquisition, and the Congregation of Cardinals in Rome, prodded by Bruno's nemesis Cardinal Bellarmine, prohibited the printing, reading, or possession of the works of Descartes. Even Jesuits were not immune from persecution, and Father Friederich von Spee was imprisoned for writing in his *Cantio criminalis* against the torture of witches, and only just escaped with his life.

Kircher's reconstruction of ancient alphabets, leading to his understanding of Coptic

Kircher, who was inclined to side with Galileo on the Copernican theory, took care to deny such an opinion, fearing the fate of Bruno, Vanini, and Campanella. Publicly he declared: ''In case we seem to assert anything contrary to the decrees and instructions of the Holy Roman Church, we declare that we deny both the idea of the mobility of the earth, and of the inhabitants of the other heavenly globes.'' Hard to swallow, for an astronomer of his caliber.

To keep well out of trouble, Kircher plunged deeper into the study of Coptic. By 1636 he had produced his first book, *Prodromus Copticus sive Aegyptiacus,* in which he attempted an interpretation of hieroglyphs, which he explained as a symbolic system for expressing the theological teachings of the Egyptians. Publication of the book caused a stir among patrons of the arts wealthy enough to acquire it. Fascinated by Egyptian antiquities, Kircher's patrons knew little or nothing about Egypt other than from the fragments passed on to them in the Renaissance from Greek and Roman authors. Next, Kircher produced *Lingua Aegyptica restituta,* or *The Language of Egypt Restored,* which in no way delivered what it implied, though it contained della Valle's Coptic-Arabic dictionary, slightly updated.

From his reading of the classics and the Neoplatonists of the Renaissance, Kircher was convinced that the temples of ancient Egypt incorporated not only the cosmology of the ancients, but their system of physics. In 1639 he sent to Egypt a young man, Tito Livio Burattini, to measure the Great Pyramid of Cheops, inside and out, to see if he could find in its dimensions a figure for the circumference of the earth, as had been correctly suggested by the Milanese mathematician and astrologer Girolamo Cardano. Excitedly Kircher awaited Burattini's return with the careful measurements he had made as well as meticulous copies of many hieroglyphic texts taken from temples and obelisks. But Burattini was seized by bandits on his way back to Rome through the Balkans, and his invaluable manuscripts were scattered and destroyed. This left Kircher with nothing to go on but the few letters with data which Burattini had managed to send from Egypt.

For Kircher to do better, he needed more hieroglyphs, hence more obelisks. His opportunity came in 1644 with the death of Pope Urban VIII and the enthronement of Innocent X (Giambattista Pamfili). In a field along the old Appian Way, in what had once been the circus of the emperor Maxentius, four broken pieces of an obelisk

The Circus of Maxentius, with its broken obelisk, etched by du Perac in 1575

The fertility gods Ceres and Consus appeared at the end of Roman circuses, and recently excavated pre-Roman Etruscan tombs show chariots in a circus racing around conical obelisks.

surfaced from the area where they had been originally raised by the emperor Domitian late in the first century A.D. What better monument, Kircher reasoned, than to raise this obelisk in honor of Innocent X? The product of an old Umbrian family which had settled in Rome in the fifteenth century, the new pope was anxious to embellish the front of the house where he had been born and which his widowed sister-in-law and "confidante," Donna Olimpia Maidalchini, had begun refurbishing into a princely palace with the help of papal funds. Appropriately, it overlooked the oblong Piazza Navona, which had once been the stadium of Domitian, and earlier still, even more appropriately, one of the circuses attributed to the founders Rome, called by them *Agona,* site of the large *Ago,* or needle.

To Kircher's suggestion, the pope replied: "Father, we have decided to raise up this obelisk of no small bulk. It will be your task to work out the meaning of the inscriptions that are on it. We would like you, therefore, since you have been endowed by God with such gifts, to give yourself wholeheartedly to the task, doing all you can so that those who are amazed by the bulk of this great obelisk may come, through your endeavors, to understand the secret meaning of the inscriptions."

A committee was formed with Father Kircher as field director to excavate the obelisk from the ancient circus; but it was soon discovered that several pieces were missing from the fractured monolith, most of which appeared to be in the hands of local antiquarians. When it became known that the pope wanted the missing frag-

ments restored, those who disliked or were jealous of
Kircher decided to withhold the fragments to see if the
Jesuit was canny enough to correctly fill in the vacant
spaces with substitutes of his own creation.

The result, according to Kircher, was to vindicate his
understanding of the subject. "Through the illumination
God gave me, all unworthy though I was, I so formed the
figures on the obelisk . . . that they fitted in perfectly with
what was there already and in no way differed from those
which were on the actual missing pieces. They were all
amazed and could think of no explanation to my skill
except that the Holy Spirit had given me the key to the
inscriptions." Later "experts," less convinced, scoffed at
Kircher for the folly of such presumption, though they
could do no better.

Next came the problem of raising the obelisk. As no one
had put one up since Fontana, models were requested
from several leading architects, including Bernini's rival
Francisco Borromini, who succeeded in obtaining the
commission by submitting a pretty but banal sketch.
Bernini, who had fallen out of grace with the Vatican since
the death of his patron Urban VIII, was outraged, yet
determined, with the help of his protector, Prince Niccolò
Ludovisi, nephew of Pope Gregory XV, to steal the
commission. As a stratagem, Bernini cast his model in
solid silver and donated it as a bribe to the voraciously
avid Donna Olimpia, with the proviso that it be placed in
her house where her brother-in-law the pope would be
bound to see it during one of his visits—regular enough to
cause rumors of a more than brotherly attachment.

Arriving for lunch on the Feast of the Annunciation, after
a hearty morning ride, Innocent was so struck by Bernini's
model that he immediately gave him the commission with
the quip: "To avoid a Bernini project, one must simply not
see it."

The architect's grandiose project to erect a relatively
short obelisk high above the piazza on a stunning baroque
fountain was not cheap. Money for the job had to be
raised through a special tax imposed on all the citizens of
Rome, which hit the poorest, cutting down their bread.
Bitterness was expressed in lampoons and pasquinades,
the most savage of which were directed against the
pope's sister-in-law, who was rightly suspected of being
behind the scheme to glorify her brother's family. Much
scurrilous play was made of her name, which lent itself to
being fractioned into *olim pia,* Latin for "once virtuous,"
implying, as have several historians, a sexual relation with
the pope. Every night as the great fragments of stone

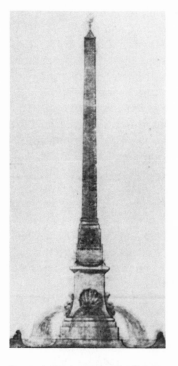

Borromini's sketch for the Piazza
Navona obelisk

were left to rest along the streets of Rome on their slow way from the Via Appia to the Piazza Navona, there were cries of *"pane, pane, non fontane."* Anonymous hands attached to the obelisk placards, one of which played on words from the Bible: "If only these stones would turn to bread!"

But once the great phallus was raised, Romans consoled themselves with the gush of delicious *acqua vergine,* the best water in Rome, which issued from Bernini's fountain symbolizing the four great rivers of the world— the Ganges, the Amazon, the Danube, and the Nile, the last discreetly represented by a figure with its eyes covered because the river's source was unknown. Jokes were soon forthcoming about how the sculpted blackamoor representing the river Ganges was holding up his hand not in awe of the great obelisk, but for fear that the façade to Borromini's Church of Santa Teresa, which forms a backdrop to the fountain, was so badly built it would fall on his head.

That the obelisk had been raised with no significance other than to honor the Pamfili family, was clear to all. To resolve any doubts, an inscription was placed on the base spelling out the Pamfili emblems: "Above the noxious Egyptian monstrosities [the heiroglyphs] rests the innocent dove, wreathed in lilies of virtue, offering the olive branch of peace." The dove triumphant was to symbolize not the Holy Ghost but Innocent X Pamfili. Bernini, driving past his opus, is said to have drawn the curtains to his carriage with the remark: "How ashamed I am of such bad work."

Innocent X celebrated the raising of the obelisk by asking Kircher to publish an account of the entire proceedings, which gave Kircher the chance to put into print in some five hundred pages his attitude toward Egyptological problems in general, and hieroglyphs in particular. Entitled *Obeliscus Pamphilis,* and adorned with elaborate prints, only its second part treated of the obelisk in the Piazza Navona. The first part included an excursus on John Dee's *Monas* glyph, which Kircher connected with the Egyptian ankh, or symbol of life, and which he interpreted as a symbol of the ascendency of spirit over matter.

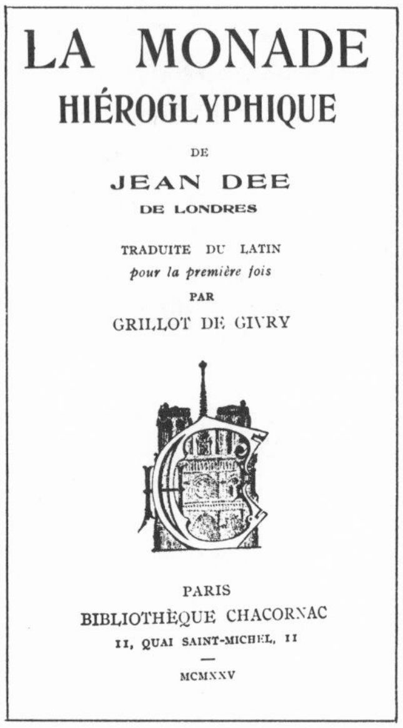

LA MONADE
HIÉROGLYPHIQUE
DE
JEAN DEE
DE LONDRES
TRADUITE DU LATIN
pour la première fois
PAR
GRILLOT DE GIVRY

PARIS
BIBLIOTHÈQUE CHACORNAC
11, QUAI SAINT-MICHEL, 11
MCMXXV

Dee's *Monas hieroglyphica,* which Frances Yates considers to be at the heart of the Rosicrucian mystery, deals with the mathematical properties of symbols—a subject as close to Kircher's heart as it had been to Dee's. Like Bruno, Dee pursued a philosophy of nature "which sought the divine meaning of the hieroglyphic characters written by God into the universe." And like Bacon, Dee presaged a scientific era in which man would compel nature to unleash forces to serve him to an extent undreamed of. Dee's notion that man could use numbers to achieve fantastic magical results is all too apparent in what passes for modern science, whose proponents, unlike Dee, do not appear to have been initiated into the secrets of alchemy and its great work of *spiritual* transformation.

Delving into the arcane and the cabalistic, Kircher's fundamental thesis about the hieroglyphs was a reiteration of the Hermetic tradition: the glyphs were not an ordinary system of writing but "a sacred instrument bequeathed by the gods to the Egyptians . . . enabling them to express their wisdom and the secrets of esoteric knowledge in symbolic pictures the meaning of which was directly revealed to initiates by divine inspiration." For Kircher, each inscription had a quadruple sense: "literal, figurative, allegorical and analogical, to express the same thing." As Erik Iversen puts it: "With an absolute confidence in the authority of his sources, and in the firm conviction that all leading metaphysicians of antiquity, Pythagoras and Plato as well as Plotinus and Iamblichus, had been directly influenced by Egyptian theology, Kircher had no doubt that his studies of their works combined with his knowledge of the Cabbala and the Hermetica, had given him a complete insight into what he considered Egyptian philosophy and thought."

With this as a premise, all that Kircher needed was to identify each hieroglyph with the basic Neoplatonic concept applied to it. The notion was genial. But despite his enormous erudition, his enthusiasm, and his almost superhuman industry, the results were inconclusive. Fortunately for Kircher, although at the time there was no one sufficiently equipped to confirm his argument, there was also no one equipped to refute it.

Kircher's translation of the glyphs on this Minervan obelisk deals with a supreme twofold spirit—the great Hemphta— whose generative powers infuse stars and sun to bring forth the bounties of life. In what sounds like a Tantric allusion, he calls the Left Hand of Nature "the Fount of Hecate."

ATHANASII KIRCHERI E. SOCIETATE IESV
OEDIPVS ÆGYPTIACVS
AD FERDINANDVM III CÆSAREM SEMPER AVGVSTVM.

Kircher next produced his *Oedipus Aegypticus,* a formidable work of almost two thousand pages, with numerous engravings, which appeared in four volumes between 1652 and 1654. New type had to be cast for the oriental languages he quoted, and for the Ethiopian, Chinese and Egyptian glyphs he reproduced. Expert printers and engravers had to be hired, which could only be done with the lavish patronage of the Holy Roman Emperor, the scholarly composer of music, raised by the Jesuits, Ferdinand III. In Iversen's words, Kircher, "as a modern Oedipus attempted to solve the riddle of the Egyptian Sphinx."

95

The Great Pyramid of Cheops as reconstructed by Kircher from Burattini's measurements

In the body of his *Oedipus,* Kircher came close to doing just that, defining a symbol as "the significant sign of a hidden mystery, whose nature is to lead one's mind through meditation on certain similarities to the comprehension of something much different from the thing presented to external senses, the nature of which can be said to be transcendent or hidden, as obscured by a veil." As an example he noted that the Egyptian scarab did not symbolize the actual sun but "the secret and mysterious operations of that body which foster growth and generation." In the body of his *Oedipus,* Kircher clarifies and explains the more important of his ideas relating to Egyptian language and antiquities, to their mathematics, mechanics, medicine, chemistry, theology, and magic. But the last part is largely a rehash of his earlier notions on hieroglyphs, the result of twenty years' study during which he consulted some three hundred ancient authors, including all the favorites of the Hermeticists.

Kircher said he regarded the Hebrews after Moses as betrayers of the Egyptian wisdom, perverting the Egyptian fertility cult into what he called crude phallic worship, and he objected to Islam because it promised a heaven of sex-fulfillment. Somewhat incongruously he also attacked the occult sciences of magic, alchemy, dowsing, divination by dreams, theurgy, and chiromancy, leading Joscelyn Godwin, in *Kircher, A Renaissance Man and the Quest for Lost Knowledge,* to wonder "whether his protestations are just a blind, enabling him to expound dangerous doctrines with impunity." Certain it is that in so doing, Kircher kept the ancient wisdom bubbling in an otherwise stagnant sludge of orthodoxy.

In his *Oedipus,* the obelisks of Rome are illustrated with glyphs that do not always resemble their originals all that closely. On the basis of Burattini's surviving tracings, Kircher was nevertheless able to add better reproductions from the two obelisks still standing in Alexandria and Heliopolis.

Kircher's method of decipherment was an identification of each glyph with its metaphysical idea. ‡ he identified with "generation"; ‡ with "force"; ‡ with "infernal"; ‡ with "supernal" or "celestial"; ‡ with "emanating from above." None, alas, was to be supported in the light of orthodox Egyptological deciphering. Yet intuitively Kircher sensed that though some of the glyphs represented ordinary material objects, they could also be used alphabetically as letters. The sign ‡ he correctly identified as "water," and went further, correctly, to suggest the phonetic value of *m,* with a reference to the Coptic word for water: *mu*. As Iversen writes: "It is Kircher's incontestable merit as the first to have determined the phonetic value of an Egyptian hieroglyph. Yet he remained more interested in the possible symbolism of the glyphs and the esoteric knowledge they might transmit."

In the *Oedipus*, Kircher follows Pico in comparing the glyphs of the Cabala with those of the Hermetica, and though he agrees with Ficino and Bruno about the magical power of the Egyptian cross, or ankh, he condemns cabalistic magic. Yet, in the end, he makes his Hermetic point by including Hermes's hymn from the *Pimander,* adding a hieroglyph enjoining silence and secrecy concerning these sublime doctrines—the colophon employed by the Brothers of the Rosy Cross!

The year after the last volume of *Oedipus* appeared, the pompous and austere Innocent X died, to be succeeded by Alexander VII (Fabio Chigi), at last a philosopher and poet, who yet favored the Jesuits in general and Kircher in particular. A patron of the humanities, who had devoted his resources as cardinal to the promotion of art and science, the new pope was to embellish Saint Peter's basilica with Bernini's stunning baroque colonnade, and to offer Kircher a decade of undisturbed study in his favorite subjects, which were becoming more catholic—in the original sense of the word. Refreshingly, the new pontiff was an extraordinary anomaly: an Hermetic scholar who took a personal interest in Kircher's hieroglyphical studies, contributing generously to the publication of Kircher's many more works, and so, indirectly, to keeping alive the wisdom of Ficino, Pico, and their Thrice Great Master.

By climbing down the maw of erupting Vesuvius, and by exploring the famous "cave of the dog," whose volcanic fumes of carbon dioxide hovering along the ground would kill that animal, but leave a man unaffected, Kircher got involved in the mysteries of the world beneath the soil, which led to perhaps his most famous work, *Mundus subterraneus.* Fascinated with astronomy (on which subject he produced his *Iter extaticum*), Kircher was a firm believer in the influence of heavenly bodies on earthly happenings and phenomena. A student of Paracelsus, he mirrored the Swiss master's notions of a panspermia, or universal seed of all things, "a certain material spirit, or something made from the most subtle heavenly aura or from portions of the elements, a certain spiritous sulphurous-saline-mercurial vapor, the universal seed of things."

Of the existence of Plato's Atlantis, Kircher had no doubt, placing it as a large island in the middle of the

The two human figures represent man surveying and measuring the planet, which is suspended by a chain to the hand of God. Sun and moon affect the twelve varying zephyrs of the cartographer's wind rose, clearly indicating Kircher's understanding of the Copernican notion of the earth spinning in the void around the sun, an earth whose circumference he correctly believed the Egyptians to have measured and incorporated into the Great Pyramid on the Ghiza plateau.

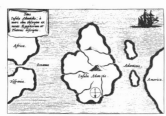

Kircher's Atlantis

Frontispiece of *Ars magna lucis*, showing the light of the sun (depicted as Apollo) shining onto earth reflected by the moon (Diana), all emanating from *IHVH* surrounded by angels

Illustration of a magic lantern as described by Kircher in his *Ars magna lucis*

That obelisks were involved with magnetic phenomena in the solar system was prophetically illustrated by Kircher in this sketch showing a large magnet in the central obelisk (symbolic of the sun) variously affecting magnets in the different-sized globes surrounding it.

Atlantic, about where the Azores now lie. On the art of consonance and dissonance Kircher wrote ten books in which are treated the whole doctrine and philosophy of sound, especially as applicable to philosophy, mathematics, physics, mechanics, medicine, politics, metaphysics, and theology. He gave numerous accounts of the curative powers of music, such as a melody to cure the bite of the tarantula and a tune to calm the frenzy of the mentally disturbed.

In his *Ars magna lucis et umbrae,* a thousand-page analysis of the phenomena of light and shadow, Kircher included methods for designing and constructing sundials. He even built a great pyramidal sundial, and designed an *horologium catholicum,* or universal clock, ostensibly to mark the different time of day in the various Jesuit colleges scattered around the globe, but more specifically to help establish longitude. The idea was a development of Galileo's suggestion that the moment of some astronomical event, such as an eclipse of one of Jupiter's moons, could be predicted with the help of tables in some standard time related to a fixed degree of longitude, and that a person in some other part of the world, observing the same event in terms of local time, could readily calculate the longitude of the place from which the observation was being made. Kircher even devised a sort of calculating machine which he claimed provided practical results to various mathematical and scientific problems.

When he was shown the remains of the obelisk found in a cellar in the area of the old Campus Martius, Kircher suggested to Alexander VII that it be raised on the spot where Augustus had used it as a great gnomon, or sundial. In his report to the pontiff, Kircher further suggested that the Vatican obelisk, which had been reraised by Fontana for Sixtus V, be similarly used as a sundial by the insertion of markers in the pavement of Saint Peter's Square. Both projects were more than Alexander VII, in a frail state of health, could face; but just before the death of the pope, Kircher found a way to repay his beloved patron by organizing for him an Hermetic monument in the form of a small but extraordinary obelisk raised by his old friend Bernini.

Some Dominican friars digging a new wall around their garden in the convent of Santa Maria Sopra Minerva, the ancient Roman dromos of Isis, had struck a pink granite obelisk buried about 15 palms beneath the surface. Alexander immediately appointed Kircher to head a committee to supervise the excavation of what turned out to be a short (5.5-meter) obelisk with remarkably well preserved hieroglyphs carved on all four of its sides.

Kircher's homage to the Hermeticist Pope Alexander VII

Kircher's reconstruction of the ancient Roman Iseum

Ironically, this monument to Isis (the Pallade Egizia of the Romans), erected on the site later dedicated to the pagan goddess of wisdom, Minerva (upon whom the Christians superimposed their Virgin Mary), was quickly seized by the Dominican fathers as their rightful property. They wished, they said, to raise it in the square before their church, on a base of six hillocks (symbols of the incumbent Chigi pope) surrounded by four dogs with torches in their mouths, a play on the words *domini cani,* or "hounds of the Lord," to indicate the bird-dog qualities of their order in ferreting out heresy. Alexander VII reluctantly gave in to the Dominicans' desire to have the trophy placed before their church, but vetoed their self-serving design, assigning Kirchner to see that this thoroughly Egyptian relic was more sensitively raised according to the old and clearly Hermetic design of the cavalier Bernini: that of an elephant with the obelisk on its back.

Just before the pope died, Kircher was further able to repay his beloved patron by underlining the Hermetic thought chiseled onto the base of the obelisk: "Oh you who here see transported by an elephant, the strongest of animals, the hieroglyphs of the wise Egyptians, heed this monument: to sustain solid wisdom, a robust mind is needed." All through the Middle Ages the elephant had been considered a wise and intelligent animal. In the works of Horapollo it was the glyph for a strong man in search of what is beneficial and essential. It was plain that the monument was specifically designed for Alexander VII, whose mind, despite his physical frailness, was considered strong enough to handle the Hermetic wisdom of Egypt. But the satirist Segardi, taking the symbolism one step further, used the fact that the elephant's rear end is turned toward the monastery of the Dominicans to compose the epigram *"Vertit terga elephas vertague proboscide clamat Kyriaci Frates Heid Vos Habeo"* or, in short, "Dominicans, you may kiss my arse!"

The Minervan obelisk facing away from the Dominican monastery

The Society of Jesus, founded in 1541 by Ignatius Loyola, adept, through the device of the spiritual retreat at conjuring visions to convince susceptible heretics to return to the Church, was to carry the standard of the Counter-Reformation. In a virtual state of war, Jesuits served as the military light horse of the church under the absolute orders of a general known as the "black pope," who was elected for life. Individual Jesuits were bound by a vow of personal obedience to both the "black" and "white" popes, ready to follow orders anywhere at any time, "manageable as a stick in his hand . . . unaffected as a corpse." A sacrifice of intellect to total obedience was considered "pleasing to God." Aware that the cause of the Reformation was the "ignorance, neglect and vicious lives of so many priests, especially in the higher ranks," Jesuits devoted their efforts to better education; and for three centuries were the best schoolmasters in Europe. By 1620 there were 20,000 Jesuits traveling to the ends of the earth, often suffering cruel martyrdom, dragging with them to death thousands of Christian converts. In Japan, when the Christianized women of the Shogun refused to perform in his harem, 250 churches were burned and 200,000 converts killed. Cardinal Bellarmine argued that since all authority derives from God, any Christian price forfeits his right to authority if his government contravenes the wishes of the Church. Subjects have no obligation to such a prince, and can take steps to remove him. The argument led to accusations of assassination against the Jesuits, including that of Henry IV. A spurious document, *Monita Secreta Societas Jesu,* purported to give secret instructions for acquiring power over princes and rich widows, and how to poison. Accused of becoming "the apostles of the rich and influential," Jesuits soon incurred universal hostility, especially from other members of the Church. In the course of the next century, the works of 27 Jesuits, including Bellarmine, were or-

dered burned by the common hangman. Another decree declared that Jesuit doctrines "contained the errors of Arius, Nestorius, Calvin, Luther, Wycliffe and Pelagius; that they were blasphemous, outrageous, and insulting to the Blessed Virgin and the saints; destructive to the divinity of Christ; favorable to Epicureans and Deists; encouraged murder and patricide, usury, vengeance and cruelty; threatened the safety of princes, and were in contradiction to the decisions of the Church, to the divine will, to peace and good order." The good fathers were accused of pederasty. In France, they gained the enmity of Madame de Pompadour by refusing her absolution while she remained the king's mistress, so she got Louis XV to expel them from France, and requested the pope to suppress the society.

From Portugal they were expelled for purported complicity in the attempted assassination of King Joseph I. Clement XIII, in his eighty-second year, is said to have died of shock when requested by France, Portugal and Spain to dissolve the society. In a brief, *Dominus ac Redemptor,* in which he referred to the suppression of the Templars, Cardinal Ganganelli as Clement XIV declared the Society of Jesus extinguished, abolished, and abrogated forever, with all its houses, colleges, schools and hospitals. Its general, Lorenzo Ricci, was thrown into Castel Sant' Angelo where he died two years later. Many of the 22,000 disbanded Jesuits took refuge in Prussia and Russia where they were used by Frederick II and Catherine II as teachers for pupils whom they considered illiterate bores.

From the frontispiece of his *Sphinx mystagoga* it was clear that Kircher believe the wisdom of the world to have come from Egypt and to have been incorporated in its tombs, pyramids, and obelisks.

Times grew rougher for supporters of the Hermetic tradition. In England, Jesuits took advantage of the civil disorders which broke out after the death of Cromwell to intrude themselves among the Rosicrucians to pervert the order and cause its apparent disappearance. No longer protected by Alexander VII, Kircher gave up his jobs at the Collegio Romano, determined quietly to devote the rest of his life to archaeology and the solution of the riddle of the obelisks and their mysterious glyphs.

In an epoch when it was the fashion to search for unicorns and mermaids, and the Rosicrucian Elias Ashmole was organizing his antiquarian's museum at Oxford, one of Kircher's main interests became his own museum of rarities and oddities which he had collected to go along with his Egyptological curios. To these he added geological specimens, preserved birds, skeletons, mechanical models, as well as his own inventions, which included a variety of musical instruments, alchemical glassware, and microscopes. From all over the world Jesuits sent him donations such as rhinoceros horns, gold embroidered vests, girdles studded with rubies, idols, icons, and strange drugs. Soon he had an exhibition hall in the Collegio Romano 300 feet long with side galleries of curios such as the skeleton of a bird with three legs, and a monstrous 10-ounce stone removed from the bladder of his comrade Father Leo Sanctius. But the principal attraction remained his central exhibit of a range of Egyptian obelisks.

As Kircher's early work had dealt with the crucial but still mysterious force of magnetism, his last book describes his experiments with a microscope which could "amplify a fly into an elephant and a flea into a camel." In vinegar and milk he found innumerable "worms," which led him, well ahead of his time, to guess that the plague, of which no one knew the cause, might be propagated by tiny living organisms.

In November 1680, almost on the same day as his old friend Bernini, Kircher died in his seventy-ninth year, to be derided, ridiculed, and even questioned in his honesty. Ever since, he has been the whipping boy of Egyptology, though as Iversen says, "His devotion, his untiring enthusiasm, and his positive contributions have been disregarded by the science he sacrificed his life to further and to serve . . . an easy prey to egyptologists who have sacrificed his reputation for a witticism, mostly without having opened his books." A fair criticism, as the volumes are hard to come by, even in the very best libraries, and their thousands of Latin pages are still judiciously untranslated into any vernacular.

As Maristang notes, Kircher's life work, in its scope, went far beyond the limits of Egyptology, representing one of the last efforts to combine the totality of human knowledge in religion, philosophy, history, and science into a theological system, a universal cosmology based on the concepts and ideas of a Neoplatonized Christianity. Iversen, in sum, wonders if Kircher's conceptions of Egyptian religion and mythology, though undoubtedly fantastic and unhistorical, "are very much further from the truth than the sterile and lifeless waxworks to which the more sober, unmetaphysical methods of modern egyptology have reduced the Egyptian pantheon." From a humanistic as well as an intellectual point of view, he adds, "egyptology may very well be proud of having Kircher as its founder." Yet three hundred years were to pass before this remarkable scholar was given the credit he justly deserved for keeping alive the torch handed down to him from ancient Egypt.

Nothing, says Kircher, on the frontispiece of his *Ars magna sciendi,* is more beautiful than to know all.

103

Summoning a spirit

6. EGYPTIAN RITES OF MASONRY

The century which followed Kircher's, the so-called Age of Enlightenment, was to see a reversal in the fortunes of the religious contestants, bringing into play the destruction of the Society of Jesus and a flourishing of the Hermetic tradition in the ranks of all manner of Freemasonic orders, including their more secret organizers—the Rosicrucians and the Illuminati.

Two revolutions, one in America and one in France, ended the dogma of the divine rule of kings in favor of republican governments with the political and religious freedoms propagandized by Freemasons and eventually protected by the Bill of Rights. But despite the banishment of the Jesuits from most European countries, the popes, especially Pius VI, who was to reign longer than any previous pontiff, fought back. Opening his pontificate with an encyclical which forbade individual freedom of conscience, Pius VI, by the intransigence of his stand against political progress in France—which he was able to enforce by threatening with excommunication a weak and believing Louis XVI—became responsible, though perhaps unwittingly, for the abortion of an orderly evolution to constitutional government, bringing on instead a grossly radical revolution in which almost every value was drowned in the blood of the Terror.

The year before the American Declaration of Independence, the elevation to the seat of Saint Peter of Giovanni Braschi was greeted by the poor of Rome with foreboding and caustic pasquinades—those satirical notes clandestinely attached by wits to two mutilated statues known as Pasquino and Marforio, whose salty dialogue constituted an outlet for the pent-up misery of citizens. Ominously, Romans pointed out that any ruler with a six in his title had always brought disaster to the city. *"Semper sub sextis perdita Roma fuit,"* they lamented, thinking of Shakespeare's villainous and bloody Tarquinus Sextus, who deprived the city's poor of their arms and set them to slave work building great monuments, and of Urban VI, an intractable nepotist responsible for executing several cardinals and initiating the Great Schism which divided the Western Church for forty years, and of that unforgettable Spaniard, Alexander VI, the Borgia tyrant.

PIVS VI PONT MAX

Pius VI was lampooned for his vanity. When he added an eagle and a *fleur-de-lis* to his escutcheon of "two winds," the people of Rome suggested he restore the eagle to the empire and the lilies to the king of France, keeping for himself the "winds." Historian Jean François de Bourgoing said of him: "his prodigality and his taste for brilliant but expensive enterprises rendered him more odious than many princes who were really wicked." When an enormously expensive sacristy was added to Saint Peter's (at a cost to the people of 200,000 crowns) Pius added a plaque which read "What the public voice demanded, Pius VI completed." To which some Roman added: "You lie. The public was never consulted. Only your vanity."

105

Nor were the poor of Rome happy with a pope who seemed determined not only to wage a war on "bad" books, but to revive the ostentatious splendor of the reign of Lorenzo the Magnificent's son, Leo X, at their expense, by diminishing their ration of bread—especially when he chose to rub salt in the wound by having engraved on the monuments he raised with their slave labor MUNIFICENTIA PII VI P.M., a practice which gave rise to such satires as the insertion of a reduced loaf of bread, engraved with the same papal inscription, into the hands of Pasquino.

Surrender at Yorktown

In the fall of 1781, as Freemason George Washington defeated Freemason Charles Cornwallis at Yorktown, and Freemason Frederich Baron von Steuben received the Englishman's sword, in Rome, lowlier masons, digging foundations for a small house by the hospital of San Rocco, struck the point of an obelisk. Further probing revealed two more pieces, plus the base, which had been broken in two. It was the same relic, the soutaned observers realized, which had been disinterred two centuries earlier in 1549, on the land of Monsignor Francesco Soderini, and quickly reburied because Pope Paul III had died before anything could be done about it.

To Pius VI the hospital of San Rocco, which specialized in caring for unwed mothers and illegitimate children, now raised a cry for compensation to remedy the damage caused by digging around their buildings. The new pope, though as profligate a nepotist as any of his predecessors—his nephew Romualdo Onesti, speculating on property sequestered from Jews soon made such a fortune he was able to acquire title to the dukedom of Nemi and have himself named both prince of the empire and grandee of Spain—continued to refuse the hospital any compensation until someone suggested raising the required 1,200 scudi to indemnify the monks through the sale of lottery tickets to the poor.

With that problem so economically settled, Pius ordered his papal architect, Giovanni Antinori, to repair the broken pieces of the San Rocco obelisk, no matter what the cost, and have it raised on the Quirinal Hill opposite his great palace, already expansively decorated by Fontana and Borromini, which served him, because of its finer air, as a summer residence. The obelisk was to stand in the Square of the Horsemen, so known because of two enormous Roman equestrian statues placed there by Pius V in the mistaken notion they represented Castor and Pollux, mythological twin sons of Leda by Zeus.

Classical horses in the Quirinal Square before the raising of the obelisk brought from Augustus's mausoleum

Veduta della Piazza di Monte Cavallo

107

How much Pius wished to raise the obelisk as yet another antipagan symbol against the wave of revolutionary ideas spreading through America and Europe, and how much he merely wished to beautify Rome, remains moot. But the times were electric with the reforming ideas of Mason, Rosicrucian, and Illuminatus. The execution of victims for supposed offenses against the Church and its tenets, though diminished, had not ceased. In the Pas-de-Calais town of Abbeville, two young Frenchmen had just been sentenced to have their tongues torn out by the roots with pincers and their severed right hands nailed to the door of the church, before being burned to death by slow fire, simply because a wooden cross on a country bridge had been found whittled away with a knife—a crime of which the boys had been accused. One of them, named d'Etallode, succeeded in fleeing. The other, La Barre, was duly executed on July 1, 1776, in the manner prescribed, thus becoming one of five million such victims estimated by Victor Hugo to have succumbed to the Churches, apart from those killed in religious wars.

It was then, just as the American Continental Congress was meeting in Philadelphia to announce the Declaration of Independence, that there appeared on the European scene a new and extraordinary young man, determined to raise even higher than Pius's obelisk the torch of freedom by reviving the Egyptian tradition of Bruno. At the very time La Barre's body was being consumed by the flames, and the last Englishwoman to be burned alive was given to the flames in Horsham, a medium-sized man of thirty, with dark curly hair and large magnetic eyes, arrived in London in the company of a stunningly beautiful wife of twenty-one. The newcomer, elegantly but soberly attired, handsomely coiffed, with a sword at his side, cut a noble figure, followed by a retinue of servants, who addressed him as Count Cagliostro.

In Whitcombe Street, Leicester Fields, where the couple took rooms, black smoke was seen to pour from the chimneys as the mysterious stranger practiced the art of alchemy over ovens and retorts, surrounded by books on the Cabala, the tables of Pythagoras, the calculations of Agrippa, and the computations of the abbé Trithenius, whose astrological magic was considered not only a form of telepathy, but a means of acquiring universal knowledge "of everything that is happening in the world." With these interests, it was only natural that Cagliostro should gravitate toward the Order of Freemasons which considered itself the repository of alchemical secrets going back to the Temple of Solomon.

Alessandro Cagliostro

Serafina Cagliostro

Masonic procession in eighteenth-century London. The Esperance Lodge 369 is said to have been frequented mainly by French and Italian residents in London, and to have been attached to the Continental Masonic Order of Strict Observance, supposedly a continuation of the Knights Templar.

On April 17, 1777, at the King's Tavern on Gerard Street, in Soho, Alexander Count Cagliostro was initiated into the Lodge of Esperance 369, with the grade of Master Mason, accorded him because of his membership in the Knights of Saint John of Jerusalem, a sovereign order recognized by the Scottish Observance, formed in the 1750s by a baron von Hund, which claimed to possess secret documents of the Knights Templar dating back to the fourteenth century, and which operated under the orders of mysterious Unknown Superiors with the object of regenerating Freemasonry in an aristocratic sense.

Ever since 1646, when Elias Ashmole had been the first gentleman "accepted" into the order of Masonry, the operative guilds had taken in more and more mystics and occultists with no relation to the actual building trade. By the beginning of the eighteenth century, these "accepted" Masons, mostly aristocrats, humanists, and rationalists, outnumbered the "operatives," who withdrew to form their own trade unions. The last Grand Master of the actual builders had been Christopher Wren, obliged to leave his post in 1702 because of his religious opinions. The new "accepted" Masons, though they considered themselves the perpetuators of the ancient mysteries of Egypt, with its higher science and deeper understanding of the secrets of nature, passed down to Gnostic, Neoplatonist, and Templar, were yet a living order, tolerant of all religions, with the fundamental tenet that "there is only one Supreme Being; He is all, the one and only."

The reason for the papal anathema, according to Freemasons, was their assertion that every man is himself the living, slain, and rearisen Christ in his own person. To which a twentieth-century 33° Mason has appended: ''Well may Catholic and freemason alike stand appalled at the stupendous blasphemy which is implied, as they ignorantly think, not knowing themselves of the stuff and substance of the Supreme Self, each for himself alike no less than Very God of Very God.''

Politically, it was the Mason's prime desire to spread knowledge, confident that once understanding and tolerance gained an ascendancy in men's minds, they would condemn and reject narrowly enslaving dogma. Believing that only in free debate, without censorship, could society develop, Masons aimed at the establishment of complete freedom of worship, freedom of speech and association, freedom of the press, and freedom from arbitrary arrest and imprisonment without trial. They wanted every man to have the right to choose his type of employment and place of residence—entailing the abolition of the serfdom still binding in Europe—and envisaged an eventual government controlled by public opinion, subject to a representative parliament. They believed that humanity, if it so desired, could attain to a social order, such as that of the ancient Egyptians, reflecting the order of the cosmos.

But the Church thought otherwise. When the Encyclopedists, a group of Masons in France, tried to bring out a translation of Chambers Encyclopedia edited by Denis Diderot, with the collaboration of Voltaire, Rousseau, Montesquieu, d'Holbach, and d'Alembert, it was banned by the Church, placed on the Index of forbidden books, and copies were burned wherever possible. Clement XII issued a bull forbidding Catholics, on pain of excommunication and the threat of hellfire, from joining or supporting Freemasons, because they allowed persons of all religions into their order, were ''depraved and perverted,'' and for ''other just and reasonable motives known to Us,'' which, not being specified, were presumed to be sexual.

In London, introduced into society by his brother Masons, Cagliostro was appreciated not only as an alchemist, but as a natural healer and producer of marvelous elixirs and rejuvenating pomades, sought after by the ladies, who were much attracted to this man of mystery. But because neither Cagliostro nor his wife could speak English well they were obliged to rely on a Portuguese housekeeper to interpret for them. This woman soon introduced into the household friends and relations who complained so pitifully of poverty, they induced Cagliostro to use his clairvoyant powers to foretell for them one set of winning numbers in the national lottery. When Cagliostro refused to continue this unconventional form of welfare, from which the beneficiaries had earned several hundred pounds, they organized a plot to denounce their benefactor to the police for theft in order to gain entry to his house with a warrant and seize the notebook in which he kept his secret computations for foretelling the outcome of the lottery.

Cagliostro with the upcoming numbers in the royal lottery

Unjustly arrested, Cagliostro was kept four months in the King's Bench jail before the beneficiaries, common London swindlers, could be brought to justice; at which point, lest one of them be hanged for theft, Cagliostro chose to withdraw charges. But the charm had gone out of residence in England. Admitting he too was perhaps unjust in attributing to the whole nation the faults of a few individuals, he nevertheless "determined to leave a place in which I found neither laws, justice nor hospitality."

The Comte de Saint-Germain—a transparent pseudonym for "holy brother"—moves in the twilight between history and legend, using many names: Baron Gualdi, Comte de Gabalis, Lord Welldone, Count Orloff. Biographer Marie-Remonde Delorme believes him to have been Prince Leopold Racoczy, one of three sons of Francis II of Transylvania, born in 1696. Paul Chacornac, another biographer, thinks him more likely to have been the son of Queen Marie-Anne de Neubourg, who had been married without issue to Charles II of Spain but had a child by her lover John Thomas de Cabrera, Duke of Rioseco, Grand Admiral of Castille, exiled with the arrival of the Bourbons. Marie-Anne's de Medici uncle appears to have fostered the exiled child in Florence. In Paris, where Saint-Germain appeared in 1744 he looked about fifty, but Madame de Gergi, daughter of the French Ambassador to Venice, remembered seeing him there in 1710, when he looked no older than forty-five. Like Cagliostro, he was said to have discovered the elixir or life. His rejuvenating pomades were much in demand by the ladies. Described as aristocratic, with large dark eyes, powerful but full of tenderness and humor, he was elegant but soberly dressed, displaying a wealth of diamonds said to have been alchemically produced. An accomplished musician, he played and composed with equal ease, and was renowned for a stock of tales he told in almost every European language. He could write a love letter with his left hand while composing a poem with the other, or compose the same text with both hands so alike they appeared identical when superimposed. He could tame bees and charm snakes. After falling into a cataleptic sleep for hours or days, he would descibe having visited the remotest corners of the planet, or even the stars. He described his past lives, including that of Menkh-Kheperseneb, son of Hatshepsut, recounting historical events as if eyewitnessed. He was as great an alchemist as

On the Continent, the Cagliostros traveled to the Hague, Brussels, Liege, Nüremberg, Leipzig, and Sarrebourg, everywhere welcomed from one Masonic lodge to the next. In Prussia they were cordially received by King Frederick II, a Mason, who, influenced by his close adviser, the comte de Saint-Germain, had become not only tolerant of all forms of religion, but intolerant of the use of torture, which was banned from his kingdom. And it was from meeting Saint-Germain that Cagliostro appears to have discovered his real mission in life: to act as a catalyst to bring Masonry—which, on the Continent, seemed to be divided into divergent strains, some no more than a vain pursuit of high-sounding titles and exotic costuming—back to the esoteric principles of ancient Egypt with a purified and regenerated ritual. For this, Cagliostro decided to organize an Egyptian rite, no longer merely speculative, but "transcendental, at once Christian, yet reviving the early rites of initiation into the Osirian myths of death and resurrection, of communion with the dead."

The grandiose goal was "to restore to man the powers which had been his in Eden before the fall, before having been obliged to struggle by the sweat of his brow"—a state in which Catholic dogma appeared to wish him kept forever. Man, said Cagliostro, following the Hermetic tradition, was fundamentally of an archangelic nature, a demigod, with power to command spiritual beings and to reign on earth. But to do so, to become once more the happy intermediary between the divine and its counterparts in nature, man must first reacquire his love and understanding of nature.

From various books on magic, but chiefly from an Egyptian papyrus discovered in the Upper Nile Valley, Cagliostro developed a rite designed to regenerate Masonry by regenerating each individual Mason.

In a castle in Holstein placed at Saint-Germain's disposal by Prince Charles of Hesse, Cagliostro and his wife were initiated into the Order of the Knights Templar. Jean Pierre de Luchet has described the scene as taking place in the fantastic setting of candle-lit dungeon with Saint-Germain seated on a golden throne; but as Luchet's object was to denigrate Masonry by concocting spurious "memoires" of Cagliostro, and as he could hardly have attended in person, the description is doubtful.

But it was from this point on that Cagliostro began to display his colors as a Rosicrucian adept, claiming to be not only capable of transmuting baser metals into gold, but of transmuting his "non-self" into his "real self"—the object of the Great Work of "spiritual alchemy."

chemist, and a series of impressive laboratories were placed at his disposal by the aristocracy and royalty of Europe. Without means of support, he was free with money, generous to those in need, arousing the suspicion he had access to the hidden assets of the Rosicrucians, perhaps the remnants of the Templar's treasure. A personal counselor to kings and princes, Saint-Germain served as intermediary between prime ministers in England, France, Austria, Prussia, and Russia. In London in 1745, he was confined to the Tower in the company of Emmanuel Swedenborg and the Marshal of France de Belle Isle, *habeas corpus* having been suspended by the landing in Scotland of the Jacobite son of James III. Known as a member of the Jacobite pro-Catholic Scottish Rite Masonry, to which the majority belonged who had gone into exile with James II, Saint-Germain's predicament was increased by the discovery on his person of a letter of thanks from the Pretender. This led to the presumption of his being on a spying mission for Louis XV, who had mounted a fleet to help the Pretender. When the aspirant James IV was defeated at Culloden, Saint-Germain was allowed to leave England, presumably thanks to his connections in the British aristocracy and his high standing in Masonic circles. From 1746 to 1758, Saint-Germain disappeared from Europe, and, according to biographer Pierre Laermier, was in the Far East with Hindu gurus to develop a deeper understanding of reincarnation, hypnosis, pharmacology, clairvoyance, levitation, telekinesis, and the secret practice of the Tantric arts already familiar to his brothers of the Rosy Cross. Back in Paris in 1758, with his old friend Marshal de Belle Isle as Minister of War, Saint-Germain was befriended by Madame de Pompadour and frequently invited to dine with Louis XV, who spoke of him as a person of illustrious birth. In her diaries she relates how he fascinated the king with his ability to eliminate flaws from gems, ren-

Exactly how much Cagliostro learned from Saint-Germain is difficult from the record to establish, but it was after seeing him that the younger man began to formulate his new Egyptian Rite of Masonry based on the ancient Hermetic wisdom as well as on the later Alexandrine Rites of Memphis.

In Berlin, Cagliostro appears to have read the *Crata Repoa,* published in Germany in 1770, a book giving details of initiation into the ancient mysteries of the priests of Egypt. A French translation had been edited by Freemason Anton Bailleul in 1778, and that same year the Abbé Rodin, a member of the Parisian Lodge of the Nine Sisters, published a description of the initiatory mysteries of ancient Egypt in his *Researches on Ancient and Modern Initiation.*

Manly P. Hall, in his *Freemasonry and the Ancient Egyptians,* has reprinted an English version of the *Crata Repoa* made at the end of the nineteenth century by a high Mason of the Rite of Memphis, Dr. John Yarker, and Hall claims that a comparison "leaves no doubt that they are from a common source and are maintained by a common inspiration."

The *Crata Repoa* is a reconstruction of the rituals of initiation into the ancient mysteries put together from hints and allusions contained in the writings of such classical authors as Porphyry, Herodotus, Iamblichus, Apuleius, Cicero, Plutarch, Eusebius, Arnobius, Diodorus Siculus, Tertullian, Heliodorus, Lucian Rufinus, and others. From these fragments insight can be gained into the degrees of initiation undergone between neophyte and adept. According to Hall, a high Mason in his own right, the third degree of the *Crata Repoa* corresponds closely to the third degree of the Blue Lodge of Modern Freemasonry.

Crata Repoa initiatory scene from Manly P. Hall's *Freemasonry and the Ancient Egyptians*

dering them more valuable, or to conjure visions of the future, frightening the king with a vision of his grandson, Louis XVI, decapitated. The object of such seances, according to Saint-Germain, was to convince the monarch that reform was essential not only in the Church but in his government if he wished to avoid revolution, urging him to move toward a constitutional monarchy such as in England, and a federated Christian Europe for which peace between France and England was the key. By 1760, Louis agreed to send Saint-Germain to England on a secret mission to negotiate with George III an end to the Seven Years War, which was ruining France. The mission was aborted because of an encounter in the Hague with the adventurer Casanova. Casanova informed French Foreign Minister de Choiseul, who was against the scheme. Forewarned of imminent arrest, Saint-Germain moved quickly to asylum with his friend Frederick II of Prussia, and from there to Russia to help Catherine II seize the throne from her impotent husband Paul III, by summoning—as one historian tells the story—the ghost of Peter the Great to give her instructions how to act. After many adventures, Saint-Germain found in the Duchy of Schleswig-Holstein the ideal prince to help him develop his Rosicrucian projects—

As reconstructed in the *Crata Repoa,* the ancient rite began with circumcision as a permanent sign of belonging, followed by several months' imprisonment in a subterranean vault where the neophyte underwent a severe fast to symbolize that in this life the body is the sepulcher of the soul and can only be released from the serfdom of darkness through the light of initiation. Bound and hoodwinked, to symbolize the limitations of the mortal state, the neophyte was shown that the evils which petrify him when blindfolded lose their power once his eyes are uncovered. Binding the eyes was also a symbol for the necessity of binding the physical senses if the superphysical world is to be perceived.

In the first grade of the ancient Egyptian rite, the neophyte was shown a ladder to climb as the symbol of metempsychosis, his foot placed on the lowest rung to indicate that the ladder of the mysteries extends from the mundane sphere to the empyrian of the wise, and that each disciple as he ascends the grades must become teacher to those directly below him in attainment. The ladder likewise symbolized seven psychic centers of the human body, a ladder to be climbed by mastery of the secrets of yoga. In the first degree, according to Hall, the robes and garments were designed to represent the changes in the auric colors of the disciple resulting from his newly directed spiritual purpose, the conical hat being a symbol of aspiration toward the light, while an apron was a sign of purification. Robed in purity, the disciple was groomed to become "a guardian at the gates of truth," and given the secret password *Amoun,* meaning, says Hall, to be discreet.

How much of this ritual Cagliostro was able to apply to his adepts presumably depended on their desire for advancement, but mostly Cagliostro appears to have used his talents as a thaumaturge and magus to attract followers to at least embark on the way.

According to Cagliostro there had been three important Egyptian practices performed in the Holy of Holies of the Great Pyramid: the convocation of disembodied entities, either of "gods" or of spirits of the dead; divination through a child medium; and, finally, some form of spiritual and physical regeneration.

From the various esoteric doctrines practiced in the temples along the Valley of Nile, Cagliostro took the idea of reestablishing "an intimacy with the ancient 'gods' of Egypt and of enticing their participation into the life of Man." In this he was following the lead, spelled out in Hermes's *Asclepius,* of Ficino, Paracelsus, Agrippa, Dee,

Charles of Hesse, son-in-law of the King of Denmark and Grandson of George II of England, who became the magus' truest friend and admirer. A student of alchemy and the magic of evoking spirits, Charles of Hesse was convinced of the existence on the planet of illuminated men, who had penetrated the secret teachings of the ancient Egyptians, Brothers of the Rosy Cross, who received precise, clear revelations from superior beings. Hesse, who was reputed to have mastered the method of intercourse with ghosts and supernatural beings that would appear at his call, was also able to describe his own past lives, which he said included one as King Josias of the Old Testament, another as Joseph of Arimathea, and most recently as the Protestant preacher Zwingli.

Baroque representation of the archangel Michael

Bacon, and Saint-Germain; and Cagliostro appears to have learned from the Rosicrucian manual *Enchiridon,* the actual steps by which adepts could be put in touch with "angels and the spirits of the dead."

In Leipzig, at the Lodge of Minerva of the Three Palms, Cagliostro learned from Dom Permety, a Benedictine alchemist who had developed a *Hermetic Rite of Perfection,* to convoke "the entities that revolve in heaven." Permety was later made a member of the Academy of Berlin by Frederick the Great, then curator of his Royal Library; eventually he formed the lodge of Illuminés of Avignon.

On the basis of these various techniques, and what he claimed to have learned in his travels in Egypt, Cagliostro fashioned his rite for summoning angels: it amounted to hypnotizing a child, usually a young girl whom he called a dove, or a boy whom he called a *pupille,* to scry in a crystal bowl, illumined by candles, wherein the child could see visions and make prophecies. The officiating magus could then tell people about their own past, including their past lives, with the hoped-for effect of waking them up to the fact that they were indeed immortal spirits, occupying different bodies, and that they were on the planet with some goal to achieve. By communicating with what he claimed to be disembodied entities, and even sometimes by succeeding in materializing some sort of visible form for those present, Cagliostro was better able to convince the participants in his rituals of the Hermetic tenets that the material world they lived in was but one level of reality, interconnected with other more rarefied dimensions, leading up through a spirit world to the divine, where, eventually, all was One.

Several of those who joined the rite brought their own children to act as mediums. In Wittau, Count von Howen brought his son, who turned out to be an expert, going into trance and immediately seeing visions, among which he described the archangel Michael, leader of the planetary spirits, as a shadowy figure robed in white, followed by other archangelic entities such as Anael, Raphael, Zodiachel, Uriel, Anachiel, and Zachariel, appearing in various guises. More instantly convincing were descriptions given to individuals of their own immediate family lives, often amazingly correct. Cagliostro also made more general prophecies. In November 1780 he declared that the empress Maria Theresa of Austria had died. Five days later, the news was confirmed. He then prophesied that the empress's daughter, Marie Antoinette, would give birth without trouble to a healthy dauphin, which she did a few weeks later.

When the chair of Canon Law at the University of Ingelstadt in the Catholic stronghold of the Southern German monarchy of Bavaria became vacant in 1774, after being held for ninety years by the Jesuits (the order was dissolved by Pope Clement XIV), the Curator of the University, Baron Johann Adam Ickstatt, a liberal member of the Privy Council of the Elector who had begun to liberalize the University, appointed to the chair his twenty-six-year-old godson, Adam Weishaupt. Adam's father, also a professor at the University, had died when the boy had been only seven, leaving him to the Baron's care. Brilliant, and well trained by the Jesuits in the conspiratorial methods of access to power, young Weishaupt decided to organize a body of conspirators, determined to free the world from the Jesuitical rule of Rome and help humanity back to the pristine Christian faith of the hermetic martyrs. He is reputed to have been initiated by a German merchant named Kölmer, who had spent many years in Egypt, into a secret doctrine based on Manichaeism. Mayday of 1776, Weishaupt founded his own sect of the *Very Perfectibles*—better known as Illuminati—with five original members, self-described as reformist libertarians, partisans of absolute equality. It was Weishaupt's contention that all that was needed to recover man's original nature was "to create the good society," a goal, he maintained, which demanded only that "men should understand the weight of prejudice and error encumbering them." Universal happiness, complete and rapid, could be achieved, he declaimed, by dis-

In Ingolstadt, Cagliostro is believed to have met Adam Weishaupt, professor of philosophy and canon law at the university, who, in 1776, had founded the sect of Illuminati. Calling themselves heirs to the Knights Templar, they declared their interest in using celestial intervention as achieved by Cagliostro for the furtherance of a program of worldwide religious reform, but one more radical than Cagliostro's, "committed to avenging the death of the Templar's Grand Master Molay by reducing to dust the triple crown of the popes and disposing of the last of the Capet Kings."

Cagliostro obliged, and described in prophetic detail the decapitation of Louis XVI, an event hardly to be envisaged at that time as anything but improbable.

posing of hierarchy, rank, and riches. "Princes and nations," said Weishaupt, "will disappear without violence from the earth; the human race will become one family; the world will be the abode of reasonable men. Mortality alone will bring about this change imperceptibily." Unable in Catholic Bavaria to achieve this utopian goal by direct means, Weishaupt determined to work from within an existing organization: the Masonic order. In 1777, just a year after Cagliostro had joined a lodge of the same Strict Observance, Weishaupt was initiated in Munich into the lodge of *Theodore of Good Counsel.* Within two years he was in control of the lodge. Further to expand membership in his Illuminati, Weishaupt recruited a youthful but effective Masonic organizer, Adolf Francis, Baron Knigge. By 1779, there were 54 members of the Illuminati, mostly young noblemen and clergymen, established in four Bavarian cities. Thereafter, with the help of a Masonic bookseller, Johann Bode, the order branched out through Southern Germany and Austria, and down into France and Northern Italy. Intellectuals, such as Goethe, Schiller, Mozart, and Herder were attracted. Bode even managed to recruit Saint Germain's friend and protector Prince Charles of Hesse, then director in Germany of the Strict Observance Ritual, though he soon withdrew, influenced apparently by Frederick Wilhelm, heir to the throne of Prussia. By the end of the 1780's, "no one could be sure how many Masons shared the Illuminati views." Already Bavarian Jesuits were preparing a massive counterattack. As with Luther, they first attacked Weishaupt on his personal life, accusing him of having fathered an illegitimate child and of having tried to perform an abortion for his sister-in-law while awaiting dispensation to marry her. Thanks to a bolt of

On the physical level, what the aspirant initiate found appealing in the Egyptian rite was a means, probably learned from Saint-Germain, of regenerating the body every fifty years. As described by Cagliostro, the method, starting with the full moon of May, required forty days of the strictest dieting and consumption of elixirs designed to eliminate all toxins from the body. At the end of the ordeal, in a climax of convulsive fever, the body was to shed hair and teeth, which with all the other cells of the body, were to regenerate and last another fifty years.

For the postulant to recover knowledge of his own immortality, Cagliostro developed a spiritual retreat of forty days leading to initiation and enlightenment.

For spiritual regeneration, the psychic objective involved the search within the male for his female counterpart, and for females the male, so that, mated, they could "flower, through the miracle of love, and give birth to a whole new self on a higher plane."

For women, Cagliostro founded the Egyptian Lodge of Adoption, with Serafina as Grand Mistress. Robed in a white-and-gold gown embroidered with the words *Virtue, Wisdom, Union,* she officiated with the symbol of will in her hand: the sword. On her apron of white leather, trimmed with blue roses, symbols of regeneration, were the words *Love* and *Charity.*

lightning which struck the house of one Illuminatus, the police seized a cache of incriminating papers. The Elector issued an edict outlawing all secret societies in the provinces. Another edict of March 2, 1785, specifically condemned Freemasons and Illuminati, offering rewards for those who would reveal what they knew of the organization. Numerous documents seized in a police raid provided the government with what were considered sensational revelations, showing prescriptions for inducing abortions, for making secret inks, and indications that the order claimed the power of life and death over its members. The Illuminati were accused by the Jesuits of seeking ingredients for abortions to be ''free to debauch women, or indulge in all manner of licentiousness.'' Dismissed from his post at the University, Weishaupt fled to a neighboring province. The order went underground; but the Jesuits continue to pursue it to this day.

As a place to settle, Cagliostro chose the Rhineland city of Strasbourg. There he arrived with a special rose powder which he said enabled him to soften hard marbles, and with formulas he claimed allowed him to transmute metals and precious stones; he also brought elixirs for health and long life. He is described as entering the city in a coach covered with magical symbols, preceded by six servants riding black horses. As news spread that the great miracle healer had taken a house in town, rich and poor flocked to his door, on crutches, on stretchers, in every state of disease. In all of these Cagliostro took a benevolent interest, soothing, restoring confidence, healing. The record is abundant, precise, and incontrovertible. Hundreds of cures were attested to by official statements and reports, including those of several physicians and priests.

But when asked how he performed his miraculous cures without orthodox training, Cagliostro replied that a spiritual healer had no need for what passed as ''medical science,'' that his was a more ancient therapeutic art he had learned in the East. Through his gift of clairvoyance, he said, he could analyze the mind as well as the body of his patients, urging them to purify their souls. The power to heal, he insisted, came not from him, but from the

118

patient; it was largely a question of finding the equilibrium of the forces that flowed from the greater cosmos through the smaller cosmos of the human body, an equilibrium which could sometimes be reestablished, as he had learned from Egyptian and Chinese medicine, with no more than a single word or a gesture.

He extolled the sublimity of nature and the limitless possibilities for spiritually regenerated man in a state of "pre-Adamic" grace. "He who is illumined by the light of Nature," he quoted Paracelsus, "will succeed in penetrating the whole structure of man, and will find the right remedy." Like a good Rosicrucian, Cagliostro not only refused to accept money for his cures, but was constantly distributing largesse to those of his patients who were too poor to feed themselves or take care of their needs in order to get well. And though the source of Cagliostro's money remains a mystery—unless he somehow had access to the remaining treasury of the Templars—he was never in any financial trouble involving the law.

News of Cagliostro's fabulous cures reached the ears of the bishop of Strasbourg, Louis René Édouard, Cardinal de Rohan, Prince of the Empire, Landgrave of Alsace, Headmaster of the Sorbonne, Grand Almoner of France, a descendant of the ancient kings of Brittany. As scion of one of the most important families of France, he held vast lands, and resided at his sumptuous Château de Saverne, where he was attended by fourteen butlers and twenty-five valets. The cardinal, who, like Cagliostro, cherished a passion for alchemy, sent word that he was eager to meet the magus. "If the cardinal is ill," replied Cagliostro, "let him come to me and I will cure him. If he is in good health he has no need for me, nor I for him."

The rebuff, instead of infuriating or insulting the cardinal, aroused his curiosity. In his luxurious coach, he drove off to visit Cagliostro on the excuse that he wished to be cured of his asthma. Cagliostro obliged, explaining that he saw no conflict between holy religion and celestial magic, the latter being sanctified by the Bible under the laws of Saint John. "Magic," said Cagliostro, "is an art due to divine goodness, dedicated to the fullfilment of the divine will." Rohan invited Cagliostro to stay at his château, where he put a laboratory at the magus's disposal and where the cardinal attested to seeing Cagliostro produce before his eyes not only gold, but diamonds. "In my place, in my presence," said the cardinal, "he has made five or six thousand pounds worth of gold."

When the cardinal's elder brother, Charles de Rohan, prince of Soubise, became seriously ill in Paris, Cagliostro

Cardinal de Rohan

119

Mesmer's baquet

agreed to travel with the cardinal by coach to the capital to effect a cure. It was the summer of 1781, just when Pius VI and Antinori were preparing to raise the obelisk in front of the Quirinal. In Paris, Cagliostro found the prince of Soubise wasting away as the result of an attack of scarlet fever. In three days the magus had the old man on his feet, and in two weeks he was back at court, where Louis XVI was so impressed he ordered special protection extended to Cagliostro.

Letters of recommendation from Louis's minister for foreign affairs, count de Vergennes, from the keeper of the Royal See, the marquis de Miromesnil, and from the minister of war, Marshal de Ségur, charged the authorities in Strasbourg in the king's name to extend every consideration to Cagliostro. But the fact that the magus performed his cures without charge, and often on patients whom the orthodox medical profession declared to be incurable, roused the enmity of the organized doctors of Strasbourg. What most irritated the faculty members of the university was his overtly authoritarian manner in matters of curing. The physicians of Strasbourg, outraged at Cagliostro, did to him what their compeers in Vienna were then doing to Franz Anton Mesmer for the very same reason: they launched a monstrous campaign of calumny, including public posters, anonymously labeling Cagliostro a quack

A French lodge of Freemasons at the reception of a Master

and a charlatan, so poisoning the atmosphere that he decided to leave.

In Lyons, center of Illuminism, and of interest in the occult, lived numerous followers of the clairvoyant philosopher who explored the spirit world in vision—Emanuel Swedenborg. There were also the followers of the so-called "unknown philosopher," Claude de St. Martin, and of Martinez de Pasqually's Elus Cohens who had returned to the Gnostic concept of the universe as a living divine organism in which man could rise through the cabalistic spheres to his true and divine self. Received with great enthusiasm by the Masons of Lyons, Cagliostro believed he had found the true setting for building a Central Masonic Lodge devoted to his Egyptian Rite. The Lyonnais were happy to contribute to the creation of a *Lodge of Triumphant Wisdom* of which Cagliostro would be Grand Cophte. Started in 1784, the splendid temple was ready in 1785, complete with huge pillars of Jakin and Boaz, red and white, as in the Temple of Solomon, symbols of the two forces which, in equilibrium, sustain the universe, represented in the temple by a great vault decorated in the image of the infinite. As in Egypt, the walls were carved with hieroglyphs, and there were statues of Isis, Anubis, and Apis, the sacred Egyptian bull.

Anubis, jackal-headed "god of the dead," is called "guardian of the secret of transformation and leads the deceased toward a state of bliss or to grievous trials." According to myth, Anubis was the son of Nephthys, who had tricked her brother Osiris into having intercourse with her. Abandoned by Nephthys, Anubis was raised by Isis. He helped find and embalm the body of murdered Osiris, through whose kingdom he then guided the dead.

From all sides, says Cagliostro's biographer François Ribadeau Dumas, adherents flocked to Cagliostro's Egyptian rite, "drawn by the beauty of its sentiments, the loftiness of its ideals, its central rule of love." In the lodge, the neophyte was to be put through the grades of initiation, applying himself to the problems of living in the world while remaining pure to spiritual law.

De Gébelin suggested that the Tarot cards were leaves of a sacred book which had descended from ancient Egypt, representing symbols of philosophical and metaphysical importance. Tarot was understood to mean the innermost nature of something, its principle, or the law of its being, one which could act as the key to ultimate reality.

In the second grade more symbolic hazards were applied, and the neophyte was taught to withstand bodily terror by being covered with snakes. Removal of the snakes meant liberation from the illusions of this world. By breath control the neophyte was to learn to master the serpent power within his own body. Instructed in the secrets of geometry, he was to measure the universe by the rule of living. As a symbol of the fall of the human race from the Golden Age of Saturn he was given the caduceus of Toth and told it was an emblem of the movement of the sun around the ecliptic.

In the third degree of the *Crata Repoa,* which Hall corresponds to the third degree of the Blue Lodge, the neophyte descended into the abode of the dead where lay in effigy the murdered Osiris, slain by Set, the animal nature in man, the mummy bonds emblems of the hampering agencies of ignorance, superstition, and fear. Here the sword of karma was placed against the neophyte's throat to remind him that if he broke the law, he would destroy only himself, that the law of society represents the law of the universe.

Hall believes that in this ritual the neophyte was actually knocked out by a blow on the head to experience seeming death in order to learn that he could exist outside his body. Alternatively he was given a drug from a goblet made from a human skull to lead him to the world of spirit.

As Kenneth Grant points out in his *The Magical Revival,* the Egyptians distilled the juice of the sycamore, the sacred fig tree, because it was noticed that mortals who drank it "were transformed into immortal spirits, able to penetrate the spirit world and hold commerce with disembodied spirits and other subtle entities." The liquor was then mythified as nectar, ambrosia, or the drink of the gods. In India the juice of the *peepul* was said to "place men on an equal footing with the gods, enabling them to see into the past and into the future, to transcend space and time, to know the secrets hidden in the regions of the universe."

After this stage came the greater mysteries in which the initiate was shown the "elemental potentates, archangels, angels and tutelary spirits and the various orders of the upper world," to demonstrate, as Yarker puts it, "the great perfection to which the Egyptians had reduced the science of theology."

In the next grade the initiate was taught the secrets of alchemy, or how to direct the power of fire to decompose substances and combine others, in order to acquire metaphysical knowledge and superphysical powers by means of which to transmute the evil in human nature into perfect "gold" or "light."

In the sixth, or penultimate, grade, the initiate was shown that the "gods" of the Egyptians were "the principles of life and the workings of universal law . . . vast beings rooted in eternal principles sustaining the universe by their emanations." Here the initiate was shown the bodies of the dishonored dead who had betrayed the secrets of the Society indicative of the occult truth that the spiritual powers of the universe cannot be perverted without fearful compensation, and that broken vows will destroy the body and unseat the reason. In the seventh grade, say Yarker and Hall, all the great mysteries were explained.

But Cagliostro could not tarry with his adepts in Lyons. He was summoned to Paris by his friend Cardinal Rohan, who, anxious to return to royal favor, and hopeful of becoming the king's first minister, pleaded with Cagliostro to use his wonder-working powers to help him regain the favor of Marie Antoinette. The queen had been displeased with Rohan ever since he had returned from being French Ambassador to the Viennese court of her mother, the Empress Maria Theresa, who disliked the cardinal for his lavish style of living and his penchant for pretty young ladies.

Cagliostro and Serafina arrived in Paris in January of 1785 as guests of the Cardinal, and were put up in his sumptuous palace, the Hotel de Strasbourg. But Cagliostro, seeking privacy, soon moved to a smaller house of his own not far away in the rue Saint Claude, now the Boulevard Beaumarchais.

French Masons were quick to welcome Cagliostro, inviting him to join the Lodge of the Nine Sisters, that "most mystical and esoteric of the French Lodges," also described as "a university of world political philosophy," grand-mastered by Benjamin Franklin, then the main link between the secret societies of Europe and America, to whom Cagliostro is reported to have prophesied that a New Atlantis would be rising in America. Among the other distinguished members of the Nine Sisters were Voltaire, Helvetius, and Thomas Jefferson. Another brother was Franz Anton Mesmer. And one of Mesmer's patients, who attested to having been cured by him, was a former Grand Master, Antoine Court de Gébelin, France's leading orientalist, first to identify the pack of Tarot cards as a reservoir of ancient Egyptian wisdom, the secret teachings of the Egyptian priests, who, he asserted, had thus disguised their arcane knowledge, their symbolic depic-

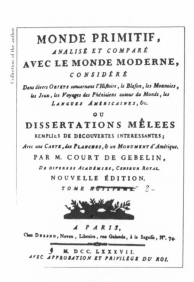

MONDE PRIMITIF,
ANALISÉ ET COMPARÉ
AVEC LE MONDE MODERNE,
CONSIDÉRÉ
Dans divers Objets concernant l'Histoire, le Blason, les Monnoies, les Jeux, les Voyages des Phéniciens autour du Monde, les Langues Américaines, &c.
OU
DISSERTATIONS MÊLEES
REMPLIES DE DÉCOUVERTES INTÉRESSANTES;
Avec une Carte, des Planches, & un Monument d'Amérique.
PAR M. COURT DE GEBELIN,
De diverses Académies, Censeur Royal.
NOUVELLE ÉDITION.
TOME HUITIÈME. 2-

A PARIS,
Chez Durand, Neveu, Libraire, rue Galande, à la Sagesse, N°. 74.

9 M. DCC. LXXXVII.
AVEC APPROBATION ET PRIVILÉGE DU ROI.

Grand Master Court de Gebelin

123

The duc de Chartres, shortly to inherit his father's title of Duc d'Orléans, was one of the richest men in France, but popular in Paris because of his gifts to the poor. Known as a liberal, with aspirations to becoming a constitutional monarch, he is described by contemporaries as "possessing the charming manners of a *grand seigneur,* never rude or cruel, full of gentle consideration for all about him, though selfish in his pursuit of pleasure." Accused during the Revolution of aspiring to replace Louis XVI, he adopted the title of Citoyen Egalité and was elected deputy from Paris to the Convention. When faced by the terrorists' guillotine, he was accused of arguing that he was not truly of noble extraction, but the son of a coachman who had been his mother's lover. Shocked by such behavior, surviving Masons are said to have celebrated his defection with a ritual degradation and breaking of his sword.

tions of the structure of the universe, received from Hermes Trismegistus so that it might survive through the ordeal of Christianity after the collapse of the pagan world.

Asked by a committee from the leading Masonic lodges of Paris to interrogate Cagliostro on ancient Egyptian philosophy, de Gébelin was struck by Cagliostro's amazing replies, as were all those present, who admitted they had met their master in such matters. Urged by fellow Masons to open an Egyptian-rite lodge in Paris, Cagliostro installed himself as Grand Cophte of the Temple of Isis in the rue de la Sourdière. There he admitted women to "the mysteries of the pyramids," attracting such high-ranking ladies as the queen's favorite, Madame de Lamballe, who was initiated at the vernal equinox of 1785. Cagliostro then formed a supreme council with the duc de Montmorency as Grand Protector, Jean-Benjamin de Laborde, farmer-general of France as Grand Inspector, and Beaudard de Saint-James, wealthy treasurer general of the French navy as Grand Chancellor. His Royal Highness the duc de Chartres, Grand Master of French Masonry, attended an Egyptian-rite ceremony, declared his confidence in Cagliostro, and announced his official recognition of the rite. Another *grand seigneur* with equally liberal tendencies, fresh from aiding the Americans in forming a republic, also joined Cagliostro's Egyptian rite and proclaimed his absolute confidence in the powers of its Grand Cophte; Marie Joseph Paul Ives Roch Gilbert Motier, Marquis de Lafayette.

The Duc de Richelieu, under an assumed name, and wearing a disguise, came to consult Cagliostro and was shown a past life as Ruggieri before Catherine de Médicis. And just as clearly as he described the past lives of the duke, Cagliostro declared he could see the rot behind the apparent splendor of Louis's police state, which was causing misery and degradation among the masses. But although Cagliostro called for greater social justice for the poor, the sick, and the underprivileged, his political principles were oriented more toward "regenerating the Christ in man," as a means of achieving a peaceful transition to a constitutional monarchy. In the more liberal forces of Masonry, and especially among the followers of his own rite—whom he confidently estimated to amount to a million souls—Cagliostro saw a determined desire to search for a better system of life, without recourse to bloody revolution.

In France, where the papal bulls against Masonry had never been promulgated, twenty-six Masonic lodges were

124

presided over by priests, and members of the clergy of all ranks constantly frequented Masonic rituals. Catholic lodges had been founded in Paris under the protection of the marquises de Girardin and de Bouillé, both royalists and friends of Saint-Germain, whose goal was to "establish communication between God and man by means of intermediary beings." Soon so many priests were attending the Egyptian ceremonies, declaring themselves highly satisfied with the rite, that Cagliostro, whose dream was to effect a union of his Egyptian science of magic with the fundamental beliefs of Christianity, was moved to hope his order might at last be recognized by the pope, as had been the order of the Knights of Saint John.

Cardinal de Rohan promised Cagliostro his support and appealed to the archbishop of Bourges, to whom Cagliostro explained his rite. A favorable report was apparently sent to Rome, and the dossier seems to have been presented to Pius VI under promising auspices.

Pius was just then admiring from the windows of his summer palace on the Quirinal the San Rocco obelisk at last being raised by his architect Antinori between the two great horses placed in the square by Sixtus V. The delay of four years in handling the needle had been caused by Antinori's failure to find a way to turn the great rampant beasts so the pope would not have to face their rear ends. Prodded by Pius, Antinori at last found a way; and the operation, in the end, required no more than ten minutes per horse.

But the Romans did not think much of the monument, nor of the expense it had entailed, and some wit changed the inscription on the base of the equestrian statues—which had been mistakenly attributed to the Greek sculptor Phidias—from OPUS PHIDIAE to OPUS PERPHIDIAE PII SEX II. And the obdurate and purblind reaction of Pius to Cagliostro's ecumenical suggestions was to dash the magus's hopes for a peaceful solution to the revolutionary fervor in France. Instead, an unexpected Parisian scandal was to pit the pope's dutiful acolyte Louis XVI against the forces of Freemasonry and accelerate the French Revolution.

7. PIOUS TERROR

The day Calgiostro arrived in Paris, Cardinal de Rohan, in his haste to get back into the good graces of Marie Antoinette, had fallen for the ploy of a scheming female, Jeanne de Saint-Remy de Valois, who called herself Countess de la Motte. The impoverished descendant of a bastard son of Henry II, the woman used a tenuous position at court to convince Rohan she had access to the queen whose favors she could obtain for the cardinal, if, with his large fortune, he would guarantee a financial transaction. The queen, said de la Motte, wanted a fabulously expensive diamond necklace which the king, considering the economic condition of the country, thought impolitic to buy for her. But if the cardinal would merely act as guarantor to the bankers who owned the necklace, the queen could acquire it immediately and pay for it in installments from her private funds. In return she would grant the cardinal her "favor," and even meet him clandestinely in the park of Versailles.

None of this had the cardinal told Cagliostro, though the latter had repeatedly warned him to beware of de la Motte as an unreliable fraud. The cardinal, already infatuated by the schemer's sexual attractions, was even more delighted by the prospect of becoming a lover of the reputedly sensuous queen. But the scheme went wrong; and when Louis XVI was informed of his wife's involvement, the la Motte woman, in a desperate attempt to save herself, tried to shift the blame onto Cagliostro whom she accused of being the Cardinal's own *eminence grise*. By chance, or good fortune, one of the financial backers of the jewelry firm which had delivered the necklace was Monsieur Beaudard de Saint-James, Grand Chancellor of Cagliostro's Egyptian-rite lodge. Promptly he informed Cagliostro of the charges brought against him by the countess, who accused him of having purloined the necklace and selling the stones in England—which was just what she had done, with the complicity of her husband, a disreputable minor guard's officer.

Foolishly, Louis XVI ordered an investigation by parliament, and by *lettre de cachet* had Cardinal Rohan arrested just as he was about to celebrate mass on the Feast of the Assumption in the royal Chapel. Into the lurid dungeons of the Bastille the unhappy cardinal was followed by Cagliostro and Serafina, all placed incommunicado.

Jeanne de la Motte managed to live at Versailles by boasting royal blood as a descendant of an illegitimate scion of the Valois family who had committed forgery under Louis XIII. Her husband, a gentleman soldier in the gendarmerie, was a rake and a gambler.

As the months wore by, without news of his wife, or of the outside world, Cagliostro kept himself sane by writing his memoirs. Outraged at the horrible injustice of a system which allowed a king by simple *lettre de cachet* to imprison in the Bastille anyone he chose, for as long as he chose, even for a lifetime, without access to a lawyer, to be tortured at the pleasure of his jailers, Cagliostro prophesied the brutal death of the Bastille's governor, the Marquis de Launay, and the transformation of the fortress into a Temple of Freedom, property of the people of France.

Brought to trial before a parliamentary court, and asked who he was, where he was from, what he did, and by what right, Cagliostro replied: "I do in God's name all the good I can. It is a right that requires neither a name, nor a country, neither proofs, nor caution. . . . Am I not a free man? Judge me by my habits, by my actions. Tell me if they are good, tell me if you have seen any that are more effective. Then do not occupy yourselves with my nationality, my rank, or my religion."

When, on the witness stand, Madame de la Motte accused Cagliostro of all sorts of crimes, saying she "only regretted not living in those blessed times when a charge of sorcery would have led Cagliostro to the stake," Cagliostro calmly replied that he forgave her, and

Jeanne de la Motte conspiring with Marie-Nicole Leguay, alias Baroness d'Oliva, who bore a remarkable resemblance to Marie Antoinette, as they arrange a meeting with Cardinal Rohan. The girl agreed to impersonate the queen at night in the rose garden of Versailles to induce Rohan to act as security for the diamond necklace. She gave him a rose and a note signed "Antoinette de France," hopeful harbingers of a sexual assignation.

Jeanne de la Motte being branded on the shoulder by the hangman with red-hot V for *voleuse,* or thief, before being exposed naked to the crowd in front of the Conciergerie with a rope around her neck. She later died in London from a fall from the window of her lodgings. The jewels she stole from the necklace, small and very blue, were bought by John Frederick Sackville, third duke of Dorset, ambassador to the court of Louis XVI, and are in the possession of the family at Knole in Kent.

that he assumed her calumnies must be inspired more by the desire to clear herself than of actual hatred against him. The parliamentary court, after due deliberation, found Madame de la Motte to be the guilty party, condemning her to be publicly whipped, naked, by the executioner, and to be branded with a hot iron on both shoulders, forfeiting all her properties. Cagliostro, Serafina, and Rohan were found guiltless and released. But the governor of the Bastille, fearing a daylight demonstration in favor of Cagliostro by the people of Paris, only let the Cagliostros out close to midnight. But a tumultuous crowd of almost ten thousand Parisians who considered Cagliostro a hero against whom the king had been arbitrary and unjust, was there to greet them and carry them on their shoulders to their house, acclaiming Cagliostro for his liberalism, his powers as a healer, his generosity to the poor, and his innocence as a victim of the hated Austrian, Marie Antoinette, whom the Parisians believed to have been guiltily involved in the affair of the necklace.

As for the queen, incensed by the release of Cagliostro, she forced the vacillating Louis to order him out of Paris in twenty-four hours and out of the country in twenty-one days. As the Cagliostros' ship sailed from Boulogne, an estimated five thousand French well-wishers waved farewell to the man they considered the greatest living benefactor of mankind.

From London, Cagliostro addressed a letter to the people of France in which he attacked Louis XVI's absolutist regime, prophesying the advent of a new constitutional monarchy in which *lettres de cachet* would be abolished, and predicting that stone by stone the Bastille would be demolished till the people of Paris could dance on its site.

Romantic cliché of the demolition of the hated Bastille

In his memoirs, written in the Bastille, Cagliostro described a childhood in Medina, under the name of Acharat, where he was tutored by an elderly Greek occultist, Althotas, confidential adviser to Grand Master Pinto, who took him to live in the palace of the Grand Mufti Salahyn, high priest of the Moslem religion. There, said Cagliostro, he was taught botany and medicinal physics while being exposed to the wisdom of Islam, eventually traveling to Mecca to be initiated into Chaldean magic and the wisdom of the Assyrian sect of the Old Man of the Mountain—the Hashishin. A further pilgrimage, similar to that of the legendary Rosenkreutz, took him to Egypt to be initiated into the secrets of the Great Pyramid, and be told of the great underground halls where the ancient priests protected a precious store of human knowledge. In Fez, said Cagliostro, while in a trance, he was further initiated into the contents of the Rosicrucian secret books of *T* and *M*.

The widespread publication of this letter in France aroused Louis and Marie Antoinette to further vengeance. Ambassadors and agents of the king were ordered to make life, wherever the Cagliostros might try to enjoy it, impossible.

Grounds for such an action were to be fabricated with the expertise of a professional blackmailer and libelist, Theveneau de Morande, a police informant who for some years had spied on the French community in London, and who lived on a yearly pension of 4,000 francs blackmailed out of Louis XV's mistress, Madame du Barry, by threatening to divulge details of her private life as a prostitute, which, in the end, he did anyway. Morande, as the editor in London of a scandal sheet called *Courrier de L'Europe*, was hired to launch a scurrilous campaign of defamation against Cagliostro and his wife. In a series of articles paid for by Louis, he set to libeling Cagliostro as a charlatan, an imposter, and a petty crook, using for ammunition the evidence fabricated by Madame de la Motte, ordered destroyed by parliament, a surviving copy of which was

Marie Jeanne Bécu, countess du Barry, known as "la sultana," the all-powerful courtesan mistress of Louis XV for whom the diamond necklace was originally designed, before the king suddenly died. In her ghosted memoires she tells how Cardinal Rohan brought Cagliostro to her house to show her her future in a "metallic glass and ebony frame, ornamented with a variety of magical characters," warning her she might not like what she saw. When du Barry looked she fainted—presumably at the sight of her own head rolling from the guillotine on December 7, 1793.

furnished to Morande by Louis's minister of state, Baron de Breteuil. Morande also managed to collect stories from those of Cagliostro's former servants who had stolen from him, or betrayed his confidence, and were now happy to defame him for money. Added to this anecdotal padding were attacks from one of the most dangerous of all sources: those women, such as Baroness von der Ecke, whose favors Cagliostro had declined.

Cunningly, Morande hit upon an assured method for defaming Cagliostro: he attributed to his victim the crimes of a pimp and petty crook, the Sicilian Giuseppe Balsamo, who was known to have been repeatedly arrested for minor crimes and for selling the favors of his pretty wife, Lorenza, to prospective victims. For Morande, it was nothing to charge that Cagliostro and Balsamo were one and the same. For Cagliostro, there was nothing to be done but deny the allegation, which he vehemently did: "It is not I who under the name of Giuseppe Balsamo was driven ignominiously from Paris in 1772. And, it is not my wife, who under the name of Lorenza Feliciani was imprisoned. No police register, no testimony, no investigation by the Bastille authorities, no notice of information, no proof at all has been able to establish that I am Balsamo. I deny that I am Balsamo."

131

But the libel spread, and as each lurid article, concocted in the best style of red-herring journalism, followed the other, the appetite of readers grew with what it fed on. Using false and anonymous letters to the police, Morande was able to print details so circumstantially lascivious that the public began to wonder if indeed it might not have been duped, if Cagliostro, at least in his early life, might have been the crook Balsamo. As Morande's *Courrier* went the rounds of Europe, Catherine the Great of Russia, turned by her Jesuit friends against Masons, used Morande's material to lampoon all of Masonry through Cagliostro in a series of plays which drew ridicule on the magus as a charlatan and mountebank. Even Goethe, a brother Mason, fell for the *canard*. In disguise he traveled to Palermo to investigate the identity of Balsamo by interviewing his family, and though Goethe obtained not a shred of evidence to support the contention that Cagliostro was Balsamo, he decided to protect his own flank by waffling.

All over Europe, such is the nature of man, people too closely associated with Cagliostro thought it best to dump their former hero. Some of the charges were wild: such as

Gillray's caricature of Cagliostro at a convivial gathering of the Lodge of Antiquity in London in November 1786, where, instead of the sympathy he expected from fellow Freemasons, the magus was ridiculed by one called Mash, an optician, who gave a burlesque imitation of the Grand Cophte of Egyptian Masonry as a quack doctor vending a spurious balsam to cure every malady. Cagliostro was so mortified he withdrew, and left the country.

those of the comte de Mirabeau—never averse to changing coats—who voiced the opinion in a pamphlet that Cagliostro had all along been an emissary of the Jesuits "hatching secret plots in Protestant countries."

In London, whereas the Lodge of Antiquity of the Scottish rite had honored Cagliostro with a magnificent reception on his arrival in November 1786, Masonic friends began to avoid him for fear of being tarred by Morande, especially when his journal accused the membership of the London lodge which had initiated Cagliostro of being composed of "valets and barbers." The atmosphere necessary for Cagliostro to create a lodge of his Egyptian rite in London no longer existed. To avoid trouble with Louis's agents, Cagliostro left for the Continent, alone and incognito.

In Switzerland he was greeted and cared for by staunch Masonic friends, but the atmosphere was no better suited for a prolonged residence. From Switzerland, where Serafina had joined him, the Cagliostros traveled to Turin; but the king of Sardinia, on instructions from Paris, ordered the refugees out of town within twenty-four hours. At Rovereto, in the Austrian Tyrol, where Dante had sought refuge in exile from Florence, Cagliostro was welcomed by old and trusted Masons, who helped him open a lodge of the Egyptian rite by the shores of the Adige. There he set about curing the sick, as usual, gratis, until the doctors, priests, and magistrates joined to force him out of town.

Friends advised him to try Trent, where the bishop, Monsignor Pier Vigilio Thun, an Austrian prince, was much taken with alchemy and occultism. The bishop welcomed Cagliostro and even accepted the possibility that his rite might be accepted by the Church, if only Cagliostro could, as he had done for him, lay out its content to Pius VI, directly, person to person. To facilitate matters, the bishop addressed a letter to the Vatican secretary of state, Cardinal Boncompagni, asking for a safe-conduct for Cagliostro to travel in the Papal States. The cardinal answered that "Cagliostro, being under no prohibition in the Pontifical States, has no need for the safeconduct you request."

Further to aid Cagliostro in his venture, the bishop of Trent addressed letters of recommendation for him to cardinals Boncompagni, Zelada, Colonna, and Albini. After a great banquet in the bishop's palace, on May 17, 1789, just as Mirabeau in Paris was challenging the will of Louis XVI in the States General, precipitating events toward a break with the monarchy, the Cagliostros set off by carriage for Rome to obtain from Pius VI approval for his

When asked to be more specific about his nationality, Cagliostro replied: "All countries are dear to me. All men are my brothers. I am a wanderer. On my way I do what good I can; but I do not tarry. As I pass I leave a little light, a little warmth, a little of myself until all shall be spent at the end of my career, when the rose will flower on the cross. I am Cagliostro. Need I say more? If only you realized that you are, as you are, the sons of God, if you were not so vain, you would have already understood." Asked to explain the secret of his nature, he replied without pomp or vanity: "I am of no time and no place. As a spiritual being I exist eternally, and if I immerse myself in my thoughts going back over the years, if I project myself towards a way of life quite far from that which you may perceive, I can become whomsoever I please. Participating consciously in the absolute being, I best regulate my actions with that which surrounds me. My name is that of my function; and I choose it, as I choose my function, because I am free. My country is the one in which I momentarily pause. Date it yesterday, or tomorrow, if it suits you, and that illusory pride of a grandeur that may never be yours. I am he who is."

133

Architect Antinori showing Pius VI the newly raised fifty-foot obelisk believed to have been part of Sallustius's circus dedicated to the festival of the goddess Flora. It was now adorned with a spherical star containing a piece of wood reputed to have come from the Most Holy Cross of the Crucifixion, with relics of saints Paul, Andrew, Gregory the Great,

Egyptian rite of Masonry, a move intended to reunite Christian and Mason in the Hermetic dream of a new and progressive order.

And so the trap was set.

Arriving in Rome at the end of May, Cagliostro and Serafina, who was happy to return to her native city and visit her aging parents, were just in time, as they put up at the small hotel della Scalinata on the Spanish Steps, to witness the inauguration of another obelisk raised by Antinori for Pius VI at the top of the steps, facing the Church of the Trinità dei Monti. Placed so that a person standing at the exit of the pope's summer palace could admire from a single spot the perspective of three separate obelisks at the end of the via Quattro Fontane, the via Sistina, and the via XX Settembre, the new monument was clearly an adornment to Rome. But its symbolic function was the more apparent in the face of political trouble in France. Like its predecessors, this obelisk was being raised as an overt symbol of the Church's determination to squash the Hermetic tradition from Egypt manifesting as it was in France through efforts of French Masons, 477 of whom were members of the States General.

Pius's plot was Jesuitical in the extreme. On the pope's direct orders, Cagliostro, from the minute he arrived in Rome, had been placed under surveillance by agents of the Inquisition, not only in the hope that they might ferret

and Pius V. Broken pieces of the obelisk had lain opposite the Lateran Palace ever since Pope Clement XII had stolen them from the garden of the duke of Sora (where they had surfaced among the flowerbeds in 1734), on the excuse that *all* the antiquities in Rome belonged to the Reverend Household. Then came the French connection. In 1765 France's minister of finance tried to buy the needle for 25,000 francs to place in front of Nôtre Dame de Paris. And on the grounds that the entire Pincian Hill had belonged to the kings of France since Charles VIII, the Minimi Friars of the Trinità, afraid the work would undermine their church, appealed to the French ambassador, Cardinal de Bernis, to have the project stopped. Pius VI remained obdurate; the needle went up just as Cagliostro arrived in town, in time to hear the complaints of the populace, who joked about its shortness. Goethe, also in Rome, described a hat at carnival made of a tiny red obelisk atop an enormous white pedestal.

Cardinal François Joachim de Bernis, French ambassador to the Vatican, whose poetry had so pleased Madame de Pompadour he was named minister of foreign affairs under Louis XV. The marquis de Sade, in *Justine*, renders one of the most pornographic poems in the French language, attributing its authorship to the cardinal.

from their secret hideouts the Masons of Rome, but in the hope that Cagliostro might be used as a scapegoat for discrediting Masonry throughout the world. A pirated copy of de la Motte's memoirs, including the false letters she had fabricated as having passed between Rohan to Marie Antoinette, had been delivered to Pius, along with the libelous articles produced by Morande.

Unaware of the trap, and secure in the protection of his letter from the secretary of state, Cagliostro first drew up a petition to Pius, laying before him the regulations and constitution of his Egyptian rite. He then called on the Vatican and left his credentials, declaring that the rise of Masonry in the heart of Catholic countries could not fail to deserve the benevolence of the Vicar of Christ, especially as the ritual had as its preamble: "Love and worship the Lord God with all your heart, cherish and serve your neighbor by doing all the good to him of which you are capable, let your conscience be your guide in all your actions."

Masonic circles in Rome, mostly in the aristocracy, and among foreign diplomats, welcomed Cagliostro, especially at Villa Malta, near Porta Pinciana, the Roman residence of the Knights of Saint John of Jerusalem, a great many of whom were initiate Masons, as was their Roman Master, the Bailly de Loras. There Cagliostro organized Masonic séances, and initiated members of Roman society into his Egyptian rite. In Malta House he was safe, since its grounds were covered by diplomatic immunity. There he performed one séance in the presence of the French ambassador, Cardinal de Bernis, and several members of Rome's nobility, which was later described by an eyewitness, the abbot Lucantonio Benedetti, as taking place in a large hall adorned with Egyptian, Assyrian, and Chinese idols.

When a young female medium described seeing a crowd surging toward Versailles, demanding the overthrow of the king, the French ambassador became much perturbed. And even more so shortly thereafter, when he heard that the revolution had actually started in France, that the scene described by the young medium had actually taken place in real life, conveyed by some occult means. On July 14, as Cagliostro had predicted, the people of Paris seized the Bastille, and slaughtered his old jailer, the Marquis de Launay.

On August 4, ecclesiastical privileges were overthrown in France, there were riots in churches, convents were sacked and burned; the clergy made plans for a civil constitution, separating themselves from Rome. A decree

Caricature of Louis XVI, over-whelmed by the gross burden of both the nobility and the clergy of France

was issued by the National Assembly declaring that all men have a right to think as they choose in matters of religion, and express their opinions on the subject, that man is accountable for his actions, not his beliefs, which are his own business. Man, said the decree, is bound to obey only laws to which he has consented.

In reaction, Pius VI issued a contract to Antinori to raise a third obelisk, in Piazza Montecitorio, before the papal Palace of Justice—ironically the seat of Italy's future parliament, and took immediate security measures to prevent the entrance into the Papal States of potential subversives. Watch was redoubled against a possible uprising among an estimated five thousand armed Masons within the Papal States, who were believed to be only waiting for a signal to rise up with the help of more groups in such Masonic strongholds as Bologna and Ancona. In Rome it was suspected by the Inquisition that Cagliostro had come as a secret agent or commissar of Weishaupt's radical Illuminati to perform just such an action.

Meanwhile, urged by Roman Masons to organize a lodge of his Egyptian rite, Cagliostro chose to do so almost within the shadow of Antinori's Trinità dei Monti

136

obelisk, in the studios of a French painter, a fellow of the adjacent French Academy, Augustin Louis Belle, in whose quarters Masons had been secretly meeting for more than two years. One room, known as the room of "reflection," was draped in black, with a small table holding a skull. A larger room, known as the "Temple," adorned with the usual two columns and various emblems of Masonry, held a throne for the Master.

There, Cagliostro initiated a Capucin monk, a professor of theology in Paris, Father François Joseph Roulier, who said he was attracted to Christian occultism and the symbolism of the Masons, and whom Cagliostro believed might be useful in Rome in furthering acceptance of his rite by the Vatican, or, in the words of Ribadeau Dumas, "uniting the Children of Hiram with the sons of St. Peter." Far from being of help, the Capucin is believed by several historians to have been an agent of the Inquisition. The first documentary piece of evidence against Cagliostro, produced after the Capucin became his secretary, was a letter addressed by Cagliostro to the French States General, over which Cardinal Rohan was then presiding, in which he asked to be allowed to return to live in France; it was passed straight into the hands of the Inquisition. The letter, evidence enough of revolutionary leanings, prompted the Inquisition's first move, which was to put pressure on the family of Serafina, obliging her father, by who knows what sinister methods, to sign a complaint against Cagliostro for practicing Masonry—a crime forbidden by law in the Papal States.

Immediately Cagliostro was warned by a fellow Mason, Giuseppe Ferretti, that trouble was at hand. Other Masons secreted their incriminating emblems and went into hiding. Cagliostro, confident of his own good faith, and of his letter from the secretary of state, did nothing to protect himself, other than send out an appeal to other Masons in Rome to come to his rescue in case he was taken prisoner. What Cagliostro did not know was that Cardinal Boncompagni was no longer secretary of state, having just been opportunely replaced by Cardinal Zelada.

On December 3, 1789, Pius VI turned over his dossier on Cagliostro to the supreme tribunal of the Holy Office. The assessor requested the arrest of Cagliostro. On Sunday, December 27, though it was the Feast of Saint John, and a holy day, on which one did not arrest, the pope, for fear that Cagliostro might flee the trap, granted the special request. Monsignor Rinuccini, governor of Rome, ordered Cagliostro seized, and Belle's studio searched.

About 10:00 P.M. a squad of papal grenadiers broke into

Cardinal Francisco Zelada, Vatican secretary of state, a Spanish Jesuit, who spent many years in charge of the secret Vatican archives

137

Cagliostro's lodgings and carted him off to Castel Sant'-Angelo. Serafina was taken to a convent. All of Cagliostro's papers and correspondence, all of his Masonic impedimenta, were seized; no effort had been made by him to hide any of this material, sufficient to incriminate any man as a Mason. Hardly the precaution of a Weishaupt agent of subversion.

Some prominent Masons were arrested in the city, including the duke of San Demetrio. The marquis Vivaldi managed to disappear in time, and his wife, dressed as a man, fled to Venice. Loras, master of the Knights of Saint John, escaped to Malta. Yet, from the documents found in Cagliostro's house, and from the contents of Belle's "Temple," the Inquisition was able to reconstruct only the secret Masonic ceremonial, and the dress of the officers, but not the inner meaning of the ritual, the mystery of which had to be revealed from initiate to initiate, as Cagliostro had hoped to do in person to Pope Pius VI.

For fear that someone might attempt to liberate Cagliostro, the guard was doubled at Castel Sant'Angelo. No one without a special pass was permitted within. So serious was the threat considered that Carnival festivities were canceled in Rome lest Masons take advantage of fireworks to pull some trick.

From his dungeon Cagliostro was brought before a group of top Inquisitors, including Cardinal Zelada and Cardinal Antonelli, head of the Church's Propaganda Office. The governor of Rome was present, as was the state treasurer, Monsignor Giovanni Barberi, acting as Inquisitorial secretary. Hardly the talent required to interrogate the petty crook Balsamo, whom the Inquisition, using Morande's Jesuitical device, now claimed to have in their hands. Forty-three times, over a period of almost a year,

Interrogation by the Inquisition at the end of the eighteenth century

138

Grilled by the Inquisition

Cagliostro was grilled by various Inquisitors. No record is available of what transpired at his so-called trial, carried on in absolute secrecy. All documents relating to it have disappeared or been suppressed.

It is even difficult to reconstruct what happened to Cagliostro during his imprisonment in Castel Sant'Angelo, or the degree to which he was tortured. It was rumored he had been strangled so that Balsamo could be put on trial in his place to show that the law was dealing not with a personage of importance, but with a mean delinquent. Though how popes, cardinals, archbishops, ministers, and the crowned heads of Europe, could, for twenty years, have had social intercourse with a creature so mean and so villainous as Balsamo was painted, was never explained; nor was the fact that everywhere Cagliostro had been in Europe he was idolized by those he met and cured and by them was considered to be a great and enlightened benefactor of humanity.

All that came out of the trial was the judgment, passed by the tribunal of the Holy Office on March 21, 1791. A week later, in chains, his head veiled in black, in the presence of Pius VI, the prisoner was forced to kneel and hear his sentence. Giuseppe Balsamo was condemned to the penalty established by Clement XII and Benedict XIV against heretics, dogmatizers, heresiarchs, masters of superstitious magic: death by burning.

139

Pius, with the excuse that he wished to allow the prisoner more time to repent—but clearly not wishing to create another martyr by blood—piously commuted the sentence to perpetual imprisonment in a fortress, without hope of pardon. Posted on the streets of Rome, between the holy figures of Saint Peter and Saint Paul, the decree stood for all to read and take warning that to be a Mason in the Eternal City was a capital crime, one the Church intended to proscribe forever. Using the occasion as pretext for a general denigration of Masons, Pius issued an apostolic edict confirming and reinforcing previous pontifical edicts against Masonry, invoking the severest corporal punishment of death against anyone practicing the rituals, especially those of the Egyptian rite.

The same day, there appeared for sale on the streets of Rome a pamphlet printed by the Pope's Reverend Household anonymously written, which purported to be a compendium of the life and deeds of G. Balsamo known as Count Cagliostro. Its author was the Inquisitorial secretary, Giovanni Barberi, not a Jesuit as most historians aver, but a lay monsignor, who chose this method—one of the grossest injustices— to defame and vilify a prisoner with no means whatsoever of defense.

What Cagliostro may or may not have said under torture is moot; the top secret dossier of the minutes of his trial has not been made available from the Vatican archives. Barberi's compendium is the sole known source for Cagliostro's supposed revelation of a secret meeting with the heads of Weishaupt's Illuminati during which he is said to have received large sums of money to spread their propaganda and "illuminize French Masonry." To this charge the French translator of the compendium arbitrarily added a preface associating Cagliostro with "the gloomy follies of the German Illuminati," accusing the German sect of "surrounding thrones, blindfolding sovereigns in error and keeping from them men of talent and vision," a charge repeated to this day by right-wing propagandists. The hero of Barberi's compendium is described as "short, dark-skinned, plump, surly-eyed, speaking a Sicilian dialect mixed with an ultramontane vernacular, without cognition, science, void of any resource that might make it beloved. . . ."

This of the Cagliostro who had constantly frequented the highest society and the greatest minds in Europe, described by those who knew him as "intelligent, sympathetic, gay, temperate, active, at ease with princes and all the great, whom he considered he could help but from whom he required nothing in return," and, by Maurice

Among Cagliostro's effects confiscated by the Inquisition was a seal consisting of a serpent pierced by an arrow and holding an apple in its mouth. This serpent has been interpreted as the green dragon of Hermetic philosophy, or the Hebrew letter *Aleph*, symbolizing equilibrated unity. Another source has interpreted it as a sigil of the three celebrated emblems carried in the Greek mysteries: the phallus *I*; the egg, *O*; and the serpent, Φ—the first being the emblem of the sun, the second of the female, the third of the destroyer and reformer, eternally renewing itself.

Magre, in his *Return of the Magi,* as having had "a broader view of events and human nature than any other man in history." It is easy to understand, says Magre, why his followers called him the "Divine Cagliostro." "A marvelous spirit had descended into him."

Is this the same person of whom Barberi asks: "How could such a man have had access to gracious women whom he managed to deviate from the path of virtue?" To which he replies: "The women he was able to conquer were all so old and so ugly they could find no other mate than Balsamo." The magus's famous cures, says the compendium, were all the result of pure chance, or not cures at all. His Egyptian elixir "was nothing but cheap wine with some aromas capable only of exciting the vertigo of sensuality." Balsamo-Cagliostro was labeled a thief, a pimp, a counterfeiter, a syphilitic, a criminal wanted by the police of several countries.

No mention whatsoever was made in the compendium of the role of Cardinal Rohan, nor of his description of Cagliostro as "the most extraordinary man, the most sublime, whose knowledge is equalled in the world only by his goodness."

Yet this libel by Barberi is what became the prime source for future historians. Thomas Carlyle, in a vicious attack on Cagliostro, whom he never met, admitted having based his entire work on Barberi's compendium.

W. R. H. Trowbridge, another major biographer of Cagliostro, sums up the case: no proof was, or ever has been, brought forth in support of the libels. Not a word of testimony was heard in support of the list of crimes of which Cagliostro was accused. No witness in court or elsewhere ever identified Cagliostro as Balsamo. The family of neither was summoned to Rome to give evidence. No proof was formulated.

Dr. Marc Haven (whose real name was Emanuel Lalande), a member of the cabalistic order of the Holy Cross, in his earlier biography of Cagliostro, calls the magus "a human being as sublime in love as in wisdom," and concludes: "No one every proved Balsamo and Cagliostro were the same person." As Henry d'Almeras puts it in his *Cagliostro and Freemasonry in the Eighteenth Century:* "From his whole life they were able to substantiate only one single crime, that he had been a Free Mason, a crime which the pontifical bulls punished with death."

By striking down a petty Balsamo, the Church hoped to discredit all of Masonry as a phony font of religious tolerance, of liberty, equality, and fraternity, a slogan attributed to Cagliostro, as terrifying to established institutions as it was appealing to their victims. Now every last Mason in Europe who had known or frequented Cagliostro would be made to feel the shame of having been deluded by a quack and a charlatan, a pimp and a snake-oil peddler. Masonry and its officials would be made the laughingstock of Europe for having fallen for such "garbage" as Cagliostro had conveyed in his "spurious" Egyptian rite. All liberal ideas would be as discredited as the Masonic leaders who had supported them.

Further to demean Cagliostro, he was forced, barefoot, in penitent's garb, with a candle in his hand, to walk between two lines of monks from Castel Sant'Angelo to Santa Maria Sopra Minerva, the ancient temple of Isis, where he was obliged to kneel before the altar and abjure his errors. In the same piazza, in the shadow of the obelisk raised by Kircher in memory of one Hermetic pope, Cagliostro's manuscript on Egyptian Masonry, declared "seditious, heretical, blasphemous, and tending to destroy the Christian religion," was given to the flames by the hand of the public executioner. With it were burned all of Cagliostro's Masonic emblems. Lost to the world, as the crowd clapped and shouted, were his *The Ritual Rules of Egyptian Masonry, Concerning the Beatific Vision, Concerning the Evocation of Higher Spirits, Physical and Moral Regeneration, The Art of Prolonging Life, The Art of Making Gold, The Divine Cabala,* and *Astrological Calculus.* Masons tried to defend Cagliostro's position, but the reaction was ruthless, and their pamphlets were bought up and destroyed by Church and police.

Of the homages paid to Cagliostro shortly after his condemnation, perhaps the most tender and lasting came from his fellow Mason Wolfgang Amadeus Mozart. In *The Magic Flute,* first produced in Vienna on September 30, 1791, Mozart portrayed the Grand Cophte of the Egyptian rite as Sarastro, the high priest of Isis and Osiris, central figure of the opera, venerated by his followers.

From Rome, Cagliostro was taken in chains by forced night marches to the fortified bastion of San Leo, atop a peak in the Montefeltro Mountains near San Marino, the most feared prison in Italy, whose inmates were known to have been driven mad in a matter of weeks. The marches across the Apennines took place in the dark for fear that someone might recognize the prisoner and make an attempt to free him. At San Leo, Cagliostro was placed in a dungeon which had served as a water cistern, deep underground, and when it was rumored that a group of French Masons might be preparing to land around the fortress from balloons, the jailers, warned by Cardinal

142

The reputedly impregnable Castle of San Leo, where Cagliostro was immured

Zelada that they would pay with their heads for Cagliostro's escape, walled the prisoner up alive, leaving only a small hole through which to spy on him, pass him his gruel, and torment him with the same question posed to Christ on the Cross: "If you are really the Son of God, why don't you call on your angels to set you free?"

Still hoping for a pardon from Pius, that he might seek refuge in revolutionary France, Cagliostro had a message sent to the pope warning him that a girl dressed as a page would try to stab him, that eventually he would lose his temporal powers and be taken a prisoner from Italy. The girl was apprehended; but it did nothing for Cagliostro, other than validate his clairvoyant powers. Pius was too busy unveiling his last obelisk in the Piazza Montecitorio before a great throng in the presence of Mesdames

143

The obelisk raised by Pius VI on Montecitorio—opposite the papal court of justice and future seat of Italy's Parliament—was his most important venture, if only because at last some attention was paid to the original point and purpose of such monuments. First raised in Heliopolis by Psamometitos II of the Saite dynasty, the obelisk is described by Pliny the Elder as having been brought from Alexandria to Rome by Augustus in 10 B.C. and set in a marble pavement in the Campus Martius marked out with bronze stripes and decorated with mosaics representing wind roses and the constellations of the zodiac; its purpose was to serve as a great gnomon, or sundial. The pavement, says

Piazza di Monte Citorio

CAMPVS   MARTIVS

Pliny, was laid out for an appropriate distance so that the shadow of the obelisk at noon on the shortest day of the year exactly coincided with its height. Bronze rods let into the pavement measured the shadow day by day, as it gradually became shorter and lengthened again. According to Pliny the device had been engineered by the mathematician Novius Facundus, though others attributed it to Manlius. Unfortunately, Pliny was not explicit enough to make it clear whether the monument served only as a *solarium,* to indicate the length of the meridian shadow, or also as an *horologium,* to indicate the hours of the day. In any case, something went wrong with the device, for Pliny reports that after thirty years its astronomical indications no longer corre-

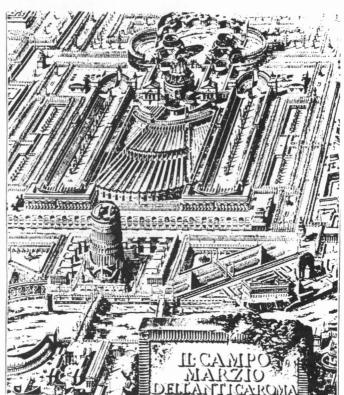

IL CAMPO MARZIO DELL'ANTICA ROMA

sponded. This he attributed to a change in the path of the sun, or to some other heavenly change, or because the earth had shifted its axis, or because of earthquakes which could have tilted the needle. Pliny even considered that the foundations could have been affected by inunda-

tions of the Tiber, though he discounted this explanation, "as the obelisk's foundations are as deep as it is tall." The needle was reported still standing in the eighth century A.D., and Iversen believes it to have been knocked down by the Norman Duke Robert Guiscard who put Rome to the sack in 1084 while freeing the tyrranical pope Gregory VII from imprisonment in Castel Sant'Angelo. It disappeared again until discovered by a barber in his cellar, where Fontana took Sixtus V to see it in 1587, though they buried it again as too burned and damaged to raise. In 1666 Kircher suggested to Alexander VII it would be easy to dig up the broken pieces, but his patron died too soon. A few years later, Cornelius Meijer, a Dutch inventor living in Rome, suggested raising the obelisk to serve as a solar gnomon, adding that because of the narrow vertical slit in the bronze ball atop the needle it might be used not only to note the passage of the sun's rays but also for sighting the north star and thus counting off the hours of the night. But Innocent XI was too weak for the job, which was left to Benedict XIV who jovially agreed to inspect the needle through a wall dug through the cellar of the Lottery. To extricate the five broken pieces without destroying the economically essential Lottery, the pope had recourse to an extraordinary old man called Niccoló Zabablia, a very rough fellow, who could neither read not write, and could barely express himself in words, but was renowned for the invention of simple machines to move great weights in restricted areas. Between May and August 1748, Za-

bablia brought out the five pieces and lay them in the filthy courtyard of the Palace of the Lotto. Benedict came in a carriage to admire, but as no architect dared raise the fragments they lay in a courtyard until Pius VI dragooned Antinori into accepting the challenge. Six days before the storming of the bastille he had it raised as a symbol against revolution. When the obelisk had first been discovered, Romans digging wine cellars and latrines had found beautifully wrought bronze constellations and a sundial clock with seven gilded degrees. This led to a dispute between what d'Onofrio calls the *eruditi* and the *matematici* as to whether the obelisk could function as a clock for Romans or merely as a rough gnomon to observe the sun's shadow from solstice to solstice. Pius's papal treasurer, Cardinal Ruffo, convinced that it could do both, hired a quarryman to carve out a series of marks in the cobbles of the piazza to indicate the hours of the day by means of the shaddow cast by the ball atop the obelisk, as well as along a meridian to mark the solstices. An immediate cry was raised by Rome's professors who argued against the "vain

design" of having an obelisk serve as a sundial. d'Onofrio quotes two illustrious opponents. One, Giacomo Pessuti, ridiculed the idea of an *horologium* "for reasons . . . obvious to anyone with the slightest tincture of optics or astronomy." Obelisks, he argued, had naturally fallen into disuse as gnomons because of "the advent of wheeled clocks." He also claimed that heavy traffic of pedestrians and carriages would render the venture useless. Another opponent, the abbot Giuseppe Calandrelli, noted ironically "that the project would make the papal states ridiculous, as if they were without an elementary knowledge of astronomy, reduced to establishing noon with the use of a gnomon." He compared the situation to "a poor lay Capucin who, in his miserable kitchen garden, has to stick a nail in the wall to indicate to his bretheren when it is noon." But Ruffo had his way, and onto the base went an inscription in Latin: "Royally raised as a pyramid marking the time on its dial, long in a dunghill it rested, broken, disdained, and forgotten. Now to new splendour and dignity called by Pius VI, proudly it counts with its shadow each of his glorious hours."

de France, Adélaïde and Victoire, the two maiden great-aunts of Louis XVI, living daughters of Louis XV, who had managed to escape to Rome from the Revolution. As an overt display of the antirevolutionary feelings rife at the papal court, the ceremony was, like the puffed-cheek Aeoli of the papal arms which adorned the obelisk's pyramidion, whistling in the wind. Two weeks later Antinori was dead. Shortly thereafter the Mesdames de France died miserably in Trieste; as for the pope, he was burned in effigy in Paris, a foretaste of what was in store for him.

In San Leo, unable to take his rejuvenating elixir, Cagliostro realized he was doomed, and made his last prophetic announcement: "I will be the last victim of the Inquisition; for when I come to eternity I will pray so hard there will come a new order upon this earth."

It was June 8, 1795.

On August 23, according to the prison record, Cagliostro suffered an apoplectic stroke. A Capucin monk, Cristoforo Cicerchia, ran to his side, imploring him to make peace with the Church: "You still have a few moments in which to buy yourself a good place in heaven," he pleaded. But Cagliostro refused. He would neither repent nor confess. On August 26, as recorded in the parish register, Cagliostro expired. As a heretic, his body was ordered by the local bishop to be buried in unhallowed ground with no religious rite.

The daughter of one of the jailers reported, some years later, that in his cell Cagliostro had painted a full-length portrait of himself using a brush made from the hairs of his beard and color from the rust on the cell bars; it showed Cagliostro dressed in pontifical robes pointing to the image of a Masonic temple on his bared chest; beneath his feet were the emblems of the Catholic Church.

An eyewitness described four men bearing his body on an old broken door. At the bottom of the hill, sweating because of the August heat, the bearers deposited their load by a well to have a drink in a nearby wineshop. Sufficiently inebriated, they dug a hole on the promontory, into which they placed a brick as a pillow for the corpse's head. Its features covered by an old used handkerchief were buried in earth.

Two years later, on December 8, 1797, as Napoleon returned to Paris to capitalize on his Italian victories, the castle of San Leo surrendered to General G. E. Dambrowski of the Polish Legion of Napoleon's Cisalpine Republic, and its inmates were released, so the story goes, to dig up Cagliostro's grave and use his skull to swill wine as a toast to their liberation. Ironically, the

French troops entering Rome
from the Flaminia to congregate
in Piazza del Popolo around the
obelisk of Augustus, reerected
by Sixtus V

presence of the French troops in the Papal States was
precipitated by the murder in the streets of Rome of the
French agent Hugo de Basseville by a group of conspirators headed by Cagliostro's inquisitors Giovanni Barberi
and the Cardinals Zelada and Albini.

When General Duphot of the French embassy, who was
engaged to Joseph Bonaparte's sister, was also murdered, Napoleon's General Louis Alescanshe Berthier,
later Prince of Wagrom, captured Rome, set himself up in
Pius's Quirinal Palace, and declared the Papal States a
republic. Barberi was condemned to death for this second
overt act of murder, done presumably on orders from, or
with the consent of, the pope. Particular severity was
exercised against Barberi, says historian Jean François
de Bourgoing, because he was "deservedly hated on
account of the influence he acquired, and of the persecu-
tions by which he had harassed all the inhabitants of
Rome—whether natives or foreigners." According to Bourgoing, Barberi's exceptional actions arose from his preju-
dices and his ignorance, "Being exclusively versed in
criminal jurisprudence, he was unacquainted either with
political affairs or with mankind." But whereas Barberi
managed to escape and hide out in what was then the
inaccessible wilderness of Monte Argentario, beyond the
lagoon of Orbetello, Pius VI, in his eighties, his legs

Pius VI taken prisoner by Napoleon's troops in Rome. In one day the pontiff's nephews, Cardinal Braschi and the duke of Nemi, sank from opulence to beggary.

Jorgen Zoëga at work on his obelisk book

paralyzed and unable to flee, was forced to cede to France the papal lands of Avignon, Ferrara, and Romagna. Taken prisoner, first to Siena, then to Florence, then to Turin, and eventually to Grenoble, Pius VI was never again to see the Rome he had adorned, nor the obelisks with which he had adorned it.

What remained of Pius's fame was an enormous folio volume of nearly seven hundred pages, *De origine et usu obeliscorum,* commissioned by him from the Danish scholar Jorgen Zoëga, who had settled in Italy in 1783, which came off the presses as Napoleon's troops invaded Rome. The volume, greeted as the most comprehensive and dispassionate survey of Egyptology that had yet appeared, contained in the first two chapters the accumulated material from classical authors on which what was known of Egypt was based. There followed an archaeological and historical description of all the known obelisks in Europe and Egypt, taken mostly from Mercati, Bandini, and Kircher, to which Zoëga added an excursus on pyramids.

Though Zoëga declared his purpose to be the collection and exhumation of all the evidence from authors ancient and modern which had any bearing at all on the obelisks of Egypt, he found the data to be "absurd," thus missing the whole point of what he was studying. He did show, by detailed measurements, that most of those proposed by his predecessors were not even consistent and he did attack the problem of the hieroglyphs. The volume contains the most extensive and carefully reproduced collection of original hieroglyphical inscriptions published till then. What is more he stressed the distinction between the hieroglyphic script and the large-scale drawings which often accompanied them, showing that the direction of hieroglyphic writing was indicated by the figures facing the start of each line.

In his attempt to classify the number of separate glyphs, Zoëga reached a total of 270 on the obelisks themselves, and 958 including all the inscriptions in European museums. From this he deduced that the total was not nearly large enough for an entirely ideographic script in which each word of the language has its own separate sign. This led him to suggest that certain figures of animals, birds, or plants used in the hieroglyphs might represent letters that could be read as sounds. This suggestion constituted the first ideational breakthrough in the decipherment of hieroglyphs; it also contributed the first modern European usage of the words *phonetic signs,* or *notae phoneticae.*

On the negative side, Zoëga concluded that there were no esoteric or symbolic secrets whatsoever involved in the shape of the great obelisks: that their slender pyramidal shape arose solely from considerations of aptness, beauty, and durability, "so that there was no mystery about it." A mystery there was: but he had missed it, as had Pius. And all the time the evidence had been within their grasp.

As General André Massena's troops went through the liberated Castel Sant'Angelo, they discovered an anonymous manuscript which had been seized in Cagliostro's lodgings on the day of his arrest. Entitled *La Très Sainte Trisophonie,* or *The Most Holy Threefold Wisdom,* it was a beautifully handwritten work with a score of colored illustrations and many glyphs. That it survived the fires of the Inquisition is due, most probably, to the apparently totally innocuous allegorical language in which it is written.

Grillot de Givry, who first commented on the discovery in his *Musée des Sorciers,* just over a hundred years later, interpreted the text as cabalized alchemy, presumably from the pen of Saint-Germain, one of the sole remaining documents attributable to this timeless sage of the eighteenth century.

Manly P. Hall's reprint of the only remaining text of this rarest of occult works

149

Illustration in *La très sainte triso-nophie* of a couple scrying. Theodore Bersterman, in his treatise on crystal-gazing published in 1924, says: "Scrying is a method of bringing into the consciousness of the scryer by means of a speculum (or mirroring surface) through one or more of his senses the content of his subconscious, or rendering him more susceptible to the reception of telepathically transmitted concepts, and of bringing into operation a latent and unknown faculty of perception."

But it was not until the middle of the twentieth century, when the Californian philosopher Manly P. Hall reproduced the book in its entirety from the original and only example, now in the library of Troyes, adding copious notes and a prefatory text, that it was shown to be "in every respect an authentic ritual of the Society of the Rosicrucians, possibly the actual record of Saint-Germain's own acceptance into the mystical brotherhood of which he finally became the Grand Master." The early sections, says Hall, seem to derive their inspiration directly from the neo-Egyptian ritual called the rite of Memphis.

That Pius and his cohorts missed the mystery, unable to decipher the Hermetic meaning behind the overtly blameless story, is explained by Edward C. Getsinger, an authority on deciphering ancient texts, who found that the volume contained the most ingenious codes and methods of concealment he had ever encountered; "a perfect example of how symbolism is used to intimate truths too dangerous to reveal."

Pius VI on his deathbed in captivity

It is clearly, says Hall, a threefold enigma. "From its symbolism, it seems that one of the keys is alchemy, or soul-chemistry; another Essenian Cabbalism; the third Alexandrian Hermetism, the mysticism of the later Egyptians." Those who wish to consult Manly Hall's notes may come as close as it is possible in an overt document to learn the truths for which Cagliostro laid down his life, truths which were only to reappear in the next century with the discovery of the Egyptian so-called *Book of the Dead.*

But none of this was for Pius. By the time he was taken from Rome, Saint-Germain had vanished from the scene. And, in condemning Cagliostro, the poor pontiff had managed to bury the one clairvoyant who might have given him a clue to the mysterious meaning of the obelisks and their glyphs, just as, in patronizing Zoëga, he had managed to bury in a tome of pluperfectly pedantic Latin, the whole subject of obelisk and glyph.

And there it lay, requiescent, but not in peace. Sadly, Zoëga admitted his failure: "When Egypt is better known to scholars, and when the numerous ancient remains still to be seen there have been accurately explored and published, it will perhaps be possible to understand the meaning of the Egyptian monuments."

151

8. NAPOLEON REDISCOVERS EGYPT

Jean Jacques Champollion (Figeac)

Jean François Champollion (le Jeune)

Frontispiece of the *Description de l'Égypte* with Napoleon's imperial *N*

As Pope Pius VI lay on his deathbed in August 1799, a young French professor of history at the university of Genoble, Champollion-Figeac, had been pulling strings to get himself named to a group of savants being selected by the twenty-nine-year-old General Bonaparte to accompany him on his conquest of Egypt.

Jean Jacques Champollion had already added to his surname the appellation of his native town of Figeac in order to distinguish himself from his eight-year-old brother, Jean-François, for whom he anticipated a great future, and whose limelight he did not wish in any way to shade. Convinced that the boy had a truly remarkable mind and deep devotion to scholarship—at four he had learned to read and write by comparing a written missal with the prayers he had learned by heart—the elder Champollion had taken the youngster into his home to give him special tutoring in advanced studies. To repay his elder brother's courtesy in calling himself Figeac, the younger Champollion added to his own name that of Le Jeune, or Junior. But because of his olive complexion, curly black hair, and slightly slanted eyes with yellow irises, which gave him an oriental appearance, his sister-in-law called him Sagir, the Arabic word for "junior," a nickname which stuck to him for life.

Despite strong recommendation, Champollion-Figeac was not selected to go to Egypt. But the Paris Directorate was only too happy to be rid of Napoleon, whom they considered an irritating and formidable rival. His overt object was to cut off Britain's route to India. A stronger motivation was his driving search for fame. "I must seek it in the East; all great fame comes from that quarter." In the footsteps of Alexander the Great, Napoleon wished to conquer the world, but first he had to conquer the East, overthrow the Turks, seize Constantinople, take Europe in the rear, paving the way for the fall of India, China, and the world.

The idea was not original. It had already been envisaged by Sixtus V in 1587 when he outlined the scheme to the Venetian ambassador, Giovanni Gritti, in his lamentably vernacular Italian: "A little money, a little money, Mr. Ambassador, and I could send an army into Egypt. Seven-

General Napoleon Bonaparte

Obelisk raised at Rouen in honor of Napoleon's victories in the Italian Campaign

ty or eighty galleons, well armed, would do the trick. I could seize and fortify Alexandria and be master of Egypt. It would buy off the inhabitants and make them into Christians, perhaps even with the help of Arabs who are against the Turks." Sixtus even had the genial notion of cutting a canal to Suez, but was afraid the difference in water level in the Red Sea might cause a dangerous flood in the delta.

An occupation of Egypt by the French had also been envisaged by another student of hieroglyphs, the German philosopher and mathematician Gottfried Wilhelm von Leibnitz, discoverer of differential and integral calculus, who had suggested the idea to Louis XIV. Leibnitz (who had been offered custodianship of the Vatican Library but had turned it down because he would have had to join the Catholic Church), like Zoëga, did not agree with Kircher's belief that the hieroglyphs contained esoteric wisdom. He considered the inscriptions on the obelisks to be merely "historical texts commemorating events and victories."

Napoleon, as a freethinker, was more sanguine about cracking the riddle, which his Masonic friends in Paris convinced him was essential to a proper understanding of political history. To do the job, he had deliberately collected some 150 scientists and artists, many of them Masons, recruited from the Académie des Inscriptions, including scholars of the highest distinction, such as Gaspard Monge, Étienne Geoffroy Saint-Hilaire, Edmé François Jomard, Claude Louis Berthollet, and Jean Baptiste Joseph Fourier. That obelisks were on Napoleon's mind is evident from the story that his wife Josephine, also a Freemason, came to see him off at Toulon, and asked him, as she kissed him good-bye, to bring her back one from Thebes, even if it were only a small one.

On May 19, 1798, Napoleon's armada sailed with thirteen ships of the line, fourteen frigates, seventy-two corvettes, and nearly four hundred transports carrying forty thousand troops. In his cabin, Napoleon carried with him the Bible, the Koran, the Vedas, a book on ancient mythology, Montesquieu's *Spirit of the Laws,* translations of Thucidides, Plutarch, Tacitus, Livy, and several books on such military commanders as Turenne, Condé, Luxembourg, and Marlborough. For lighter reading, he took along Cook's *Voyages* and forty English novels.

His archrival, Horatio Nelson, somewhere at sea in the Mediterranean, was cruising with his squadron in the hope of intercepting and destroying the French armada. But the two great fleets, each commanded by a Freemason, silently passed in the night, narrowly missing an encounter.

Six weeks later—after stopping in Malta to loot the treasure of its Knights—the French squadron reached Alexandria on July 1. Napoleon's troops quickly seized the town, once a sophisticated metropolis of half a million souls, with 4,000 public baths and 400 theaters, which had been reduced under the Ottoman Turks to no more than a village of four thousand souls. A miserable march through the desert took the expedition to the Giza plateau. There, at the great Battle of the Pyramids, Napoleon defeated sixty thousand Mameluke warriors by letting their intrepid horsemen shatter their silk-and-gold-laden bodies against the firepower of his classic infantry squares.

In three weeks, Bonaparte's generals chased the remnants of the Mamelukes up the Nile as far as the Aswan cataract. With the entire country subdued, Napoleon declared Egypt a French protectorate. Promising to treat local citizens with restraint and respect, he set up in Cairo a government which included prominent Egyptians. It was then safe for his savants to be let loose to loot the country of its ancient treasures as they unearthed temples, dug into pyramids, and measured obelisks for transfer to Paris. Soon they had collected antiquities from all over the country, housing them in a special collection in Cairo. Thus came to light a slab of black basalt found by a detachment of French soldiers working on fortifications near the village of Rashid or Rosetta. From this discovery it looked at last as if the key to the unravelment of the secrets of Egypt was at hand. The stone was covered with inscriptions in three distinct scripts: one hieroglyphic, one mysterious, one clearly Greek.

But the French had counted without Albion. A short distance from Rosetta, in the Bay of Aboukir, Nelson caught the French fleet by surprise. As brilliant at sea as Napoleon was on land, the young admiral trapped the French between two fires and sank all but one of their ships of the line, leaving the French army stranded in Egypt in the midst of a population rapidly growing hostile.

From this victorious Battle of the Nile there mushroomed a coalition of British, Turks, and Arabs, determined to expel the French from Egypt. When an uprising in Cairo caused the death of several hundred French soldiers, Bonaparte retaliated by shooting and beheading the insurgents, rolling their heads in the squares. En route to attack the pasha of Acre, who had raised an army, Napoleon captured Jaffa, but unable to feed or guard three thousand prisoners, he had them shot to a man, wiping out the male population of the city, an act of cruelty so heinous it put marrow into the defenders of Acre. Thus this

Nelson wounded during the Battle of the Nile

last stronghold of the Templars, which had fallen to the Moslems in 1290, now cost Napoleon an empire. When the town would not surrender, blocking the would-be world conqueror's way to the East, Napoleon bitterly remarked: *"J'ai manqué ma fortune à Saint Jean d'Acre,"* and began his first retreat.

To save his reputation at home, this general of the French stole secretly from his troops, sailing on the sole frigate that had survived the British attack. Once more slipping past Nelson's fleet, Napoleon reached Corsica well before the news of his defeats, to be greeted as a hero, a welcome which paved his way to the coup of 18 Brumaire and his being named consul of France, then first consul.

Cartoon lampooning Napoleon's clandestine flight from Egypt

Meanwhile, the British general Sir Ralph Abercromby had landed an army at Aboukir Bay, 14 miles northeast of Alexandria, and attacked Napoleon's abandoned forces.

156

General Abercromby dueling with French dragoons

The Rosetta Stone, described in the *Courrier d'Égypte* as of very fine-grained black granite, found by Pierre François Xavier Bouchard, an officer in the French engineers, at Fort Jullien, Rosetta

So stalwart was the conduct of the foot soldiers of the Twenty-eighth Gloucestershire Regiment, heavily engaged by the French *par devant et par derrière,* that they gained the unique distinction thereafter of wearing their badges both at the front and back of their headdress. Even Sir Ralph distinguished himself by engaging in personal combat with some French dragoons, until the French, facing capitulation, fired a few volleys and quit. From one of these last volleys a spent ball struck Abercromby in the head. Succumbing in the moment of victory, he left to his number two, General Hely Hutchinson, the honor of receiving the surrender of the French. Gallantly, the Englishman gave the debris of Napoleon's army free passage back to France.

But all the antiquities collected by the French, including the Rosetta Stone, were claimed by the British as spoils of war. Hearing the terms, the savants rose in rebellion and refused to part with their trophies. Saint-Hilaire did not mince his words: ''You are taking from us our collections, our drawings, our copies of hieroglyphs; but who will give you the key to all that? . . . Without us this material is a dead language that neither you nor your scientists can understand. . . . Sooner than permit this iniquitous and vandalous spoilation we will destroy our property, we will scatter it amid the Libyan sands and throw it into the sea. We shall burn our riches ourselves. If it is celebrity you are aiming for, very well, you can count on the long memory of history: you too will have burnt a library in Alexandria.'' General Hutchinson, a man of vision, was sufficiently impressed to allow the French to keep their collection. But he insisted on retaining the Rosetta Stone. Lost to France, it went to reside in the British Museum, where no one, as Saint-Hilaire had warned, could make head or tail of its glyphs.

In a Grenoble bookstore, the younger Champollion, then nine years old, came across a copy of the *Courrier de*

157

l'Égypte with a description of the discovery of the Rosetta Stone. Spurred by the suggestion that a decipherment of the hieroglyphs might eventually open up the whole of Egyptian history, he plunged into the study of Latin and Greek so as to be able to read for references to Egypt in the classics. It was to take him several months.

By this time the senate in Paris had proclaimed Napoleon emperor of the French. Abandoning for the moment his dream of conquest in the East, he decided instead to concentrate on reorganizing his empire at home. One of his first moves was to establish the University of France, which he linked administratively to all the regional universities and to all the public *lycées.* As a result, Champolloion-Figeac, a good Bonapartist, managed to obtain for his younger brother a scholarship to the Grenoble *lycée.* Fourteen years old, Champollion-le-Jeune was not tall but had a firm, slender body full of strength. According to his major biographer, Hermine Hartleben, the boy's handsome features, fine-boned and full of magnetism, caught people's attention; and when he talked on matters he liked, such as Egyptian history, he seemed to vibrate with an intense desire to be understood. Adults, startled by his self-assured manner and the ease with which he conversed, were drawn to him and indulged him.

Grenoble was then a university town of twenty-five thousand inhabitants, standing on the left bank of the river Isère in a lovely fertile plain with hills and mountains that swept up steeply toward the distant peak of Mont Blanc. The seat of the bishopric, with fortifications dating back to the Roman emperor Diocletian, its people were nonetheless independent *dauphinois,* strongly democratic, intellectual, boasting of many learned societies.

The town of Grenoble in the Piedmont of Dauphiné Alps

ALKSANTRS
(Alexander)

PTLOMÊS
(Ptolemy)

When a new prefect was appointed to the district by Napoleon, it turned out to be Jean Baptiste Joseph Fourier, the engineer-historian who had been to Egypt with Napoleon and served as secretary to the French Institute in Cairo. In Grenoble, when Fourier was asked to become a member of the learned Académie Delphinate, its secretary, Champollion-Figeac, asked if he could introduce his younger brother. Amazed at how much the boy already knew about Egypt, Fourier showed him the small museum of Egyptian antiquities he had collected, including stelae, amphorae, statues, stone tablets, and fragments of papyri covered with hieroglyphs. Most exciting to young Champollion was a rough parchment copy of the three texts of the Rosetta Stone. When told that no one could either read or understand the glyphs, the boy replied firmly: "Then I will."

From the Greek text, which he could readily translate, Champollion saw that the stone carried a decree issued in Memphis in 196 B.C. by an assembly of Egyptian priests in honor of King Ptolemy V Epiphanes, to commemorate his benefactions to the indigenous priesthood. More interesting was a colophon which decreed that the stone be engraved in three different characters: hieroglyphs, native letters, and Greek. From this it seemed clear that the stone carried three versions of the same text. Unfortunately, the top and both sides of the Rosetta tablet had been broken away, so that only half of the hieroglyphs were left, not one line of which was complete.

Fourier explained that so far the best efforts at deciphering the tablet had been achieved by working on the nonhieroglyphic text, the so-called demotic script, to see if any relation, letter to letter, could be found between it and the Greek text. Sylvestre de Sacy, Europe's leading orientalist, had tried his hand at the problem by picking out the proper names which appeared in the Greek text and then searching for the equivalent letters in the demotic. In this way he had managed to locate the names of Alexander and Ptolemy.

A Swedish diplomat, John David Akerblad, widely traveled in Egypt, to whom de Sacy had lent a prepublication copy of the inscription, had identified Arsinoë, Verenice, and Aetos, establishing that such words as *Greek, Egyptian, temple, love,* and *abundance* were written with the same alphabet, of which he identified twenty-nine letters. Fourier explained to the boy that the demotic words deciphered by Akerblad were almost identical with Coptic words for the same concepts, which seemed to vindicate Father Kircher's notion that ancient Coptic had been the language of Egypt.

Thanks to Fourier, Champollion was now able to obtain rare material that would otherwise have been impossible for him to consult, including the works of Kircher. Promptly the boy launched into a study of Coptic, and produced a map of Egypt following the Coptic names, disregarding the Greek and Roman ones, which he considered suspect. He also began to study Arabic, Chaldean, Syriac, Ethiopian, Sanskrit, Send, Pehlevi, Parsee, and Persian, hoping to find other clues to the langauge in which the hieroglyphs might have been written. He even launched into Old Chinese, because some authorities maintained the ancient Egyptians had come from China to settle on the Nile.

By the time he was seventeen, Champollion had made his first table of the succession of Egyptian pharaohs, based on data culled from the Old Testament, and from ancient works in Greek, Latin, Arabic, and Coptic. Shortly thereafter, he was invited, despite the opposition and hostility of several members of the faculty, because of his youth and his intolerance of ignorance and prejudice, to read a paper to the faculty of Grenoble University. Trembling slightly, agitated by some inner emotion, the slim, dark-skinned youth stood erect before the gathering of professors, then announced that he proposed to regale them with an encyclopedic view of ancient Egypt in all its aspects. As the young scholar spoke, brushing a hand through his dark curly hair, the audience became enthralled. Never had they heard anything like it. There were gasps of amazement as he mentioned rare sources he had consulted, ancient Coptic scripts, Hebrew and Arabic sources, sources which represented hundreds of hours of concentrated reading in many ancient languages, mostly from obscure books that the professors had not even heard of. He described the country as if he had lived there, creating the illusion he had stepped out of ancient Egypt into the nineteenth century. As one historian put it, he had so thoroughly absorbed the ancient Egyptian culture, he gave the uncanny feeling to those in his presence that he was an ancient Egyptian reincarnated.

When Champollion finished, there was a hush, followed by a buzz of excitement. His conviction and sincerity had carried all before him. The president of his lyceum jumped up and embraced him. Professor Renauldon told him he could immediately join the faculty of the university. Unanimously he was accepted as a corresponding member of the Academy of Grenoble. From humble student he found himself a highly regarded teacher, but not for long. Such precocity could only engender jealousy. To escape it, and the antagonistic atmosphere of academia, Champollion wanted more than anything to be allowed to go to Paris to pursue his study of the Rosetta Stone and its hieroglyphs, admitting to his brother that he had the weird feeling he had been present in Memphis in 196 B.C. when the stone had been raised.

Napoleon's victory at Austerlitz

It was 1808. Napoleon had defeated the Austrians at Austerlitz, and by taking Berlin replaced what was left of the Holy Roman Empire with a French-controlled Confederation of the Rhine. In Paris, he set up a court as precise and rigid in its etiquette as that of the *ancien régime,* rivaling the splendor of Louis XIV, though it could be said for the empire that it did not restore the feudalism, privileges, and exactness of the Bourbons.

In Paris, Champollion became a student of Sylvestre de Sacy, the head of the Académie des Inscriptions, who had finally managed to obtain a plaster cast of the Rosetta Stone. Champollion was soon lost in the dusty archives of the Paris libraries, only coming out to wander into another institute or museum, searching constantly for anything to do with ancient Egyptian or with Coptic. In the Bibliothèque Nationale, he found and annotated Kircher's *Lingua Aegyptiaca restituta* and was able to work on the Coptic manuscripts stolen by the revolutionaries from the Vatican.

In the Louvre Museum, Louis XVI's former palace, which had been opened to the public in 1793, he could admire the works of art accumulated by a series of French monarchs, or more recently looted by Napoleon from the churches, galleries, and museums of Italy, the Netherlands, and Germany. There, Baron Dominique Vivant Denon, named by Napoleon director of the museum, had formed the Egyptian collection from the enormous quantity

Silvestre de Sacy, head of the Academy of Inscriptions, founded to supply Louis XIV (the Sun King) with "learned ornamentations for his pleasure."

161

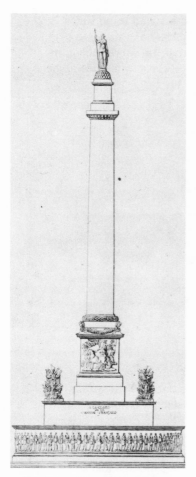

Napoleon, whose Arch of Triumph stands at the top of the Champs-Élysée, planned an even bolder and grander monument to outdo the glory of Thebes and Rome—a 180-foot obelisk to replace the statue of Henri IV on the Pont Neuf near where de Molay was burned. This colossal needle was to be formed of six superimposed granite monoliths, the lowest of which was to weigh a million pounds. The sculptured faces were to cover more than 10 million square feet (or about 24 acres). Calculations were made and plans drawn by Charles Le Père, who had accompanied Napoleon to Egypt, where he had been responsible for *mis*-measuring the Great Pyramid of Cheops. No more than the foundations were laid for Napoleon's needle before the plans collapsed along with the empire.

of antiquities brought back by Napoleon's savants, to which he continued to add.

Convinced that Coptic was to Egyptian what modern Italian is to Latin, Champollion tried to find someone in Paris who could teach him to speak the language. There was no one, other than a Coptic priest who said mass at the church of Saint Roch, by the rue de Rivoli; from him he was able to learn something of the pronunciation of contemporary Coptic, but little more. For practice, Champollion spoke Coptic to himself whenever he was alone, which was most of the time.

With no money other than what his brother sent him from his own small earnings, the young man found a room next to the Louvre, cheap, shabby, with an iron bed, rickety sofa, and two chairs. It was damp and cold. His meals consisted of bread, cheese, and onion, with an occasional bowl of stew, eaten rapidly and sparingly. His coat was threadbare, and his shoes were stuffed with paper. The gray dampness which hung over Paris induced a cough with spasms which developed into a severe pain in the chest.

In 1809, when Napoleon began drafting recruits for military service in his new campaigns, the young Champollion only just managed to be exempted through the intervention of Fourier and de Sacy. But his money ran out, and his landlady, catching him speaking to himself in Coptic, threw him out as a lunatic, leaving him no choice but to go home without having solved the riddle of the glyphs.

In Grenoble, his brother managed to get him the post of assistant to the octogenarian professor of history at the university, but a jealous group of professors soon banded against him, determined to force the young savant from the faculty. They could not tolerate his pointing out the errors in their instruction. "I do not like to compromise with truth," he insisted, "it is shameful to play politics with education." Believing that teachers had to be intellectually free and immune from pressure, Champollion began to write satirical sketches attacking both the royalists and the Bonapartists, which endeared him to neither.

By this time Napoleon had divorced his childless Josephine to marry the archduchess Maria Luisa of Austria, thus allying France with Austro-Hungary. As the ersatz Holy Roman Emperor he decided to emulate his predecessor caesars and pontiffs, and in a decree issued from Schoenbrün, ordered the erection of an obelisk made of Cherbourg granite in memory of the campaigns of Iena and the Vistula, bearing the inscription "From the Emperor Napoleon to the People of France."

Louis XVIII caricatured as interested mostly in the problems of his mistresses

Ten projects were submitted, in one of which two elephants on either side of an Egyptian colonnade rendered homage to the "new Alexander." But the jury chose a more sober design by the architect Jean François Chalguin. The foundations were laid, but Napoleon, retreating from Moscow, was badly defeated at Leipzig. Pursued by his enemies into France, the depressed dreamer was forced to abdicate on April 11, 1814, and go into exile to Elba. The obelisk was stillborn.

As the Bourbons reclaimed the French throne upon which to seat a fat, lazy, and inept Louis Xavier Stanislas, comte de Provence, brother of Louis XVI, as Louis XVIII, Champollion buried himself in his work. That year he published his *Egypt Under the Pharaohs* in two volumes; it was dismissed as fanciful. Stung by the critics, Champollion realized the only way to prove his point would be to decipher the hieroglyphs and show a truer history and chronology of Egypt.

Then came the "hundred days," not only to reprieve Napoleon, but by chance to bring Champollion and the emperor together. Tired of his island prison, the ex-emperor slipped past his guards on Elba and landed unopposed at Antibes in the south of France. "I shall reach Paris without firing a shot," he predicted. To avoid the royalist towns of Provence, he headed toward Savoy and republican Grenoble, where an old friend was in command. Just before Grenoble, a body of royalist troops barred his way. Stepping forward, Napoleon threw open his coat to reveal his well-worn uniform and the ribbon of the Legion of Honor. "Soldiers, if any among you wishes

Napoleon's return from Elba

to kill his Emperor, here I am!'' An officer gave the order to fire, but the soldiers refused, crying *''Viva l'Empereur!''* Crowding around him, they tore off their white Bourbon cockades.

In Grenoble, Napoleon put up at the Auberge des Trois Dauphins and asked for a competent man with a clear mind and lucid style to translate his verbal instructions into written orders. The mayor suggested Champollion-Figeac, then head of the faculty of letters at the university.

The elder Champollion, who had now legally changed his name to Figeac, arrived at Napoleon's quarters in the inn with his younger brother, whom the emperor began to cross-examine about Egypt, becoming so impressed that he kept the youth in his small room while a crowd fidgeted anxiously outside.

Napoleon in Grenoble. Leaning against the still-barred gates, he is said to have taken a pinch of snuff and then tapped with his silver snuff box until the gates were opened by a welcoming crowd.

The next day, to pursue the conversation, Napoleon sought out Champollion in his quarters at the university library to tell him he admired the courage with which he imposed his views: "I would never have taken Toulon in 1793 if I had not done the same," said the emperor. "I was just your age." Champollion talked to Napoleon in Coptic, which enthralled the emperor, who agreed it was the key to understanding ancient Egyptian, and said he intended to restore Coptic as the national language of Egypt. He promised to have Champollion's dictionary printed at government expense as soon as he got to Paris. "I will do it by decree," said Napoleon, "just as I ordered the publication of Ptolemy's *Almagest* translated by de Sacy, and the great Chinese dictionary which had been languishing for a hundred years."

Wanting to know more about Egypt for his future plans, which involved a great irrigation project to make the country bloom, Napoleon spent several hours with Cham-

299. Serment de Ney — Serrement de nez

Cartoon playing on the French word *nez* (pronounced "ney") for "nose."

pollion, pumping him on every facet of the subject. When Napoleon set off to reconquer Paris, he took with him Figeac as an aide, leaving young Champollion to edit the Bonapartist newspaper started by his brother, the *Journal de Isère,* the first number of which described Napoleon's triumphant march from Elba toward Paris, emphasizing the democratic ideals of liberty on which the new regime was to be founded, rather than the former imperial pomp.

By the time Napoleon reached Lyons, he was addressing everyone as "citizen" and promising a liberal constitution. Republican sympathizers disillusioned with the Bourbons who had shown themselves incapable of ruling, and had deliberately broken every stipulated agreement made with Napoleon at the time of his abdication, flocked to his tricolor banner with shouts of *"Vive l'empereur!"* Even Napoleon's old marshal, Michel Ney, Prince of Moskowou, who had suggested to the Bourbons bringing Napoleon back to Paris in a cage, took one look at the approaching tricolor and came over to the emperor's side, quickly imitated by his troops. Louis XVIII, hearing of the triumphant reception given the returning hero, slipped quietly out of Paris.

Napoleon welcomed back to his old quarters in Paris

At the Tuileries, officers and soldiers seized the emperor and carried him up to his old apartment on the second floor. Figeac, who was with Napoleon all the way to Paris, now became a member of several committees charged with projects of reform.

But the "hundred days" were soon over; the combined reactionary forces of Europe proved too strong. Figeac was with Lucien Bonaparte at the Palais Royale on the evening of June 20, 1815, when they received the news of Napoleon's defeat at Waterloo by a combination of English, Dutch, Belgian, and Hanoverian troops under the command of the duke of Wellington. Louis XVIII slipped back into the Tuileries just as quietly, this time protected by Scottish muskets. Everywhere in France, royalists were forcibly put back into power by foreign bayonets. In republican Grenoble, which held out against the royalists, raising barricades, Champollion rushed about to hide the rarest volumes and manuscripts of the library from a vicious royalist artillery bombardment.

As Napoleon abdicated at Fontainebleau, Austrian soldiers were installed in Grenoble. Champollion's paper was taken over by antirevolutionists who cried for Napoleon's accomplices to be shot. Blood flowed. Thousands, including Marshal Ney, were executed. Champollion got away with a mere dismissal from the university, and exile to his native town of Figeac. The Bourbons were back, having, as Talleyrand remarked, "learned nothing, and forgotten nothing."

Frontispiece of the *Description de l'Égypte* with the bust of Louis XVIII replacing the imperial *N* of Napoleon.

When Napoleon seized power as emperor he initiated the reestablishment of orthodox Catholicism in France, with Pius VII as pope, but kept him a virtual prisoner at Fontainebleau. When the new pontiff requested the suppression of Masonry, Napoleon decided instead to make use of it. The Grand Orient and the Grande Lodge were united, and the emperior's brothers, first Joseph, then Lucien, were named Grand Master of the joint body. Dignitaries of the new empire quickly followed suit. But it was a chastened Masonry, deprived of its Illuminist tendencies, anxious to integrate itself in the new structure of patronage. With the defeat of Napoleon, Pius VII was restored to the Papal States, so relieved, they say, that he levitated during the celebration of Mass. Masonry was once more forbidden. The Inquisition was revived along with the index of forbidden books. The church threw its support to absolute monarchs, while parliaments and democracies were termed "atheistic," and the Jesuits again sought to make every sovereign the vassal of Rome.

Cameo of Thomas Young

The Inquisition, abolished by Napoleon's brother Jérôme as King of Westphalia, was reestablished by Pius VII. In Paris, Figeac obtained the protection of the Masonic group which, under the leadership of Edme François Jomard, was allowed to continue to edit and bring out the remaining folio volumes of the *Description de l'Égypte* minus the imperial "N" which had decorated the earlier volumes.

To keep alive, young Champollion managed to give private lessons, slipping up to Paris on holidays to consult the copious and magnificent illustrations in the huge volumes of the *Description,* which were causing a sensation in Europe among those who could afford to read them, and were strong enough to lift them.

In Grenoble the new prefect was the baron d'Haussez, a former revolutionary from the Vendée who had rallied to the empire and then reverted to the royalists with the return of Louis XVIII. More royalist than the king, he now hated liberals, and especially Champollion, whom he accused of conspiring against the safety of the state. A cold, unpleasant man, who kept a guard at every window, he showed Champollion copies of his Bonapartist letters to Figeac intercepted by Fouché, the chief of police, who had survived every regime from the Terror to the Reaction. Unable to work in Grenoble, Champollion sought refuge with his brother in Paris. There, in a top-floor attic on the rue Mazarine, he survived the stagnation of the Bourbonic restoration by devoting himself entirely to cracking the secret of the hieroglyphs, working mostly with material provided by his brother, who had been collaborating with André Dacier, the permanent secretary of the Academy of Inscriptions, where thousands of reproductions of glyphs had been accumulated.

A competing researcher in England, Thomas Young, a physician by profession and a physicist by inclination, had found a direct relation between hieratic and demotic, and published his results in 1818. By noticing a collection of characters that occurred thirty times in the demotic script of the Rosetta Stone and comparing them with where their equivalent appeared in the Greek text, Young concluded that they stood for the word *king,* yet he could not tell which letter stood for which hieroglyph. Nevertheless the system enabled him to establish the correct significance of such words as *Osiris, immortal, victory, year,* and *likewise.* But he had no idea of how to read the individual letters, most of which he got wrong or transposed. He did correctly guess that a cartouche was a convention indicating a royal name; but otherwise, with the hieroglyphs, he

PTOLMÊS
(Ptolemy)

KLEOPATRA
(Cleopatra)

The island of Philae (now submerged by the Aswan Dam) lay about 5 miles south, or upriver, of Aswan, beyond the first cataract and before the second. The obelisk found by Bankes was 20 feet long and weighed 6 tons. It was inscribed with the names of Ptolemy IX (184(?)–116 B.C.) and his sister-wife Cleopatra. Bankes later found the lower half of its matching pair, which he had removed to England.

made no further headway, considering, as did everyone else at the time, that they were purely ideogramic—that is, standing for words or ideas, not sounds.

Champollion had at first thought likewise. But when he counted the number of words in the Greek text of the Rosetta Stone and the number of signs in the hieroglyphic text, he found there were three times too many of the glyphs; this led him to conclude that they *must* represent sounds, not words. By transcribing the Greek name *Ptolemaios* letter by letter from demotic to hieratic and then to cursive hieroglyphic, Champollion was finally able to find virtually the same hieroglyph in the Rosetta Stone. This meant that the proper names of Greeks, such as *Ptolemy* and *Cleopatra,* must be written phonetically, letter by letter, in all the hieroglyphs. Unfortunately, there was no *Cleopatra* in the Greek text of the Rosetta Stone; but in a text known as the Casati papyrus, he found the demotic form for this last of the Ptolemaic queens. What he needed now was another Rosetta Stone. And in 1891 he got it in the form of an obelisk.

Some years earlier, a French traveler, Frédéric Caillard,

Giovanni Battista Belzoni

had found an obelisk on the island of Philae above Aswan, between the Nile's first and second cataracts, smaller than most, only 22 feet long, but which weighed about 6 tons. Unable to move it, Caillard bequeathed it to the French consul, Bernardino Drovetti. But Drovetti's competitor in the racket of ravaging Egypt for treasures to sell to wealthy antiquarians, the British consul Henry Salt, also got wind of the find and hijacked it. With a wealthy young English antiquarian, William Bankes, an adventurous friend of Byron's, Salt arrived on the scene and arranged with the gigantic Italian explorer and adventurer Giovanni Battista Belzoni, to have the obelisk floated down the Nile so it could be shipped to Bankes's estate in England.

Belzoni's men had built a rough stone causeway from the bank but the weight of the obelisk sank the stones into the mud of the Nile until only the tip was visible above the swirling waters. In despair Belzoni had divers lay heavier stones underwater until the obelisk could be gently levered back onto land. With heavy ropes tied upstream a boat bearing the obelisk was delicately manuevered through the steepest part of the cataract until it shot out into clear water to be safely navigated downstream to Aswan and Alexandria for shipment to England as a successful coup for the British.

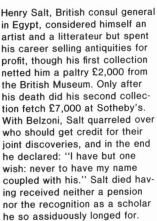

Henry Salt, British consul general in Egypt, considered himself an artist and a litterateur but spent his career selling antiquities for profit, though his first collection netted him a paltry £2,000 from the British Museum. Only after his death did his second collection fetch £7,000 at Sotheby's. With Belzoni, Salt quarreled over who should get credit for their joint discoveries, and in the end he declared: "I have but one wish: never to have my name coupled with his." Salt died having received neither a pension nor the recognition as a scholar he so assiduously longed for.

While Bankes continued up the Nile with an elderly Prussian nobleman, Baron Sack, Belzoni immediately ran into difficulties and nearly lost the obelisk when it got loose and slipped into the Nile, requiring enormous exertion and some sharp engineering to recover. Next he had to float it down the cataracts, a job so dangerous the boat captain buried his head rather than watch. Finally, he had to overcome Drovetti, who did everything in his power to recover the obelisk, including making threats to Belzoni's life. At one point Drovetti even tried to convince a native sharif that the obelisk was his property because the hieroglyphs on it said it had belonged to his family!

The French consul Bernardino Drovetti (seen here with his gang of trusties) was a Piedmontese born in Barbaria who accompanied Napoleon to Egypt as a colonel. Like his great rival Salt, he had difficulty selling his Egyptian loot to Catholic Charles X because it was feared it would show the Egyptian civilization to be older than the 4004 B.C. accepted by theological dogma. Eventually he disposed of it with the Berlin Museum and with the king of Sardinia for the monarch's Turin collection. After 27 years on the Nile, Drovetti ended his days in an asylum for the mad.

The Philae obelisk, which W. J. Bankes financed Salt to steal from Drovetti, as it stands in Kingston Lacy House in Dorset.

In the end Belzoni got the trophy safely to Cairo, where it was shipped to England, to be set up on Bankes's Dorset estate, Kingston Hall, in the presence of Arthur, duke of Wellington. On the base of the obelisk was an inscription in Greek in honor of Ptolemy Euergetes II and of Cleopatra, his wife. Of the two hieroglyphic cartouches, Ptolemy's was immediately recognizable. It was hoped that the other would bear the name of Cleopatra. In 1821 a lithograph was made of both the Greek and the hieroglyphic texts, a copy of which reached Champollion in January 1822. Immediately he recognized the second cartouche as that of Cleopatra, spelled nearly as in the transcript of the demotic name, only more fully. It confirmed for Champollion the value of the letters *polt,* which appear in both *Ptolemy* and *Cleopatra.*

Altogether this gave him fourteen recognized alphabetical signs among the hieroglyphs; but what puzzled Champollion, as it had puzzled Young, was that different signs appeared to express the same sounds, a fact for which neither expert could account. Some signs, like the egg at the end of the Cleopatra cartouche, Champollion realized from other research was simply a designation of the feminine. But he was now convinced that he was on the right track to decipher the lot, and that nothing could stop him. Locked up in what he called his "arsenal" attic studio, he began to apply the system to all the available texts on obelisks. A cartouche from a Karnak obelisk reproduced in the *Description de l'Égypte* quickly gave

170

him ALKSDR, for Alexander. The Barberini obelisk, which had first brought Kircher to Rome, gave him HADRIAN, and SABINA his wife. Furthermore, as the general inscription on the obelisk contained a repeated group of eight letters, obviously a proper name, and since Hadrian's favorite was the youth Antinoüs, Champollion deciphered the name as ANTEINS, proving the stone to have been carved in his memory.

Kircher's next obelisk, the Pamphilian, raised by Bernini in Piazza Novona, referred to VESPASIAN and his son TITUS. Other obelisks of the Roman period carved with hieroglyphs gave Champollion the names of LUCILIUS, SEXTUS, AFRICANUS, TIBERIUS, DOMITIAN, NIRVA, and such titles as CAESAR and AUTOKRATOR. It was now clear that late Egyptians had used phonetic glyphs to spell out foreign names and titles. If only there had been some Egyptian names of pharaohs in the Bible, Champollion mused, he could see if the principle also applied to native pharaohs; but there were none.

Like a caged beast, Champollion paced his arsenal, begging everyone to send him more texts. Then it happened. In September 1822 he received copies of some inscriptions from a French architect, Huyot, who had copied them from the famous rock temple of Abu Simbel between the first and the second cataracts. One of the

Temple of Ramses II at Abu Simbel

171

texts contained a cartouche with a royal name written with the picture of the sun, which Champollion recognized as the glyph for Ra, followed by an unknown sign, ⵮ , like an *m,* and two ⌐ ⌐ . Champollion then found another cartouche with the same ⵮ and ⌐ glyphs preceded by the glyph for an ibis, which he knew to be the representation of the god Thoth. Thus he had the names of two pharaohs: Thoth (⵮⌐) and Ra (⵮⌐⌐), obviously Thothmes and Ramses.

It was a breakthrough. Unmistakably the ancient Egyptians used phonetic glyphs to spell out not only foreign names, but also Egyptian names. Could it be that all of the hieroglyphs were phonetic? It was a step Champollion dared not yet take, though he sensed that success was at hand.

In a fever of excitement, he rushed to the institute, where he threw the papers onto his brother's desk, pronouncing the now famous statement: *"Je tiens l'affaire!"* I've got it! Then his legs buckled and he fell into a coma which lasted three days.

When Champollion recovered, he was able to transcribe the names of a score of ancient Egyptian gods and pharaohs. From the next text given in Greek by Hermapion for the Piazza del Popolo obelisk, brought to Rome by Augustus, and raised by Sixtus V, Champollion deciphered the title *Whom Amon loves,* and established that the Egyptians gave their pharaohs a name and a title in two cartouches joined by the phrase *Child of the Sun.*

Soon he had read fifteen more glyphs of pharaohs going back as far as the eighteenth dynasty. From the Campus Martius obelisk raised by Antinori for Pius VI he got PSMTK for the pharaoh known to the Greeks as PSAMMETICHOS. He also discovered that proper names were followed or preceded by signs indicating a species, such as god or man.

He now had the alphabetical equivalent of twenty-four Egyptian glyphs. But knowing the letters of a language does not mean one can read the language. His only hope was the Coptic connection. Had Coptic not existed, Champollion would have seen no way to reconstruct any of the language other than its personal names and places. But if he could find a group of hieroglyphs that coincided with an ordinary word in Coptic, the meaning of which he knew, he might have a start on the language of ancient Egypt.

Before launching into this strange new world, he decided to announce his limited breakthrough to the Académie des Inscriptions, which he did in a letter, since famous, addressed to its permanent secretary, Dacier. On Septem-

172

ber 22, 1822, under the great cupola of the institute, Champollion gave the substance of his discovery to twenty-five academicians. Each was issued a leaflet with the names of the pharaohs Champollion had deciphered, along with their equivalents in Greek and Coptic, dramatically bringing home to his audience the fact that they were witnessing the beginnings of true Egyptology, a means of opening up the ancient civilization of Egypt.

De Sacy was quick to appreciate and approve Champollion's thesis. But neither Young nor Jomard, both jealous of Champollion, would accept his system of decipherment; they refused to attribute importance to his discovery. In England and Germany, Champollion's translations were rejected out of hand, though few of those who voiced their criticism bothered to test his method on other inscriptions. Only the brothers Humboldt, in Germany, gave Champollion credit for one of the great discoveries of mankind. Finally, Salt, who had helped with the seizure of the Bankes obelisk, admitted that Champollion's system had enabled him to decipher several words.

By this time Champollion was analyzing and translating not only phrases but small inscriptions and whole sentences, proving that the system he had discovered was applicable to the entire body of Egyptian glyphs. These results he wrote up in his *Précis du système hiéroglyphique,* dedicated to Louis XVIII, in which he showed in more than four hundred quarto pages with forty-six plates that the hieroglyphs were both phonetic and ideographic, that some could be read phonetically as letters, others as ideograms—in other words, that some could be used to indicate the object represented, such as a man, or bird, and at other times stand for the alphabetic value of the initial consonant of that Egyptian word. The précis has been called "one of the most important and original works of modern scholarship."

A short while later, a distinguished, well-dressed man called at 28 rue Mazarine and asked to see Champollion. When his sister-in-law asked whom she should announce, she was told: the duke of Blacas, first gentleman-in-waiting to Louis XVIII. Blacas said he had come on behalf of the king to present Champollion with a gold snuff box with his initials in diamonds and the inscription: "From King Louis XVIII to Monsieur Champollion, on the occasion of his discovery of the hieroglyphic alphabet." The king ordered Champollion's précis printed at state expense, and encouraged him to create an Egyptian grammar and a dictionary of hieroglyphs.

With this success Champollion was able to marry and

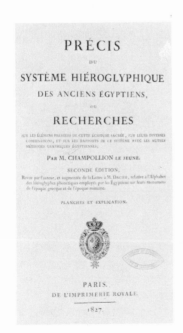

have a daughter, Zoraide, who was born on March 1, 1824. A few weeks later he was received in private audience by Louis XVIII, who asked him to travel to Turin to consult and reorganize three hundred cases of Egyptian antiquities, including two hundred papyri with hieroglyphs and assorted stelae looted in Egypt by the French consul Drovetti and bought by the king of Sardinia for his Turin museum. Champollion was to copy the inscriptions so as to create a more correct version of Egyptian history, and at the same time negotiate in Leghorn for the acquisition for Louis XVIII of the valuable Egyptian antiquities "collected" by Henry Salt.

In September, Louis XVIII died and was succeeded by his reactionary younger brother, the count d'Artois, who came to the throne as Charles X, to set up what Wellington called "a government by priests, through priests, for priests." Luckily, the new king, though violently antirepublican, confirmed Champollion's commission to travel to Italy. In Turin, Champollion made a sensational discovery: the work of Clement of Alexandria, who had

Charles X, brother of Louis XVI, and chief of the ultra-royalist reactionaries at court, passed his youth "in scandalous dissipation" incurring a debt of 56 million francs. Claiming to reign by divine right he threw power into the hands of the extremist Jesuits and declared, "I would rather hew wood than be a king under the conditions of the king of England."

lived about A.D. 200, an expert on "heretics," who may have been an initiate into the "mysteries," and who, by his knowledge of the ancient Egyptians convinced Champollion that all of what passed for Egyptian history would have to be rewritten. He also found the only then known example of a great Egyptian literary work, transmitted directly from the time of the pharaohs: 165 chapters written in pure hieroglyphics. Eventually published as *The Book of the Dead,* it proved to be one of the most vital documents ever discovered in Egypt, and enabled Champollion to begin to tear away the veil from that country's past.

Champollion worked hard at transcribing the glyphs, but his notes for a book were stolen by a fellow researcher, Salvolini, and did not surface till long after Champollion's death. From Piedmont, Champollion went to Rome to study the hieroglyphs on the obelisks there and to make a catalogue of the Egyptian antiquities in the Vatican. Received by Pope Leo XII, he was told that with his discovery, he had done a great service to religion— though not to which.

Back in France, Champollion was awarded the Legion of Honor; he was also named curator of a special Egyptian collection at the Louvre which Charles X wished to form with the cases of antiquities bought from the king of Sardinia. On November 4, 1827, the collection was inaugurated in the presence of Charles X, and opened to the public on Christmas Day. To decorate the entrance of his new museum, the King decided to have an obelisk transported from Alexandria, where Champollion was to travel in order to check out the obelisks there, then mount an expedition to copy and bring back correct drawings of as many Egyptian antiquities as possible.

The young Sagir's dreams had at last come true.

Called *The Book of the Dead* by early Egyptologists, these ancient texts dealing with the awakening of the soul at death are more aptly called *The Book of Coming into Light.*

175

9. CHAMPOLLION PARTS THE VEIL OF ISIS

On July 31, 1828, Champollion sailed from Toulon on the frigate *l'Egle* with seven young French artists and one medical doctor, Pariset. At Civitavecchia they were joined by a group of five Italians sent by the duke of Tuscany under twenty-eight-year-old Ippolito Rosellini, an Egyptologist and professor of languages at Pisa. The Italians were to help Champollion transcribe inscriptions and make drawings of temples and monuments. As the group approached Alexandria, their ship was caught in a storm and several of the adventurers, fearing *l'Egle* would sink, put messages in bottles and tossed them overboard. Then the sea calmed, and early on the morning of August 18, they spotted the landmarks of Alexandria: Pompey's Pillar, and close by, the standing silhouette of Cleopatra's Needle. Champollion jumped ashore and kissed the soil of Egypt.

His first endeavor was to copy the inscriptions from the second of the obelisks raised by Augustus in front of the Caesarium which had fallen beside its still standing neighbor, Cleopatra's needles, and required excavation from the sand. From its inscriptions, Champollion concluded that both it and its companion had once stood before the Temple of Thothmes in Heliopolis. But why the obelisks had stood in pairs, he could not fathom.

Drovetti, who had done all he could to prevent Champollion from coming to Egypt because he was afraid the visitors might constitute a danger to his various looting schemes, now refused to take responsibility for their expedition. Nonetheless, he was obliged by orders from Paris to take them to see the khedive or viceroy of Egypt, Mohammed Ali.

When the British left Egypt in 1803, such chaos had followed, with rampant plundering and assassinations, that the religious leaders in Alexandria had appealed to Mohammed Ali, commander of the Turkish troops in Egypt, to restore law and order. A reliably cruel and unscrupulous tyrant from the hills of Albania, he did just that, seizing the opportunity to establish a certain independence from his Ottoman masters. By treacherously murdering the entire corps of the Sultan's Mameluke beys, he turned the Ottoman province of Egypt into what amounted to his own independent state, one in which foreigners could vie to

Denon, in the Louvre, among the treasures looted by the French in Egypt

177

Mohammed Ali, a converted Christian orphan from Macedonia, wished to bring Western technology to Egypt, harness the Nile for agriculture, and introduce industrial manufactures into Egypt. He was in no way interested in ancient temples except to use their beautifully hewn blocks to build factories that would never go into production. His prime addiction was to the pleasures of his harem of five hundred lovely women—two hundred in Alexandria, three hundred in Cairo.

On the eastern point of Phoros stood the great lighthouse, first of the Seven Wonders of the World, reputedly as high as the Washington Monument. Begun by the first Ptolemy, it was completed by the second. Originally an island, the point was later joined to the mainland by a half-mile mole called the *hepastadion,* six stadia long. At the head of the mole stood the Temple of Hephaestus, and behind the emporium the great Caesarium with its two guardian obelisks.

Palace of the khedive

invest, and where their consuls as virtual ambassadors could collaborate with the autonomous viceroy in looting the country.

On August 24, in the very hottest days of summer, Consul Drovetti came with horse and carriage to fetch Champollion and the captain of *l'Egle* to meet Mohammed Ali. The rest of the party followed on donkeys. To Champollion the sumptuousness of the pasha's palace, on the peninsula of Pharos where the great Alexandrine lighthouse had stood, came as a shock because of its stunning contrast with the poverty of the people in the streets.

Mohammed Ali, then 60 years old, with a long white beard, received the Frenchmen in one of the cool rooms of the palace, seated between two windows, dressed in a simple robe. Of medium height and cheerful countenance, his eyes full of vivacity, the Pasha smoked a long pipe decorated with diamonds as he asked Champollion about the sort of voyage they planned. Champollion replied that all his life he had dreamed of visiting this most beautiful of countries, and that to read the hieroglyphs and rediscover the ancient history of Egypt, he wished to go as far up the Nile as the second cataract, studying the ancient sites along the way.

Mohammed Ali stroked his beard and offered them coffee. To show that he was privy to what was going on, he remarked that everyone seemed to be trying to prevent the voyage. "They don't want you to see too many antiquities too close," he said with a wry smile. "But don't worry, I'll give you a *firman* [a passport], and two of my personal body guards." All he asked in return was a translation of the inscriptions on the Alexandrine obelisks, which Champollion, working all through the night, delivered the following morning.

Typical Nile boat

Thanks to the pasha's support, Champollion was able to bypass Drovetti and rent the largest and best equipped boat on the Nile, the *Isis*. As they set sail, Champollion felt he was reliving the dreams of his youth. "Everywhere I go," he wrote in his diary, "and everywhere I look, everything I touch is like renewing acquaintance with things I have known and loved all my life." Between Alexandria and Cairo he followed the map drawn by the editors of the *Description de l'Égypte,* carefully correcting the names of the towns which the members of Napoleon's expedition, in their ignorance of either the Egyptian or the Coptic language, had misnamed or misplaced.

In Cairo, as he wandered through the twisted streets, stopping from bazaar to bazaar, Champollion found himself back in the world of *A Thousand and One Nights.* He had grown a long handlebar moustache, and shaved his head, which he covered with an enormous brightly colored turban. At his side hung a large scimitar. With his dark skin and extraordinary command of the language, he passed easily for an Arab. Eyeing his companions, dressed in native pantaloons and bright brocade, with the yellow pointed boots much favored by rich Turks and Egyptians, Champollion said with satisfaction: "I am a completely new person! I don't feel tired as I did in Paris." Much taken with the beauty of the native females, he describes in detail the erotic dances of the ubiquitous *aalmas,* or dancing girls, but gives no details of his own amorous adventures.

179

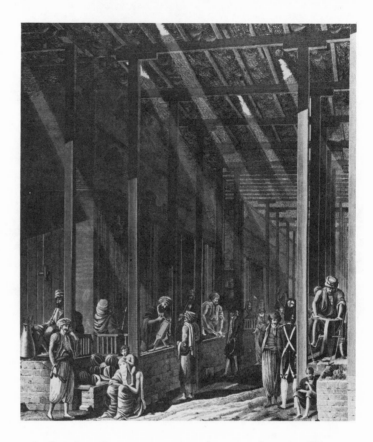

Cairo bazaar

In October the group prepared to travel up the Nile aboard the *Isis*. At Memphis, where, according to the Rosetta Stone, King Ptolemy V Epiphanes had been deified, Champollion correctly classified architecture of different epochs by a mere glance at the ruins. As the group roamed about, sketching and measuring, or copying inscriptions, the natives who followed them laughed at these people "who could read stones."

Sakkara, with its ancient stepped pyramid, they found largely destroyed, plundered for building material for the pasha's palaces at El Difdjar. Everywhere they went, they saw that agents of antiquities dealers such as Salt and Drovetti had ruined the sites, rendering them impossible to study. Tombs had been devastated, pillaged, and refilled. Fragments of mummies had been scattered so profusely they made what Champollion called "a plain of mummies."

At Antinoe, rebuilt by Hadrian for his boyfriend, they found nothing left of the beautiful monuments described and drawn by the members of the Commission de l'Égypte: the inhabitants had destroyed and burned the limestone blocks to extract the lime. Little was left standing other than the indestructible granite columns.

Since the Renaissance, Egyptian graves had been systematically robbed to provide Italian cardinals with private collections. By the time Richard Pococke, a British traveler, visited Egypt in 1737, he complained, "They are every day destroying these fine morsels of Egyptian Antiquity; and I saw some of the pillars being hewn into millstones." Champollion saw that thousands of movable objects were being exported by collectors, dealers, tourists, and unscrupulous consular agents such as Salt and Drovetti, subjecting Egypt to an orgy of destruction. Not only amulets, scarabs, papyri and whole mummies were being taken, but entire rooms, freizes, and tombs were stripped and shipped.

Still, Champollion was able to buy a heavy granite head of Ramses II for one piastre, and make the owner drag it himself to the boat.

At the end of October they arrived at Esna, where they wanted to visit the temple on the west side of the river, greatly admired by the Commission de l'Égypte. Too late. Twelve days before their arrival, the temple had been pulled down by the pasha to strengthen a quay on the river. Luckily the temple of Esna has been spared as a

Temple of Esne

181

storehouse for government cotton; but Champollion found its decadent Ptolemeic sculpture quite detestable.

At Armant he described the temple, and copied many of its reliefs—which was lucky, for it was later in the century destroyed by the viceroy Said for stones to construct a sugar factory. Denderah they encountered by moonlight.

At Denderah they found six rooms within the thickness of the walls, and six more underground, access to which was very difficult as the passages were full of bats and there was little air. The walls and the colossal columns were covered with scenes in relief, including a great zodiac painted in two bands along the ceiling of the portico. The famous ceiling zodiac had already been blasted out with dynamite in a cops-and-robbers duel between Salt and Drovetti, and shortly thereafter a quarter of the temple was quarried away for a saltpeter factory.

Without native guards, but well provided with arms, they set off through the night, singing arias from the latest operas as they marched to find the temple, most likely from Rossini's *Semiramide* which had premiered a few years earlier.

When the temple loomed before them, bathed in soft moonlight, they saw that it was the best-preserved structure they had yet encountered. To enter its vast halls they lit torches, which revealed hundreds, even thousands, of inscriptions, from which Champollion deduced that the temple was not dedicated to Isis, as everyone maintained, but to Hathor, whom he identified with Venus or Aphrodite, the goddess of mirth and love. Champollion saw that two pharaohs of the New Kingdom, Thothmes III and Ramses II, had added to the original construction, as had succeeding monarchs down to the Ptolemites, followed by the Romans, the last deducible from the carved names of Augustus and Antonius.

At El Kab they went ashore to see the temple, but found it, too, had disappeared, destroyed by Mohammed Ali, as were the two temples of Amenophis III and Thothmes II, of which nothing was left but the drawing done by the commission. In November the party reached Karnak at Thebes, where they visited the Temple of Seti I, the

These seated colossi on the plain of Gournah, across from Luxor, were identified by Greeks with Memnon, a mythical king of Ethiopia, known as "Son of the Dawn." The statues were renowned for giving off harplike sounds at dawn (apparently caused by expansion of the stones in the morning sun); but the Persian troops of Cambyses, curious to know what made the giants howl, broke up the stones. They were further damaged by an earthquake in Roman times. Egyptologists saw in the statues representations of Amenophis III (or Menephtah), son and successor to Ramses II, which had once stood before his mortuary temple, already destroyed in Augustus's time. Champollion found their bases covered by 15 feet of accumulated dirt. Later measurements showed that the bases were linked by cubit and proportion to the king's chamber in the Pyramid of Cheops.

Memnon Colossi, and the Ramesseum; but Champollion, seeing that "it would take a lifetime to copy all the glyphs," decided to spend more time on his return.

Further up the Nile, at Edfu, he found an immense and magnificent temple also dedicated to Hathor and to her mate, Har-Hat, the personification of celestial science and light, whose son Hawsont-Tho Champollion considered the equivalent of Eros, or "love," in the Greek myths. Sculptured representations of the three divinities, with qualifications and titles, threw a new light for him on the Egyptians' theogonic system, or genealogy of gods. At Abydos, Champollion found dynastic sites mixed in whith those of the Greco-Roman period, all badly ravaged by vandals. Sliding almost naked on his belly to enter the buried interior passages of temples, he nearly stifled, but obtained some extraordinary drawings. Found lying in a dead faint in one of the tombs, he joked on reviving that he "needed complete silence in order to hear the voices of his ancestors." On the walls of an ancient tomb he found more than a hundred different kinds of birds carefully depicted, and more than a dozen different dogs, several not native to Egypt.

The Temple of Edfu with its two immense pylons half-buried in the sand, rebuilt in the Ptolemaic era at the end of the first millennium B.C. Champollion deciphered glyphs on its walls dating back to the third millenium B.C.

At the first cataract, the group had to abandon the *Isis* and proceed to the second cataract in three small barques lent them by the commander of the province of Esne. Champollion was excited to see Philae, the lovely island where the Bankes obelisk had been discovered. From the river it appeared unspoiled, with temples and colonnades overgrown with fragrant tropical plants, shaded by tall palm trees. But they soon found that Christians, with hammer and chisel, and in the name of God, had ruthlessly obliterated inscriptions and friezes on the porticos of the Temple of Isis, lopping off heads, hands, feet, and phalli.

In Nubia, in the Temple of Kalabschi, Champollion got a better insight into the basic religion of the ancient Egyptians. He saw that Amon-Ra, their supreme and primordial being, was not only his own father, but husband to his mother, the goddess Mouth—that is, the feminine portion contained within himself, at the same time male and female—and that all the other Egyptian gods were merely forms of these two principal constituents. Most important, Champollion found that no matter how far back he went into Egyptian history, the people had been highly civilized, possessing hieroglyphs, mathematics, music, and an understanding of embalming. There seemed to be no beginning. Only under the Ptolemites had they become decadent. By this time Champollion had the long black beard of a Capucin monk, and had assumed the dress of a desert Arab, eating pilaf with his fingers, smoking three pipes a day, and keeping healthy by drinking nothing but Nile

water, possibly on the advice of his predecessor up the river, that intrepid seventeenth-century traveler responsible with Francis Bacon for organizing a New Atlantis in Virginia, George Sandys, who recommended Nile water "for it procureth liberal urine, cureth the dolour of the reins, and is most sovereign against the windy melancholy arising from the shorter ribs, which so saddeth the mind of the diseased."

Nubia, for Champollion, grew desolate, with crocodiles asleep on the sandbars, and unexpectedly cold at night.

Reading the stones

Crossing the Tropic of Cancer in January 1829, Champollion complained that he almost froze. So they turned back, also because Drovetti had held up their mail and the money due Champollion.

Slowly coming back down the Nile, the party stopped and made careful drawings and notes of hieroglyphs on all the temples they could find, "hoping to bring back all of Egypt in our portfolios." This time they stayed seven months in Thebes, which Champollion described as the most magnificent work produced by the hand of man, the grandest and the most marvelous. No nation on earth, he concluded, either ancient or modern, had ever conceived architecture so noble, and on such a scale. "The Egyptians of old," he said to Rosellini, "thought like men a hundred feet tall. We in Europe are but Lilliputians."

Hypostyle temple of Esne

In Thebes, Champollion learned that a British engineer in Alexandria was studying the means of removing to England the recumbent obelisk which Mohammed Ali had now donated to the British. To Drovetti he wrote that he was delighted the Englishman wished to waste his country's money on removing such an inferior obelisk. Instead he recommended that if France were to put up an obelisk in Paris, it should be a Theban one. To his brother in Paris he described in detail just how the obelisks could be felled and dragged to the river, and told him that the natives could be hired for a few sous and the sharifs easily bribed, especially one—"who had the soul of a Frenchman." Champollion pleaded with his brother to convince the French government to increase the budget for the extra cost of transporting one or even both Theban obelisks. "It would not be amiss to put before the eyes of the nation such a monument, so as to disgust it with the knickknacks [*colifichets*] and gewgaws [*fanfreluches*] which we call public monuments, veritable boudoir trinkets, perfectly suited to our great men, and worthy of architects who are but meticulous imitators of all the poverty of the Bas Empire."

In Cairo, Champollion was amiably received by Mohammed Ali at a palace luncheon, where they met the pasha's adopted son, Ibrahim, a pockmarked man of forty, who suddenly fell to the floor stricken by an attack of apoplexy. Mohammed Ali, thinking his son had died, allowed his eyes to fill with tears. But Dr. Pariset rushed to Ibrahim's side, and the pasha was amazed to see his son revive. Thereafter he treated both Frenchmen with extraordinary regard, and would talk to them for hours, saying: "One of you has restored the life of my son, the other has restored the glory of my country."

Before bidding them farewell, the pasha asked Champollion to write for him a short history of ancient Egypt from all of the new inscriptions he had copied, and this

Champollion did, pleading in return that the pasha forbid further destruction of Egypt's ancient monuments and prohibit the export of its valuable antiquities, requests which the pasha eventually incorporated into a decree. Not that Champollion let the decree affect his own immediate export of all that he and his group had collected.

Back in Alexandria in September, Champollion became friendly with a young naval lieutenant, Raimond Jean Baptiste de Verninac Saint-Maur, commander of the corvette *Astrolabe,* which was to take the party and all its loot back to France in November. Finding in Verninac a fellow Bonapartist, Champollion plotted with him the means of bringing back to France one of the Theban obelisks, which they hoped to have raised in memory of Napoleon's conquest of Egypt.

On December 6, 1829, after a year and almost four months in Egypt, Champollion sailed from Alexandria on the *Astrolabe,* with an enormous collection of notes and sketches, plus two thousand pages of hieroglyphic inscriptions, entirely transcribed by hand. He also had notes on all the monuments still standing along the Nile from the Pyramids to the second cataract, reproduced with great fidelity. Fifteen hundred drawings, many colored *in situ,* had corrected virtually everything published in the *Description de l'Égypte,* whose sketches, though esthetic, turned out to have been lamentably inexact, some of the inscriptions, in Champollion's opinion, having evidently been invented by a doubting or lazy draftsman who could not believe that the hieroglyphs would ever be deciphered.

Champollion arrived in Toulon just before Christmas, to find the port in great turmoil, preparing for an expedition against the Barbary pirates of Algiers, to which his new friend Lieutenant Verninac was promptly assigned.

In Paris, Champollion found his brother at a new address, by the Bibliothèque Royale (now Nationale), to which he had been appointed curator. As a present, the young Champollion had brought him a small piece of crocodile meat, too far gone to be eaten. Figeac had duly passed on all of Champollion's recommendations about bringing back the Luxor obelisks, and the minister of the navy had been quick to support the notion, going so far as to suggest the commissioning of a special vessel to do the job; but, being the same Baron d'Haussez who had gotten Champollion into trouble as a Bonapartist in 1815, the minister intended to see that Champollion was cut out of the picture and take for himself all the glory of the

188

project, a feat he managed to accomplish so successfully that in the two volumes of d'Haussez's memoirs, Champollion is not even named.

With Drovetti (who also hated Champollion), d'Haussez organized a committee which obtained from Charles X the order to bring back to France not only the two Theban obelisks standing before the Temple of Luxor but also Cleopatra's Needle and its recumbent partner in Alexandria. To negotiate with Mohammed Ali the cession to France of the Luxor obelisks, d'Haussez decided to send a special envoy to Alexandria. As a suitable ambassador, because of his taste in art and letters, and because he had traveled widely in the Near East, d'Haussez selected the king's commissioner to the Théâtre Français, Baron Isidore Taylor, who had been aide-de-camp to General d'Orsay during the Spanish campaign against Wellington. To advise on the engineering problems of removing the obelisks, Taylor was to take with him a French naval engineer, Lefebure de Serisy, who had recently served as Mohammed Ali's adviser in reconstructing the Egyptian fleet, destroyed two years earlier in the Battle of Navarino when British, French, and Russian squadrons had defeated the Turks and established the independence of Greece.

In May 1830, Taylor and Serisy sailed from Toulon with an initial purse of $20,000 for expenses, plus various presents to entice the Egyptian viceroy. Among these, for propaganda purposes, was a richly bound folio edition of the twenty-volume *Description de l'Égypte.* There were also some socially prized items such as Sèvres porcelains, cut glass, and table crystal, as well as items considered suitable to an oriental potentate, such as arms, helmets, and breastplates. On the recommendation of Consul Drovetti, some artificial pieces of anatomy were included for the school of medicine in Cairo.

Arriving in Alexandria, Taylor found that Mohammed Ali was still in his winter palace in Cairo. He was received instead by Ibrahim, who gave the baron a stunning piece of bad news. The French had been so tardy in removing Cleopatra's Needle that it had been given away, after much soliciting, to the British consul, Mr. Barker. Upset, and in receipt of urgent requests for his return to Paris from the intendant of the king's household, who complained that his absence was prejudicing the success of the Théâtre Français, Taylor nevertheless decided to try to salvage the situation by awaiting the arrival of Mohammed Ali.

After lingering another month in Cairo, the pasha at last

Karnak, slightly north of Luxor, consisted of a group of temples occupying about 150 acres, its walls covered with intaglios of the god Amon and scenes of pharaonic splendor. It was the national shrine of Egypt for more than two thousand years. The great obelisk in the foreground was raised by Thothmes I. Other, smaller obelisks were raised by Hatshepsut and Ramses II.

turned up, sufficiently mollified by the French diplomat's manner and by his lovely presents to reverse his decision, reconfirming to Charles X of France the gift of Cleopatra's Needle. As a bonus he added both the Luxor obelisks. Mr. Barker was to be assuaged with what the pasha considered an equitable solution: an offer to the British of quite another prize, the great obelisk of Queen Hatshepsut still standing in the Temple of Karnak—the pasha being convinced that the British could never remove it.

Taylor wrote at once to Paris that the Alexandrian and Luxor obelisks were now the property of Charles X. But by July, events in France had taken a turn. News reached Alexandria of a three-day revolution in Paris which had forced the reactionary Charles X, King of France, to abdicate in favor of the bourgeois Louis Philippe, King of the French, helped into power by a conspiracy of Masons. Mohammed Ali changed his mind and refused to allow the embarkation of Cleopatra's Needle onto the ship *Dromadaire,* specially sent out by d'Haussez. Mr. Barker, seizing the advantage, quickly conceived a plan to remove the obelisk to England, placing several of the pasha's agents in his pay.

Taylor did his best to convince Mohammed Ali that nothing was fundamentally changed in France by the revolution, that the gift had not been to the person of the king, but to the nation, to the people of France. Mohammed Ali pondered, and finally changed his mind, reconfirming the gift to the government of Louis Philippe "in gratitude to France for numerous tokens of favor and friendship," but mostly in the hope of obtaining naval equipment for his infant Egyptian navy.

By this time Taylor had learned that there was no hope of getting heavy timbers from Caramanie in Cyprus needed to load the Alexandrine obelisk, so he decided to return to France to speed up the building of a special vessel to fetch the Luxor obelisks before there were any more changes of mind. In Paris, Taylor found that d'Haussez had fled to England, accused with several of his colleagues of being responsible for the reactionary ordinances which had brought about the revolution of July. His successor at the naval ministry, General Horace Sébastiani, had, however, been on a mission to Egypt under the consulate, and saw no reason to change the arrangements for the obelisks made by d'Haussez. Only there was no ship in the French navy capable of sailing 1,800 leagues across the Mediterranean, 200 leagues up the shallow Nile to Thebes, then back again loaded with a single 250-ton obelisk, let alone one capable of facing the contrary winds of the Atlantic's Bay of Biscay before being towed past the low and narrow bridges of the Seine all the way to Paris.

Such a ship would have to be specially designed and built, breaking all the rules of naval architecture. In order to hold an 80-foot obelisk, the ship would have to be at least 100 feet long. To sail the Atlantic it would have to be well keeled. To sail up the Seine it could be no wider than 25 feet. To cross the sandbanks at the mouth of the

Nile it would have to be as flat-keeled as possible, yet sturdy enough to be beached on the banks of the Nile and receive a load of 250 tons. For such an extraordinary craft it was decided to lay five separate keels specially reinforced with extra strutting to spread the weight of the obelisk evenly over its bottom.

As a name for this novel ship, the one which Champollion had originally suggested, the unnovel *Luxor,* remained. And now that d'Haussez was gone he was also able to suggest as captain Lieutenant Verninac Saint-Maur, who had just distinguished himself in the French operations against Algiers by bringing back in the *Astrolabe* 10 million French francs in gold looted from the Casbah.

No sooner had Verninac deposited the gold in the French treasury than he heard of his appointment as captain of the *Luxor.* Verninac took over his new command with some doubts as to its seaworthiness, and immediately lightened its load by ordering a reduction of most of its armament. As a second-in-command, Verninac selected another young naval officer, Lieutenant M. de Joannis. Three more officers were to command a crew of 136 sailors, along with two naval surgeons, Dr. Angelin and Dr. Pons.

To handle the actual operations of felling the obelisks, the maritime prefect of Toulon recommended a diminutive naval engineer with the appropriate name of Lebas. Monsieur Jean Baptiste Apollinaire Lebas's orders were to fell the right-hand obelisk facing the palace at Luxor, as selected by Champollion, and embark it on the ship. During the felling and embarkation, Lebas was to be in sole command; otherwise command rested with Verninac. To help Lebas with his job, he was allowed to select from the Toulon base a master carpenter with assistants, smiths, caulkers, jointers, stone cutters, and several first-rate boatswains.

While Verninac loaded the ship with a year's worth of supplies, including pistols, sabers, rifles, and ammunition, Lebas loaded equipment necessary to lower the obelisk, including several 50-foot beams almost 2 feet in diameter, forty 16-inch boards of the same length, and 4 inches thick, 1,200 meters of rope as thick as a man's arm, 400 meters as thick as a man's leg, several heavy capstans, block and tackle, pulleys, and a forge. Lebas was empowered to hire as many men ashore as he needed for the job, payments for whom would be provided by the new French consul in Alexandria, M. Mimaut, who had replaced Champollion's enemy Drovetti.

On April 13, 1831, fully loaded, the *Luxor* sailed from Toulon with a favorable breeze, carrying a band of adventurers who hoped to duplicate an engineering feat which had not been accomplished since the time of the Romans—the removal to Europe of one of the great Egyptian obelisks. As the extraordinary vessel passed the boom, all the ships of the French navy lined up in Toulon harbor sounded general quarters. Toulonnais massed on the quays waved handkerchiefs; mothers, sisters, and sweethearts dabbed their eyes.

10. BOURGEOIS ADVENTURERS

With the wind either abeam or astern, the *Luxor* breezed along at a comfortable 8 knots, but it was soon clear to Captain Verninac that she was not a seaworthy craft. When the wind shifted to the east, obliging him to sail close-hauled, the keels would not hold, and the *Luxor* progressed sideways like a crab. Hit by a storm, the ship was unmanageable. As the storm died, Verninac realized that for the return trip with the obelisk aboard, he would have to have one of the navy's newfangled steamships tow him to Toulon.

On May 3, at dawn, the sandy dunes of Africa appeared against the blue sky above Pointe d'Aboukir, reminding the crew nostalgically of both Bonaparte's victory on land and of Admiral Brueis's disastrous defeat in the bay. At 10:00 A.M., the ancient landmarks of Alexandria—for both sailor and bedouin—Pompey's Pillar and Cleopatra's Needle, appeared on the horizon, and the *Luxor* anchored in Alexandria harbor opposite the sparkling white palace of

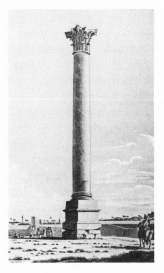

Pompey's Pillar

the viceroy of Egypt, Mohammed Ali Pasha, and Captain Verninac went ashore to call on the khedive's son Ibrahim, whose prime preoccupation at that time was the instant recruitment of an army with which to attack his Ottoman masters, who had insulted his father.

When Mohammed Ali and his suite arrived at the palace, Verninac, Lebas, and Angelin, all in full French naval uniform with huge epaulettes and fore-and-aft hats, were received by His Highness in the large hall with arched porticoes and thick Turkish carpets. Raising himself on his cushions, pipe in hand, Mohammed Ali asked for the engineer Lebas, as if he were so small he could not see him. Laughing at his own joke, the pasha then honored Lebas by asking him to sit beside him and tell

him all about the problems of the obelisk. Captivated by the pasha's deep probing eyes, Lebas, as he later recounted in his report on the operation, listened carefully to "His Highness' refined, perspicacious, and profound ideas."

Mohammed Ali, as he had done for Champollion, graciously accorded the expedition a *firman* for free circulation in all his states, plus the protection of two janissaries to see that his *firman* was obeyed. He ordered that everything possible be done to facilitate the enterprise, even producing for the French, as dragoman, or guide, an ex-Frenchman who had stayed in Egypt after Napoleon and had adopted the oriental name of Youssouf Kachef, an exotic fellow who spoke excellent Arabic, and knew most of the sheikhs up the Nile.

Alexandria, at the extreme western edge of the Nile Delta, was not on an actual estuary of the Nile. The main mouth of the great river emptied into the Mediterranean just north of the town of Rosetta. Navigation on this estuary was only possible for the *Luxor* at floodtime, which would come toward the end of June, a month or more away; and even so, shifting sandbanks blocked the mouth, which became most dangerous when whipped by sudden winds. The *Luxor's* third mate, Midshipman Juarez, sent ahead to the mouth of the Nile to sound out the depth of the sandbars, returned with a competent pilot.

At dawn on June 11, Lebas set off with a flotilla of small flat-bottomed barques called *dgermes,* loaded with the heavy equipment from the *Luxor,* heading across Aboukir Bay for the westernmost mouth of the Nile, about 12 leagues east of Alexandria. As the water at the mouth of the Nile was 6 feet deep over the sandbars, and the *Luxor* drew 8½ feet, Verninac had been obliged to lighten the ship to the utmost, and as it could no longer sail on the open sea on its own without ballast it had to be towed by a French thirty-cannon brig, the *d'Assas,* which opportunely appeared in Alexandria harbor.

Lebas, in his *dgerme,* noticed the sea was taking on a
yellowish tint. From the frown on the pilot's face, he
concluded they were approaching the mouth of the Nile.
Small mounds of sand appeared on the surface of the
water, forming sinuous passages of unequal depth, wide
enough for the small boat to negotiate, but difficult for the
Luxor. To guide the *Luxor* through the treacherous sandbars Verninac had found a single-toothed Arab pilot who
had spent a lifetime negotiating what the Turks called the
boghaz, or narrow maritime passages. At daybreak on the
seventeenth, the *Luxor,* cast adrift from the *d'Assas,*
headed for the *boghaz.* Small boats lined each side of the
narrow frothy passage, which continued to shift under the
impact of waves, current, and a stiff breeze. On the way
through, Verninac caught sight of the wreck of a ship
which had missed the passage and been battered against
the banks. Moments later, a heavy shock signaled that all
five keels had struck bottom. If the *Luxor* could not
surmount the bank, she risked being caught by the sands
and held for the rest of the year, putting a quietus on the
whole expedition.

Heavy waves raised and lowered the ship. Sails
strained in the quickening breeze. With a groaning lurch,
the ship was carried across the barrier into what Verninac
described as "the tranquil waters of the most beautiful of
rivers." The Arabs shouted hurrahs. Cannons from the
Turkish forts guarding each side of the mouth fired a
welcome. Unable to respond with salvos, because they

197

had dismantled all their guns, Verninac flew pennants and made up for his apparent rudeness by a donation of Bordeaux and Champagne to the local Turkish garrison.

There was a brilliant sun. The sky was alive with swallows and terns. Broad-beaked pelicans circled overhead as the ship slid slowly past an island which had not been there when Napoleon had charted the area thirty years before. Along the banks of the river, date palms framed a delightful panorama where the Rosetta Stone had been discovered. On the gently flowing Nile, the *Luxor* was a novelty. Natives ran from their cottonfields and rice paddies to stand at the river's edge and admire the mountainous ship. Children left their sheep and buffalos unherded to stare in wonder at what they called a floating mosque.

Three hours later the *Luxor* anchored off the actual town of Rosetta, surrounded by a cool green landscape. It was explained to the Frenchmen that many of the town's lovely houses were uninhabited since the newly dredged Mahmudi Canal, shorter and safer, had siphoned off traffic directly from the Nile to Alexandria, leaving Rosetta commercially high and dry. While the *Luxor* waited for the waters of the Nile to rise sufficiently for it to proceed upstream, Verninac and his crew were able to enjoy Rosetta and its surrounding wonderland of orange groves, banana plantations, and cool shady gardens lined by avenues of sycamores.

The town of Rosetta on the east Nile

But Lebas could not linger. He had to reach Thebes in time to dig a berth for the ship on the riverbank, as close to the obelisk as possible, so that the *Luxor* could be floated over it at floodtime and be left in a level drydock when the waters eventually withdrew.

There were four types of boats on the Nile: the *dgermes*, with large lateen sails, svelte enough to scoot up the river in any season; *agabas*, heavy flatbottomed barges, drawing very little water, used for towing supplies when the waters were at their lowest; the *masch*, known as the storeship of the Nile, a craft of 400 to 500 tons, used to sail only during the inundation of the river; and *canges*, narrow boats, light and elegant, with the fine lines of a yacht.

Midshipman Juarez and surgeon Pons, with ten sailors and a detail of sixteen carpenters, smithies, and stone cutters, were to go ahead to Cairo, 40 leagues up the river in a mixed flotilla of native boats loaded with equipment.

Lebas, Juarez, and Pons boarded a light *cange,* which could travel speedily either by sail or by scull, and installed themselves on the stern, where a small superstructure had been divided into two rooms—a messroom and sleeping quarters.

On July 19 the whole flotilla abandoned the *Luxor* off Rosetta and set sail for Cairo. As Lebas put it, "All was new to us, the countryside, the trees, plants, costumes, and the language of the Arabs." Avidly taking stock of the varied products, many of them unknown in France, the Frenchmen let their eyes wander happily over the passing delta. The banks were bordered with flowering hedgerows, forests of date palms, and fragrant mimosa. Beyond the fertile fields, a wasteland of desert stretched to the horizon.

Here and there the Frenchmen spotted land, once fertile, which had fallen into the most depressing poverty. Nearby villages lay in ruins, replaced by hovels of sun-dried mud, roofed over with palm fronds. They noted that despite the fertility of the delta, the Arab population appeared to be miserable and half-starved, lining the riverbanks to implore assistance, displaying their naked half-starved children. Everywhere the Arab men were covered with rags, prematurely aged by ill-treatment and privation. The only social institution appeared to Lebas to be the caprice of the Turk, who could have any Arab lashed on any pretext with a *courbache,* or heavy whip of hippopotamus hide.

199

On the roof of every house or hut Lebas was surprised to see a pigeon coop, from which at dawn myriad of pigeons would fly out, darkening the sky, and return at noon to rest through the heat of the day. No one seemed to shoot or eat these birds; they were raised solely for their excrement, a powerful fertilizer for field and garden.

At Abou Mandour they passed a famous mosque where female pilgrims came to perpetuate their bondage by obtaining fertility from the waters of a reportedly magic fountain. Every evening Lebas and his colleagues would go ashore to study the manners and customs of the people, whom they were surprised to find essentially gay, despite the ever-present threat of the *courbache.* The curious natives stared at the Frenchmen's clothes and asked many questions.

By day Lebas would flit from bank to bank of the Nile in his light *cange,* trying to keep the Arabs, with their heavier *agabas,* constantly on the move. Like a cabby with a tourist, the river captains, or *reis,* of the *agabas,* would take the longest time, dallying wherever possible to increase their salaries, running onto sandbanks they could easily have avoided. At one point there was a near disaster when one of the grounded *agabas* sprung a leak and threatened to wet and ruin the heavy cordage needed for lowering the obelisk. Luckily the French sailors saved the day by using their leather hats, or *bousingots*, to bail the leaking craft long enough to remove the cordage.

Eleven days after leaving Rosetta, Lebas reached Cairo and complained to the Turkish governor about the malingering of river *reis*. The Turks forthwith produced the *courbache,* and it was all Lebas could do to insist that he wanted efficiency, not punishment. With a shrug the Turks assigned to him four janissaries, whose job was to keep the river captains on the mark.

Cairo from the river

They also visited the nearby plain of Memphis, where Menes, the reputed founder of the First Dynasty, is said to have changed the course of the Nile. There also his great capital city had once stood, described for the Frenchmen by Herodotus and Strabo; but the Frenchmen found only rubbled ruins among the date palms. In the evening they walked to where their *cange* was moored in sight of the earliest known pyramid, the Stepped Pyramid of Saqqarah, said to have been built for King Soser of the Third Dynasty by Imhotep, the most renowned of architects in ancient Egypt.

At Cairo, the lower-river pilots were replaced by upper-river pilots. These were of a different race, called Barbarin, the inhabitants of lower Nubia, darker-skinned, more supple in their movements, with a grace which Lebas found almost pretentious. Their faces were more like those sculptured on the monuments of ancient Egypt, their voices softer and fluted, ending in sharp notes as they spoke a dialect quite different from the Arabic of the delta.

Before starting upriver, Lebas and his companions left Cairo for a short visit to the pyramids of Giza.

The pyramids of Ghiza seen from the Nile

201

Everything that Lebas saw of ancient Egypt was a pleasure to him. He found his eye lighting agreeably upon the forests of columns in the temples because their number and size were harmoniously designed for the heavy roof they were intended to bear. The plans of the buildings he found simple and precise, and therefore easy to comprehend. Egyptian paintings, reliefs, and sculpture he found charming and extraordinarily descriptive, the figures admirably expressing the passions and pains which animated them. So deeply was he affected by what he saw, he found it difficult to tear himself away from the hypnotic lure of the amazing ruins.

Sailing up the Nile is favored in July by the northwest or northeast winds, which predominate throughout the period of inundation. With the wind abeam or astern the sails could easily overcome the current, except where the river looped so widely that the wind came head-on. There the Arab sailors would jump ashore and pull the *cange* with heavy lines, cadencing their footsteps with a song. As they moved further south, on either side of the Nile the plains began to be bordered with limestone mountains from whose flanks the stones of the Great Pyramids had been quarried. Here the progress of the boat was slow enough for Lebas and his colleagues to take short excursions into the Arabian hills, where the ancient monuments attracted them, temples they knew from Denon's beautiful etchings and from those of the *Description de l'Égypte.*

Lebas found the heat of Upper Egypt stifling and nearly insupportable for a European. The Frenchmen constantly quenched their thirst with water from the Nile and took advantage of every cooling breeze caught between the riverbanks, which at some points rose to high peaks where the river cut between the Libyan and Arabian chains. Sailing in the evening, refreshed by the northwest breeze, was pleasantest. As the Nile below the cataracts is bereft of rocks, there was little danger of nocturnal mishaps. Stars, barely visible in Europe, sparkled brightly in a deep blue sky, while the Arab sailors, bunched around the mainmast, chanted nostalgic songs.

202

The cange's great lateen sails, like butterfly wings on its antennae masts, heeled the barque through the swift current, churning up a frothy wake. On the riverbank the shadows of sycamore and palm tree slid past with a mysterious calming effect. The only sinister note was occasioned by mournful wails that would drift across the water from some darkened village.

They passed Atfyr, Beni-Sonef, Sbou Girgeh. Lebas would have liked to linger over the sights, but the threat of not reaching Thebes in time to berth the *Luxor* before the Nile receded from the apex of its inundation pressed him on. It was not till Siout, the capital of Upper Egypt, where he was required to deliver a letter to the governor, that Lebas stayed ashore a whole day.

North of Abou Fedda, Lebas learned from the pilot that they were in for trouble. Here the Arabian chain rises straight from the east bank to a height of 100 meters. Forced through a narrow passage, the Nile boiled along with enormous force, and the wind swirled and hit the *cange* from every direction. To overcome the hazard, the Arab master resorted to some magic, jabbing his knife into the mast, throwing a handful of salt into a hastily built fire, praying to the Prophet. He then tore off the head of a chicken and sprinkled its blood on the masts, anchors, and doors, attaching a few sticky feathers here and there, all the time appealing to the divinity of the river. Mixing a concoction of oil, tea, alcohol, and salt, he poured it on the turbulent waters of the Nile.

The *cange,* struggling with all its sails against a current of 4 or 5 knots, had barely covered a third of the way through the Abou Fedda passage when it was hit by a stronger squall. A bolt of lightning cracked the mainmast.

It was the forerunner of a tornado. The wind shifted around the compass, buffeting the frail barque forward and backward. Sailing on its forestay, but mostly blown along like a straw, with its keel scraping bottom, the *cange* was in constant danger of being crushed against the sheer side of the cliff. The ordeal lasted more than two hours; then the wind calmed and the skipper managed to pull the craft through to safety. Three hours later they were at Manfalout.

The wind was now favorable and propelled the *cange* so fast that in five days they were in sight of a superb forest of doums that preceded the ruins of Denderah. Lebas would have liked to visit the Temple of Hathor, from which the already famous but still undeciphered zodiac looted by Drovetti had been brought to Paris at great expense, but again he was afraid to tarry. Instead, he obtained permission from the local Turkish governor to return later and cut a hundred doums as lumber for felling the obelisk at Luxor. "For a little money," said the indifferent Turk, "the natives will bring you a whole forest."

The great Gamouleh bend in the Nile was handled by the Arabs with ropes. As they came around it the vestiges of the ancient city of Thebes appeared, lit by the last rays of the sun. To starboard stood the ruins of Gourna; beyond

Gerald Massey explains the magic involved in mummification. As the embalmer rolled up the mummy in its bandages, he would, by the rhythm of his gestures and the formulas he chanted, fix the "shadow," or *shout,* of the deceased into the body, for fear it would wander about as a demon or unleashed passionate force. Embalmed and drugged and tranquilized by incense and music, it would not waken unless grave robbers (or Egyptologists) freed it from the shackles of its bonds. If so it would take off in search of human fluids to keep itself alive. A freed shadow, says Massey, could obsess a person to death, or take over the fetus of a pregnant woman. Destroying the mummy would no longer help. A special chant was needed to destroy the name.

R. Brendamour X.

Across the Nile from Luxor, beyond the Valley of the Dead, with its line of funerary temples, lies an arid, savage mountain chain riddled with deep passages and vaults—tombs for the pharaohs, where their mummies lay in richly ornamented sarcophagi in exquisitely decorated rooms filled with the treasures of Egypt. All around, more tombs for queens, princes, viziers, generals, priests, and important personages were dug into hill and valley above the floodline of the waters of the Nile.

them, against the distant Lybian chain, the temples of Medinet-About and the sinister Valley of the Tombs of the Kings. To port rose the columns of Karnak, with its immense pylons, dominated by the giant obelisk of Hatshepsut, higher than the ones at either Alexandria or Heliopolis. A mile or so up the river, still to port, stood the colonnade of the Palace of Luxor, its two pink granite obelisks, russet in the sunset, barely visible as they guarded the immense gateway.

Musing at the ruins of Thebes, Lebas was struck with wonder at the thought of a city of a hundred gates, with colossi, monoliths, and colonnaded palaces, all of which he had heard described by Champollion. But his prime preoccupation was to reach the obelisk he was to fell. He could just see it, in the twilight to the right of the great entrance to the Ramesseum at Luxor.

One by one the *agabas* drew up at Luxor on the eastern bank of the river by a sandy beach which climbed gently toward the village, a conglomeration of mud huts nestling among the ruins of the great palace of Ramses II.

Arrival at Thebes

The inhabitants, attracted by the appearance of barques flying the French *tricolor,* and the possibility of *bakshish,* lined up along the bank, covered in rags, hands out, bemoaning their misery. As Lebas's *cange* dropped its anchor, he jumped ashore, followed by the French sailors, who clambered across the sand, disappearing among the mud huts to get a closer look at the one great pink granite obelisk which was the object of their journey. The natives would not believe the French had come to remove the obelisk. They considered such an idea so fanciful it had to be a ruse to disguise some ulterior motive. They believed the foreigners to be making a reconnaissance of the area before returning to take over as conquerors. "Do you not know," they explained, "that these needles were set up with a special mastic hardened by the sun which it is impossible to pull apart without cutting up the stone?" Where, they inquired, was the man big enough to perform such a prodigious feat? When they saw the engineer Lebas, they burst into friendly peals of laughter, laced with cries of "Allah! Allah!"

Lebas and his sailors crowded round the base of the obelisk, which stood in a mass of rubbled stone, its shaft deeply buried in the sand, touching it tenderly and making estimates of its height and weight. The master stone cutter they had brought from Toulon, an Italian named Mazacqui, gently tapped the eastern face, listening carefully to the resounding surface, then cried out in a mixture of Italian and French: *"Moussu, la pietra, elle est felée, mais je ne crois pas qu'elle soit routta; lou son est sano, on pourra l'enlever pourvu qu'elle tombe piano, piano"* which translates as "Sir, the stone has a lesion, but I don't think it is cracked through. It sounds quite whole. We will be able to take it, providing we lower it slowly, slowly."

Lebas was dumbfounded; there had been no mention of a fissure in any of the works he had read on Luxor. He was also worried that he might be accused of having cracked the obelisk in the process of felling it. In a sort of stupor he returned to his *cange.* The next day, more cheerful after a good rest, Lebas set to work with some hired *fellahin.* Clearing away sand and debris they traced the fissure all the way to the base, twelve feet below the surface. But Mazacqui had correctly deduced from the sound that the fissure was not deep enough to cause trouble. It appeared to be as old as the obelisk.

What did provide an obstacle were the one-story huts the natives had built so close to the obelisk they would be destroyed by its felling.

Object of the quest

Native huts nestling in the great palace of Sesostris, or Ramses II

Lebas concluded that clearing a way to fell the obelisk would mean destroying thirty of the native huts, which would have to be valued for expropriation. For this purpose, and to cope with the oriental custom of *bakshish,* Verninac had been provided with 40,000 francs, and Lebas with 20,000. But Lebas found to his surprise that for once the sight of gold had no effect upon the Arab owners, who could not be induced to give up their homes.

The dragoman Kachef then explained to Lebas that the Arabs were merely waiting for nightfall so as to be able to remove from their houses the goods they had harvested and secreted from the Turkish overlords. The next day, negotiations were resumed before an expropriation committee consisting of Lebas, the local Turkish governor, or nazir, and the local judge, or cadi, plus the headman of the village, who wore a green turban to indicate a doubtful descent from the prophet Mohammed. Ibrahim, the local interpreter, a tall, lean figure with a huge protuberance of a nose, heatedly waved his arms and kicked his legs, alternating threats with persuasion, and making a thousand grimaces. The Arab families pressed hard around the committee table, the men's faces pouring with sweat, the women, veiled, displaying their emotional distress through darting black eyes, uttering sharp guttural cries.

This brouhaha reached a paroxysm and died suddenly—at which point the interpreter told the stupefied Lebas: "We are in agreement. His Excellency the nazir

Luxor natives in the ruins of Ramses' palace, whose columns are half submerged in a millennial accumulation of dirt.

invites the committee to dinner." The indemnity amounted to 4,000 francs. Each hovel owner came personally to kiss the hand of Lebas and thank him for his munificence.

At the nazir's table, Lebas, dressed in his grand naval uniform, did not feel too comfortable, squatting before a common dish, feeding with his fingers, dipping his bread into the communal sauce, and tearing the meat with his teeth. Each dish was on the table only a few moments before it was whipped away. In all, Lebas counted thirty-five dishes, including two whole muttons, which the brin-bachi, or town major, carved up, handing Lebas as the choicest morsel, the liver, dripping like a sponge.

The meats were followed by sweets, creams, fruits, and rice cakes, all washed down with water from the Nile. To Lebas's distress, there was no wine or liquor, only Turkish coffee. After the ritual rinsing of hands, he was offered the first smoke from a hookah with an amber mouthpiece, which was passed from mouth to mouth. When Lebas expressed his surprise to Kachef over the sudden happy ending of the expropriation ceremony, he was informed with a smile that the whole performance had been a *mise-en-scène* by Ibrahim to merit a proportionate reward. All he had needed to say was: "The government wants your house. The *courbache* is at hand!" Still smiling, Kachef told Lebas of Ibrahim's first words upon the Frenchman's arrival at Thebes: "Well, friend, how much do you think this gentleman is worth?"

209

11. MUDDLING ON THE NILE

From what the Arabs said, and from signs left along the riverbank, Lebas could distinguish the limits of the previous year's flooding of the Nile, which had reached just 400 meters from the base of the obelisk he wished to remove. His problem was to dig a berth deep enough not only to house the *Luxor* when it arrived, but to float it again with its extra load of 250 tons at the peak of the river's coming flood.

Lebas's announcement that he would pay a daily wage, instead of merely administering the lash, brought hundreds of ready hands. But the French overseers soon found the Arabs capable of digging a simple hole, not a trench, which required the use of rules and lines; so they had to instruct them at every moment just where to dig and where to level.

Four hundred *fellahin,* dressed in cotton trousers, and equipped with spades, raised a great cloud of burning dust that hid them from the village. While the men dug, the women and children hauled dirt in wicker baskets, boys and girls in two long lines, all equally naked. They would help each other load a basket on the head, then set off all together chanting to the cadence of what Lebas called an extremely obscene song. "Such customs," he remarked in his puritanical manner, "which in Europe are repugnant to our mores, should not astonish in a country where it is the custom to call each part of the body and its function by its proper name."

At certain times of the day the heat was so intense that the young carriers, whose soles were not yet hardened, would upturn their baskets and put them on their feet while the Arab overseers, wielding palm fronds, shouted *"Yalla volet, Yalla benti!"*—Come on boys, come on girls! Drenched in sweat and covered in dust, the workers were constantly quenching their thirst from special urns of Nile water placed at regular intervals. At the drumbeat signal that ended the day's work, men, women, and children would rush to soak in the Nile, oblivious of the menace of crocodiles, then come and squat in circles of forty or fifty on the beach where Lebas would make the round to pay them their daily wage of 15 centimes. In five days the natives dug Lebas a channel 50 meters long, 12 meters

Five leagues from Thebes, at Maximianopolis, with the wind head on, and no means of hauling the anchor, the *Luxor* was obliged to stop, but the local nazir, or vice-governor, a thin-faced beardless man with a large aquiline nose, ordered his janissaries to impress the inhabitants of four local villages. From a cloud of dust appeared 400 naked men, dark-skinned, goateed, and with leather feet, reluctantly ready to do the pulling. Beaten by the janissaries, they started at a slow cadence. Inch by inch the *Luxor* moved forward to the sound of a monotonous chant in praise of the "Sultan of Fire," or Napoleon Bonaparte, who, according to the song, had "led his Western men safely to the shores of the Nile to destroy the Mameluke oppressors who dissolved before him like the mists of the Nile before the morning sun!" Under the lash, it took the gangs ten hours to move the *Luxor* 3 leagues around the Gamouleh bend. Starved, worn out from fatigue, some thirty fellahs fell by the way. But by dawn the *Luxor* could once more hoist its sails. For their efforts the surviving fellahs each received 35 centimes, a liberality which filled them with such joy they crowded round to kiss the hands of their Gallic benefactors.

wide, and 1.5 meters deep, perfectly suited as a berth for the *Luxor*.

The Nile was rising fast, its waters changing from deep green to russet, undermining the crumbling banks. By July 7 it had risen sufficiently for the *Luxor* to leave Rosetta and set sail upstream. Three weeks later, after a trip that included sailing before favorable winds, being towed by four hundred naked men, and many exotic sights for Verninac and the crew, the *Luxor* was able to anchor offshore in sight of the obelisk, loudly acclaimed by the populace, who were most amazed to see such a monumental ship being maneuvered by no more than the thin shrill sound of a whistle, without word or other signal being given.

On August 16 the *Luxor* slipped into the end of its berth, carried forward little by little by the waters of the Nile until it could be lashed into its resting place, pointing directly at the obelisk. A month later, on September 16, the retiring waters left the *Luxor* firmly grounded in its sandy berth. Two more banks of sand were built up along the ship's flanks to be watered daily so as to keep the hull from cracking in the heat. Further to protect the hull, several rows of reed matting were raised on palm beams all around the sides. The ship's masts were lowered, and

Matted against the 120° sun

212

The Memnonium of Thebes

all its gear was housed in a room of the great palace of Sesostris—better known as Ramses II.

Lebas had installed his engineers in the great hall of the south palace of Emenophis Memnon. Verninac now set up quarters for his crew in the two main galleries of the south portico—"where the pharaohs had once dispensed justice and the priests preached mystic lessons"—stringing hammocks between the ancient hieroglyph-encrusted columns. Sailors' lockers at the foot of each hammock gave the appearance of a regular naval barracks. In the adjoining rooms the Frenchmen created a storehouse for supplies, a bakery with an oven, a carpenter and joiner's shop, an arsenal with a powder room, a forge for the smithies, and a stable for the horse which milled the grain for their daily bread. To accommodate doctors Angelin and Pons, a hospital was built with thirty beds in a long airy hall lighted by twelve windows.

The officers were quartered on the roof of the palace, where they were given the three-room residence of the brinbachi, who was evacuated on orders from the nazir. On this rooftop, between the south wall and the northern extremity of the vestibule, Lebas arranged for a small room, 15 feet square, to be built for each officer out of Nile brick. All gave onto a broad terrace overlooking the neighboring countryside with its rolling plain, dotted with

View from the French compound

213

To make a solid roof atop its ancient pillars, Lebas had several palm trees ripped into joists with which he replaced the missing architraves. Filling the empty space with palm fronds, he had them covered with a mixture of Nile mud and chopped straw, which was quickly baked by the sun into a useable floor. Though a good rain might have washed it away, there was little likelihood of a downpour in the serene blue skies of Egypt.

mimosa and dates, which ran up to the foothills of the Arabian chain.

On this platform were also built a reception room, a mess hall and a common room, or divan, all neatly whitewashed and furnished with the officers' effects from the *Luxor*.

The quarters, which could easily be reached from a ramp of sand banked against the palace walls by the desert wind, were comfortable enough, says Verninac, except for the heat, which normally stood about 100° in the shade, and except for the scorpions which kept crawling out of cracks in the wall, and the vipers that rested in the ceiling, and the great gecko lizards which ran wild along the walls.

The actual village of *Luxor* had been built within the millenial crumbling walls of the two great palaces, on a ridge 700 meters long by 350 wide, 3 meters above the level of the plain, on foundations dating back at least thirty-four centuries and most likely more. The gateway between the two great obelisks led into the heart of the village where a garrison of five Turks ruled a population of eight hundred Arabs. Everywhere the mudbrick huts of the modern inhabitants were nestled in among the ancient columns, walls, pylons, and obelisks, like an incrustation of bird's nests. Where the propylaeum had stood, a mosque with a low minaret rose up for the muezzin to summon the faithful to prayers. Streets in which the windblown sand accumulated in uneven piles wound tortuously between the Arab houses, one-story affairs of sun-baked adobe brick, mainly clustered around the north end of the place of Sesostris, each surmounted by a pigeon coop with cut branches for the pigeons to roost on protected from the midday sun. Camels knelt in the dust, donkeys slept on their feet; everywhere were flies. Dogs, almost wild, the descendants of an ancient Egyptian species with long fur, pointed noses, broken ears, and narrow hips, barked almost incessantly.

The road from Luxor to Karnak, once lined with 1,500 sphinxes

One main road—possibly the ancient avenue which had once linked the quarters of Thebes to the eastern bank of the Nile—led through the town to a colonnade composed of fourteen gigantic columns, each 45 feet high with a lotus capitol. From there the avenue had led between two rows of fifteen hundred sphinxes, half-woman half-lion, almost 2 miles to the palace of Karnak. A few tamarisk trees with filiform leaves relieved the monotony of the sand.

Each sailor was assigned a plot to till, and in a few days the area around the palaces took on the aspect of a French hamlet, sailors preparing gardens and building private huts in which to spend leisure hours.

French gardens at Luxor

The flooding of the Nile had brought the countryside to life, turning dust to soil. Everywhere hedgerows sprouted with sweet-scented flowers. From France, the men had brought a variety of seeds and grains, and the land was of such vitality that stringbeans bore leaf within a few days and were edible within the month. Tomatoes, basil, sweetpeas, grew almost before their eyes. For meat the Frenchmen were provided by ambulant butchers who would slaughter their cows on the spot, spread the entrails on the ground to attract the flies, then cut off pieces to sell to the passerby. From the Nile, Coptic fishermen brought fish. Of the forty-odd species in the river only three were considered edible—the finni, the voult, and the ketcher. Turtles also flourished in the Nile, about a meter long, but were not considered by the French good enough for the table.

Auctioning fish in the market

The sailors would have liked to swim in the Nile, but on the very first day, an Arab who had gone down to fill a jar begun to scream, and before their eyes was dragged under by a 20-foot crocodile, leaving a large bloodstain on the surface. Eventually the Frenchmen discovered that the crocodile was not so dangerous, and would normally run when approached. But they kept their distance, learning to locate the reptile by a strong musty smell recognizable at 15 feet. The French were more startled by a large variety of amphibious lizard called *tupinambis,* which grew to a length of 4 feet; but they were pleased to find them good to eat.

What these hot-blooded Mediterranean Frenchmen did for women during their stay at Luxor is not spelled out in the memoirs of the chroniclers. But Lebas says they were

216

Bedouin market

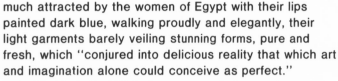

Dancing girls

much attracted by the women of Egypt with their lips painted dark blue, walking proudly and elegantly, their light garments barely veiling stunning forms, pure and fresh, which "conjured into delicious reality that which art and imagination alone could conceive as perfect."

And in his veiled Victorian manner, Lebas makes no bones about the availability of the Egyptian women, despite their premium on virginity, pointing out that on marriage, although the mother ritually ripped her daughter's maidenhead in the presence of a few relatives who then carried the bloodied linen through the streets to hang in the window of the house of the bride-to-be, such a custom "left leeway for a certain chicanery on the part of the mother of the bride." While an Egyptian girl could be condemned to death for losing her virginity to a European, her head being cut off and her body thrown into the Nile if she were caught *in flagrante,* the culprit, says Lebas, could still save the girl if he had himself circumcised on the spot and espoused the faith. "That being as it may," adds Lebas, "any other form of complaisance is perfectly tolerated and entrains no particular danger."

By the end of September, while the natives finished digging a 400-meter causeway along which to drag the obelisk to the bow of the sand-berthed *Luxor,* Lebas was ready to fell the western monolith. When its base had been cleared of sand and rubble, the men found a pedestal of granite which had become friable from the effect of mineral salts below the surface. The base was formed of three blocks of granite atop a single slab, the south side of which was carved into four cynocephalous or dog-headed baboons, each bearing on its breast a legend to the glory of Sesostris.

217

Causeway along which the obelisk was dragged to the *Luxor*
for embarkation

As the base was about even with the *Luxor*'s berth, it
would have meant removing an extra 45,000 cubic meters
of dirt to make a horizontal causeway. It would also have
meant knocking down more intervening houses, and running the risk of unearthing some ancient ruins that would
have been difficult if not impossible to move. Lebas
decided it would be better to attempt to twist the obelisk
on its base and bring it down to rest on the higher
embankment of sand and rubble which had accumulated
round it. He could then dig a more shallowly inclined
slipway down to the river, along which it would be easier,
with the help of gravity, to drag the monolith.

Lebas' method for delicately lowering the obelisk, so as not to
break it

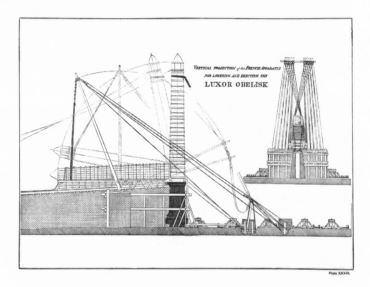

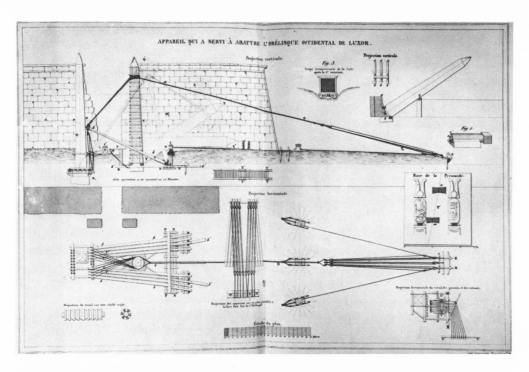

Equipment for lowering Ramses' needle

The main problem in lowering the obelisk was to do so—in the words of the mason Mazacqui—*"piano, piano."* Lebas believed the reason so many obelisks had been smashed, especially in Rome, was because they had been felled with ropes tied only around the top, and with no counterpull to slow the descent.

On August 1 three long ladders were raised one above the other along the south face of the obelisk. At a signal from Verninac, the tricolor was unfurled from the pyramidion, and the Frenchmen saluted with shouts of "Now it belongs to France! Soon to be in Paris!" Lebas, more circumspect, was reminded of La Fontaine's "one should never sell the bearskin till one has it on the floor."

The whole job of lowering the obelisk had to be done with no more sophisticated equipment than the winches, block and tackle, and the hoisting gear brought from France. The carpenters built a wooden scaffolding and then a wooden casing to protect the obelisk, economizing as best they could on the hard-to-come-by lumber. No matter what method was used to fell the monolith, its sharp edges had to be protected by boards that could not be less than 16 centimeters thick, nailed together with crosspieces and doubly bound with iron bands and screw bolts. To protect the edge of the base, on which the obelisk was to pivot and rotate, a special oak beam was hollowed to fit.

219

To rip auxiliary beams of date palm, and to cut through the rocklike beams of oak which the French had brought from Toulon, Lebas organized special teams of Arabs who soon became proficient at cutting either straight or curved lines as requested by the master carpenter. Such ripping in such a climate was too arduous for Europeans. In a short time the Arab children had learned the names of all the French tools, and could fetch them in an instant, saving the Frenchmen much time, which was badly needed, as a race was on to accomplish the work before the oncome of the *khamsin,* a wind from the south which lasted fifty days, making life unbearable with tempests and tornados of sand.

Then came the bad news. Some boatmen coming up the river told of cholera ravaging Alexandria and Cairo. Soon the river was filled with the *canges* of Europeans fleeing upstream, closely pursued by the plague. The French consul informed Lebas he had lost a son. Fifteen of Verninac's men caught the plague, but no one abandoned his post. Work on the obelisk proceeded as usual, and Angelin and Pons took such good care of the French victims that none succumbed.

Not so the Arab workmen. Of the village's eight hundred inhabitants, more than one hundred died, at the rate of about ten a day. The workers would suddenly keel over in the middle of their work, or would be stricken just as they were being paid their salaries. This caused an almost constant wailing from the habitations of the Arabs, where women bared their breasts, covered themselves with ashes, rolled their dark eyes, and addressed pitiful entreaties to the defunct.

Ibrahim Pacha, son of Mohammed Ali, terrified by cholera, came up the river in his red-sailed *cange,* standing alone in the bow, speaking to no man, fixing his own food, and daily washing his only change of linen in the water of the Nile. He had panicked and abandoned his army outside Cairo. At the First Cataract, he placed guards on either bank and forbade anyone to pass. This caused a backflow of refugees, many of whom docked their boats at Luxor and camped out on the beaches, spreading the plague.

A few days later, Ibrahim, shamed by an insulting message from his father, slunk back down the river to Cairo to lead his army into battle against his Ottoman masters. When the refugees saw him go, they too followed suit.

On October 1 the sun rose with a lovely tint of autumn. The obelisk was entirely sheathed in lumber, the trestles holding the block and tackle were raised and abutted. The scaffolding was removed and the tricolor once more unfurled from the top of the flower-wreathed trestle. A heavy cable was attached to the pyramidion, leading to several blocks and tackle, and half a dozen winches. Men pushing on the winches were to tilt the obelisk forward far enough to shift its center of gravity so that it would wheel and then fall by itself. To steady this movement and control the fall of the monolith, Lebas arranged for a trestle of huge poles 40 feet long to act as a fulcrum over which cordage could pull the obelisk in the direction opposite its fall. This cordage was anchored round the solid base of the second obelisk. To keep the bank from crumbling and falling as the obelisk came to rest on it, a brick wall had been built up, capped with a cylindrical pole of oak.

One hundred and ninety Arabs manned the winches. Eight men controlled the braking rope, great anxiety showing on their faces as the moment of trial arrived. The French commanders were armed with naval whistles. The villagers—Turks, Arabs, Egyptians and Copts, men, women and children, all those not engaged on the ropes, including the very old men with green turbans—were in attendance at the historic scene. So was the hawk-nosed nazir of Thebes. Sir James Gardiner Wilkinson, described by the French as an antiquary, draftsman, and geographer, turned up with three English travelers and a Greek named Triandafilon, who lived in a nearby cave. Sunlight illuminated the silent faces of the colossi of Memnon, which, before they were vandalized, had resounded harmoniously to the touch of sunrays.

Verninac gave the order. The winches turned. The tackle stretched through the blocks. Tension increased as the windlasses oscillated on their axes. Unfortunately, instead of rolling, the oak cylinder at the base ripped like cloth. The wooden casing of the obelisk began to creak and crack. Heavy vibration caused the hoisting shears to tremble. The obelisk's head leaned slightly toward the river, traversing an arc of 8°, then came to a stop. All was still.

The officer in charge of the winches issued a warning that under the heavy strain the anchor points of the blocks were slipping forward in the sand. The relieving tackle was excessively taut. He suggested moving faster so as to take the obelisk past its vertical center of gravity, and shift the strain from the winches to the

braking cables and the trestle. Slowly the center of gravity swung past the vertical, and the obelisk began to fall of its own weight. It was now a question of whether the braking mechanism would hold as planned. It depended on the thrust being equally distributed. For this, Lebas had made a movable cylinder with eight necks for the ropes. Though apparently useless, it proved itself essential in this crucial descent until the obelisk lay safely on the sand in one piece.

Lebas then had the carpenters make use of the demolished scaffolding to build a 21-meter cradle in three movable parts on which the obelisk could be slid toward the river. As the rear section was freed it would be shifted to the front. But the quality of the lumber was such that the cradles could not be made as solid as required, and there were not enough pieces left over to repair a section if it were damaged. The master carpenter reported that every particle of wood had been used. If anything should break, he would be unable to repair it.

On November 16 Lebas got 160 Arabs to man the winches. The pulleys whined under the tension. Frenchmen incited the Arabs with hurrahs, but the obelisk would not budge. Two of the heavy tackles parted, causing irreparable loss. Lebas was puzzled. The effort exerted was twice what was necessary to move the obelisk, but because the cradle was completely buried in the sand, he could not spot the trouble.

It took two days to clear the cradle and see that a snapped oak pole directly beneath the obelisk had been driven 45 centimeters into the brick wall, causing an insurmountable obstacle. Lebas noted that under the heat and pressure of the strain, the soil at some points had been virtually turned to rock, too hot to handle. As for the pole, it had sheared into annular sheets like a telescope.

Ten jacks beneath the obelisk finally raised it into proper sliding position; and this time, when full pressure was exerted, the obelisk moved forward a few centimeters. Thereafter it was a matter of time and sweat—almost a month of painful hauling, averaging fifteen hours a day, while the Arabs pushed on the winches singing the ancient chant of the galley slave: *"Where is my homeland? When will we see it? When will we return to the home of our fathers?"*

All along the way the obelisk had to be controlled with sturdy props on either side to keep it from rolling off its cradle. By December 18 the pyramidion had reached the berth of the *Luxor*. To fit the monolith into the ship, the whole bow had to be cut through with a great saw, 3 meters behind the bowsprit, in a great vertical slice. As one Frenchman put it: "The ship was deflowered to receive the great phallus." The severed segment of bow was then hoisted aloft by several hoists. To slide the obelisk into the ship without crushing the hull, a ramp of packed dirt on a foundation of heavy stones was built right up to the raw cut. To drag the obelisk within the hull precisely to where its center of gravity would coincide with that of the ship, two cables had to be passed through holes in the stern and anchored in the sand some

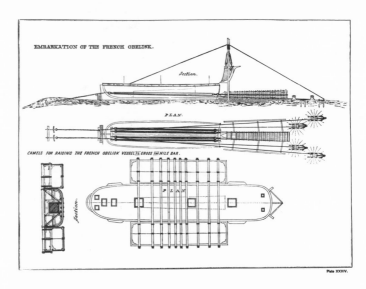

distance away, symmetrically placed on either side of the main longitudinal axis. A brick wall raised these cables to prevent any ripping of the ship's stern—also to protect the hull in case the tackle were to snap under the pull of forty-eight men.

On the morning of December 19, Lebas ordered the winches in motion. In less than two hours the obelisk was safely aboard. It had taken four and a half months of excruciating work, sleepless nights, worry, and anxiety. All together, they had moved 90,000 cubic meters of sand, cut through a sizable hillock of debris, demolished thirty houses, cared for and fed 140 Frenchmen in a country with few resources, in the desert, in the midst of a cholera plague, all the while working in clouds of burning, choking dust, with the temperature mostly above the 100° mark. It was hard, says Lebas, to describe the joy of the assembled sailors and workmen.

The next day, when the bow of the ship was refastened, the mark of the saw was virtually imperceptible. The governor, thinking it would take the French at least two weeks to place the obelisk aboard the *Luxor,* had not turned up on the nineteenth. Now neither Turk nor Arab could understand what had happened. They kept looking at the ship and the place where the obelisk had lain, and could not believe their eyes till they had touched the obelisk inside the ship. Even so, they attributed the translation to the work of *afreets,* or *jinns.* On his arrival, the governor, amazed at the performance, announced that Mohammed Ali would pay for all the expenses of lowering and embarking the obelisk, forthwith reimbursing Lebas with 25,000 francs.

The solitary obelisk which still stands guard at the gates of Luxor

But the work had taken just a few days too long. The Nile, pulling back into its channel, was leaving the *Luxor* with its heavy load high on the drying sand. There was no longer any hope of leaving before the next inundation, sometime during July 1832. It was a heavy blow. It meant the Frenchmen would not see their families for another whole year; and it meant another twelve months of living in makeshift quarters in the palaces of Luxor.

Resigning themselves to the situation, the men set about securing the obelisk within the hold of the ship; struts and crosspieces had to be fashioned, which would take the carpenters some time, working with nothing but the detritus of lumber still available. As their work aboard the *Luxor* needed no supervision, Lebas decided to take a trip up the Nile to visit the temples and ruins of ancient Egypt, at least as far as the first cataract, where Napoleon's army had come to a halt after scattering the remnant of the Mameluke forces, and where all the great obelisks had originally been quarried. He was determined to see for himself the greatest of them all, which lay half-quarried near Aswan, and discover why this particular spot had been the source of so many obelisks.

12. GALLIC COCKCROW

On January 9, 1832, Lebas embarked with his servant—"a good looking young man of seventeen with a lovely figure"—aboard a *cange* crewed by five Arabs. Casting off, they intoned a favorite chant: *"Habouzale, habouzelphi."* A favorable breeze, filling their lateen sails, glided them past an island rich in vegetation situated opposite the sanctuary of the temple.

The next day at 2:00 P.M. they reached the Temple of Esne, 15 leagues upstream from Thebes, by a small town on the banks of the Nile built into the ruins of the ancient city of Latopolis. Remnants of the old port and docks were still visible, and Lebas admired the great colonnade, which the natives used as storage space for firewood. The local mamour, or prefect, gave Lebas a letter to the nazir of Syene, assuring him that "with this, they will take you up the cataract faster than the water rushes down." What had made the mamour so complacent was a sudden infatuation with Lebas's young servant, an infatuation which engendered from Lebas the caustic remark that in the Ottoman Empire any young man could rise the faster by lying down.

The next day Lebas visited Edfu, whose gigantic temple dominated like a citadel the small town built on the slope of the hill. While anchored by a sandbank at two in the morning there was a cry of *"Arame! arame!,"* or thief, thief! His servant, afraid, says Lebas, of falling into the hands of bedouins and "suffering what might be justly considered a degrading ordeal, or repetition of the favors extended to him by the Turkish mamour," beat against the

After the evening meal, while the cabin boy fed the fire, there was always a routine of song and dance initiated by a saucy tale from some sailor, followed by a graver tale from the *reis,* usually about money and the sultan. To the sound of two hollow reeds and the vibrations from a skin glued to an earthern funnel held beneath the arm and beaten with both hands, the sailors would abandon themselves to raucous and lascivious dancing. Lacking females, the sailors' entertainment tended toward the homosexual. A sailor, his sole garment a long shirt, would make progressively more indecent movements to an applauding audience.

227

door until Lebas appeared with a gun. On both knees the pilot also implored Lebas to fire his gun to scare away the thieves who were known to come from underwater, their naked bodies heavily greased, to swim away with whatever they could seize, including other pretty bodies. Lebas fired in all directions, and returned to his slumbers, only to discover in the morning that the pilot had taken advantage of the fracas to seduce his servant. To dissuade the pilot from further advances, Lebas threatened to have him given two hundred strokes of the *courbache* as soon as they reached Aswan.

At Djebel Selseleh they passed large quarries dug into a hillside. Between there and Aswan they came across the temple of Loum Ombou with its grand façade consecrated to the crocodile, its vast edifice partly demolished by the river, which had undermined the foundations. As they approached Aswan, the bed of the river, which had been muddy, became studded with dangerous black protuberances of granite, highly polished by the flow of water, which, according to the Arabs, had been hurled down from the mountains by the gods who wished to close the channel.

Moored in Aswan harbor they found a *cange* flying the Turkish flag, aboard which were Mohammed Ali's doctor, Monsieur Botta, the French consul general, Monsieur Mimaut, and a desert Arab of some renown, called Baraka, meaning Providence. After a daily fare of eggs, rice, fish, and dates prepared in a hundred ways by his servant, Lebas was relieved to be invited to dinner on the Turkish *cange,* where he was feasted with choice viands and game.

Aswan (so-called by the Arabs) was the ancient Egyptian town of Sun-t ("allowing the entrance"), called Syene by the Greeks. Just below the first cataract, it formed the border between Egypt and Nubia and was an important geodetic and astronomical site. Opposite Aswan lies the island of Elephantine, the largest rock formed by the first cataract. Close to the Tropic of Cancer, it is the only location in Egypt from which an accurate observation can be made at the solstice to establish the circumference of the earth. Lebas found that Elephantine had been stripped of the lovely temple depicted in the *Description de l'Égypte.*

Lebas found the Lybian hills around Aswan to be the source of a fine-textured, rose-colored granite, normally free from seams and flaws, known as syenite, consisting of quartz, feldspar, and hornblende, from which all the great obelisks of Egypt appeared to have been quarried.

A ten-minute ride into the hilly hinterland brought Lebas to the area from which all the great obelisks were said to have been quarried. There, on a flat surface, he found the outline of an enormous obelisk half carved out of solid red granite, apparently abandoned after three faces had been shaped because of an unexpected fissure. It was difficult for Lebas, because of the effect of foreshortening, and because parts of the obelisk were buried by windblown sand, to estimate the length of the monolith, but he figured it to be one third again as long as the largest obelisk at Karnak, and to weigh three times as much, or a thousand tons. This, he concluded, would have required at least 12,000 men to slide along a greased runway as he had done with the much smaller obelisk at Luxor.

Six-inch holes drilled into the granite at eighteen-inch intervals around the recumbent stone indicated to Lebas that plugs of soft palmwood could have been introduced into them. Soaked with water, these would have frozen in the cold nights of that latitude, causing the plugs to expand and split the granite. To flatten the top, he surmised that fires could have been lit which would have made the granite crumble. The sides of the obelisk appeared to have been worked to a finish by pounding with six-inch dolerite balls which abounded naturally in the surrounding hills. The underside of big stone was pierced by a number of tunnels which led Lebas to surmise they had served for the insinuation of timbers to act as a sledge with which to move it once the entire underface had been cut away.

229

The largest known obelisk, half quarried from a vein of Syene granite

Classical authors gave the region an eerie reputation by reporting that the inhabitants for miles around were all as deaf as the cataract stones because of the terrible roar of the waterfall.

All of which caused Lebas to marvel at the brilliance and endurance of the ancient Egyptian engineers. Considering the trouble it had cost him to move his obelisk he could not imagine how they had managed to quarry, move, ship and raise one four times its weight without even the winches and tackle available to him.

As a final exploration on the Upper Nile he decided to study the great temple of Abusimbel, to see how the Egyptians could have carved it out of a solid mountain as described by Belzoni and recently visited by Champollion.

Back on the river, teams of camels were employed to drag the *cange* up the cataract, past the date-burdened island of Elephantine, where the ancient Egyptians had an

astronomical observatory, and a nilometer to measure the flooding of the river. Dark Nubians, excellent swimmers, skipped from rock to rock, attaching lines as brakes to prevent the *cange* from being swept away by the swift flow of current and crushed against the rocks. Overhead, swarms of black crows circled to inspect the maneuver while sand swallows darted to and fro.

Twelve leagues above the second cataract, in a wasteland of sterile mountains devoid of all vegetation, Lebas sought out the two cyclopean temples of Abusimbel, carved deep into the vertical side of the mountain, one with its entrance flanked by 60-foot standing colossi, the other, bigger still, with eight identical colossi of Ramses, seated on either side of the entrance.

From Abusimbel Lebas decided to turn back to Luxor, traveling more leisurely, taking sidetrips after duck, snipe, hare, partridge, and doves. The river itself abounded with an extraordinary variety of birds: eagles, falcons, storks, plovers, ibis, and the percnotaire, a huge beast with lovely plumage.

Lebas was most fascinated by the idiosyncrasies of three peculiar birds. One, which he called the scissor bird, because of the scissor shape of its beak, would cut its fish into morsels before swallowing them, then regurgitate the bones in a round white ball. Another odd bird, the *Sharadrius niloticus,* a sky-blue bird with black bands, called a *cak* by the Arabs, would spend its day cleaning the teeth and gullet of the sleeping crocodiles, whose open mouths were a lure for swarming insects. Lebas was also intrigued by the sacksack, a black-and-white bird, with a gray back, which acted as the sentinel of the Nile, screaming at the sight of anything unusual, and alerting birds and animals for miles around of the possibility of danger.

Back at Luxor, Lebas found that his fellow Frenchmen had spent their time tending their gardens. The acacia trees planted barely a year earlier were now 15 feet tall and as thick as a man's arm. A fig tree the size of a thumb, planted at the door of a garden, was 12 centimeters thick and covered with fruit. Some, like Joannis and Verninac, had gone on hunting trips into the interior, or on voyages of exploration up the Nile. All together, during Lebas's absence, ten Frenchmen had died from one cause or another, mostly dysentery. One sailor, failing to follow Angelin's strict rationing orders, had got into the larder and consumed 2 pounds of raw rice. Within forty-eight hours his stomach had exploded.

The year's stay had turned the rest of the Frenchman into shadowy figures. Fifty were laid up in the hospital, mostly with dysentery; and even Angelin had sickened. To relieve twenty of the sickest, Verninac ordered them sent ahead by boat to Alexandria. Though their cases weren't serious, the doctor recommended a different regime and the more European climate of the delta. All were anxious to get back to France for fear they could not survive much longer in the climate. As the Nile approached flood time, there were just enough healthy men to recommission the *Luxor* and see to clearing the sand around it. When this was done the planks were found to be tight enough to hold water, whereas the deck, which had been exposed to the sun, had cracks they could see through.

To receive the waters of the Nile around the keels, a large hole was dug. Each year the Nile announced its flooding by tiny oscillations, which took place at the latitude of Thebes sometime in late May, and a gradual change in color caused by rains in the Abyssinian highlands. At first the water would lose its transparency, taking on a greenish tint. Gradually the green would grow deeper until it could be seen in a scooped-up handful. According to the Arabs, the deeper the green, the bigger the inundation. Eventually the water turned brick-red.

That year the Nile was slow in flooding; its telltale oscillations only became evident during the first few days in June. Everyone became agitated, rushing to the river's edge to look and examine. Small twigs were placed in the ground from which to note the smallest change in level. News bulletins of the rise were posted on the door to the mosque. Faces lit up with excitement. Arab women celebrated by singing religious chants up and down the river's edge.

As late as July 30 the water continued to rise rapidly and evenly, without causing any damage. Many of the Frenchmen spent their nights by the river to watch the markers being swept away. They would even feel for them in the dark. By August 5 the water of the Nile had turned deep red, and the *Luxor* was an island. It needed only thirty more centimeters to float. Everyone believed it would float the next day, or, at the very least, the day after. On August 6 the river began to subside, and continued to fall back until August 12. The French were stunned. It meant the prospect of spending another whole year in the Theban heat. Anxiously they consulted Arabs for opinions. The imam, or priest, said the Nile was just catching its breath, and would rise again. He suggested a donation of two muttons to the mosque, to propitiate Allah.

Among the harbingers of the flooding of the Nile were beetles that rolled up their seed into a small ball of dung which they buried by the riverbank for safety against the coming flood. Nile beetles figured in the constellation of the Crab, the point along the Zodiac at which the inundation began, known as the month of Mesore.

According to Lebas, the Arabs consumed very little, especially by comparison with their Turkish overlords. He figured the yearly cost of feeding and clothing an Arab would not exceed 15 francs, his daily fare being based on three small loaves of millet bread, or *doura,* augmented, depending on the waters of the Nile, by some cucumbers, watermelons, chicory, dates, onions, or their favorite, lentils. All of the good land of Egypt, and all its produce, belonged outright to the Pasha. Only the land closest to the channel of their river, the last to be uncovered in April and May, was considered common, because of the short time it remained unflooded. Here the fellahin were allowed to sow at will their quick-growing products by the simple process of making a hole with a stick and covering the seed with the foot. Often they would have to wade into the rising water to gather late sproutings. When the waters of

On August 13 the water rose again. Verninac fixed a line to the stern of the *Luxor,* had an anchor carried out into the middle of the Nile, and attempted to winch the ship free. For three days the French pulled, but the *Luxor* would not budge. On the eighteenth, with a supreme effort, they managed to move the *Luxor* a few feet. The water rose again, a hair, and by evening the ship was once more afloat on the Nile. The greatest problem now was to get it safely down the river.

Worried about sailing the flooding waters with the heavily loaded *Luxor* facing treacherous currents and unforeseeable hazards, Verninac had ordered from Toulon two *peniches,* or pinnances—small two-masted vessels rigged like schooners, which could be propelled by oars. Though announced by a courier, they had failed to arrive, and Verninac was afraid to wait any longer lest he fail to arrive at the mouth of the delta while the water was still high enough to float him across the sandbars.

During the night, the inhabitants of Luxor and Karnak crowded the riverbank to be ready to bid the *Luxor* farewell when it hauled its anchor in the morning. At 11:00 A.M. the breeze freshened and the *Luxor* set its sails. Two

the Nile subsided in November, the first crop planted was always broad beans. On the next land uncovered in December, wheat, barley, peas, and lentils were planted. In February the fresh beans were harvested, in March the poppy seeds, in April the lentils, in May the peas. During the season of the pointed peas the natives would economize on their *doura* by walking through the fields avidly eating the peas directly from the pod. In April, when the trees were in flower, the natives would fertilize the females by hanging well-developed male fronds from the female branches. Wheat and barley were harvested in May and June. In July and August, on land not yet covered by the rising waters, corn was planted, to be harvested in October and November. But legally all of this was the property of the pashas. With the natural resources of the Nile, Lebas was convinced that in a short time modern Egyptians could be brought to a much higher standard of living in which the arts and sciences could once more flourish. Were the land distributed to the native farmers, he believed, it would bring Mohammed Ali a hundredfold in revenues. As things stood, the pasha only managed to collect a tiny portion of what the natives could be induced to cultivate, the rest being hidden or stolen by the middlemen.

janissaries came running up with a present from the nazir for Dr. Angelin: a pet hyena. It was a pathetic cortege. As the *Luxor* had been preparing to sail, and the janissaries had been unable to catch the creature, and the nazir had not been specific as to how this should be done or whether the gift was to be dead or alive, the janissaries had stoned the hyena to death and now ceremoniously brought along the carcass, already in a state of putrefaction, as a farewell gift for Angelin, who had loved the nazir's living pet.

Slowly the *Luxor* moved downstream. The crowds ran along the bank, waving; some swam out to cling to the ship's side; others followed in small boats. The French were amazed by this demonstration of affection, especially as they had seen the same Arabs totally impassive under the *courbache* of the Turks.

With the wind head-on, as it prevailed during the period of inundation, Verninac figured he could zigzag downstream from bank to bank by presenting alternate flanks to the wind. But he soon found the rudder would not respond sufficiently to keep the ship in control. The *peniches* arrived, but were 3 meters too short for the job. When Verninac tried them, they caused the *Luxor* to run up hard against the bank, luckily without damage. To solve his problem, Verninac decided to emulate the system of the ancient Egyptians as described by Herodotus. According to the Greek historian, the Nile boats of his day sailed downstream by means of a sieve of heather reinforced with rushes lashed to the bow; this caused the rapid current to propel the boat forward. A heavy rock dragged along the bottom served as a brake to help maneuver from side to side.

Turkish nazir wielding the courbache

Verninac threw a heavy anchor over the stern to use as a brake. Thereafter he was able to make his way downstream irrespective of wind or current. Unfortunately, on the thirty-first, the anchor stuck and there was no way to raise it. The ship was about to go under when the pulley snapped, its fragments being hurled to a great distance, luckily without killing anyone aboard. The next day the tiller struck ground. With the ship immobilized, the Nile waters, on the opposite side from the current, heaped a sandbank straight up against its flank; by midnight the *Luxor* was almost submerged. Luckily a sudden gust, filling the sails, dragged the ship off the embankment.

The famous Gamouleh elbow gave them plenty of trouble. At one point, they found themselves with full sails whirled completely about, moving at full speed backward down the current. Date palms whizzed past at such a speed that if the *Luxor* had hit the bank, it would have been crushed to kindling. Luckily the river began to bend in the opposite direction, and the *Luxor* was able to wheel in time.

With another anchor, Verninac managed to control the boat safely to Cairo. There they took a break from their ordeal long enough to enjoy a festival known as the dalmees, a local saturnalia, where, as voyeurs, they could enjoy the dance of the bee, in which an Arab woman pretending to have a bee in her galabia removed all her clothes in a series of wild dances. But Verninac could not dally. It had taken him as long to come down the Nile as it had to go up. He was worried about reaching the mouth in time to cross the sandbars. Any time in the past two weeks he could have crossed with ease; but September, with its great flights of pelicans, had come and gone.

On October 1 the *Luxor* arrived at Rosetta to find the water at the sandbars 20 centimeters too low to pass. Lebas thought of raising the ship by means of two large flanking pontoons, but it was too heavily laden to withstand the strain. On the off chance that a sudden change in the wind might cause a break in the sandbars, they anchored by the mouth of the river.

It was not an uncomfortable wait; the more European climate with its autumn air revivified the crew. But weeks dragged into December and its dangerous storms. It became unwise to linger. Back at Rosetta, Verninac demasted and decommissioned the *Luxor,* storing its gear on dry land, and began to look for winter quarters for officers and men. Rosetta had its compensations. There were still plenty of bananas, oranges, and grapes. The men could pass their days at the Turkish baths, smoking pipes, or drinking coffee. The crew, says Joannis, "soon managed to create such pleasantly domestic situations they were enabled to forget the postponement of their return to France," till an unexpected event changed their plans. An Anatolian ship loaded with oranges, struck by a gust of wind, crashed into the sandbanks and sank, causing a breach of 2.5 meters in the bank, where there had been nothing but sand. The pilot who had witnessed the crash rushed back to Rosetta to inform Verninac that the breach was wide enough and deep enough for the *Luxor* to pass through.

In thirty-six hours the ship was recommissioned and reached the sandbar on January 1, 1833. By noon the weather was perfect, the wind favorably astern. Beyond the sandbank, riding at anchor, was the steamship *Sphinx,* sent from Toulon to tow the *Luxor* back to France. Inch by inch the *Luxor* moved through the breach, followed by the *peniches* holding anchors in case of trouble. A freshening breeze and sudden rough seas caused the *Luxor*'s keel to ground on the sandy bottom. As darkness fell, the ship was once more immobilized. Everyone aboard was in a state. The pilot clutched at his beard, crying "Allah! Allah!" Hardtack and wine were distributed. An anchor was rowed forward and attached to a winch. By 10:00 P.M. the slight Mediterranean tide reached its peak; with a lurch, and a great hurrah, the *Luxor* slipped over the final barrier into the salty sea.

Raising its *huinier,* the *Luxor* went to anchor by the *Sphinx* which, the next day, towed it safely to Alexandria harbor. There the *Luxor* was flooded with visitors. Ball

Alexandria harbor

237

after ball was given in honor of the Frenchmen, while Verninac waited for suitable weather to sail. Winter in the eastern Mediterranean can be rough and foul. Several times the departure of the French was delayed by storms and heavy winds. Apart from the lovely Pointe des Figures, and Mohammed Ali's palace, they found the French Quarter, with its wide avenues and squares, the only pleasant part of the city. There the local merchants and consuls opened their houses to the men. Lebas was again received by Mohammed Ali, who expressed great satisfaction at the successful removal of the obelisk, and was only macabre in his curiosity to know how much weight the obelisk would lose under water, if the ship should sink. When Lebas thanked Mohammed Ali for his generous help in securing to France the Luxor obelisk, the khedive replied: "I have done nothing for France that France has not done for me. If I give her the relic of an old civilization, it is in exchange for the new civilization of which she has spread the seeds in the Orient. Let the obelisk be a tie between our two countries."

Finally the *Luxor* set off from Alexandria, on April 1, towed by the *Sphinx* at a speed of 4 knots. On the night of April 2 a breeze from the west turned into a violent storm. By noon of the third the *Luxor* was dwarfed by enormous waves. The *Sphinx* was making no headway, and to avoid wasting coal, it let itself drift toward Rhodes. As a result, the *Luxor* began to roll so heavily the seas were washing over the gunwales, threatening to loosen the obelisk and sink the ship before the horrified observers aboard the *Sphinx*. To salvage the situation, Verninac spread all his sails. This inhibited the heavy rolling, but risked demasting the ship. Finally the winds subsided. By the sixth, both vessels were able to anchor in the harbor

The *Sphinx* with *Luxor* in tow

of Rhodes, which the French found depressingly Turkish, with no sign of the ancient Knights of Saint John, or the famed Colossus.

About 6 leagues away, at Marmara, on the Caramanian coast, they found a pleasant cove called La Bonbonnière. There they spent some time having their clothes washed and hunting in the mountains, where there was much game and a landscape with windmills run by pretty falls of water. Next they went to Milos in search of coal. Finding none, they went on to Navarino and Zante, still with no luck. At Corfu the British high commissioner, Lord Nugent, obliged them with supplies from the British naval base. Both the British and the Corfiotes were most cordial in their welcome, sumptuously feasting the French. Crowds came aboard the *Luxor* to admire the obelisk and compliment the officers and crew.

Leaving Corfu, the *Sphinx* and the *Luxor* bucked another storm all the way to Cape Spartivento. On May 4 the wispy outline of Etna appeared to the west, and they slipped unharmed between Scylla and Charybdis. The Liparis were shrouded in fog, but Stromboli lit up the night sky with eruptions every ten minutes. In honor of Homer's Strombolian god of the winds, Verninac uncorked the last of the Champagne. It helped them double Cap Corse and drop anchor in Toulon harbor on the tenth of May, 1833, just two years and twenty-seven days after they had left.

For fear of the Egyptian plague, the Toulonnais refused to let the crew ashore, obliging them to submit to the excruciating ordeal of a month's quarantine within sight of their homes and loved ones. Only Lebas was allowed to go ahead to Paris to prepare a berth for the *Luxor* on the city's embankment.

On June 22 the *Luxor* sailed for Gibraltar on the first leg of its journey around Iberia. Across the bay, in Algeciras, they stopped to obtain permission from the authorities to put in at any Spanish port in case of trouble or bad weather. As it was the anniversary of the birth of Fernando VII's queen, Maria Cristina, the festivities were brought aboard. Crowds of dignitaries came to examine the obelisk; in the stateroom converted for the occasion into a ballroom, everyone danced the fandango and the bolero.

Approaching Cape Saint Vincent, the southernmost tip of Portugal, in a strong west wind, the convoy was obliged to lay off Lagos, on the Portuguese coast, where the crew of the *Luxor* witnessed the extraordinary spectacle of two warring battle fleets tied side by side. The corvettes, brigs, frigates, and schooners of Don Pedro, contender for the Portuguese throne, had just captured the superior forces of his rival, Don Miguel, despite the latter's ships of the line. On August 11 the *Luxor* caught sight of the coast of England and headed east for the military port of Cherbourg, just in time: the hurricane season had begun to ravage the channel ports, whose coasts were littered with wrecks and corpses.

At Cherbourg, Verninac received orders from the maritime prefect to await the arrival of King Louis Philippe, who was traveling with his family in western France. The king, accompanied by his wife and all the young princes, came aboard to decorate Angelin and Joannis with the Legion of Honor, and to inform Verninac of his promotion to *capitaine de corvette*. After listening to a description of the felling of the obelisk and being introduced to the ship's officers, Their Majesties were taken aboard the *Sphinx* for a naval review with lots of gun-firing and cries of *"Vive le roi!"*

The *Luxor* now had to be towed up the Seine to Paris. On September 12 the *Sphinx* took her as far as Cap de la Heve, at the estuary of the Seine, where there were more dangerous sandbanks to negotiate as far inland as Quilleboeuf, the actual mouth of the Seine. At La Heve the *Sphinx* was replaced by the river tug *Heva* for the trip to Rouen, where the *Luxor* would have to wait, tied to the Quai d'Arcourt, for the first autumn rains to raise the waters of the Seine sufficiently for the ship to be towed the rest of the way to Paris. But the rains were late; not till the middle of December did the river rise enough to move the *Luxor*.

Lebas rejoined the ship and ordered her lightened of all unnecessary equipment, including her masts, so as to pass under the twenty-two bridges between Rouen and Paris. Midday on December 14 the *Luxor,* which now resembled a flat *peniche,* negotiated the Pont de l'Arche and began its slow ascent up the Seine, drawn by eight pairs of horses. At points where the current was particularly strong, as many as thirty-two horses had to be engaged.

When the ships docked near the Bridge of Meulan, the water of the Seine was so high the *Luxor* could no longer pass under the arch nearest the towpath, and the local authorities, worried about damaging their precious bridge, made a lot of trouble before they would allow the more complicated maneuver of towing the ship through the central arch. When the *Luxor* reached the Bridge of Saint-Cloud, on the outskirts of Paris, at midnight of December 22, the bridgemaster refused to let it through, despite a

Louis Adolphe Thiers (1797–1827), historian and statesman from Marseilles, author of a history of the French Revolution, was one of the Freemasons involved in the enthronement of Louis Philippe in 1830. He became prime minister in 1836, and president of the republic in 1871.

written order handed him by Verninac. The water was rising so fast the ship risked being blocked below the bridge for several months. After an hour's harangue the bridgemaster finally relented, and the *Luxor,* just in time to avoid being caught, was winched through in the early hours of the morning.

In a thin misty rain a Parisian crowd had gathered along the Quai d'Orsay and on the Pont de la Concorde to see King Louis Philippe ride past on his way to open the 1834 joint session of the chamber of peers and of deputies at the Palais Bourbon. As the *Luxor* hove through the mist drawn by its teams of horses, word quickly spread that the obelisk from Luxor had arrived in Paris; but the crowd was disappointed to look down on the dirty, mastless ship with its tired crew in workaday waxed slickers. It had now passed from the jurisdiction of the minister of marine to that of the minister of commerce and public works, in the person of another diminutive Frenchman, described by Lebas as one who accorded to the arts and sciences "an enlightened protection," but who was to become better known as "the greatest little man of French history," the first president of the Third Republic: Louis Adolphe Thiers, a professed Freemason.

To beach the *Luxor,* with its five keels, and to avoid the risk of breaking either its stem or its cargo, Lebas had prepared another solid berth on ground near the Pont de la Concorde, just high enough to be left dry as soon as the waters of the Seine retreated from their peak.

The authorities could not make up their minds whether the obelisk should be placed at the Rondpoint des Champs-Élysées, in the courtyard of the Louvre, as a sentinel before the Madeleine, or in the Place de la Concorde as a symbol of a reunited France. Under various authorities of the Restoration, the center of the great square had been successively occupied by various monuments, the last of which was an equestrian statue apotheosizing Louis XVI on the spot where he had lost his head.

On December 24, King Louis Philippe announced he would visit the *Luxor,* which was rapidly spruced up for the occasion. Among the dignitaries assigned to greet the king was Geoffroy Saint-Hilaire, member of Napoleon's Institut d'Égypte and president of the Academy of Sciences. Arriving in his ceremonial palm-fronded uniform, complete with bogus épée, the old gent slipped on the narrow gangplank and plunged into the icy waters of the Seine, whence he was retrieved by two sailors and taken to Angelin's quarters, where his lobster-red body was toweled back to normal. The king, arriving by launch from the river-side, climbed aboard without mishap, and having inspected the obelisk in the ship's hold, gave Verninac 2,000 francs to be distributed to the crew.

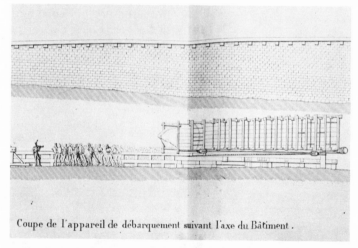

Coupe de l'appareil de débarquement suivant l'axe du Bâtiment.

To drag the obelisk up the embankment, Lebas impressed a company of artillerymen. To house the obelisk, pending the decision whether or not to place it in the Place de la Concorde, Lebas hired a pavilion. Once more the bow of the ship was sawed off. As at Luxor, a wooden cradle was built to slide the obelisk on a wooden track. Two hundred and forty artillerymen pushing on winches managed to drag the obelisk safely out of the ship, and, the next day, up the ramp. Thereafter, the obelisk lay for eighteen months in the pavilion, while a suitable pedestal was being devised. It took till August 1835 to find the right granite, in a town with the odd name of Later-il-Dut, on the coast of Brittany, for a pedestal which weighed 236½ tons—more than the obelisk itself. The *Sphinx* was sent to retrieve the finished pedestal and did not arrive back in Paris until April 1836. Three hundred artillerymen manned winches as the obelisk was dragged to the very spot where Louis XVI and Marie Antoinette had been decapitated barely forty years earlier, there to be raised with a trestle similar to the one which had felled it in Luxor. Inch-by-inch the monolith advanced across the square, eased by the old Egyptian method of pouring boiling grease onto the runners. But three more months were to pass by before the raising equipment was in position, and most observers began to wonder if the obelisk could actually be erected.

On October 24, 1836, all was ready. Ten winches, each of which could lift 15,000 kilograms, were to lift the obelisk's 125,000 kilograms past the crucial point of equilibrium. By eleven-thirty 350 artillerymen stood in an elliptical enclosure, ready to man the winches at an order to be sounded by a trumpet. It was a dangerous operation. Were a single order to be misinterpreted, the obelisk could come crashing down to kill or maim hundreds of workers and onlookers. The idea of clearing the Place de la Concorde of all spectators had been considered, but was discarded as unpopular. By noon more than 150,000 Parisians had gathered as close as they could get to the action.

At the sound of the trumpet the winches began to turn, the hoisting gear tightened, tension built up, and the trestle straightened almost imperceptibly. The master carpenter called out, "The obelisk has moved!" At noon the clarion sounded. Winches began to turn to the cadenced march of the artillerymen. The point of the pyramidion left its berth and began to describe a slow arc upward. But, as the foot of the obelisk described a similar arc in the opposite direction, its sharp edge dug into its wooden base, causing the juices to squirt from the lumber under pressure.

No harm came of it, and by the time the king and queen and members of the royal family appeared on the specially decorated balcony of the naval ministry, the obelisk had reached an angle of 38°, almost the point of utmost strain before the center of gravity could shift. There was the sudden cracking sound of splitting timber, and Lebas

243

The Paris authorities, hoping to use the occasion to show the populace the great advances of modern engineering over that of the ancients, had decided to use the raising of the obelisk to publicize a newly developed steam engine, virtually unknown to the public—"a mysterious and formidable creation which could terrify with its noise like thunder." By demonstrating to the public that a single man at the controls could lift the whole of Sesostris' monolith, the authorities hoped to impress upon the populace how well those at the helm of the ship of state were in command of science, or, as they put it: "man's most glorious conquest over nature."

Fortunately a banal defect in the equipment voided the experiment, which was to have proved that "nature, working for man, would be the sole serf of the future."

shouted for an immediate stoppage. The tension on the braces was such that they resounded to the touch like the strings of a violin. Bolts began to buckle. Obelisk, trestle, and base all risked being hurled by the strain in the direction of the Madeleine. The workers, though in imminent danger of being crushed, did not budge. To overcome the danger point, Lebas ordered accelerated pulling.

Minute by strained minute the obelisk rose, until at last it was upright, suspended a few inches above its base. All seemed in order when Lebas realized that in the excitement he had omitted to give the order to have the retaining chains loosed from the pyramidion. Two sailors quickly climbed the obelisk to cast them off before any damage could ensue.

Now the problem was to let the obelisk down onto its base gently enough not to crack it. To accomplish this delicate maneuver, winches were ordered to make three turns, two turns, one turn, then half a turn. Thus, five years from the day it had been felled where it had stood for four millennia, the obelisk once more rested upright on a solid base. There was wild applause as carpenters climbed the scaffolding to raise the tricolor above the pyramidion.

Louis Philippe uncovered his head to salute the same colors which had been raised thirty-five years earlier by

244

The obelisk in the Place de la
Concorde, with Napoleon's Arch
of Triumph at the end of the
Champs Élysées

Napoleon's savants over the ruins of Thebes. Lebas
crossed the square to join the king, who had summoned
him for congratulations and to invite him to dinner that
night at the Tuileries. As a reward for raising the obelisk,
Lebas was named engineer first-class, curator of the
marine museum, and member of the counsel of admiralty.

From the Château of the Tuileries that night, Lebas
could see the pyramidion of the obelisk, which his carpenters had specially illuminated. After dinner the king gave
Lebas 3,000 francs to distribute to the workers who had
raised the obelisk. Everyone appeared to be astounded
that Lebas had managed to place the obelisk within 2
centimeters of where it had been meant to go, overlooking
the fact that, originally, ancient engineers had erected it
squarely on a base exactly as they had intended.

Local chroniclers, remarking that the obelisk would
probably survive the splendor of Paris at least as long as
it had survived the splendor of Thebes, praised its beauty,
grandeur, solemnity, durability, simplicity, proportion, polish, harmony, and even its phallic qualities. But no one
mentioned or seemed to have any idea as to what might
have been the original purpose of the obelisks of Luxor.

The one person who might have cracked the riddle for
them, Jean François Champollion, recently elected a

245

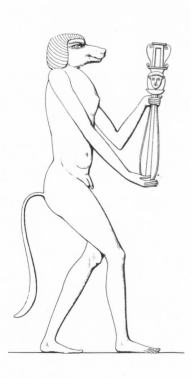

I
MONUMENTI
DELL'
EGITTO E DELLA NUBIA

DISEGNATI DALLA SPEDIZIONE SCIENTIFICO-LETTERARIA TOSCANA IN EGITTO
DISTRIBUITI IN ORDINE DI MATERIE INTERPRETATI ED ILLUSTRATI

DAL DOTTORE
IPPOLITO ROSELLINI

TOMO TERZO
MONUMENTI DEL CULTO

PISA
PRESSO NICCOLÒ CAPURRO
M D CCC XL IV

member of the Académie des Inscriptions and named by Louis Philippe to an archaeological chair specially created for him at the Collège de France, had just finished his *Grammaire Égyptienne*—which he considered "my visiting card to posterity"—when he was struck by apoplexy and confined to bed. In January 1832, just as Lebas had been embarking to travel up the Nile to Aswan, Champollion had become too sick to lecture and was obliged to retire to Figeac. There the doctors diagnosed his strange disease as something brought back from Egypt which manifested itself in the form of bronchitis, gout, galloping tuberculosis, and partial paralysis. A career, which was about to flower brilliantly, was struck in the bud. On March 4 of that year Champollion was dead.

With this first real giant of Egyptology out of the way, a small but energetic clique of envious and malicious enemies began to poison his memory by continued efforts to minimize and ridicule his findings, questioning, as they had with Kircher, his honesty and integrity. "It is sad," remarks Erik Iversen, "that every scientific achievement must submit to the disgraceful ordeal and mock trial of envy, ignorance and stupidity, painful and often fatal to the victim, even if truth prevails."

For the next several decades after his death, Champollion's claim to having deciphered the hieroglyphs was hotly disputed. The English refused to accept the evi-

dence; the Germans rejected his method. It was left to Ippolito Rosellini to publish in ten volumes, over a period of eight years, the results of their expedition to Egypt. Not till 1866 was Champollion properly vindicated, when what amounted to another Rosetta Stone was found by the German Egyptologist Karl Richard Lepsius in the delta ruins of Tanis, inscribed in hieroglyphics, demotic script and Greek. The stone bore a decree in honor of Ptolemy III and Berenice II, his queen, inscribed in 239 B.C. in the ancient Egyptian seaport of Canopus on the western mouth of the Nile. With this newly discovered text, Lepsius was able to corroborate Champollion's dictionary of hieroglyphs and prove the accuracy of his grammar.

Sixty-four years after Champollion's death, Sir Peter le Page Renouf at last addressed the Royal Society in London to pay homage to the brilliance of Jean François Champollion le Jeune as the true founder of modern Egyptology. Egyptologists were able to forge ahead with translations of glyphs to reveal laws, rituals, literature, customs, and manners of the ancient Egyptians. From these efforts a picture emerged of a people who had carried art and science to a height which modern man had only begun to match. At last Pico, Dee, Bruno, Cagliostro might come into their own.

To drive home to the world the importance of this revival of Egyptian wisdom, a group of British Freemasons decided to erect a symbol to it in London by bringing back from Alexandria the obelisk donated by Mohammed Ali which the French had negligently left in place.

13. VICTORIAN VANITY

Napoleon's troops had already fastened a cable around Cleopatra's upright needle in Alexandria and were on the point of felling it to bring back to France in commemoration of their 1798 victories in Egypt when they were rudely interrupted by General Sir Ralph Abercromby's Twenty-eighth Gloucestershires, who forced the French to abandon the attempt. Victory gave the British the idea of bringing back to England the obelisk to celebrate the defeat of Napoleon. But instead of the upright needle, which seemed tricky to lower without breaking, Major General the earl of Cavan, in command of the small force of Britishers left to garrison Alexandria, decided it would be easier to ship to London the prostrate monolith beside it. Cavan sought permission from the local Turkish authorities to remove the fallen needle, and schemed with his military engineer, Major Alexander Bryce, on how to embark the trophy.

To finance this operation, the British troops were "graciously" invited by their officers to "voluntarily" subscribe a certain number of days' pay to "meet the expenses of an undertaking in which their feelings were deeply interested." Officers and men—so goes the official report—"vied with each other in offering their contribution to the furtherance of an object so gratifying to their national and professional pride." Seven thousand pounds were collected to build a jetty from which to load the obelisk into the stern of a captured French frigate, El Corso, where it would lie on a bed of timbers.

Work was begun, and "pay issued to the working parties from the funds they themselves had contributed"; but after the soldiers and sailors, aided by a gang of Arabs, had expended a week of heavy labor they only managed to move the obelisk 6 inches. Then a gale washed away the jetty, and in London the British commanders of the army and navy ordered the project canceled, the official reason given to avoid displeasing the Ottoman sultan to whom the obelisk technically belonged, but unofficially for reasons of state. El Corso was disposed of; what was left of the money was returned to the troops.

Not to be totally frustrated, Cavan had a tablet inscribed to the memory of Britain's exploits against the French in Egypt. Afraid the Turks would destroy it as soon as the British left, he had it buried beneath the base of

249

the prostrate obelisk, where no one could possibly see it. In the words of the official account: "They found the pedestal to Cleopatra's Needle and having heeled it to starboard they made a cavity to receive the tablet and replaced the heavy stone."

Once the last of the British had left Alexandria in 1803, the monolith was allowed to disappear again beneath the sand, there to be forgotten until Mohammed Ali, as the new khedive of Egypt, realized he might use the trophy as bait to obtain from the British enough corvettes to develop a navy and so defend himself against his former master at the Ottoman Porte. Renewing his offer to donate the prostrate obelisk to Britain, Mohammed Ali even volunteered to pay for it to be loaded onto a ship. But the admiralty, who did not wish to see the upstart viceroy develop even a weak Egyptian fleet along their route to India, allowed the offer to dangle.

Not so the generals who had served in Egypt in 1801, and who were still hankering and agitating for their prize. But as the years stretched into decades without their being able to change the admiralty's mind, they finally presented a memorandum to Queen Victoria's consort, Prince Albert, to see what he could do. Dutifully, the prince addressed a letter, signed "Albert," to the queen's minister, Lord John Russel, in which he supported the notion of having "this universally renowned work of art brought to London." But even his royal efforts were of no avail against the admirals.

Cartoon lampooning the khedive for walking off with Cleopatra's Needle

Only when it was rumored that Mohammed Ali was flirting with the French in the hope of improving his navy, and had offered them *both* obelisks in Alexandria, was a new ruckus raised in Parliament. But when the French unaccountably refrained from taking the obelisk, it too died down. What was needed by the military survivors of the Egyptian campaign to get their obelisk was more propaganda, and it came in the form of two reports, neither too subtle. A London magazine carried the story of a Briton having been seen sitting astride the prostrate obelisk, knocking off chunks of the inscribed stone with a hammer as mementos for himself and his fellow tourists. When the writer of the article had expostulated with his fellow Briton, reminding him that the relic belonged to the British nation, the vandal was quoted as replying: "I know. And as a member of the British nation I mean to have my share." That the story was apocryphal is evidenced from the fact that the obelisk was still buried deep in the Alexandrine sands of the delta. Some smart propagandist was pulling at Albion's heartstring.

The second story, with a French villain, induced even greater Bullish choler. It was reported that the Greek owner of the land on which Britain's obelisk lay had hired a French engineer to dynamite the monolith into pieces small enough to be used for building material.

That did it. General Sir James Edward Alexander, a ranking Freemason and great-nephew of Sir Alexander Bryce, who, as Major Bryce, had originally helped Lord Cavan try to remove the obelisk in 1801, went into action. It was March 1875. "I determined," wrote Alexander, "to endeavour to save the national disgrace of the loss and destruction of the trophy, and resolved to do my utmost to have it transported to London to grace the metropolis with a monument similar to those at Rome, Paris and Constantinople."

Alexander's first move was to go to Egypt and confirm permission from Mohammed Ali's grandson, the reigning khedive, or viceroy, Ismail Pasha, to remove the obelisk. From the British government Alexander received partial assistance in that Lord Derby, then foreign secretary, gave him a semidiplomatic status by instructing the British agent in Egypt, General Stanton, to introduce him to Ismail Pasha. In Cairo, General Alexander put up at Shepherd's Hotel, full pension, for 16 shillings a day. Among the guests were Lord Grey, whom Alexander described as keeping up the British sporting reputation abroad. He had just spent eighteen thousand cartridges on pelicans, ducks, quail, and one on a crocodile.

Alexander found the khedive, Ismail, who had been educated in Paris, a pleasant-looking man, in good condition, wearing the usual red fez, dark surcoat, and white vest, but no sign of rank, a mode he had adopted since the opening of the Suez Canal six years earlier, when he had begun to claim rank as a European sovereign. But his administration was so expensive and his aides so corrupt he was soon obliged to sell to Britain his shares in the canal, which signaled the beginning of his downfall.

Alexander's audience with the khedive took place on March 25, in the Palace of Abdin, guarded inside and out by a reconstituted body of Mamelukes, in crimson and gold. For the occasion, Alexander wore a general officer's undress uniform with a sword and a sash. In French, the khedive said to Alexander: "This obelisk was presented to the British nation by my ancestor Mohammed Ali Pasha, for services rendered to Egypt. It belongs to Britain. I give it up freely. How is it to be removed?"

Alexander explained, as best he could, and accepted the gift with good grace, knowing that the khedive was being generous because he wished to sell to Great Britain his shares in the Suez Canal to help defray part of the 100-million-pound debt he had run up with a swarm of foreign concession-hunters, who had helped him to loot the country. Taking his leave, Alexander returned to Alexandria, where he asked his dragoman, Mustapha Ali, to show him the obelisk.

"There," said the dragoman.

"Where?" said Alexander. "I see nothing."

Mustapha gave orders to an Arab standing nearby, and when a large amount of sand had been cleared away, a portion of the obelisk came into view. It lay near the seawall, which was wasted by the water of the Mediterranean. For some distance out, the sea was very shallow and choked with the remains of ancient buildings, broken columns, and other debris from centuries past. So encumbered was it that an ordinary vessel capable of carrying a 200-ton load could not possibly come close to shore, especially a shore that was frequently exposed to gales.

Several people came forward with suggestions to Alexander as to how he could move the obelisk.

First, the obelisk had to be completely uncovered, so as to examine its condition and accurately estimate its weight. A working party of Arabs was engaged, and Dixon was able to establish that the obelisk was 68½ feet long, with a base 7½ feet wide. From this data he estimated the obelisk had a volume of 2,517 cubic feet and a weight of 186⅓ tons.

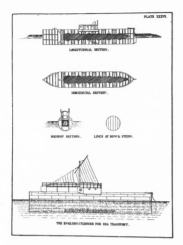

Dixon's plan for transporting the obelisk to England

Alexander settled instead on the advice of a civil engineer from the North England Iron Company to whom he had been introduced by an officer of the Porte, Chamberlain Bey. The engineer, Waynman Dixon, also a high-ranking Mason, explained to Alexander that he and his brother John has been interested in the obelisk for some years and had worked out a careful scheme for getting it back to England.

Having had a good look at the obelisk, Dixon was convinced that the only method of getting it into the sea, and back to England, was to encase it in an iron cylinder which could be rolled down the slopes till it floated. If the cylinder were built in properly watertight segments and given a keel, it could be towed by a regular steamship— all the way to England. Such segments, said Dixon, could easily be built in a British naval yard, and shipped out to Egypt. Only, who was to pay for the job?

In a letter to a friend and fellow Mason in England, Dr. William James Erasmus Wilson, Alexander had already referred to "Cleopatra's Needle." Wilson, a doctor in his middle sixties, who had piled up a fortune as Britain's leading dermatologist, augmented by shrewd investments in gas- and oil-company shares, offered to meet and discuss the matter with Waynman Dixon. An indefatigable traveler in the Near East, particularly interested in Egyptian antiquities, Wilson was renowned as a generous benefactor of charities, having bequeathed no less than £200,000 to the Royal College of Surgeons.

When Wilson found out that Dixon was also a high-ranking Mason "all formality and ceremony were at once banished." Dixon told Wilson he could encase the monolith in boiler plates, steady the cylinder with bilge plates, ballast it, fix on a rudder, a cabin, and a spar deck, then tow the whole thing to England for about £7,000. Would Dixon, Wilson asked, undertake safely to set up the obelisk in London on the banks of the Thames for £10,000—"no cure, no pay"?

"Willingly," replied Dixon; and Wilson's only further stipulation was that Dixon converse with another Freemason, civil engineer H. P. Stephenson. They met in a solicitor's office in Bedford Row and agreed upon a contract.

But by this time, back in Alexandria, Alexander had found himself stymied. The obelisk had been entirely surrounded by a tall palisade, put up by the owner of the land on which the obelisk lay, a Greek named Giovanni Demetrios, who had been complaining to the khedive for a score of years to get the obelisk removed from his property as it was a hazard to its development. Now the

Greek complained that by giving away the obelisk without consulting him, the khedive had wounded his feelings, adding that the khedive had no right to allow strangers to trespass on his private property. Demetrios refused to allow anything to be done unless he received a heavy indemnity for the removal of the obelisk.

To resolve the situation, Alexander called on Demetrios with a lady friend—a Mrs. Gisborne—in the hope, he said, that female influence might affect the old Greek. Alexander found him living in a handsome residence in a beautiful garden, a man of culture, with his personal physician in attendance, Dr. Neroutsas Bey, "a very intelligent antiquary." After much coffee-taking and palavering, Demetrios gave in, explaining that as a Greek, who was thankful to Great Britain for what she had done to help liberate his country, and as a connoisseur and collector of antiques in his own right, he had no desire but to help. There was only one condition: that he be considered the donor of the monument. Alexander readily agreed, and a deed of gift was drawn up which showed that both Demetrios and the khedive had made a present to Britain of the obelisk.

It was now only a question of receiving the iron cylinder segments from England and of assembling them about the obelisk. To superintend the job, Waynman Dixon had commissioned an old salt, Captain Maximilian Carter, who had served twenty-two years with the Peninsular and Orient Line. He was to inspect the segments of the vessel being constructed at the Thomas Iron Works Company under the instructions of a naval architect.

Meanwhile, Dixon recruited another gang of Arabs to remove all the sand from about the obelisk. With hydraulic jacks capable of lifting 100 tons, he had them raise the shaft onto a solid bed of long pine beams and railway sleepers, uncovering in the process several skulls and

human arms and legs, which he promised to the British Museum. When Captain Carter arrived in Alexandria, he was pleased to find the obelisk lying parallel to the sea, but concluded he would have a hard time rolling the completed cylinder into the water because of the hundreds of building stones lying about the shore front and extending far into the sea; many of them were relics of old Roman pavement, others, more ancient, were covered with Egyptian hieroglyphics. Divers were hired to remove enough of these enormous blocks of stone—some of which weighed more than 20 tons—so as to make a path for the obelisk through the shallow water to where it could be floated in a depth of about 10 feet. But some of the blocks were so large they had to be blasted with dynamite, as did some buildings further out to sea whose huge walls appeared to be the foundations of an enormous Roman bath.

Cleopatra's Needle encased in its iron cylinder, 9.8.1877

When the cylinder was finally wrapped around the obelisk in ten watertight compartments, it looked like an enormous boiler, 93 feet long and 15 feet in diameter. Dixon figured that if the center of gravity of the obelisk inside the cylinder was kept 10 inches below the main axis of the cylinder, it would—once it was a vessel—

255

remain in a state of equilibrium in the sea, no matter which way it was rolled by wind or wave. To protect the outer surface of the cylinder while it was being rolled into the sea, timber rings 9 inches thick and 18 inches deep were strapped around it, near the ends, making huge wheels on which the vessel could roll. To start it rolling, hawsers were passed nine times round the vessel and taken to winches on board heavy lighters moored some distance out. Other hawsers were fastened on land to check any undesired movement.

On the day set for the launching, August 28, 1877, a terrible fog shrouded the scene, but it soon cleared, and several thousand spectators turned up from the mixed population of Alexandria to view the operations in what developed into a heat wave of 90° in the shade. A select group of visitors, protected by parasols, included Princess Said, sister of the khedive, and the British consul general, Mr. Vivian.

At the appointed signal, the winches began to pull, hawsers strained, and the cylinder slowly turned, its movement hardly perceptible. By noon it had made one full revolution, covering a distance of 50 feet. Then the anchors began to drag out to sea, and the ropes had to be shifted to tugboats which steamed away at full power, just managing to keep the cylinder rolling. By 5:30 P.M., the cylinder had reached the water's edge and by seven it was in 3 feet of water; there it was left for the night.

Soon after daylight on the twenty-ninth, tugs began to

Floating the cylinder

The cylinder being towed to the Alexandria docks

With the use of heavy jacks, the obelisk was placed 4 inches below this axis and forced into place with heavy timber struts. The other 6 inches were gained by loading 12 tons of iron rails into the vessel's bottom as ballast. Further to steady the craft, its fore and aft compartments were completely filled with concrete.

tow again, and by noon the cylinder should have floated. But it didn't. It was half full of water, and there was no way to get inside because the manholes had rotated to its underbelly. Arab divers were summoned, but could not figure out what had happened. When a hole was cut in the surface, above water, and a double suction pump set to work, it had no effect on the level of the water within the cylinder. A deepsea diver in proper suit found that a large stone, hidden in the sand, had penetrated the bottom of the cylinder. Water had mysteriously flooded all the compartments. It was then discovered that in the excitement of the event, everyone had forgotten to close the bulkhead manholes.

To remove the half-ton stone took several days. The cylinder had to be rolled so that its 18-inch hole could be riveted from above water. Two more days and the cylinder floated. Safely towed 9 miles to a great floating dock belonging to the Egyptian government, it was to be fitted with 40-foot bilge keels riveted to the bottom, plus a cabin, a bridge, and a rudder. As soon as the latter was hung from the stern, the vessel was ready for the open sea.

For a crew to man the cylinder under his command, Carter had hired five Maltese sailors and a Maltese carpenter, who agreed to make the run to England for £20. A boatswain insisted on fifty. To tow the cylinder, Dixon had obtained the *Olga,* a steamship belonging to William Johnson and Company of Liverpool, for £900, half to be paid in advance and the remainder on safe arrival, with the obelisk, in Falmouth.

On September 19 a party was held aboard the cylinder, attended by "a hundred and fifty ladies and gentlemen" who watched as the daughter of the British admiral Mac-Killop Pasha christened the cylinder *Cleopatra* with a bottle of Champagne broken against the stern. On September 21, 1877, despite remonstrances from the Maltese crew that it was bad luck to set off on a Friday, Captain Carter, who had worked himself into a state of exhaustion to get the *Cleopatra* shipshape, agreed to sail. Dixon, traveling on the *Olga,* was anxious to get the obelisk to London and avoid having to wait for fair weather in the spring. Slowly the *Olga* steamed out of Alexandria harbor, with the *Cleopatra* in tow.

The odd-shaped vessel showed herself to be staunch and buoyant, but not easy to steer. She yawed wildly, and in an undulating sea pitched severely, causing great and uneven tension on the 700-foot wire towline. Even at a moderate speed the *Cleopatra* would sink her bow, obliging the *Olga* to go dead slow.

Captain Carter spent all of the first night on deck. The next night the heat was so oppressive his men could not sleep below. Stretching themselves on the narrow deck, wherever they could find room, they tried to snatch fitful half-hours of sleep. Then the breeze freshened, and the *Cleopatra* began to plunge, making sixteen to seventeen dives a minute, completely submerging her bow, which required the crew to hold on with both hands as the sea swept over the entire vessel.

The boatswain got sick from an inflamed liver, and the crew asked to put into Malta. Lest they all bolt, the captain refused. Instead, he gave them each a glass of grog and opened a bottle of Champagne for himself and

The *Cleopatra* towed by the *Olga*

The captain in his cabin

Taking care of the boatswain

Longitudinal section of the cylinder with ballast and bulkheads

the invalid boatswain. One man short, Captain Carter had to stand watches, assist in the cooking, and even trim the lamps at night. He no longer took off his clothes except to wash them and put them on again. Every six hours he took pains to examine the compartments below deck to see that all was secure. To reach the obelisk, he had to wriggle down a small hole in the floor of the saloon, crawl through the manholes in the various divisions, and examine each diaphragm. When the candle he held in his mouth as he crawled beneath the obelisk began to burn his nose, he had to drop it, obliging him to grope his way back for a full half-hour before he could reach the open air. It was not, said Carter, using a Britisher's understatement, "drawingroom work." At first he had difficulty squeezing through the narrow manholes. Later he joked that the regular but simple diet enabled him to slip through "like a halfstarved rat."

Near the island of Galita, the ship ran into much thunder and lightning. A ball of fire danced on the masthead, and there were wild screams from the *Cleopatra*'s crew of "the devil! the devil!" Carter explained it was nothing but Saint Elmo's light, not unusual in the Mediterranean in stormy air full of electricity.

On October 2, the *Olga* signaled she had to put into Algiers for coal. There the ship's crew got so drunk they assaulted their chief officer, tearing out one side of his whiskers. At Gibraltar, when Dixon went ashore and engaged two more sailors, he was warned by naval men that October was a singularly bad month to head across the Bay of Biscay, especially with such a tricky cargo. There was also a report from America warning that a hurricane was expected to cross the Atlantic in mid-October. But Dixon was determined not to have to leave the *Cleopatra* in Gibraltar for the winter. So they sailed on as planned.

On October 10, at 2:30 A.M., the two vessels spotted the light off Cape Saint Vincent. At six thirty they rounded the cape itself. From the west-northwest a long Atlantic swell

Rough going in the Bay of Biscay

set in, over which, according to Carter, "the *Cleopatra* rode like a duck." As they passed the mouth of the river Tagus, steamers came out to have a look at the strange craft. On Saturday, October 13, at 5:00 P.M., Carter reported seeing Cape Finisterre, the westernmost point of northern Spain. There was a light southerly wind; but he also noticed unmistakable signs of an approaching storm.

On the fourteenth, Captain Booth of the *Olga* noted in his logbook that at latitude 44°55′ north and longitude 7°52′ west, off the northernmost tip of Spain, the wind freshened, increasing with squalls and fast-rising seas. But with the *Olga*'s engines going dead slow, the *Cleopatra* was doing all right. Nevertheless, to steady the *Cleopatra* against the rising waves, a sea anchor was prepared in the form of a conical canvas bag 6 feet long by 15 feet in circumference, its mouth kept open with crosspieces. When thrown overboard at the end of 40 or 50 fathoms of rope, it would help keep the vessel's head to the wind.

By noon a furious squall came up from the south-southwest, accompanied by hail and rain. The wind increased till it was blowing a heavy gale. So long as the vessel was before the wind, Carter felt he had no cause for anxiety, although the whole of the after part of the vessel was frequently immersed, the sea occasionally rolling over the cabin. All afternoon the barometer contin-

260

ued to fall, while the wind began to veer to the west. As the sea became more quarterly, it broke heavily against the deckhouse, and Carter had serious fears of the whole superstructure being swept away.

By 5:00 P.M. he made up his mind to heave to, and lie with his head into the wind to ride out the storm on his sea anchor. Captain Booth on the *Olga* acknowledged his signal and replied, "Greater risk to tow line if heave-to!" Nevertheless, he set a mainstay sail and just before sundown proceeded with what Carter called "consummate skill and judgement" to bring his ship well round to the wind. Only just too late. The *Cleopatra*'s broadside was struck by a tremendous sea which overwhelmed her, hurling her over on her starboard beam, where she remained with a heavy list. The timberwork securing the iron rails employed as ballast had given way. Shifting about, the rails caused the vessel to lay over at an angle of more than 45°.

Carter, who had already been wrecked three times before, and had been on an Indian ocean liner when it caught fire, did not panic. Instead, he opened the manhole door in the saloon floor and went down with his crew into the hold to try to right the ballast. The gale was now at its height. Though the seas were breaking completely over the *Cleopatra,* she was only making water at the upper bolt-holes. With the hull half full of water and 12 tons of railway iron sloshing around, the job wasn't easy. After an hour's work, the crew finally got the ballast shifted sufficiently to right the vessel. Then a huge wave struck the starboard side and the ballast shifted again, causing the ship to list to port at an even worse angle than before.

Slowing her engines almost to a stop, the *Olga* came as close as practicable, distinguishing signals of distress

from the *Cleopatra.* At this point the gale began to
slacken. Toward 9:30 P.M., Captain Booth decided to risk
lowering a boat, and called for volunteers. The second
mate, William Askin, a young man of twenty-six, immediately volunteered, along with five seamen, all from Liverpool.

Captain Booth stopped the engines and got a lifeboat
safely clear of the ship and into the water. In the dark,
Booth could just distinguish the lifeboat as it approached
Carter's vessel. A line thrown from the *Cleopatra* was
caught by Askin and one of his mates, but they were
unable to hold onto it. As the rope slipped through their
hands, the boat drifted past the *Cleopatra*'s leeward side
into the dark night.

On the *Olga,* Captain Booth waited for the reappear-
ance of his lifeboat, which he assumed to be on the far
side of Carter's vessel. When it hadn't arrived by eleven,
Booth maneuvered as close as he could to the *Cleopatra,*
and hailed her, to ask about the boat. He could make
nothing of the answers, except that the men were in
serious distress. The *Cleopatra* was listing very heavily to
port, and he noticed that they had cut away her mast.

Booth's only recourse was to launch a "messenger
buoy" to sweep the *Cleopatra* with a line in the hope that
its crew might grapple it and haul it aboard. The wind was
moderating slightly; but a heavy sea was still running,
causing the *Olga* to pitch and roll so heavily she was
shipping much water, and the attempt failed.

As there were no volunteers to man another lifeboat,
Booth concluded he had no other choice but to keep as

Captain Carter's sketch of the problems encountered in the heavy sea

close as he could to the *Cleopatra* and wait for daylight. All night Carter and his crew continued in their efforts to right the ballast. As often as they did so, the merciless sea threw it back. When day dawned, the gale had moderated considerably; though the sea was still running high. As the *Olga* approached, it found the *Cleopatra* settled heavily on her port beam, its crew still alive and in full force. Of the lifeboat, not a sign.

Booth slipped another cask overboard as a buoy, but again it failed to reach the *Cleopatra*. Edging closer, he managed, after several ineffectual attempts, to throw a line aboard the crippled vessel by means of which a 5-inch hawser was hauled in to keep her in position. Standing to leeward, Booth lowered a boat which managed to reach the *Cleopatra* and take Captain Carter and his Maltese crew safely aboard.

Booth then cut loose from the vessel, leaving her on her beam end, expecting her to sink at any moment. At full speed he proceeded in search of the missing lifeboat. With lookouts aloft he steered westward and soon passed a boat hook and then a messenger buoy, but saw no sign of the lifeboat. By ten thirty, there being nothing in sight from aloft, Booth bore up and ran down to leeward, passing the *Cleopatra*'s severed mast, but saw nothing of her hull, or of the lifeboat.

At noon, hopes of finding either the boat or the *Cleopatra* began to fade. Booth concluded that the lifeboat had been swamped and the crew lost. The *Cleopatra*, with her precious needle, must have gone to the bottom. Heading for Falmouth, he prepared a signal to the effect that six men had perished in a lifeboat, and the *Cleopatra* and her cargo had been lost in a heavy gale in the Bay of Biscay.

In London, where the press and the public had been following the moves of the *Cleopatra* from dispatch to

THE ILLUSTRATED LONDON NEWS

REGISTERED AT THE GENERAL POST-OFFICE FOR TRANSMISSION ABROAD.

No. 1998.—VOL. LXXI.   SATURDAY, OCTOBER 27, 1877.   WITH TWO SUPPLEMENTS } SIXPENCE. BY POST, 6½D.

ABANDONMENT OF CLEOPATRA'S NEEDLE IN THE BAY OF BISCAY, AT DAYBREAK, OCT. 15.
FROM A SKETCH SUPPLIED BY CAPTAIN CARTER, OF THE CLEOPATRA.

London reports the abandonment of Cleopatra's Needle in the Bay of Biscay

dispatch, arguing as to where the trophy should be placed, the news was stunning. Everyone was suddenly glum and silent. Only Dixon refused to believe the *Cleopatra* was lost. He insisted that the vessel had been left with eight watertight compartments and only a small amount of water in her hold, leaking from the bolt-holes on her top. The huge stone, according to Carter, had been perfectly secure when the ship was abandoned. All the seams were tight, and all of the manholes fastened. The worst that could happen, said Dixon, was that the 12 tons of rail ballast could roll from side to side, listing the vessel alternately from port to starboard, but with the fore and aft compartments filled with cement, Dixon maintained, the vessel could not capsize.

Furthermore, he pointed out that the 200 fathoms of steel cable hanging from her bows would act as a sea anchor, keeping her head to the wind, and that if she were to run into shallow water, the cable would act as a regular anchor. Convinced the *Cleopatra* was still afloat, Dixon appealed to the first lord of the admiralty to dispatch a steamer in search of her, pointing out that she was a serious hazard in the track of passing vessels, especially as she had no lights.

On October 15, the *Fitzmaurice,* a small iron screw steamer of 297 tons, bound from Middlesbourough to Valencia, Spain, with a cargo of pig iron, encountered heavy winds in the Bay of Biscay and was forced to lie to until the seas calmed sufficiently for her to resume her course. Off the northern coast of Spain, some 90 miles north of the port of Ferrol, and 15 miles northeast of Corunna, the *Fitzmaurice* sighted a strange object in the sea. As the *Fitzmaurice*'s captain Evans reported the event, at about 5:00 P.M. he spotted what appeared to be the bottom of a ship on the lee beam. Putting the helm hard up, he bore down upon the object and just at dusk realized it was the *Cleopatra,* about which all Britain was agog.

As there was too much sea to board her, he waited, with great difficulty, on account of the rough weather, till dawn of the following day, when he was able to fasten two 9-inch hawsers to the vessel. Two hours later the strain of the heavy sea caused both lines to part. The captain launched another boat and screwed more hawsers to her, setting off at a very slow pace through the heavy sea.

The next morning such a heavy gale blew from the southeast that the ropes parted again, and the captain was only able to refasten them with the greatest difficulty. Limping along, the *Fitzmaurice* finally managed to tow the *Cleopatra* into the pretty little port town of Ferrol, one of the best harbors in Europe. As soon as he was able to inspect the way in which the obelisk had been packed, Evans saw that it was still in perfect shape, but concluded that whoever had arranged the ballast had been a soldier, not a sailor. When the news reached London of the safe discovery of both *Cleopatra* and obelisk, there was general rejoicing, except for the fate of the six missing sailors. From Balmoral, Dixon received a message that Queen Victoria had suggested inscribing the names of the six drowned men on the pedestal to the needle.

At Falmouth, another message, undelivered, awaited the drowned second mate, William Askin, to inform him that his wife had given birth to their first child. A fund was immediately set up for the widows and dependents of the drowned sailors. Dixon put up the first £250, and the owners of the *Olga,* who had thought highly of Askin, and had placed him first in turn for promotion in their service, undertook to organize the fund.

Meanwhile, John Dixon, Waynman's brother, set off with Captain Carter for Glasgow to sort out the salvage costs with the owner of the *Fitzmaurice,* a Mr. Burrell. They did their best to induce the Scot to be moderate in his charges, on patriotic grounds, explaining that it had been a great honor for him, in the eyes of the nation, to have been owner of the vessel which had picked up the *Cleopatra* and towed it to Ferrol. They suggested he be content with that honor, providing the crew was paid a moderate sum for their trouble. Burrell claimed £5,000 in cash. When Dixon offered him £600, the "hard-headed Scotchman" could not be moved.

In Liverpool, Carter went to retrieve from Captain Evans his sextant and other instruments, as well as his log book. His portmanteau had been broken open and thrown overboard with all his private papers, and about £20. His clothes were gone. So were several antique coins and rings. The *Fitzmaurice*'s mate was wearing his shirtstuds. Yet Captain Evans declined to relax the lien on the *Cleopatra,* or on the obelisk, until the claim for salvage was met in full.

Taking the case to an admiralty court, Dixon was able to obtain a reduction in the salvage price from £5,000 to £2,000. As soon as the sum was paid, Captain Carter was able to proceed to Ferrol on a Spanish steamship with a fresh crew from Liverpool to refit the *Cleopatra* with 2 tons of nuts, bolts, chains, and varied ironwork.

At Ferrol, which was well provided with dry docks and warehouses, Carter was able to fit out the *Cleopatra* with a new mast, sails, steering yoke, and tiller. Water and

266

provisions were taken aboard on January 1, 1878. To tow the vessel to England, a 270-ton, 140-horsepower iron tug, the *Anglia,* arrived from Liverpool with a well-known artist aboard from the *Illustrated London News,* who was commissioned to make sketches of the *Cleopatra* and her obelisk for an avid British public, more anxious than ever for the arrival of the trophy. Dixon was worried that the *Anglia* would have to weather another 350 miles across the Bay of Biscay; but he had received a good meteorological forecast from the *New York Herald,* and he estimated that there would be a long moon starting January 19.

The *Cleopatra* resumed her journey on the fifteenth, moving at 5 knots on a tow line of 120 fathoms. Again the ships ran into a gale, which sent huge waves breaking over both vessels, tossing them badly.

"Shall we bear up and turn back?" signaled the captain of the *Anglia.*

"Not if I were in your place," answered Carter. "Better proceed at half speed."

One more boisterous night with heavy rain, and on January 21 *Anglia* and *Cleopatra* pulled into Gravesend in the mouth of the Thames to a chorus of cheers from a crowd on land, and a telegram from Queen Victoria congratulating Dixon on the safe arrival of the needle. *Anglia* and *Cleopatra* responded by dipping their ensigns.

At London's East India docks, the dockmaster, sensing the patriotic air in the wind, generously allowed the *Cleopatra* to dock free of all the usual charges.

But now that the obelisk was safely in the British capital, the great dispute was renewed as to where it should be placed. The earl of Harrowby maintained that

The *Cleopatra* at Gravesend, in the mouth of the Thames, as drawn by the artist aboard the *Anglia*

the choice of the site should be determined by what he called "moral fitness." His idea of a morally fit place was Parliament Square, where the trophy could recall its associations with the victories of Nelson and Abercromby in "surroundings which remind us of the most venerated memories of national history."

"In any other position," said the earl, "it would be a mere tall stone, a mere monolith, only remarkable for its dimensions, and for imperfectly seen configurations upon its surface, but having no significance, telling no story, awakening no associations. . . ."

Imaginative illustration of the obelisk already raised in Parliament Square.

Even more imaginative scene of the obelisk being paraded through the streets of London

The needle by moonlight

In *The Times,* "A Peer in Reply" thought otherwise, saying that Harrowby had failed to see the moral fitness of placing this relic of tyrannical pharaohs in a spot "hallowed by centuries old associations with the development of our parliamentary institutions and Christian religion." The anonymous peer summed up his argument: "it would be the violation, not the fulfillment of all moral fitness."

Still others wished to place the trophy in front of the British Museum, where it could be closer to other Egyptian antiquities, but the spot was ruled too dark and too small and it was feared that underground utilities would be endangered. At last it was decided to raise the monument on the Adelphi steps of the Victoria embankment, where the obelisk could be admired from a distance (especially by the crowds coming over Waterloo Bridge), where it could have a small park around it, and where, because of its proximity to the river, it would not crush in transit, with its 186 tons, any of the gas or sewer lines of London. Yet even the embankment was objected to by a fellow of the Royal Institute of British Architects, John Holden, who raised the question of possible dangers to the needle from the pressure of the wind, suggesting it might be blown over. John Dixon, with a heavy sigh, pointed out that, from his calculations, whereas less than 30 pounds of pressure per square foot could send a man flying, level Charing Cross station, or sweep a passenger train from the rails, 130 pounds of wind pressure would not upset the obelisk.

269

"No obelisk," said Dixon, "has ever been overturned by the wind."

As an ornamental base of the obelisk, it was arranged that an architect and an engineer with the Gilbert and Sullivan names of Vulliamy and Bazalgette provide four bronze sphinxes. These colossi, 19 feet long, 9 high, and 6 wide, were to be copies of an authentic Egyptian sphinx set up in the garden of the duke of Northumberland's castle whose sphinx was thought to be of the same period as the obelisk because of a Thothmes III cartouche on its base. Vulliamy and Bazalgette also filled with solid concrete two arches in the embankment that had been used as reservoirs for water with which to flush the steps, thus providing the obelisk with a solid base 4 yards thick and with an area of 1,500 square yards, the lot resting on a tenacious stratum of London clay.

To raise the obelisk onto these sphinxes, four immense uprights had to be fashioned out of six heavy balks of timber, 60 feet high and a foot square. They were to be braced together by tie beams, and supported in their vertical positions by struts thrown out on all sides.

THE ENGLISH METHOD OF ERECTING THE LONDON OBELISK.

Dixon's method of raising the obelisk on the embankment
The obelisk was fitted with an iron sheathing, 20 feet long, forged in four pieces, so as to be raised 40 feet on a pair of iron girders which fitted into the grooves of a great wooden framework, there to be allowed to swing on its axis from a horizontal to a vertical position.

While the "battle of the sites" was still in progress, the *Cleopatra* lay in the East India docks, with a few plates removed so that the public could catch a glimpse of the great butterfly dormant in its cocoon. General Alexander, who had worked so hard to bring the needle to England, naturally rushed to see it, taking with him a popular military figure, Colonel Lennox Prendergast, whose fame derived from having been with the Scots Greys, in the celebrated charge of the heavy dragoons at Balaclava.

While waiting for the completion of the pedestal, it was decided to moor the *Cleopatra* off the steps of Saint

The *Cleopatra* at Westminster in
the shadow of Big Ben

Thomas Hospital, opposite the Houses of Parliament.
Shortly before noon on Saturday, January 26, 1878, the
Cleopatra left the East India docks wearing a holiday
dress of bunting, to be towed by one tug, and steadied by
two others, up the Thames on a sluggish tide. Salutes
were fired from the wharves as the cortege passed, and
cheers rang out from the bridges. Watermen made a profit
from towing passengers round the *Cleopatra* at three-
pence a head; and, as no one had a clue as to why the
obelisk had originally been raised in Egypt, let alone the
meaning of the hieroglyphs, hawkers did a brisk trade in
penny histories, published by W. Sutton, 91 Saint John
Street, W. Smithfield, which purported to be ''A complete
history of the romantic life and tragic death of the
Beautiful Egyptian Queen Cleopatra, and all about her
needle, 3,000 years old, and the events that led to its
arrival in England, complete with an interpretation of its
curious hieroglyphic inscriptions.''

To explain the hieroglyphs, the pamphlets quoted the
incomprehensible translations of Dr. Birch of the British
Museum, who amused and amazed with such passages
as: ''Horus, the powerful bull, beloved of the Sun! the King
of the south and north, Menkheper-Ra, his father Tum has

271

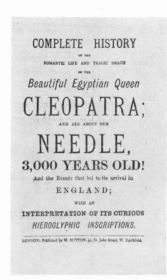

set his name up to him in the palace attached to Heliopolis giving him the seat of Seb, the dignity of Khepera, the son of the Sun Thothmess III, true ruler, beloved of the Benu of An, ever living.'' The penny histories further pointed out that whereas the inscriptions on three sides had been deciphered, those on the fourth side had not, and ''therefore any representations to the contrary in other accounts are spurious.''

Four months later, on May 30, the *Cleopatra* left her moorings off Saint Thomas Hospital for her last cruise— almost running into a string of coal barges. Luckily, Captain Carter, who stuck with the vessel to the last, managed to avoid a collision. At high tide, the *Cleopatra* was floated between two pairs of graduated posts, 65 feet apart, to her final resting place, where she was promptly put up for sale. When no one felt inclined to buy such a relic, even as a souvenir, she was ordered dismantled and stripped. Curious onlookers watched her slow disintegration, and the striptease revelation of her phallic cargo. Most visitors were only allowed by card or appointment, among them such notables as the prince and princess of Wales (later Edward VII and Queen Alexandra), Benjamin Disraeli, Earl of Beaconsfield, and Dr. Erasmus Wilson, who was later to pick up the check for the whole party—in return for a knighthood.

Dismantling the cylinder

When the carcass of the *Cleopatra* had been stripped clean, the obelisk was raised by hydraulic jacks and slid onto the embankment by screw traverses until its center of gravity came to rest over the proposed site. So delicately was the obelisk balanced that Dixon was able to make its apex describe an arc of several inches with nothing but the pressure of his own weight.

The needle about to be erected. In the pedestal were placed a collection of curious objects considered important to the Victorian world: 1878 photographs of twelve beautiful Englishwomen, a box of hairpins and other articles of feminine adornment, a box of cigars, several tobacco pipes, and an Alexandrian feeding bottle. To this were added a set of toys, a shilling razor by Mappin, a Tangye hydraulic jack, specimens of wire ropes and cables used to raise the obelisk, and a complete set of British coins plus one rupee. Along with samples a standard foot and pint went a portrait of Queen Victoria, a map of London, several current newspapers, and copies of the Bible in various languages. Finally there was inserted verse sixteen of chapter three of the Gospel of Saint John, translated into 215 languages, Francis Bacon's version of which is: ''For God so loved the world, that he gave his only begotten Son, that whosoever believeth in Him should not perish, but have everlasting life.''

On September 13, an hour before the obelisk was to officially swing on its pedestal, a heavy downpour scattered the gathering crowds. But the sun returned at 3:00 P.M., and from behind a line of constables barricading the embankment, thousands watched as the great rose granite obelisk of Thothmes III, controlled by ropes and chains, swung slowly to an angle of 45°, then 60°, then firmly came to rest on its new London base just as Big Ben chimed three thirty.

The crowd burst into cheers, which reechoed from the roads, the river terraces, and the bridges. A Union Jack was run up on the flagstaff overtopping the pyramidion on the north side, and a Turkish flag was raised on the south, in honor of the khedive, who was to be disposed of by the British within the year and sent into exile on the Bosporus for not having paid his debts. There were more cheers for the queen and for Waynman Dixon.

The penny pamphleteers, awed by the hoary antiquity of the monument, pointed out that it might have been seen by Abraham when he went down into Egypt, that Joseph, who married the daughter of Potiphar, a high priest of On, may have witnessed its first erection; that Moses, brought up by the priests of On, may have brushed against it daily.

Others pointed out that the obelisk had been standing in Egypt when Troy had not yet fallen, when Homer was not yet born, when Solomon's Temple was not yet built, and that it was still standing when Rome had risen, conquered the world, and passed into history.

An American naval officer and fellow Freemason of Waynman Dixon's, by name Henry Honeyman Gorringe, whose hope was to raise Cleopatra's still standing sister needle in New York, and who was to have a great deal more to say about obelisks, summed up the London bystanders' satisfaction that afternoon with his lapidary: "The time-worn shaft will remain erect for many years to come."

But the penny historians had the last word when they augured that the needle would look down "upon all the present and future stupendous creations of human genius, until the advent of the yet unborn but surely approaching time when IT and the land whereon it stands and the ancient life-teeming, wealth-laden Thames shall sink out of sight, and the British Empire be no more."

14. MANHATTAN'S MASONIC MONUMENT

William H. Vanderbilt

The obelisk of Thothmes III as it stands on Greywacke Knoll. First raised in Heliopolis in the sixteenth century B.C., as one of a pair, with Cleopatra's Needle, it stood at the east entrance to the Temple of the Sun, its orientation deducible from the glyphs on its face. Most likely knocked down by Cambyses when he destroyed the temple in the sixth century B.C., it was raised by the Romans in Alexandria, where it stood through the burning of the Caesareum in A.D. 366 and the sack of the city by the Saracens in A.D. 640. The English traveler Paul Lucas who visited Alexandria in 1714 found the lower portion of the shaft buried to a depth of 12 feet.

The first suggestion that an obelisk be removed from Egypt to the United States appears to have been made by Ismail Pasha, at the time of the opening of the Suez Canal in 1869. He made the offer to William Henry Hulbert, editor of the *New York World,* and a leading American Mason, who was in Cairo for the festivities. In September 1877, when the prostrate obelisk at Alexandria was being removed by Dixon, Hulbert was informed by an English friend, Louis Sterne, then in New York, that because of the good relations Dixon had developed in Egypt, he could definitely secure, as a gift to the United States, the standing obelisk in Alexandria. He would also undertake to remove it to New York if someone could be found to defray the cost, which Dixon estimated at £15,000.

Hulbert discussed the offer with fellow Masons Judge Ashbel Green, and Chauncey M. Depew, then proposed to William H. Vanderbilt, the railroad tycoon, reputed to be the richest man in the world, and also a Mason, that he provide the funding. When Vanderbilt agreed, Hulbert spoke with the secretary of state, William M. Evarts, who instructed the consul general in Cairo, E. E. Farman, to take up the matter formally with the khedive, using "all proper means at his disposal."

On March 4, 1878, Farman reported to Evarts that the khedive made no special objection to the transport of the obelisk to New York, but warned that it would be best not to make too much noise about its removal. There was evidently considerable local opposition to the idea, especially among the foreign residents of Egypt. Hulbert informed Dixon that the upright needle had been given to the United States and that Vanderbilt had agreed to pay the £15,000 needed to move it. But Dixon, who had just been obliged by a higher admiralty court to pay the full £5,000 salvage for the *Cleopatra,* was so out of pocket he complained that he would have to raise the ante to £20,000 to deliver the obelisk to New York. Hulbert rejected this increase, without even consulting Vanderbilt, and began to solicit tenders for the job, immediately snaring Lieutenant Commander Henry Honeyman Gorringe, USN, who read the announcement in the *New York World* of June 17, 1879, and promptly offered his services.

Henry Honeyman Gorringe

Thirty-eight years old, Gorringe had been employed in the United States Hydrographic Service, where he had recently been commissioned with a fellow naval officer, Lieutenant Seaton Schroeder, to cruise through the Mediterranean on a navy paddlewheeler, the *Gettysburg*. During a stay in Alexandria in 1878 the two officers had several times inspected the standing obelisk and conceived a vague plan of conveying the monument to America if the chance ever presented itself. Gorringe even studied the method used by Lebas to remove the Luxor obelisk, and the method used by Dixon for Cleopatra's Needle, deciding that both plans were unsuited to the transport of the standing obelisk to New York.

Hulbert and Vanderbilt were sufficiently impressed by Gorringe's plan to present to him an outline of Vanderbilt's terms. If Gorringe would undertake to bring over the obelisk and raise it on whatever site might be approved by the New York commissioner of parks, furnishing the underground foundations at his own expense, Vanderbilt would pay him $75,000 upon completion of the work; but he would assume no liability whatsoever until the obelisk was securely in place. Within two days, Gorringe accepted the proposition and its conditions.

At the request of Secretary Evarts, Gorringe and Schroeder were granted a leave of absence from the navy. Evarts also sent a dispatch to the United States vice-consul in Cairo, N. D. Comanos, asking that all proper official and personal aid be rendered to Gorringe so as to accredit him to the government of the khedive as the officer authorized to receive the obelisk on behalf of the City of New York. Gorringe's only remaining problem was to raise the money necessary to carry out the venture, an endeavor which led him straight into what he termed "almost insurmountable difficulties." At length, a fellow Freemason, and friend of long standing, Louis F. White of New York, offered him sufficient funds to start his operations.

Though neither of the vessels transporting the Paris and the London obelisks had been motored, Gorringe figured the ship that would carry the New York obelisk had to be constructed with her own motive power and be large enough to care for herself under all conditions of weather. But he abandoned the idea when he found that construction of such a vessel around the obelisk would cost the whole amount promised him by Vanderbilt. The alternative was to embark the obelisk on an ordinary ship. Here again, there was no precedent for the loading into a steamship such an enormous weight. The largest and heaviest masses yet placed intact in a steamship's hold

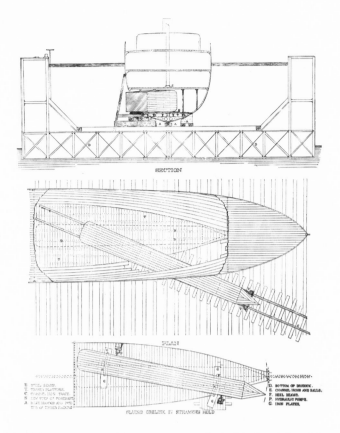

Gorringe's sketch indicating how to place an obelisk within the hold of a ship

SECTION

PLAN

H STEEL BEAMS.
T TIMBER PLATFORM.
C CHANNEL IRON TRACE.
N END WEDB OF FOREMAST.
A S IN BEAMS AND INTE-
      TOP OF TIMBER PACKING

SLIDING OBELISK IN STEAMER'S HOLD

D. BOTTOM OF DERRICK.
E. CHANNEL IRONS AND RAILS.
F. HEEL BEAMS.
P. HYDRAULIC PUMPS.
G. IRON PLATES.

had been some 100-ton guns made in England for shipment to Italy. As the obelisk could not be carried on deck without specially strengthening the vessel, at great expense, the only place for it was in the hold below the waterline. How to get the obelisk into the hold was the problem.

Gorringe's plan called for embarking the monument into the steel hull of a steamer through an aperture made in the bow, as Lebas had done at Luxor. But when he and Schroeder searched for a suitable American vessel, they could find none.

On August 24, 1879, Gorringe and Schroeder sailed for England on the *Arizona,* reaching Liverpool eleven days later. There they spent two weeks searching for a suitable English steamer to charter; again, none was available. The rates quoted for a charter were equivalent to the cost of purchase. So the naval officers decided to go ahead to Alexandria and prepare the obelisk in the hope of finding a suitable ship when and if the time came to load it.

From England they traveled through France and Italy to Trieste, still part of the Austro-Hungarian Empire, with the intention of buying timber for felling the needle. There they

279

were told they could purchase timber just as cheaply in Alexandria, whither they sailed from Venice on the S.S. *Ceylon.*

Arriving in Alexandria on October 16, they found a great agitation had been started among the foreign residents to prevent the removal of the obelisk. A howl had gone up when the news leaked out that some Americans proposed to remove the needle. Violently abusive articles appeared in the press; meetings were held and petitions to the khedive were circulated for signature. Threats of personal violence were made, openly and by letter, against anyone who would attempt to start work on the removal of the obelisk.

Egypt was no longer the country it had been under Mohammed Ali or under his son Said Mohammed, or even under his grandson Ismail Pasha, who had been forced three months earlier to abdicate and retire to exile in a palace on the Bosporus, where he remained a state prisoner of the sultan; because of his wildly extravagant expenditures and the debts he could not repay, the Great Powers had seized the opportunity to intervene in Egypt and establish a joint Anglo-French control commission.

As Alfred Milner puts it in his *England in Egypt,* trying to take some of the blame off Ismail: a series of unfortunate conditions had been necessary for Ismail's personality to become "as pernicious to his country" as it did. "It needed," says the historian, "a nation of submissive slaves, not only bereft of any vestige of liberal institutions, but devoid of the slightest spark of the spirit of liberty. It needed a bureaucracy which it would have been hard to equal for its combination of cowardice and corruption. It needed a whole gang of swindlers—mostly European—by whom Ismail was surrounded."

Gorringe was amazed by all the clamor over an obelisk which, until his arrival, nobody had bothered about in the least, even to the extent of preventing its defacement and the accumulation of offal around it. Two men had been allowed to make a business of breaking off pieces from the sharp edges of the shaft and from the edges of the intaglioed hieroglyphs to sell to relic hunters. It would not have been impossible, said Gorringe, for anything to have been more neglected and less appreciated by the residents of Alexandria and the tourists who passed through the city en route to the Nile, than was the Alexandrian obelisk. "The disagreeable odors and clamors for backsheesh hastened the departure of strangers," said Gorringe, "and they rarely devoted more than a few seconds to its examination."

Unlike his brothers, Tewfik Pasha, had not been educated in Europe, and was so displeased with the news of his succession to the viceregency of Egypt he beat up the servant who brought him the message.

As soon as the two American naval officers had established themselves in apartments in Alexandria, near the site of the obelisk, they set off for Cairo accompanied by vice-consul Comanos to obtain an audience with the new khedive, Tewfik Pasha, Ismail's son by a simple *fellah* woman. Tewfik received Gorringe and Schroeder very cordially and inquired about their plans for transporting the obelisk, cautiously expressing the hope that it would not be taken down unless they were sure of being able to remove it. To speed up such an operation, he gave them an order to the governor of Alexandria, requesting him to formally deliver to them the obelisk on condition they be charged with all expenses incurred in its removal.

Gorringe took the first train back to Alexandria and presented the order to Governor Sulficar Pasha. Within three days a formal transfer of ownership was accomplished. To the protests and petitions from the European consuls and other resident foreigners to prevent the transfer, the khedive and his ministers replied: "Too late. Cleopatra's Needle is in the possession of the United States Officer sent to receive it."

The foreign residents now attempted to physically prevent Gorringe from removing the obelisk. When a force of laborers started clearing away the ground around the base of the obelisk on October 27, an individual arrived and ordered the work stopped. He claimed to Gorringe to be the owner of the ground on which the obelisk stood, and said that if work continued, he would apply to the Italian consul, whose janissaries would be sent to forcibly eject the Americans and their employees from the premises.

Gorringe immediately fetched the American vice-consul, and together they called on the Italian consul, who informed Gorringe that any Italian subject occupying a property which belonged to him had the right to the Italian consul's protection, if necessary by the armed force of the Ottoman sultan's janissaries. The owner, explained the Italian consul, had been given authority by Mohammed Ali to build a bathing establishment by the seashore near the obelisk, but his property had been destroyed by the sea during a gale. Claiming compensation from the Egyptian government, the Italian had commandeered the land around the obelisk and built on it a shanty as insurance against losing his case.

Gorringe discovered that the claim had indeed been pending since the international courts had been organized in Egypt for the trial of cases between foreigners and the Egyptian government, and between individuals of different nationalities. But so absurd was the claim, it had never been placed on the docket, and was only kept current at the insistence of the Italian consul. To remedy the situation, Gorringe notified the Italian consul general that he would institute a suit for £15,000 against anyone who attempted to interfere with his work of removing the obelisk, and limited the time to four o'clock that afternoon for an amicable acceptance of his proposition to rent the ground.

There were some surprised Italians, but their consul shortly thereafter informed the American consular agents that the Italian claimant had accepted Gorringe's offer to lease the land, and proposed the appointment of arbitrators to fix a suitable sum. Before nightfall the lease was effected.

On the morning of October 29, a hundred Arabs, varying from ten to seventy years of age, began work, divided into three gangs. The middle-aged dug and filled baskets; the old lifted them to the backs of the young; these carried them to the shore and emptied them into the surf. This hivelike activity continued for a week until 1,730 cubic yards had been removed. The pedestal and steps to the obelisk had been cleared, and enough space created in which to construct a caisson to transport the obelisk to the port for embarkation.

When Gorringe found the bottom of the lower step below the pedestal to be nearly at mean sea level, he felt certain that the foundation could not have sunk so nearly uniformly, and that a subsidence of the ground of about 17 feet must have occurred since the obelisk had been erected nineteen hundred years earlier. The sea had gradually approached the site of the obelisk, and the constant washings of the surf had begun to affect the foundation. For some fifteen years the obelisk had been inclining gradually toward the sea, leading Gorringe to the conclusion that in a few years it would have fallen, doubtless breaking.

At some point in its history, all four edges of the base of the obelisk had been broken away, and four bronze crabs, shaped like sea crabs, had been inserted at the corners, the better to support it. Only two crabs remained; the others had long since been stolen by thieves who inserted stone blocks in their place.

While the excavations were still in progress, another attempt was made to prevent removal of the obelisk. A creditor of the Egyptian government applied through the international court to seize the obelisk and keep possession of it until his claim was paid. Gorringe realized that

Demolishing the foundations under the obelisk, without blasting, was difficult, as the cement had set to an unexpected degree. But as soon as it was broken up, the pedestal steps were moved out from under the obelisk. To raise the pedestal clear of the steps, steel wedges were driven under it until there was room enough for the end of a bent steel bar to be inserted. Hydraulic pumps acting on the upper part of this bar raised the pedestal clear of the steps and held it suspended until channel irons and cannonballs could be placed beneath it to move it with greater ease.

the entire proceeding was simply aimed at stopping his work, getting the obelisk under the jurisdiction of the court, and keeping the case pending until his attempt to remove it had been abandoned. So he raised the American flag atop the obelisk and, in his words, "prepared the means of defending it in a manner that carried conviction." When the court was advised that the American was taking no notice of the writ, and intended to use resistance against anyone who tried to take possession of the obelisk, it withheld the writ.

No sooner had this affair quieted, when some of the consuls general in Cairo, at the instigation of resident European archaeologists, again attempted to have the work suspended, so that the matter could be referred to their various governments, arguing that by the terms of a convention entered into by several powers, the Egyptian government had agreed to prevent the exportation of any object of antiquity. Gorringe met the threat by pointing out that no attention had been paid to this convention when the English had removed their obelisk, and that the consuls and archaeologists themselves were constantly shipping articles to Europe. To clinch his argument, he showed that the Ottoman *firman* which gave legal assistance to the Egyptian government stipulated that Egypt should not make treaties with foreign powers, and that therefore the convention was without legal basis. But fearing that pressure might be put on the khedive or his ministers, Gorringe negotiated through a prominent and powerful pasha in Constantinople, whom he had befriended, to ensure prompt confirmation of the gift of the obelisk from the Ottoman Porte, if such a *démarche* became necessary.

More determined that ever, Gorringe now set his men to work day and night, to get the obelisk off its pedestal. The material and machinery for removing the obelisk had been shipped from New York via Liverpool and arrived on November 11. But there was no truck in Alexandria suitable to transport the great trunnions, or truncated arms, like those of a cannon, on which the obelisk was to be turned from a vertical to a horizontal position. Placed on the only vast truck available, the heavy trunnions were hauled to the site by a gang of Arabs on the Christian sabbath—when there was less traffic on the narrow streets of Alexandria—for which effort an American missionary roundly abused Gorringe and his Arab workers from a borrowed pulpit, denouncing the holiday removal of the obelisk as the work of the devil. As Gorringe described the situation, the Arab Mohammedans spent their sabbath, or Friday, in a rational manner, sleeping during

Machinery and trunnions designed by Gorringe for raising and turning the obelisk

the morning, attending services at the mosque at noon, and devoting their afternoons to social intercourse and amusement. The Christians, almost to a man, said Gorringe, "would devote the thirty-six hours from Saturday evening to Monday morning drinking, gambling, fighting, and other excesses, and return to work drunk, sleepy and bruised."

Before the obelisk could be turned, timber had to be provided onto which it could be lowered. As the Egyptian prime minister, Riaz Pasha, had ordered the governor of Alexandria to offer Gorringe the same assistance in removing the obelisk as had been offered the British, Gorringe was convinced he was to have the use of the timbers which had been left by the British, still in a government warehouse. But the officer in charge, a European, was against the removal, and managed to evade the order. The only alternative was to buy some soft planking at the exorbitant price of $4,300.

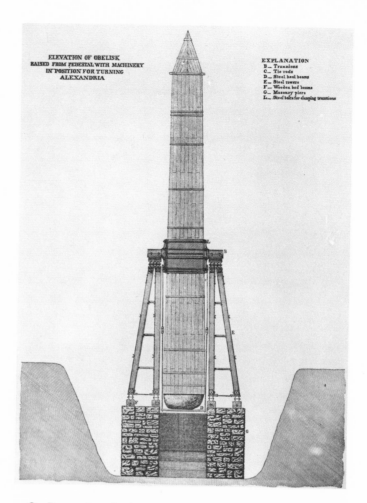

ELEVATION OF OBELISK
RAISED FROM PEDESTAL WITH MACHINERY
IN POSITION FOR TURNING
ALEXANDRIA

EXPLANATION
B — Trunnions
C — Tie rods
D — Steel heel beams
E — Steel towers
F — Wooden bed beams
G — Masonry piers
L — Steel bolts for clamping trunnions

The obelisk raised sufficiently to remove the bronze crabs securing it to the base

On December 2, the turning structure was placed in position. Three days later the obelisk was lifted clear of the pedestal, and the heavy bronze crabs removed. Rumors had been circulating that a demonstration by the foreign residents was to take place when the obelisk was turned horizontal in the presence of the governor of Alexandria. But Gorringe had found a friend, and fellow Mason, in Rear Admiral Aslambekoff, of the Russian Imperial Navy, who, from aboard his flagship, the *Qminim,* in the port of Alexandria, promptly landed a large force of unarmed but trained seamen to form a cordon around the obelisk.

On December 6, the day set for the turning, large crowds of Greeks, Italians, and other Europeans gathered in the vicinity, becoming noisy and unruly when they were prevented by the Russians from entering the cordoned-off enclosure. The moment the obelisk began to move there was absolute stillness; the only sound came from the

285

rendering of the ropes around the posts and an occasional creak of the structure as the point of the obelisk slowly described an arc. All seemed in order when a very loud crack occurred, followed by an even sharper snap. One of the tackles had parted. Gorringe gave the order to slack the other tackle, to retard the motion but not arrest it. Instead of slackening his line, the man attending the fall "lost his wits," held fast, and the second tackle snapped.

The obelisk, moving slowly at first, gathered speed. There was intense excitement. The Arabs and Greeks around the base began to flee. An ear-splitting sound reechoed, and the obelisk heavily struck the stack of timbers, splintering three courses of balks, and rebounded twice, finally coming to rest in an almost horizontal position. By some miracle the needle was intact. The Alexandrian crowd, giving vent to what Gorringe called its first manifestation of friendliness, raised a loud cheer.

Shattered timbers break the fall
and preserve the needle.

The man attending the first tackle explained that having looked up to see what had caused the noise, he had involuntarily checked the passage of the rope through his hands. This brought the whole strain onto his tackle, causing it to break. The man on the second tackle, unaware of the accident until he saw his companion flee precipitously from the obelisk, excusably, said Gorringe, lost his self-control, and down went the obelisk.

As soon as the weight had been transferred to the stacks of lumber the towers and trunnions were removed, and demolition of the piers gradually began in order to lower the obelisk 43 feet to ground level, at the rate of 3 feet a day. An iron truss cradle which moved on cannon balls had been specially designed and made in the United States to transport the monolith overland to the port of embarkation. This distance was less than a mile, and the route was over comparatively unfrequented streets, except for a short stretch across what had once been the ancient causeway connecting Eunostos island with the mainland, now the most important part of the city.

The foreign merchants were determined not to allow the obelisk to be moved through the city, using the excuse that it might crush the sewers. Gorringe's guarantees of repairing all damage were of no avail. Nor could the

287

The streets of Alexandria

Egyptian government intervene and overrule the foreigners. In return for keeping the streets paved and clean, the government had transferred control of the streets to the foreign merchants.

The alternative method, sea transport in a wooden caisson—covering a distance of 10 miles—was expensive and very dangerous. The transportation cradle, which had cost $5,100, became a dead loss and had to be thrown away. The cost of constructing the caisson was another $2,200. But preparations for launching a caisson over a shallow bank still encumbered with heavy blocks of marble and granite was even more expensive. Despite the passage cleared by Dixon, the submerged foundations of the famous palaces of Alexandria were still directly in the way. These obstructions could only be removed by divers, a difficult task along an open coast, with the surf breaking two-thirds of the time.

Diving operations, whenever the sea would permit, continued until March 1880, during which time the divers had to be paid whether at work or not. A single day of heavy surf often destroyed the work of diving operations of a whole week. A pier with derricks had to be constructed to lift out the blocks. The estimated weight of material removed, ranging from 3 to 7 tons apiece, was 170 tons. The difference in cost to Gorringe, owing to the refusal of the foreign merchants to allow the obelisk to move overland, was close to $21,000. A wooden caisson 83 feet long, 11 feet deep, 22 feet wide at one end, and 30 feet at the other, was built around the obelisk in order to float it to a dry dock. Inch by inch the caisson was pushed forward till it finally floated. Armed with two keels and two

288

Much lubricant was used on the ways to facilitate the caisson sliding into the sea, and every precaution was taken against fouling the sliding surfaces, but after the caisson had slid rapidly for 20 feet, it abruptly stopped. As with the *Cleopatra,* a towline was run out to a tug, and two anchors were planted offshore with cables leading to the caisson; but the combined force of the tug and threefold purchases on the cables did not move it an inch, even when a pressure of 100 tons was exerted. The cause was found to be a foreign body, washed in by a heavy sea, which had stripped the sliding ways.

The wind turned to a gale, and the waves threatened to break the caisson and the obelisk within it. To save the situation, water was let into the caisson. When the seas subsided, water was pumped out and the obelisk, still intact, was floated to Alexandria.

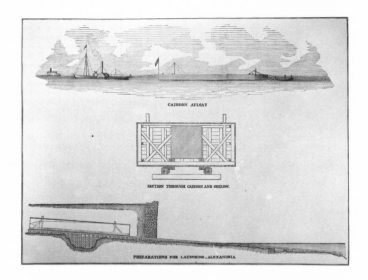

CAISSON AFLOAT

SECTION THROUGH CAISSON AND OBELISK.

PREPARATIONS FOR LAUNCHING—ALEXANDRIA.

keelsons, the caisson was successfully towed to the port of Alexandria.

Meanwhile, Gorringe had been negotiating for the purchase of an English or Italian steamer, when his attention was attracted by an old tramp, the *Dessoug,* chiefly, as he put it, because of "the fullness of her form and particularly of her low line." Lying dismantled in the Alexandria arsenal, she had been built in England in 1864 and employed in the Egyptian postal service between Alexandria, Smyrna, and Constantinople, until extravagance and corruption in the service had caused her withdrawal. Careful measurements showed that there was just enough room under her lower-deck beams to take into her fore compartment the full length of the obelisk. Though her hull was perfect, her hold, said Gorringe, was filthy, for she had been neglected "to a degree that cannot be imagined." To refit her and repair her, which was to be Schroeder's job, a large expenditure was necessary, which made it essential she be purchased at a low price. To accomplish this, Gorringe decided not to make an offer at once, but to treat the matter with apparent indifference.

Leisurely he commenced negotiations via the assistant postmaster general. After several informal conferences, an offer of £5,000 sterling was made to the postmaster general, who affected, said Gorringe, to regard such an offer as a joke, suggesting that the matter of price be treated seriously; other negotiations, he added, were pending for the purchase of the *Dessoug.* This simply meant that a firm of shipbrokers, who had been trying to charter or sell Gorringe a vessel, when informed of his negotiations for the *Dessoug,* had made an offer to the

Egyptian government in the hope of being bought off by the American. A member of the firm even offered to withdraw if he was paid a commission of 10 percent on the purchase money.

To bring matters quickly to a head, Gorringe informed the postal ministry in Cairo that his own offer would be withdrawn at noon the next day, unless formally accepted before then. Quickly, the Egyptian government accepted the offer of the shipbrokers, but demanded an immediate guarantee of payment. The brokers, who had no use for the vessel except to sell it to Gorringe, offered it to him for £6,000, but were informed that he would not purchase her from them under any circumstances.

When the brokers could not give the required guarantee, and the time allowed had elapsed, Gorringe was notified by the government that he could have the vessel for £5,100. The money was paid, and the transfer effected on December 3, in the strictest secrecy. This was because another government vessel, laid up in the same arsenal, had been seized, along with the money paid for her, on a warrant issued by the court on behalf of someone who had a claim against the Egyptian government, so that transfer could not be effected from the government to the purchaser.

Legal transfer to Gorringe was quickly effected in the office of the director of postal services, whose represent- ative then went straight aboard the *Dessoug* with Gorringe to haul down the Egyptian flag and raise the United States ensigns on mastheads and peaks in the presence of the amazed Arabs in charge of the vessel. When ordered to gather their personal belongings and leave, the Arabs made no protest, but insisted first on delivering what Gorringe called "formal and fervent prayers."

This was lucky; for Gorringe discovered that a seizure of the *Dessoug* had only failed because of his quick and secret action. A notice in Arabic, Greek, Italian, French, and English was posted on each gangway, prohibiting anyone from coming aboard, at the peril of his life, without permission. "As there was no one to whom I could call for protection," Gorringe wrote, "I was bound to protect my property myself, with all the means in my power." Several boats approached the gangways, but seeing the signs and the welcome Gorringe had prepared for them, no one attempted to board.

One condition of the purchase was that Gorringe be allowed to use the government's floating dock for embark- ing the obelisk as soon as it was felled. Orders from Prime Minister Riaz Pasha, acting for the nervous khedive, were specific, but when the obelisk and the *Dessoug* were

The *Dessoug* as Gorringe found her

ready to be mated, the Egyptian official who had control
of the dock refused to comply, ordering several small river
steamers to be hauled into the dry dock instead of the
Dessoug. Before Gorringe could appeal to Cairo, the
official had the dock pumped out and the plates torn off
the bottom of the steamers; that way they could no longer
be floated, no matter what the ministry ordered. When
Gorringe realized that the riverboats could just as easily,
and much more cheaply, have been hauled out on shore
than into an expensive dry dock, he knew the official had
been acting deliberately. He attributed the maneuver to
the widespread belief in Alexandria that the obelisk could
not be embarked in the manner he proposed, and felt that
this had caused the official to speak of the embarkation
as if it would entirely destroy the dock, or occupy it to the
exclusion of all other business for a long period.

Nearly five weeks passed before the dock was disen-
gaged, but Gorringe did manage to get the caisson
slipped in earlier by having the level of dock water
altered, which did not affect the small steamers "beyond
washing out their filthy holds and destroying some of the
vermin for which they are justly celebrated." Even so, the
official refused to follow direct orders from Cairo and only
let Gorringe enter the caisson on condition that he allow
another big ship to dock before the *Dessoug*. To this
Gorringe was obliged to agree because the caisson was
leaking so badly there was danger of its being sunk by
accident or design. As soon as it was in the dock,
Gorringe had the caisson demolished, not so much to
advance the work of embarkation but to ensure that the
obelisk could not be removed from the dock other than
aboard the *Dessoug*.

291

On May 10, 1880, the *Dessoug* entered dry dock. A foreman shipwright was brought from Glasgow expressly to superintend the opening and closing of the hole. Three gangs of thirty Arab boilermakers went to work day and night without intermission. Seven thousand rivets, sixteen frames, and thirty plates had to be removed from the starboard bow to make a hole large enough to admit the obelisk at an angle of 21° to the axis of the keel, the greatest angle at which it could be embarked without having to turn it twice during embarkation.

The caisson had been placed in the dock in just the right position for the shaft of the obelisk to be slid into the *Dessoug* as soon as her hole was readied. Gangs of carpenters were engaged in the difficult job of packing timber under the forward run of the hull, and under the track of the obelisk, to prevent straining the frames. The bed of the track was laid continuously from where the obelisk lay, through the aperture, and into the hold. The

Inserting the obelisk

292

obelisk was then rolled in on cannon balls. To ensure uniform pressure on the balls, soft wood was packed in between the iron channel and the stone.

It took ten days for these nuptial preparations, and eight hours to consummate the insertion of the obelisk. Almost as soon as the pyramidion had disappeared within the cavity, the last frame was up and riveted again. Inside the hold, a force of the best shipwrights that could be hired in Alexandria shored and stowed the obelisk against the serious danger of its shifting at sea. To obviate the risk of being broken by the inner working of the ship, the obelisk was placed on a bed of Adriatic white pine, very spongy and soft, while 10 feet at the extremities was left without support. When this was done, Gorringe felt that the vessel could be laid on her beam-ends without causing the obelisk to break adrift.

On June 1, three weeks from the day the vessel had entered dry dock, she was floated out with the obelisk within her. It was then necessary to ballast the vessel and load the pedestal and base. The largest of the base steps weighed 7 tons, the smallest nearly a ton. The pedestal itself weighed nearly 50 tons, and had to be placed in the after hatchway, on a special iron frame, to distribute the weight; but the most powerful crane on the quay could only lift 30 tons.

Gorringe decided on a wild gamble. He would try to lift the pedestal with the additional and simultaneous help of an available floating derrick that could lift 25 tons. Slowly the pedestal was raised 30 feet in the air; but just as it was being swung over the hull of the steamer, a sharp sound was heard, and the pedestal began to oscillate. Were the pedestal to fall, it would destroy the vessel, which Gorringe ordered instantly moved. The steel wire with which the pedestal was slung had stranded; only two of the seven strands remained intact. A chain cable was quickly substituted, and the pedestal safely stowed away.

At last, the *Dessoug* could sail; but the nationality of the vessel remained a delicate question to settle. Under the laws of the United States, she could not be registered as an American vessel. Sailing under the Egyptian flag would have involved serious risks. The British or another European flag, according to Gorringe, would have been even more objectionable, especially in terms of the evasion of laws relating to ownership. Finally Gorringe concluded there was no course available but open defiance of the law, which he felt the circumstance warranted. To make the voyage to New York, he determined to sail without registry of nationality, thereby taking the risk of having his

The 50-ton pedestal about to break loose over the stern of the *Dessoug*

steamer seized by any vessel at war, or by the authorities of any port at which he might be obliged to touch. Gibraltar was the only port he intended to call at for coal, and there he had a personal acquaintance with the chief military and naval authorities, whom he felt confident would not examine the ship's papers too closely. Further to lighten the risk, he made arrangements for taking on coal from lighters on the eastern side of the Gibraltar peninsula.

Providing a crew and securing a reasonable rate of insurance for the voyage had been the cause of endless trouble and negotiation from the day the vessel was purchased. By insisting that he would pay no more than a 2-percent premium, or make the voyage without insurance, Gorringe finally got the agents to lower the premium from 25 percent to 5 percent, and finally to 2 percent.

For a crew he was obliged to send to Trieste, and for officers, to England. The second and third officers turned out to be confirmed drunkards. One had to be dismissed to prevent him from killing himself, as he twice fell from the second deck to the hold, and twice overboard while drunk.

294

The quartermaster, according to Gorringe, would have done credit to a pirate ship. Only the engineer was useful, but hard-drinking. Before the ship was even ready to sail, forty-eight men deserted, convinced that the obelisk would sink at the first touch of weather. As the ship had no nationality, deserters could not be arrested; and without the means of enforcing discipline, the only available method, as Gorringe put it, "was the summary one." To get a full crew, Gorringe sent a power of attorney to a ship's agent in Trieste, stipulating that the next lot arrive in Alexandria only the day the vessel was ready for sea, so they could not back out. With this ruse, Gorringe managed to keep all but three men aboard; but of the lot only four could speak or understand English.

Back from Cairo, where he had rushed to make his personal farewell to the khedive and thank him for having resisted the pressure of foreigners to revoke his father's great gift to the City of New York, Gorringe took command of his unusual charge. On Sunday, June 12, moorings cast, the *Dessoug* steamed slowly out of Alexandria harbor amid a general dipping of colors and the sound of steam whistles and the cheers of the other ships' crews. But could she, Gorringe wondered, cross the Atlantic? Or even the Mediterranean as far as Gibraltar?

At Gibraltar, instead of being seized as a prize, the ship was visited by the governor, Lord Napier of Magdala, and Lady Napier, accompanied by the staff of Government House. Taking on coal and fixing two leaking boilers delayed departure three days, but at midnight on June 25 the *Dessoug* steamed out into the Atlantic. The weather was rough, but all went well till they passed the Azores. Fifteen hundred miles out of New York there was a terrible noise from the engine room and the engines came to an abrupt standstill. The after crankshaft, which had a flaw, had broken in two.

Fortunately Gorringe had had the foresight to place aboard a spare section, obtained at great difficulty as part of the articles of purchase. With all the men available working day and night, the brasses were bored and the shaft reconnected in six days, during which the *Dessoug,* progressing on its sails, covered a little less than 100 miles. To add to this ordeal, the weather turned foul and a waterspout formed to windward, moving directly toward the ship. With too little wind to maneuver, and being without cannons to fire into the spout and break it up, Gorringe realized they were in for a heavy dowsing. All the hatches and skylights were quickly covered, and the bulwark ports opened in the hope of excluding as much

295

water as possible from below. There was a suspenseful five minutes, then the spout changed its course, passing 50 yards to starboard. Had it burst on the *Dessoug*'s deck with its 50-foot column of water, it could have seriously endangered both ship and cargo.

On July 13 the vessel ran into another heavy gale, with high seas that almost completely arrested its progress. Two huge waves did considerable damage to boards and skylights; but a close watch was kept on the obelisk and its fastenings, and no movement was detected.

Steaming ahead as hard as the boilers would allow, the *Dessoug* stood off Fire Island on July 19, where, by a prearranged signal, her position was reported to New York. At 2:00 A.M. on July 20, she anchored off Staten Island, at the quarantine station, and after having been granted pratique, or permission to communicate with shore, moved up the Hudson to moor off Twenty-third Street.

There now occurred, on a smaller scale, the same "battle of the sites" which had taken place in London. Before leaving New York, Gorringe had consulted with William Hulbert and F. E. Church as to William Vanderbilt's preference for a location. All had expressed a preference for the area of Central Park near the Metropolitan Museum, rather than the other favored sites, which were the circle at the intersection of Fifth Avenue and Fifty-ninth Street, and the southwest entrance to the park, the chief objection to these sites being the fear that the monument would be lost among the tall buildings surrounding it. On July 27 it was decided that the obelisk would be erected on the top of Graywacke Knoll, in the park by the Metropolitan Museum, one of the highest points on Manhattan, in the midst of pretty drives and walks. To avoid further needless discussion, strict secrecy was maintained about the choice.

Gorringe would have liked to land the obelisk from the East River, within easier reach of the knoll, but the strong tidal currents and the short intervals of slack water made this impossible. The best landing he could find for the obelisk was at the foot of Ninety-first Street and the North River; but first he had to land the pedestal, and as it was impossible to move it by truck over the roadway of this street, the *Dessoug* was first moored along the wharf at the foot of Fifty-first Street, where a derrick was able to land the pedestal with a speed strongly in contrast with its embarkation at Alexandria.

This was the largest and heaviest stone on record (with the exception of the obelisk itself) ever to have been

moved on wheels through the City of New York. Thirty-two horses in sixteen pairs were attached to the truck for hauling; the first forward impetus was given by hydraulic pumps applied to the tires of the rear wheels, and as soon as the truck was in motion, the horses were started and kept going at a slow trot. But the weight was too great; the wheels sank into the pavements. When this occurred, the slings which bound the pedestal were slackened until the truck was released and timbers could be slid on the pavement beneath the wheels.

The route to be followed was along Fifty-first Street to Fifth Avenue and up to the East Eighty-second Street entrance to the park. From there to the site, the pedestal was successfully moved on greased skids, just as it had been originally in Egypt. But there it came to a rest. No action had been taken by the Department of Parks to prepare the knoll for the foundation. Four laborers from the department had merely removed the young trees to clear away the surface. A few days later their work was even suspended without apparent reason. Gorringe complained that it was the invariable custom for the department to prepare foundations for the reception of monuments and statuary contributed by individuals for the adornment of the city, and that in this case the custom was being violated.

Anxious to get the foundation prepared before winter, Gorringe decided to go ahead on his own and sought from the department almost daily the requisite authority to proceed with the work at his own expense. This was withheld for several weeks, and only granted under onerous conditions that involved a large increase in the cost of the work. Political and religious bias had evidently been behind this attempt at sabotaging what was seen to be an enterprise designed to enhance Masonic prestige in the city. But the delay could not be extended indefinitely, and by the beginning of October the earth was removed from the top of the knoll, the surface of the granite leveled and the cavities filled in with cement. Over this a thin layer of concrete was laid and the foundation replaced, so that it stood exactly as it had in Alexandria, each piece in the same relative position to the others, and to the points of the compass.

There only remained the 7-ton syenite base which was reserved for the Masonic ceremonies, this being the last piece to be placed before the 50-ton pedestal was moved into position. The Most Worshipful Jesse B. Anthony, Grand Master of Masons in the state of New York, was invited to lay the "corner-stone," and, after consultation with the commissioner of parks, fixed October 9 as the date.

On that morning nearly nine thousand Freemasons paraded past an estimated thirty thousand New Yorkers lining the sidewalks between Fifteenth Street and Eighty-second Street. Each commanderie of Masons was headed by a band. At the entrance to the park, the crowd grew more dense, and in the park itself it was so great that policemen were unable to keep spectators out of the spaces reserved for the ceremonies. The column of Masons, having marched to the base of the pedestal, opened ranks three deep and faced in.

The line extended all the way to Sixtieth Street, where the Grand Master and the Grand Lodge officers left their carriages and marched through the line to the platform on the Graywacke Knoll, followed by the Masters and Wardens of the lodges. The ranks were closed, and the commanderies were massed on the west side and the lodges on the north and east sides, while the south side was crowded with spectators, some occupying as a vantage point the great pedestal at the foot of the knoll.

When order had been obtained, the Grand Master addressed the brethren: "This monument in its associations brings forcibly before us that period of which at present we know so little and of which the researches of the scholar, the calculation of the astronomer, the study of the rocks by geologist, and the skill of the engineer, are each year adding to our information and startling us with wonderful results. This trophy comes from that land the history of which was long lost in the mist and obscurities of ancient fable and tradition,—a land of wonderful creations of human power and genius, that has been, and long will continue to be, a place of interest and curiosity to the learned."

Looking up into the gray autumn sky, the Grand Master continued: "The Egyptians were the first to have observed

Jesse B. Anthony, Most Worshipful Grand Master of Masons of the State of New York, laying the cornerstone of the future monument

the course of the planets, observations which led them to regulate the year from the course of the sun." He then suggested that the great pyramids which were believed to have been constructed as tombs might also have been designed for astronomical purposes. He attributed to the ancient Egyptian priesthood, twenty-five hundred years before Christ, knowledge of the precession of the equinoxes and the ability to predict with certainty the position of stars over periods of thousands of years.

As the Masonic marshals kept order in the crowd, the Grand Master continued: "Egypt itself is a book of history,—one of God's great monumental records, on the face of which He has written with His own hand many of the strange events of the past. It was the birthplace of literature, the cradle of science and art, the garden and garner of the world. The people of those days excelled in many respects the advanced growth of the present century. Could we but know that which time will yet unveil, we should be astonished at the revelation and ashamed of our littleness."

Pausing to survey the multitude, he asked: "Should we not take a broader ground and look to the principles which antedate the time assumed for the origin of Masonry as at present constituted? There can be no question but that in the secret societies of Egypt are to be found some elements now embraced in the principles or symbolism of Masonry of the present. . . ." Then with full Masonic rites the Grand Master laid the cornerstone.

All that now remained was to disembark and raise the obelisk. Ever since Gorringe had docked in New York, he had been occupied with the problem of getting the obelisk ashore. Unfortunately the owners of the docks had also discovered this fact. On opening negotiations with their representative, it became evident to Gorringe that as the dock owners had the right to fix whatever price they pleased and make their own conditions for the use of their property, they were going to dictate their own terms without regard to the customary charges. In fact, they fixed a price far in excess of that charged for other steamers, and made Gorringe give security for any injury to their property that might result from disembarking such a load.

Gorringe offered the owners the same rates paid by other steamers, and proposed the appointment of a commission of experts to watch the operation of disembarking the obelisk and decide what amount of damages, if any, should be paid them resulting therefrom. The dock owners answered that unless he accepted their terms and conditions *at once,* they would not agree to take the *Dessoug* into the dock at any fixed rate, according to turn, but would leave the disembarkation of the obelisk till some time when there was no immediate demand for the facilities. Without replying, Gorringe left the office, determined to devise some other plan for disembarking the obelisk.

At first he thought of taking the *Dessoug* to Philadelphia or Baltimore, disembarking the obelisk in the spacious dry dock in either of those cities, and bringing it to New York on floats by canal. But negotiations with the dry-dock owners and their representatives developed the same feeling as in New York about extra charges. Besides, Gorringe realized there would have been no end to obstacles in connection with the Customs authorities and navigation laws. The *Dessoug* had neither register nor nationality, and could not legally leave the port of New York.

Gorringe next planned the construction of a marine railway at the foot of Ninety-sixth Street, where the obelisk could be landed directly onto Manhattan island.

But this was found to be impracticable because of the Hudson River Railway, which skirted the shore, and because of the abrupt decrease in the water's depth close to the riverbank. The Dock Department insisted that the structure be removed entirely and the piles pulled out after the disembarkation of the obelisk, which would have cost almost as much as building it.

Having almost despaired of being able to accomplish his object without yielding to the demands of the dock company, Gorringe reached a solution which he summed up in one word: *tide.* He determined to make the rising tide lift the obelisk onto any available marine railway, and the falling tide land it. There would thus be no lack of power, and no need of a dry dock.

Before communicating his plans to anyone, Gorringe visited incognito all the marine railways on the shores of New York bay, and fixed on a new one at Staten Island as the best adapted to his purpose. The proprietor had no knowledge of his plans until the terms of an agreement had been entered into for the occupation of his ship. When everything was satisfactorily arranged, only the *Dessoug's* bow was hauled out of water on August 21 on the east shore of Staten Island while iron shipwrights worked at opening a hole in it.

News that the obelisk was to be disembarked on the morning of September 16 brought to Staten Island a crowd of spectators who occupied every available spot from which to view the work. The weather being favorable, pontoons were pumped out at low water and adjusted to their proper position under the obelisk. The rising tide caused them to gradually raise the cross-timbers clear of

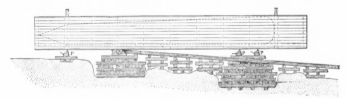

PIVOT FOR LOWERING CAISSON ON LAUNCHING WAYS.

A. ANCHORS
B. TIMBER BACKING
P. HYDRAULIC PUMPS
T. PIVOT

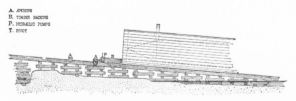

ANCHOR FOR HYDRAULIC JACKS TO PUSH CAISSON AFLOAT.

Front and side elevation of the pontoon for floating the obelisk ashore the capping on the piles until the weight of the obelisk had been transferred from the stage. At high water, 4:00 P.M., they were hauled out of the ship into the bay, bearing the obelisk on their decks.

At the foot of Ninety-sixth Street, a landing stage had been prepared for the obelisk, identical in principle to the one at Staten Island. The steamer *Manhattan,* belonging to the Dock Department of the city, was in readiness to tow the pontoons from Staten Island. The steamer *Rescue* of the Coast Wrecking Company stood in attendance to escort it. The time of high water at the foot of Ninety-sixth Street was about two hours later than at Staten Island. The distance was 12 miles. At 4:55 P.M. the *Manhattan* started ahead with the pontoons in tow. As she proceeded up the bay, tugs and steamers diverged from their course to greet the strange object with vigorous and prolonged blasts of their steam whistles. The obelisk reached the landing stage at Ninety-sixth Street at 7:15 P.M. The evening was very dark, and it was difficult to adjust the pontoons between the rows of piles. After one or two failures, owing to the swiftly running tide, the job was finally accomplished. As soon as the pontoons were in position their valves were opened to admit water, and in a few minutes the obelisk had been landed on Manhattan.

The next hurdle was the Hudson River Railway tracks skirting the riverbank, which carried passenger trains at frequent intervals, the longest time between trains being only an hour and a half at noon. To have blocked the road for more than two or three hours would have involved serious loss and much inconvenience to travelers. Orders were given by the railway officials to stop all trains at

Disembarking the obelisk from the *Dessoug*

302

11:00 A.M. Immediately after the passage of the last train, a temporary bridge was thrown across the track and in one hour and twenty minutes the obelisk was resting on the roadway of Ninety-sixth Street. One freight train had been delayed twenty-five minutes. The regular passenger trains were not delayed at all.

Gorringe first tried rolling the obelisk on cannon balls in iron channels, but the channels crushed under the weight, and he could find no economic way to reinforce them. So he reverted to the ordinary cradle, rollers, and track of a marine railway. The traction to be overcome averaged 38 tons—that is, the strain on the purchase was equal to a lift of 38 tons before inertia and friction could be overcome. To keep the cradle from slipping back in case the rope or anything connected with the pulling purchase should give way, men were stationed in the rear of the obelisk with large iron wedges, held close against the rollers. The least retrograde movement could be caught by the points of the wedges, and the weight of the large end of the obelisk would then act as a brake.

Rainy weather, difficulty in finding suitable men, and other varied factors delayed the work, and the obelisk did not reach West Boulevard until October 27. A heavy fall of snow on December 28, followed by intense cold, delayed the operation of hauling the obelisk into its trestle. It wasn't till January 5, 1881, that the center of gravity was placed directly over the axis of the pedestal and foundation, and the tedious land journey was completed. In the end it had taken 112 days to travel the 10,905 feet to the knoll in Central Park, at the rate of about 97 feet a day.

On January 15 the obelisk was lowered from the trestle by hydraulic pumps until its entire weight rested on trunnions in the turning structure. When tested, the obelisk turned easily in either direction. As the bottom of the obelisk was imperfect from injuries received in ancient

303

Gorringe's plan for land transportation

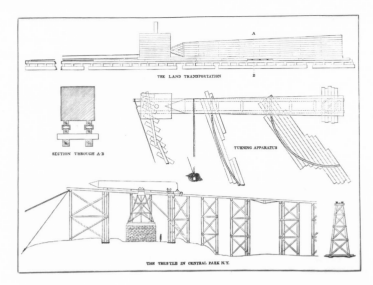

Trestle crossing the main drive in Central Park

times, and not more than two-thirds of its area would come in contact with the pedestal, Gorringe decided to give it maximum stability by supporting its corners with four bronze crabs exactly like the ones used by the Romans. These were cast at Gorringe's own expense from plaster models of the originals by a sculptor, Theodor Baur, who endeavored to make them as nearly as possible the same as the crabs cast by the Romans nineteen centuries earlier, and they averaged 922 pounds each. More than merely ornamental, they gave the obelisk an added bearing surface on the pedestal so that it would require a severe earthquake to budge it.

On January 22, long before the hour fixed for turning the obelisk, spectators occupied every available space in the park and its vicinity from which a good view could be obtained. In spite of the piercing cold wind and thick bed of snow that lay on the ground, Gorringe noted that ladies formed at least half of the estimated ten thousand per-

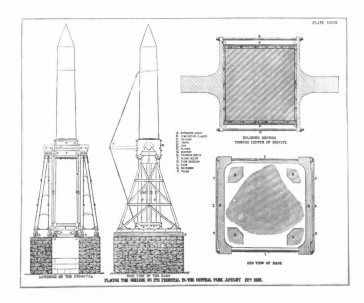

sons who came to witness the erection. A cordon of park
keepers encircled the immediate vicinity of the site, and
with difficulty kept the crowd from encroaching within the
space reserved for workmen. A platform had been raised
on the north side of this space to accommodate distinguished persons and officials, guarded by a battalion of
sailors and marines from the Brooklyn Navy Yard, who
arrived at the park a little before noon, headed by the
Marine band.

Five thousand cards had been issued as a souvenir of
the event, bearing on one side a picture of the obelisk as
it had stood in Alexandria, and on the other an announcement that it would be placed on its pedestal in Central
Park at noon. The mayor, the aldermen, and other officers
of the city, many of the civil and judicial officers of the
state, many civil, judicial, army, and navy officers of the
United States, nearly all of the foreign consuls residing in
New York, a large delegation of the members of the Grand
Lodge, almost all the members of the Anglo-Saxon Lodge
in a body, and a large number of distinguished citizens
and professional men, accompanied by their wives and
families, crowded onto the platform. A few minutes before
noon the Honorable William M. Evarts, secretary of state,
the Honorable Nathan Goff, Jr., secretary of the navy, and
Mr. William Henry Hulbert, editor of the *New York World,*
drove up to the foot of Graywacke Knoll, and took
positions reserved for them on the platform.

As Fontana had instructed the workmen in Saint Peter's
Square, the men now handling the raising tackle and those
handling the withholding tackle had been told, respective-

305

Turning the obelisk

A number of lead boxes of different shapes and sizes had been prepared to fit into available spaces enclosed by the steps to the base, and into these were placed articles contributed by the various government departments in Washington and by individuals who considered them suitable relics of nineteenth-century civilization in America, such as the *Congressional Directory* for 1880. The Treasury Department sent a full set of medals of U.S. presidents, plus a full set of silver and minor coinage for the year 1880. The Department of the Interior contributed such enlightening items as the *Report of the Commission of Education* for 1877. The War Department sent along the weather record for July, as well as the general orders announcing the death of General Myer. The Navy Department outdid itself with silver medals commemorating its victories in the War of 1812, and a model of an improved anchor.

Gorringe tried to secure a complete system of the newly invented Bell telephone, but failed. When he asked a representative of the American Bible Society to contribute editions of the New Testament, or any part of it, in all the ancient and modern languages and dialects into which it had been translated and published, he was referred to a bookstore where he could buy them. He did; and they were carefully deposited in a lead case, where he hoped "they would be preserved for an indefinite period." To fill vacant spaces in the boxes, a variety of books were inserted, such as *Webster's Unabridged Dictionary,* the works of William Shakespeare, a New York City directory, a map of the city, the *Nautical Almanac, Hayden's Dictionary of Dates,* Wilkinson's *Egypt,* an *Encyclopedia of Mechanics and Engineering,* and a *Compendium of Electricity and Magnetism,* unaware that the ancient Egyptians might have already encoded such secrets in the dimensions of the obelisk.

ly, to haul and slack away only when Gorringe held up his hand, and for as long as it was held up, and to stop as soon as he lowered it.

After a moment's conversation with Evarts, the signal was given, and 220 tons of obelisk slowly turned, while the spectators preserved a silence that was almost unnatural. When the obelisk reached an angle of 45°, Gorringe gave the signal to stop so that it could be photographed. This broke the spell, and when the obelisk resumed its motion, a loud cheer went up which was prolonged until the shaft stood erect, and the Marine band played national airs while the sailors presented arms. Only five minutes after the first signal was given, the obelisk was vertical on its pedestal. Congratulations followed, and the spectators dispersed.

Fifteen months had elapsed from the day the work of removal had begun in Alexandria. During that time the obelisk had traveled 5,380 miles by water, and 11,520 feet by land; it had been lowered 39 feet, and lifted 230. The expenses, much exceeding the original estimate, ultimately amounted to $102,576. But Gorringe was relieved that his work had been completed with no accident or incident to spoil its success.

The ceremony of formally presenting the obelisk to New York City was fixed for February 22, and the use of the grand hall of the Metropolitan Museum nearby was ten-dered by the trustees. From noon on, not a train on either of the elevated tracks, nor a car on the several street railways, went uptown that wasn't loaded with passengers. By 2:00 P.M. an estimated twenty thousand people were in Central Park between Graywacke Knoll and the museum, filling all the adjacent walks and drives.

At 2:10 the doors leading to the museum were opened and the holders of tickets were admitted by a platoon of park police specially pressed into service. Gorringe compared it to the crush of a favorite opera night ten times intensified. The mayor, W. R. Grace, was there to receive the gift to the city, seated next to Secretary Evarts, Gorringe, and the president of Columbia University, F.A.P. Barnard. Dr. Crosby, a Protestant minister, began the ceremonies with a prayer somewhat different in tone from that of the Masonic dedication:

"Almighty God, our Heavenly Father, Who hast given to us a goodly heritage in this land of liberty and peace, and hast afforded us opportunity and means for growth in wisdom and knowledge, we desire to lift up our hearts to Thee with Humble and grateful acknowledgment of Thy mercies and to ask for Thy continued favor. We thank Thee for the prosperity of our beloved city, for its health and thrift, for its wealth and enterprise, and for its institutions of charity and education. We thank Thee for the centers of refined culture Thou hast enabled our citizens to establish by which to elevate and enlighten the public mind, and now this day we do give Thee our hearty thanks that Thou hast permitted the enterprise which connects us with an extreme antiquity to be brought to a successful termination; and we pray Thee, most gracious Lord, that those who have been especially instrumental in forwarding this work may be rewarded by seeing its utility, both as an ornament and a teacher among us, adorning the city, while it contrasts our light and privileges with the darkness and tyranny of the older time. We beseech Thee, Almighty God, to accept our petition for Jesus' sake. Amen."

A hymn, which had been adapted to the music of Martin Luther's "Ein' Feste Burg," rang out with greater fidelity to the object of the ceremony:

> Great God, to Whom since time began
> The world has prayed and striven;
> Maker of stars, and earth, and man—
> To Thee our praise is given!
> Here, by this ancient Sign
> Of Thine own Light Divine,
> We lift to Thee our eyes,
> Thou Dweller of the skies—
> Hear us, O God in Heaven!

307

15. E PLURIBUS UNUM

Masonic lodges were introduced into the American colonies at the time they were being proscribed by Clement XII in 1738. By the beginning of the Revolutionary period, there were lodges in each of the thirteen colonies, including seven Provincial Grand Lodges.

Whether or not the idea for a union of the colonies originated among colonial Freemasons, it was certainly achieved through their leadership. Boston Masons organized the Tea Party at the Green Dragon Tavern, described by Daniel Webster as "the Headquarters of the Revolution" and by the British as "a nest of sedition." Paul Revere was a Master Mason, as was every general officer in the Revolutionary army, starting with Jospeh Warren, Grand Master of the Massachusetts Grand Lodge, the first to die at Bunker Hill. Two thousand more Masons were among officers of all grades, including Catholics and a score of the Jewish faith, such as Colonel Isaac Frank, aide-de-camp to George Washington, and Major Benjamin Nones, on General Lafayette's staff.

Of the fifty-six signers of the Declaration of Independence, some fifty were Masons, as was its prime author, Thomas Jefferson. The same was true of the Constitutional Convention.

In colonial times Freemasonry had been the only institution in which leaders of the different colonies could meet on common ground—Protestant, Catholic, or Jew. Local government differed too widely, from the town-meeting system of Puritan New England to the vestry system of the Southern colonies. In the Lodges men of the most diverse religious and political views, rich and poor, could come together in a spirit of mutual harmony and confidence. Founded on the broad universal principles of the brotherhood of man, the immortality of the soul, and the existence in the universe of a Supreme Architect, the lodge became a sanctuary in which any man, from general to private, could meet on an equal plane—something the princes of the world found hard to tolerate.

As Americans began to rebel against the injustice of George III's government, the lodges became divided into "modern" and "ancient," the former patronized by royal governors and British civil military officers, mostly sympathetic to the Crown; the "ancient," composed primarily of merchants, mechanics, and laborers, was intensely demo-

Drafting the Declaration of Independence

George Washington as a Master Mason

cratic, in favor of independence. With the progress of the war, independent American lodges superseded those of English, Irish, and Scottish jurisdiction.

In Virginia, when the members of Alexandria Lodge No. 22 declared themselves independent of any foreign jurisdiction, they named George Washington as First Master of the Lodge. Washington, at the age of twenty, had been entered on November 4, 1752, as an apprentice Mason in the lodge at Market House in Fredericksburg and nine months later, in his twenty-first year, was raised to the degree of Master. In the midst of hostilities, in 1780, when the idea was suggested at the Grand Lodge of Pennsylvania of creating a Grand Master of all the Grand Lodges formed or to be formed in the United States, George Washington was unanimously elected to fill the post. But the commander in chief, too busy with the war, was obliged to decline.

At last, when peace came, it was the Grand Master of New York's Grand Lodge, Robert Livingston, who administered to Washington his oath of office as first president of the United States. When the cornerstone of the nation's new Capitol was laid on September 18, 1793, the ceremony was performed in concert with the Grand Lodge of

310

Masons from Lodge 22 parading in Alexandria, Virginia

Maryland and with several lodges under the jurisdiction of Washington's Lodge 22, with the new president clothing himself for the occasion in a Masonic apron and other insignia of the brotherhood.

At George Washington's burial on his estate at Mount Vernon, 20 miles south of the District of Columbia, six of the pallbearers and three of the officiating clergymen were brother Masons from Alexandria Lodge 22. And "the mystic funeral rites of masonry" were performed by the new Grand Master of the Lodge, as, one by one, Washington's Masonic brethren cast upon his bier the ritual sprig of acacia, Osirian symbol of the resurrection of the spirit. On the coffin with two crossed swords was placed the Masonic apron specially made for Washington by the Marquise de Lafayette. So it is not surprising that the idea to raise to Washington's memory the greatest Masonic monument in the world, an obelisk of marble to tower majestically 600 feet above the waters of the Potomac, visible from his home in Mount Vernon, should have been conceived in the minds of America's Freemasons.

Within hours of Washington's death, his fellow Mason, Representative John Marshall of Virginia, later the country's first chief justice, rose in the House and moved that a monument be raised to the man "first in war, first in peace, and first in the hearts of his countrymen." Promptly in both Houses a bill was passed to raise $200,000. But no money was appropriated; and for a quarter of a century no step was taken to implement the resolution. Instead, the infant nation, founded on the tenets of the great liberating movement of northern Europe, which aspired to

311

Obelisk marking Washington's tomb in Mount Vernon, Virginia

religious liberty and the right of every man to worship God according to the dictates of his conscience, found itself swept by tides of religious intolerance almost as deadly as those of the sixteenth century, and the waves of controversy ebbed and flowed around the building of the monument.

The trouble all started in England in 1797, when a reactionary French Jesuit named Augustin Barruel fled to London from the September massacres of the French Revolution and brought out a five-volume opus, *Memoirs pour servir à l'histoire du Jacobinism,* in which he placed the blame for the bloodbath of the Terror squarely on Freemasons, singling out Saint-Germain, Cagliostro, and Weishaupt as the major Masonic villains. Tracing the slogan of "Liberty and Equality" back to the early Templars, Barruel declared that the secret of Masonry *did* consist in those two words, but that "in the higher degrees the twofold principle of liberty and equality is unequivocally explained not only by *war against kings and thrones,* but by *war against Christ and his altars."*

To Barruel, the Jacobins had instituted the Terror as members of a vast plot to overthrow society and religion, the worst villains being Weishaupt's Illuminati, cuckooed into Freemasonry. In his early volumes, Barruel claimed that a formal and systematic conspiracy against all religion had been formed and zealously prosecuted by the encyclopedists Voltaire, d'Alembert, and Diderot, assisted by Frederick II of Prussia. In his third volume Barruel attached the "wickedest anti-Christian conspirators: devoted to atheism, universal anarchy and the destruction of property, boring from within to undermine every government, wishing for the nations of the earth to be directed from their nocturnal clubs." Imagine, wrote Barruel, "thou-

312

sands of lodge rooms converted into nests of human vipers, men possessing warped intellects with one uncontrollable impulse surging through their arteries—destruction! destruction! destruction!—and you will be getting down to the true cause of the holocaust which drenched the French nation in human blood."

Barruel charged that not only the lower orders of Masonry were duped by Weishaupt, but also those of Weishaupt's own Illuminati, for whom he had provided another top-secret level of direction known as the Aeopagus, a withdrawn circle of directors of the whole order, who alone knew its secret aims. To Barruel, such revolutionary leaders as La Rochefoucauld, Lafayette, and the duc d'Orléans, had become Illuminati agents and dupes of the more extreme radicals such as Danton, provocateurs who sparked the Illuminati-directed rebellion. Barruel further charged that the entire French Masonic establishment had been converted to Weishaupt's revolutionary ideas, its lodges turned into secret committees which planned bloodshed. "Masonic units, dotted by the thousands all over the map of Europe, were thus transformed into places of anarchy, devoted to creating mob violence."

In his fourth and fifth volumes, Barruel went into the minutiae of how the holocaust had been carefully plotted in a secret meeting between Saint-Germain and Cagliostro, who had organized "six hundred thousand masons into a conspiracy with the duc d'Orléans as the chief villain, ambitious to possess the throne of France." Barruel attributed to Saint-Germain, Cagliostro, and Weishaupt the deliberate steering of the Revolution into the Terror. "The power to govern France was vested in the *Comité de Salut Public* composed of three hundred men, all leaders in the Illuminated Order." And, according to Barruel, these same Illuminati had spread to America and infiltrated American Masonry.

Jefferson, after reading one volume of Barruel's *memoirs,* called it "the ravings of a Bedlamite." Historian Vernon Stauffer, more politely dismisses the connection between Illuminati and the French Revolution as "suffering from the fatal defect of lack of historical proof." And John Morris Roberts, in his recent *The Mythology of Secret Societies,* sums up the conclusions of more rational historians: "It is difficult to grasp, let alone understand, the success—and enduring success—of this farrago of nonsense." Not only, says Roberts, does Barruel "mistranscribe and misreport," he is "careless about ideological and doctrinal distinctions. He wrote nonsense about Swedenborg and the Martinists, and he cribs, uncritically, stories which weaken his case in the eyes of anyone who has some acquaintance with the world of which he is writing." And yet, Roberts concludes, almost audibly sighing: "Few objective scholars have dictated the shape of their subject for so long as this unbalanced and indiscriminate priest."

Hardly was Barruel's book off the presses in England when a Scottish Freemason, John Robinson, professor of natural philosophy at the University of Edinburgh, with the excuse that he was anxious to disculpate English Masonry from having been involved in the French Revolution, brought out a sequel echoing Barruel's "data" in *Proofs of Conspiracy Against All the Religions and Governments of Europe, Carried on in the Secret Meetings of Free Masons, Illuminati and Reading Societies.* The book was a quick best seller; with the result that as further editions were brought out in Edinburgh, Dublin, and New York, a wave of anti-Masonic and anti-Illuminist feeling spread across America, carefully enflamed by Barruel's brother Jesuits. Even Washington was accused of having been an Illuminatus, and was obliged publicly to play down his Masonic connections.

When, in 1799, a German minister, G. W. Snyder, sent Washington a copy of Robinson's book with the warning that the Illuminati were preparing to "overthrow all government and religion," asking the ex-president to prevent the plan from "corrupting the Bretheren of the English Lodges over which you preside," Washington replied that he had heard "much of the nefarious and dangerous plan and doctrines of the Illuminati, but never saw the book until you were pleased to send it to me." Subtly, Washington added that he wished to "correct an error you have run into, of my presiding over the English Lodges in this country. The fact is, I preside over none, nor have I been in one, more than once or twice, within the last thirty years—I believe notwithstanding, that none of the Lodges in this country are contaminated with the principles ascribed to the society of the Illuminati." All of which was palpably true, though perhaps somewhat sophistical, as the lodges to which Washington belonged after 1776 were not English, but American.

In another letter, written a month later, Washington further corrected Snyder's misunderstanding. "It was not my intention to doubt that the doctrines of the Illuminati, and principles of Jacobinism, had not spread in the United States. On the contrary, no one is more fully satisfied of this fact than I am. The idea that I meant to convey was that I did not believe that the Lodges of Freemasons in *this*

President George Washington in the Alexandria Masonic lodge

country had, as societies, endeavoured to propagate the diabolical tenets of the first, or pernicious principles of the latter, (if they are susceptible of separation). That *individuals of them* may have done it, or that the founder, or instrument employed to found the Democratic societies in the United States, may have had these objects—and actually, in my view, had a separation of the people from their government, is too evident to be questioned." And although the next four presidents of the United States were all Masons, an organized surge of anti-Masonic feeling swept the country, threatening the institutions of Masonry and testing the fidelity of its members. To be seen wearing a Masonic emblem meant risking social ostracism.

In these circumstances, the prospect of erecting a Masonic monument to Washington grew dimmer. On January 15, 1824, Representative James Buchanan (later president) proposed that something be done about the 1799 resolution. His proposal was tabled. And even when John Quincy Adams, the first non-Masonic president, reminded the members of Congress of the resolution in December 1825, no action whatsoever was taken.

In the country the anti-Masonic movement had increased as there came into being the first third party in American politics, the Anti-Masonic party, which grew rapidly as a result of the hysteria generated by the disappearance in 1826 of a brick mason named William Morgan, little known other than for his penchant for the bottle, and for a dubious past as a Mason. In May 1825 Morgan had been mistakenly exalted to the degree of Royal Arch Mason in Batavia, New York, on the basis of his oath that he had received the earlier necessary degrees in Canada, where the Masonic ritual was somewhat different. But Morgan's drinking habits and his financial looseness aroused suspicion, and when it was established that he had not been initiated into the lower degrees, he was dropped from the order. In revenge, Morgan decided to publish a book containing the ritual secrets of Freemasonry, for which he obtained a contract from a printer of the *Batavia Republican Advocate,* also a former Mason who had failed to advance in his lodge in Albany, and ever since had cherished a grudge against the brotherhood.

As Morgan set to work on his book, keeping the local barrooms advised of his progress, feeling began to run high among Masons that a stop should be put to what they considered Morgan's treachery. News of the intended publication finally roused Masons in New York State to take action, though most counseled that if the book were greeted with silence it might become stillborn.

William Morgan

315

John Whitney, an ardent New York Mason, incensed by Morgan's behavior, went to Governor De Witt Clinton, Grand Master of New York Masons, but was advised to purchase Morgan's manuscript, for which $1,000 would be made available, and warned to do nothing that might conflict with the law.

On September 11, 1826, Morgan was arrested on a warrant sworn out by a tavern keeper in Canandaigua, New York, and charged with theft. Acquitted, he was re-arrested for a debt of $2.68 and jailed for his inability to pay. On September 12, Morgan was released on payment of the sum by a third party, who, with several companions, drove Morgan away in a coach. Morgan was later traced to Fort Niagara, where he had been confined in an unused military depot. Thereafter he disappeared completely. As

Depressing military depot where Morgan was held captive

a *cause célèbre* for anti-Masonic propaganda, the disappearance was a true bonanza. A great cry was raised, and his abductors were accused of being Masonic murderers, fulfilling their secret oath to dispose of traitors in the most gruesome way. According to formal allegations of the Anti-Masonic party, the ritual manner of inflicting death on traitors among Masons was "cutting the throat and tearing out the tongue, tearing out the heart, severing, quartering and disemboweling the body, and burning the ashes—tearing the breast open, and throwing the heart on a dunghill to rot—smiting the skull off, and exposing the brains to the sun—pulling down the house of the offender, and hanging him on one of the timbers—striking the head off, and placing it on a lofty spire—tearing out the eyes, chopping off the hands, quartering the body, and throwing it among the rubbish of the Temple."

To calm a population outraged by this further "farrago

of nonsense," Governor Clinton issued three successive proclamations urging all good citizens to cooperate with the authorities in helping to find Morgan and punish his abductors. A $2,000 reward was offered for information leading to his recovery and for bringing to justice his assailants. A free pardon was offered to anyone involved who would uncover the offenders.

The discovery that certain Masons had arranged for the change of horses and drivers for the 125-mile drive from Canandaigua to Fort Niagara, brought jail sentences to those involved. And every possible effort was made to prove as murderers these Masons; only lack of a body made it impossible. When a man's corpse was washed ashore on the beach of Oak Orchard Harbor, New York, about 40 miles below Fort Niagara, Morgan's widow, though she admitted the clothes were not those of her husband, expressed belief that the body might be his. But whereas Morgan had been bald, with a smooth face and the peculiarity of long white hairs in his ears and nostrils, this body had a heavy beard and a full head of hair.

To remedy the discrepancy, a leading member of the Anti-Masonic party, Thurlow Weed, editor of a Rochester paper, present at the inquest, was accused of having had the corpse shaved and hairs plucked from his forehead to thrust into its ears and nostrils. Result: a verdict that the body was Morgan's. Publicity about the verdict, as it brought on another wave of anti-Masonic outrage in the country, also brought to Oak Orchard Harbor the widow of a man, Timothy Munroe, who had fallen from a boat and drowned. So minutely did the widow describe the clothing worn by her husband and so accurately did the details tally with marks she said were identifiable on his body, that another inquest was ordered and the verdict reversed. The corpse was declared to be that of Munroe.

Of Morgan, nothing more was heard, and though stories continued to be circulated that a group of Masons had drawn lots to dump him in the river with a weight around his neck, Masons stuck to the story that Morgan had been taken across the river to Canada, where Canadian Masons near Hamilton, Ontario had given him $500 to make himself scarce—after which he had disappeared without a trace.

Not that the disappearance of Morgan did anything to halt publication of what was purported to be his book, put together by Miller, his contractual publisher, from manuscripts in the possession of his widow. To arouse sympathy and to publicize the book, Miller even appears to have set fire to his printshop, for which he was then indicted.

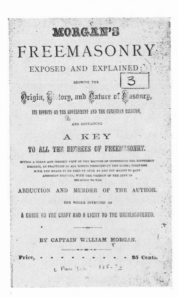

The book, quickly pirated, sold by the hundreds of thousands of copies, adding fuel to the anti-Masonic blaze.

That one such disappearance could bring down the wrath of a whole country on the Brotherhood of Masons, whereas the Church could historically be held responsible for several million agonized deaths under torture and execution, seemed to Masons unaccountably unequitable, especially as no other "ritual murder" could be attributed to American Masons, who pointed out that by their own code of ethics, they, above all, were bound to obey the law of the land, "with respect for God, country and their fellow men."

Clearly, the Morgan incident had only been a spark, like Marie Antoinette's affair of the diamond necklace, which lighted a well-prepared pyre designed to destroy the fraternity. Social, racial, religious, and political forces had been working beneath the surface to capitalize on the frenzy of the anti-Masonic movement.

Conventions of anti-Masons convened throughout the country, to sweep anti-Masonic candidates into office. Again the principal ammunition at these conventions were the works of Barruel and Robinson, freely excerpted and produced as the sacrosanct evidence of history. Illuminism, said Ethan Smith, chairman of the Committee on the Connection between French Illuminism and the higher degrees of Free Masonry, at the 1832 anti-Masonic Republican convention in Massachussets, was designed to bind the world with invisible hands, and had been infiltrated into America well before 1786. "Both Robinson and Barruel," said Smith, "testify to the fact. Barruel mentions a lodge of this order in Portsmouth, Virginia, and two lodges as having descended from it. Illuminism exists in this country; and the impious mockery of the sacramental supper, described by Robinson is acted here." Smith then quoted from Christoph Girtanner's book on the French revolution: "active members of the propagandists in 1791 numbered fifty thousand, with funds of thirty millions of livres. They are extended over the face of the world, having for their object the promotion of revolutions, and the doctrines of Atheism. And it is a maxim in their code that it is better to defer their attempts fifty years, than to fail of success through too much precipitation."

Smith also quoted from a printed sermon of a Reverend Dr. Morse, who assured the public of an official communication from the Illuminated lodge Wisdom, of Portsmouth, Virginia, to the Illuminated lodge Union. "The letter," said Smith, "was intercepted. In it were the names of their officers, and the number of their adepts; being then 100,

Tanzania Hemingway: old-fashioned standards of service and comfort, with 16 days in Nairobi, Mt. Meru, Lake Manyara, Gibb's Farm, the Serengeti and the Ngorongoro Crater. A deluxe safari, from $4315.

Out of Africa: the ultimate Kenya and Tanzania classic. A luxurious 20-day tented safari including Nairobi, Mt. Meru, Lake Manyara, the Serengeti, the Ngorongoro Crater and the Masai Mara. From $5400.

Tenting On The Zambezi: an adventurous excursion on the banks of one of Africa's mightiest rivers, including Victoria Falls, Mana Pools and Lake Kariba. From $4690.

Special Programs. Abercrombie & Kent can also take you "off the beaten track" on your own tailor-made itinerary in Africa. Possibilities include:

- walking safaris in Zambia's unspoiled Luangwa Valley
- bird watching in the Okavango Delta
- fishing for 100-pound Nile Perch on Lake Victoria
- camel safaris in northern Kenya

Though most tour planners do not offer this specialized service, A&K can create an African adventure just for you, crafted to fit your own schedule, budget and special interests.

mostly French. In this letter, it appeared that there were thousands of such Lodges of Illuminism in the world; and many in the western world." Smith came to the point of all the fuss: he produced the same charge which had been leveled against Pico, Ficino, Dee, and Cagliostro: Illuminism had been most secretly planted by the side of Speculative Masonry to indulge in *gross infidelity and licentiousness*. Here, at last, was the note needed to enflame a "Christian" opposition.

The churches joined in the general attack, barring Masons from their pulpits as "irreligious." Ministers preached the "satanic nature of the Masonic lodge" and called it incompatible with the Christian faith. Baptists were told to dissolve their ties with Masonry or risk having "the Hand of Christian Fellowship" withdrawn from them. Other denominations announced they would support no Mason for any office in either town, country, or state. Masons were stricken from jury rolls; hostile crowds formed to prevent Masonic meetings; and individuals were so persecuted that in many cases they were driven to emigrate. In the early 1830s, of 227 lodges in New York State, only 41 remained. New York's membership dwindled from 20,000 at the time of the Morgan incident to a mere 3,000. All the lodges in Vermont surrendered their charters, and it was the same in all the other states of the Union. As one historian sums up the carnage: The Temple of Masonry was shattered, the brotherhood scattered.

Many politicians campaigned on an anti-Masonic platform and rose to eminence, such as Millard Fillmore, who worked his way up to the White House, and William H. Seward, governor of New York and a United States senator, who narrowly failed to occupy the White House, but was to become Lincoln's secretary of state. There was a slight respite when Andrew Jackson, Grand Master of Masons in Tennessee, was elected president for a second term; and then gradually the halls of Masonry once more began to throng with candidates who, after the lesson of Morgan, were more warily chosen from among those whose "pure lives and characters would make them an ornament to the order." As the lodges multiplied, Grand Master James Willard was able to announce that thanks to the constancy of members, Freemasonry was once more held in respect and honor in the country, as was the memory of its founder, George Washington.

In Washington, D.C., what was described as "a number of patriotic citizens" assembled to revive the plan for erecting a national monument, asking for voluntary contributions from all the people, rich and poor, in the amount of

Washington, D.C. in the 1830s, showing Navy Yard and Capitol

$1 each. That this group, which called itself the Washington National Monument Society, was fundamentally Masonic is evidenced by its first president, Washington's brother Mason, Chief Justice John Marshall.

Ads were placed by the society to elicit designs from American artists for a monument "harmoniously to blend durability, simplicity and grandeur" at an estimated cost of $1 million. As to form, there was no limitation, but, as might be expected, a committee selected the design of Freemason Robert Mills for a 600-foot obelisk surrounded at its base by an olympian rotunda.

By 1847 the society had collected and gained from judicious investments a total of $87,000, and seemed on its way to success. A liberalizing trend in the country echoed a similar trend in Europe, especially with the election to the papacy in 1846 of Giovanni Maria Mastai-Ferretti. As Pius IX, the new pope auspiciously inaugurated his reign with a political amnesty and several badly needed reforms in the judicial and financial systems of the Papal States, proverbially the worst run in Europe, cutting down ecclesiastical graft. Censorship was mitigated and,

Peaceful capital of the United States at a time of revolutionary ferment in Europe.

Architect Robert Mills's design for a grandiose Washington monument, with an expensive circular colonnaded building (250 feet in diameter and 100 feet high) from which a 70-foot-wide obelisk was to rise 600 feet above the city. The columns were to stand 45 feet high, 12 feet in diameter, surmounted by an entablature 20 feet high, the lot crowned by a massive balustrade.

in March 1848, wonder of wonders, the pontiff promulgated a constitution with a parliament consisting of two chambers, to which many Italian Masons were elected.

In this happy atmosphere the United States Congress passed a resolution authorizing the Washington National Monument Society to erect the obelisk designed by Robert Mills, granting them, as a suitable site to build on, a 30-acre lot overlooking the Potomac south of the White House. There beautiful marble from the Symington Beaver Dam quarries in Baltimore County could easily be brought by water or by rail. The estimated cost of construction was $55,200 for the obelisk and $1,122,000 for the entire job, which Congress agreed to provide.

Mills was authorized to contract for the required material and to have a rail line laid right up to the base of the monument. And so thoroughly had the atmosphere changed that the laying of the cornerstone—a 24,500-

pound block of Maryland marble donated by Freemason Thomas Symington—could be performed with a suitable Masonic ceremony scheduled for July 4, 1848.

Stands were built around the site to make a vast sloping amphitheater of seats. Near the Fourteenth Street Bridge (then called Long Bridge), a triumphal arch was decorated with the same live eagle, now forty years old, which had hailed the arrival of Freemason Lafayette when he had visited the capital twenty years earlier. A parade of carriages led by President James Knox Polk was followed by the Masonic fraternity, headed by their Grand Marshal, J. B. Thomas; and the ceremonies were opened with a prayer led by the Grand Chaplain of the Grand Masonic Lodge of Maryland.

It was a lovely day. Recent rain had laid the dust and turned the sod a fresh green. Bells tolled solemnly as close to twenty thousand people crowded around for the ceremony, fares having been reduced by rail and stage-coach lines into the city.

Among the spectators were past and future presidents Martin van Buren and Millard Fillmore, as well as Mrs. Alexander Hamilton, Mrs. John Quincy Adams, and a delegation of Indians with whom George Washington had originally signed treaties of peace. Benjamin B. French, Grand Master of the Grand Lodge of Free and Accepted Masons of the District of Columbia, deposited articles in a cavity beneath the stone, using the same gavel and wearing the same Masonic apron and sash worn by George Washington when he laid the cornerstone of the Capitol in 1793.

Having applied the square, level, and plumb to see that the stone was "well laid, true and trusty," the Grand Master placed on the stone the ancient Masonic elements

Masonic ceremony laying the cornerstone with the same silver trowel used by Washington to start the capital in 1793

of consecration: corn for plenty, wine for joy, oil for health. He then turned to his brother Mason, Robert Mills, and presented him with the square, level, and plumb, the working tools he was to use in the erection of this monument, saying: "You, as a Freemason, know to what they morally allude: the plumb admonishes us to walk upright in our several stations before God and man, the square to square our actions with the square of virtue, remembering that we are traveling upon the level of time to that 'undiscover'd country from whose bourne no traveller returns.'"

The Honorable Robert C. Winthrop, Speaker of the House, then delivered an address which reflected the encouraging political mood of the times, alluding to the rash of liberating revolutions of 1848 as the "mighty movements which have recently taken place on the continent of Europe, where events which would have given character to an age have been crowded within the changes of a moon." In these changes, said Winthrop, "we see the influence of our own institutions . . . we behold in them the results of our own example. We recognize them as the spontaneous germination and growth of seeds which have been wafted over the ocean, for half a century past, from our own original Liberty tree."

That the occasion was intentionally and intensely Masonic was unmistakable from Winthrop's words: "Everywhere the people are heard calling their rulers to account and holding them to a just reponsibility. Everywhere the cry is raised for the elective franchise, the trial by jury, the freedom of the press, written constitutions, representative systems, republican forms." And in an unusual tribute to Pius IX, Winthrop continued: "In some cases, most fortunately, the rulers themselves have not escaped some reasonable symptoms of the pervading fervor for freedom, and have nobly anticipated the demands of their subjects. To the sovereign pontiff of the Roman States in particular belongs the honor of having led the way in the great movement of the day, and no American will withhold from him a cordial tribute of respect and admiration for whatever he has done or designed for the regeneration of Italy. Glorious indeed on the page of history will be the name of Pius IX if the rise of another Rome shall be traced to his wise and liberal policy."

But this was not to be. In November of that same year Pius fled from the republic of Rome to the Kingdom of Naples, and there, completely reversing his liberal policy, threw himself into the arms of the Jesuits, calling on France and Austria to help him back into power. Rein-

Handsome, but epileptic, Pius IX managed by his Jesuitically enflamed "ultramontanism" to concentrate all ecclesiastical power in the person of the Roman pontiff. By 1870 the Vatican Council had squashed all the independent power of the bishops, who lost their autonomous standing and became mere papal delegates. Pius then proclaimed the dogma of the infallibility of popes and the much-disputed notion of the immaculate conception of the Virgin (to whom he wished to raise an obelisk but instead erected a great pillar opposite the Office of the Propagation of the Faith).

Column raised by Pius IX in honor of the Virgin Mary

stated in Rome with foreign bayonets in April 1850, Pius inaugurated as violent an antiliberal reaction as had occurred after the defeat of Napoleon in 1815 and one which was to swing the political pendulum to the farthest opposite extreme. Absolute autocracy was restored in the Papal States, and anyone could be thrown into Castel Sant'Angelo without a trial.

By 1851 Pius showed the absolutist direction he was taking by proclaiming Roman Catholicism as the sole religion of the Spanish people, to the exclusion of all other creeds, a principle which was then applied to Latin America with the hope of doing likewise in North America. By 1854 Pius, well on his way to announcing his stunning dogma of the infallibility of popes—an idea strongly disputed by a great many Catholic bishops—defied the whole trend of liberal thought by branding as false the basic beliefs of democracy and liberalism. Reinforcing his predecessors' bans against Masonry, Pius attacked public education, free libraries, and the right of men and women to choose their own religion, claiming for the Catholic Church control of all culture, all science, and all systems of education, declaring: "The pontiff neither can nor ought to be reconciled with progress, liberalism and modern civilization."

Arguing that the Son of God had established one religion and imposed on all men the obligation of embracing it, Pius branded all Protestants and Jews as heretics, doomed to damnation, there being no salvation outside the Roman Church. Catholics were forbidden to read certain books or to discuss their religion without approval of a priest, who, in turn, could be reprimanded and punished for proposing mercy for heretics. Catholics were to be held to the dogma that hellfire was real, and that the unfortunate non-Catholic damned would never lose consciousness of their torment throughout all eternity.

Unashamed, the pontiff declared himself to be Father of Princes and Kings, Ruler of the World, Viceroy of the Lord Jesus Christ, claiming for himself absolute political power and declaring it to be the duty of all states to carry out orders from Rome, that only the Roman Church could decide whether a law was "good" or "bad" and that obedience to a law unpleasing to the pontiff was not binding on the citizens of any state.

Summed up, these clearly expressed political principles of the Roman Catholic Church, to which was applied the epithet *ultramontanism,* appeared formidable to American Masons. According to Pius IX's famous *Syllabus Errorum,* the ultimate source of law and government in the United

States lay not in the people but in the "will of God as interpreted and expressed by the Pope." The primary and ultimate functions of the government of the United States were to carry out the principles of the Roman Church as promulgated by the pope. Freedom of speech and the press were to be permitted only to the extent they did not interfere with the principles and activities of the Roman Church. Public funds were to be used to support the Catholic Church and its schools. Most alarming, Catholics who were citizens of the United States owed a primary political allegiance to the Roman Catholic pontiff who could lawfully use force to overthrow their government. Catholics were not to approve a policy of separation of Church and State, and states had no right to legislate in matters such as marriages, only to be recognized by the Church, which forbade contraception and abortion even if required to save a mother. A leading Jesuit writer in the United States classed with prostitutes those American wives who used contraception, and called them "daughters of joy," maintaining that birth control resulted in sin which was no more than mutual masturbation.

All of which, not unnaturally, was unpalatable to American democrats, especially when the Catholic clergy insisted that the laws of Rome superseded the laws of the republic, and that Catholics were duty-bound to force all people into the pattern laid down by the Church. What made the system intolerable to its opponents was the fact that Catholics in America had no say whatsoever in the choice of their own priests, bishops, or cardinals, all of whom were appointed from Rome to perpetuate the system of management and control, bishops being deliberately selected for their subservience to the Vatican. The country began to be flooded with Catholic immigrants—as many as 300,000 a year, mostly poor, illiterate, and superstitious—Irishmen fleeing the potato famine, or Germans escaping crop failures and political persecution, all under the control of foreign priests. American Protestants found themselves faced with an army officered by disciplined bishops under a single omnipotent commander in chief whose chiefs of staff were the Jesuit generals. Whereas at the time of the founding of the republic there had been perhaps 1 percent of Catholics in the colonies, now there were as many as 10 percent who could effectively influence elections in which Yankees could even find themselves reduced to minorities. As the established Protestants saw their longtime position of privilege being eroded, religious intolerance flared up to a degree almost comparable with the horrors of the Counter-Reformation.

The country was flooded with salacious literature accusing priests of seducing their pretty penitents.

Protestant ministers rose in their pulpits to denounce Catholics as un-American because they were obliged to take orders from an autocratic, antidemocratic foreign power. These ministers, believing in human sinfulness and predestined damnation, became, in the words of historian Carleton Beals, "a band of neck-swollen, hate-mongering tub thumpers." In the streets scores of Protestant antipapist magazines began to appear, and masses of anti-Catholic literature were put out by Protestant Bible societies. As sex was the easiest and most obvious peg on which to hang an inflamed propaganda, religious presses gave free reign to stories of secret orgies in nunneries, the rape of young girls by priests, the killing of bastard babies, with headlines such as "Six Thousand Babies' Heads Found in a Nunnery Fishpond." Most popular were the "confessions" of escaped nuns who described being forced into carnal intercourse with priests. *Awful Disclosures* by Maria Monk, the joint effort of "a disordered whore and unprincipled religious demagogue," sold 300,000 copies before the Civil War.

When a Catholic priest in Carbean, New York, outraged at the distribution of Protestant Bibles to his parishioners, angrily burned several copies publicly, the whole country reacted. Nor did it help when Bishop Hughes of New York defended the act, saying: "To destroy a spurious corrupt copy of the Bible was justified and praiseworthy." Described by pro-Catholic Carleton Beals as "pretty much a Torquemada deprived of rack and screw and hot irons," Bishop Hughes gave an outrageous sermon in Saint Patrick's Cathedral, boasting that the pagan and Protestant nations were crumbling before the force of Rome.

"The true Church," thundered the bishop, "would convert all Pagan nations, even England, with her proud Parliament. . . . Everybody should know that we have for our mission to convert the world—including all inhabitants of the United States—the people of the cities, and the people of the country, the officers of the Navy and the Marines, commanders of the Army, the legislatures, the Senate, the Cabinet, the President and all."

To counter the bishop, his opponents made use of a firebrand named Allessandro Gavazzi, a former priest and teacher turned revolutionist who had fled from Italy to the United States under the auspices of The American and Christian Foreign Church Union, a scandal-making organization formed to fight the "Corrupting Catholic Church." Gavazzi wanted nothing but to annihilate the papacy, and swore to devote his life to "stripping the Roman harlot of her barb." Although a renegade, he wore a long monk's robe embroidered with a blazing cross. Six feet tall, with an "almost savage physical energy," he caused riots wherever he went.

Protestants turned against Catholics as they had against Baptists, Methodists, Shakers, and Quakers, using the same methods of "torture, whippings, brandings, arson and murder, looting and raping in the name of the democracy they claimed to support." Everywhere "native" American parties began to mushroom, waving the Stars and Stripes, and raising up mobs to burn Catholic convents, churches, houses; to assault nuns and murder Irish and other European immigrants. As the nation became torn with bitter sectionalism and seething social unrest, there was repeated rioting, in Boston, New York, Philadelphia,

Opening battle between the Bowery Boys (Know-Nothings) and the Dead Rabbits (Tammanies) from Beals's *Brass-Knuckle Crusade*

A contemporary print illustrating the Astor Theatre riot of 1849

Baltimore, Providence, Hartford, New Orleans, Saint Louis, Cincinnati, Louisville, and San Francisco.

According to Herbert Asbury in his *The Gangs of New York,* at least thirty thousand men in the city were active members of gangs, and not only men but women fought in the streets. "One notorious female," says Carleton Beals in *Brass-Knuckle Crusade,* his description of early fascism in America, "carried a tomahawk, knife, and gun and wore boots cleated with broken glass. Another sheathed her nails in steel and filed her teeth to needle point. *Hell Cat Maggie,* they called her." Tammany Hall's "Sons of Saint Tamina," started, as Beals says, "by hatchetman Aaron Burr who first made secret gangsterism into a political system," found themselves pitted against Protestant bully clubs who sought to control the polling booths with sticks, knives, and guns.

That the times were rough is evidenced by miscreants in New Jersey being branded on the cheek and given public floggings. A girl convicted of petty theft was sentenced to 210 lashes on her bare back. Joseph Smith, founder of the Mormons, taken by a mob from an Illinois jail, was murdered, as was his brother. Abolitionists were dragged through the streets at the end of ropes and frequently killed. Southern states imposed the death penalty for preaching to "blacks" or teaching them to read and write. And, although Washington, in his will, had emancipated his slaves and left a trust fund for their education and for the schooling of their children, the Bible Society refused to send Bibles to slaves.

As the whole country, aroused by the fervor of prejudice, prepared to square off for the bloodiest civil war in history, there came into being a secret society known as the Supreme Order of the Star-Spangled Banner. To avoid the Constitutional guarantee of religious freedom, its mem-

328

bers pledged to vote only for non-Catholics selected by their secret upper tier caucuses, swearing never to betray the society's secrets, under pain of expulsion and implied penalty of death, and to deny affiliation by replying to the curious with the simple phrase: "I know nothing." Multiplying like rabbits, they soon numbered five million members, with new ones enrolled at the rate of five thousand a week. By 1855 they were a power in the land, controlling Maryland, Delaware, Kentucky, New Jersey, Pennsylvania, California, all but one of the New England states, and nearly every state in the South. Millard Fillmore became president standing on the Know-Nothing platform, and U. S. Grant rose to fame in the same way. But the proudest "claim" of the Know-Nothings was that George Washington had been the first of their party, citing his apocryphal words at Valley Forge: "Tonight let none but native-born Americans stand guard."

Unwittingly they were to do their assumed hero a gross disservice. By this time the Washington Monument had reached a height of 170 feet at a cost of $230,000. But the Washington National Monument Society, complaining that the turmoil of the times had dried up subscriptions, appealed for money to the various states. Alabama replied that it could give no money, but offered to contribute a stone of the requisite dimension—4 feet by 2 feet, by 1½ feet. Other states followed suit, including municipalities and associations, as did foreign governments such as Switzerland, Turkey, Greece, China, Japan, and the Vatican—from which Pius IX sent a block of marble, ironically taken from the Pagan Temple of Concord in Rome.

But even these contributions were nowhere near sufficient to do the job, and the society's board of managers appealed to Congress to take whatever action it deemed proper. A select committee recommended a subscription of $200,000, the exact sum originally voted in 1799, but never provided. It too was to be canceled, by the occurrence of an extraordinary event.

On March 6, 1855, between 1:00 and 2:00 A.M., a group of men rushed out of the darkness round the foot of the monument and seized the night watchman, whom they locked up in his shack, so as to break into a shed where the pope's stone was boxed. With skids, bars, and blocks they rolled the stone out to a scow in the nearby canal basin, then ferried it out into the Potomac almost to Long Bridge, and dumped it.

The men, nine members of the Know-Nothing party, had drawn lots for the job, announcing that the marble block represented "a designing, crafty, subtle scheme of the

far-reaching power that was grasping after the whole world to sway its iron scepter with bloodstained hands over the millions of its inhabitants.'' The same night a group of about 750 members of the Know-Nothings, many of whom had surreptitiously joined the Washington National Monument Society, called a meeting and voted their own officers into control of the society, defenestrating the others. On the morrow Know-Nothings announced they were in possession of the Washington Monument. Congress's reaction was speedy. They tabled the recommended appropriation, effectively killing it.

The disappearance of the pope's stone angered ''a large body of citizens'' and also discouraged further contributions; so all construction ceased. Two weeks later Robert Mills died, and with him went what appeared to have been the last ray of hope for continuing the monument. During the next three years, as the battle continued between the old members of the monument society and the new Know-Nothings, only 13 courses, or 26 feet of masonry were laid, consisting mostly of rubble rejected by the master mason. By 1858, unable to raise any money—in 1855 they only managed to collect $51.66—the Know-Nothings finally surrendered all their records to the original society with the entire treasury of $285. As a national party the Know-Nothings were through.

In February 1859, to prevent any recurrence of such events, Congress incorporated the Washington Monument Society with President James Buchanan presiding *ex officio*. But the Civil War was looming, and in all of 1860 the society was only able to collect $88.52, 48 cents of which came from Washington's native Virginia, and 15 cents from Mississippi. With the outbreak of war, the

Cattle grazing around the monument to supply Union troops

monument stood 176 feet high, less than a third of its prospected height. In the words of Mark Twain, it "looked like a hollow oversized chimney." All construction was halted during the war while the grounds on which it stood were used to graze cattle for the Union commissary.

Following the war these swamplike grounds came to be known as Murderer's Row—"the hangout of escapees, deserters, and other flotsam of the war"; and it wasn't until ten years later, with the approach of the first centennial of independence, that Congress once more went into action. But there was now a real question as to whether to try to continue the building or simply tear it down and write off the quarter of a million dollars already spent. The problem lay in the foundations—81 feet square

331

and 25 feet deep, solid masonry—which was now considered too weak a base onto which to raise the projected 600-foot obelisk. It was feared the structure would sink into the swampy terrain or be blown over by the wind. In the House, there were complaints about asking the people of the United States for money to "finish this unsightly and unstable shaft upon this unsafe foundation . . . this ill-shapen badly put together structure of mixed blocks." It was said that "storms, the uncertain foundation, the swaying to and fro of such a column will sooner or later bring it to earth."

The ignorance of some of the politicians was exemplified by Representative Samuel S. Cox of New York, who pompously declared: "If you raise this obelisk which

Monument's surroundings as a dumping ground and storehouse

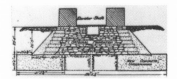

Engineers' plan to remove 70 percent of the old foundation and insert a new concrete pad capable of supporting an 82,000-ton shaft

First, the center section of each side was removed and replaced by fresh concrete.

Next, the corners were filled in.

Thirty-six feet beneath the surface, the new foundation weighed 37,000 tons and covered more than three times the previous area.

comes from Egypt, a barbarian country that never had art, I don't believe it will succeed in impressing the American people in a proper way with the virtues and greatness of George Washington.'' Representative Jasper D. Ward of Illinois argued that the monument had been stopped because ''when the unsightly column reared itself so high that they could see it they (the people) did not feel like contributing more to it.'' John B. Storm of New York, on the other hand, declared that though he might have preferred it had the monument never been started, he was ''unwilling that the hundredth anniversary of our existence as a nation should dawn upon us with that monument standing there as a testimony that republics are ungrateful.'' R. C. McCormick of Arizona agreed that ''no greater disgrace, certainly no greater calamity, could possibly befall than that the shaft after once being completed should fall to the ground,'' but argued that the chief reason for adopting the simple obelisk was its permanency and imperishability. Norton P. Chipman of the District of Columbia backed him up, suggesting there was something special in such a simple, majestic obelisk, ''eminently proper as commemorational of the character of Washington, aside from the fact that the early fathers preferred it. . . .''

In the end, Congress appointed an engineer to study the problem and give an estimate for completing the job of raising a simple obelisk, abandoning the expensive pantheon at the base designed by Mills in favor of a massive terrace with a balustrade for statuary, which would cost only $65,000. When the first engineer gave an unfavorable report, the matter was allowed to slide; and only when the actual centennial was at hand did Congress decide to hire another engineer, who after much probing beneath the monument finally agreed it would actually be possible to raise a 600-foot obelisk, provided Congress was willing to

The monument, in 1874, as depicted in *Leslie's Weekly*. Trams were horse-drawn, and the canal was busy with water-borne commerce.

spend the extra money needed to put a whole new foundation beneath the present one. But by now Congress had delayed so long, the centennial was upon them and no real progress had been made.

Not until the first day after the centennial, July 5, 1876, was Senator John Sherman of Ohio able to introduce a resolution asking for $2 million to complete the monument. On August 2, the House dutifully passed the bill to retake possession from the society of the 30 acres and its truncated shaft and appropriate the necessary money to complete the monument.

Some consideration was given to alternative designs, especially one suggested by the American sculptor William Wetmore Story, who wanted to build what he called "an ornamental Lombardy tower," which would have required demolishing 41 feet of the shaft already built, so as to insert several windows. But the advice of George Perkins Marsh, United States minister to Italy, prevailed, and the form of an authentic Egyptian obelisk was retained. However, as nobody knew exactly what constituted an authentic Egyptian obelisk, or in what proportion the pyramidion should stand to the shaft or at what angle, the State Department sent out a circular eliciting information. From Rome, Minister Marsh, an accomplished scholar who had previously been United States consul in Cairo and said he had made sketches of all the known standing obelisks in Egypt, came up with a reply. An obelisk, he warned, was not an arbitrary structure which anyone was free to erect with such form and proportions as might suit his taste and convenience, but that its objects, form and proportions were fixed by the usage of thousands of years, so as to satisfy the cultivated eye. Marsh laid down

334

The 1834 proposal for an obelisk half the height of the Washington Monument to stand on Bunker Hill. Horatio Greenbough's design was approved by Gilbert Stuart and Daniel Webster.

The completed monument drawn by Edwin A. Abbey and engraved by A. U. S. Anthony

the law that the pyramidion should be one-tenth of the height of the shaft, with its base two-thirds to three-fourths the size of the monument's base. He was categoric in insisting that it would be as great an aesthetic crime to depart from these proportions as it would be to make "a window in the face of the pyramidion or shaft, both of which atrocities were committed in the Bunker Hill monument." If one had to have a window, said Marsh, it should be the exact size of one stone and be supplied with a shutter of the same color so as to be invisible when closed. "And throw out," he concluded, "all the gingerbread of the Mills design and keep only the obelisk." His advice was taken, and a joint commission of Congress was formed to oversee the completion of the monument as Marsh had suggested, $94,474 being voted to stabilize the foundation. Lieutenant Colonel Thomas Lincoln Casey, a forty-two-year-old army engineer, was hired to raise the monument to 555 feet, ten times the size of the base; architect Gustav Friebus was assigned to design the pyramidion with which to top the shaft. It was estimated that $677,000 more would be needed to complete the monument.

On January 28, 1879, five boom derricks were erected on the top of the existing shaft with block and tackle and an 8-foot safety net to catch any workmen—none of whom fell or were injured. As a first step, so that building could start in July 1880, the top three courses laid by the Know-Nothings were removed. An iron framework 20 feet high went up first, around which the new courses of blocks

335

During the entire construction of the monument it settled only 4 inches. In the end, its 81,720 tons were so well distributed that a 145-mile-an-hour wind—almost three times the wind pressure that might be expected—would not topple it. A 30-mile-an-hour wind would only cause the shaft to sway .125 inches at the peak.

The pyramidion in place with security scaffolding and net ready for the Masonic ceremony of laying the aluminum capstone. This pyramidal capstone consisted of 3,765 cubic feet of dressed marble in 262 separate pieces which took thirty days to set. In December 1884 it was successfully raised without incident.

could be laid, with marble on the outside, and a granite backing. By the end of 1880, as Gorringe's obelisk was steaming toward New York, 22 feet of masonry had been laid, each course containing 32 blocks of marble and 24 blocks of granite, raising the monument to a height of 250 feet.

During 1882, as the shaft thinned, the number of blocks hoisted each trip was doubled and another 90 feet were added. In 1883 another 70 feet brought it up to 410. After the 450-foot level no more granite was to be used, only marble, so that during 1884 the shaft could be brought to 500 feet, ready for the 55-foot pyramidion whose 300 tons were to be lifted into place as one piece.

To finish off the obelisk at its apex, an aluminum capstone weighing 100 ounces—the largest single piece of aluminum cast to that time—was to be placed atop the pyramidion on Saturday, December 6, 1884. Placing the capstone required another appropriate Masonic ceremony, and a special scaffold was constructed on which the principal officials might stand. When the day came, a 60-mile-an-hour wind came with it, and thousands held their breath as they gazed up from the Mall at master mason P. N. McLaoughlin, the project superintendent, who successfully placed the capstone. The American flag was unfurled, and the crowd raised a cheer. Cannons brought from Fort Meyer, Virginia, boomed out a hundred-gun salute, and all was ready for the dedication on Washington's Birthday, February 21, 1885.

On dedication day, which dawned cold but clear, the obelisk stood majestic and serene, the tallest monument of masonry then in the world. A sharp wind blowing down the Potomac put a snap into the flags, and the marine band played patriotic tunes as troops and citizens gathered on the snow-encrusted turf around the base. A short address was delivered by Senator Sherman of Ohio. And Myron M. Parker, Most Worshipful Grand Master of the Grand Lodge of Free and Accepted Masons of the District of Columbia, began the Masonic ceremonies, reminding the audience that "the immortal Washington, himself a Freemason, had devoted his hand, his heart, his sacred honor, to the cause of freedom of conscience, of speech and of action, and that from his successful leadership the nation had arisen." As props for the Masonic ceremony there was the same gavel which George Washington had used to lay the cornerstone of the Capitol, the same Bible on which he had taken the oath as president, the same apron made by Madame Lafayette, plus a golden urn containing a lock of Washington's hair passed down by

View of the ceremony seen by the crowd through binoculars as Colonel Casey holds his derby against the gale, and motions to Master Mason McLaughlin to cap the monument.

Tourists ascending the monument

every Grand Master of the Grand Lodge of Massachusetts. In conclusion the Grand Chaplain of Masons brought out the same ritual corn, wine, and oil. Then the official procession, headed by President Chester Alan Arthur, marched down Pennsylvania Avenue to the Capitol to hear an address written by former Speaker of the House Robert C. Winthrop, the same sponsor who had given the oration at the laying of the cornerstone thirty-seven years earlier.

Regretting that the monument could not have been hewn from a single stone, like an Egyptian obelisk, Winthrop said he nevertheless took pleasure in the idea that the united stones standing firm and square could serve as a symbol for the national motto, *"E pluribus unum."* John C. Palmer, speaking for the fraternity, declared that Masons were no longer builders of cathedrals and castles, "poems in marble and granite," but of human society whose stones were living men, "their minds enlightened with divine truth, their hearts radiant with discovering the joy of pure love, their souls cherishing—like the ancient Egyptian worshippers of Osiris—the hope of immortality."

Within a year ten thousand citizens had climbed to the top of the obelisk to look out across the tranquil Potomac at the gentle slopes of Mount Vernon, where Washington lay buried, but few among them realized—any more than did the admirers of the Chartres Cathedral or the great pillars of Karnak, except perhaps through a sense of awe—the phenomenal significance of the majestic work of masonry upon which they were supported.

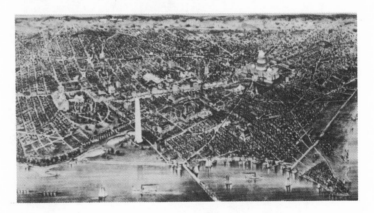

G. BELZONI ESQ.ᴿ

16. ATLANTIS IN AMERICA

In January 1880 the United States consul general in Egypt, E. E. Farnam, sent a dispatch from Cairo to the Department of State in Washington reporting that in the course of removing the foundations of the obelisk sent to New York from Alexandria, a "very important historical discovery was made relating to the order of Freemasons, confirming its claim of ancient origin." Farnam referred the department to a further report by the senior Masons Commander Henry Gorringe and Grand Master S. A. Zola, Sovereign Grand Commander of the Supreme Council of the Ancient and Accepted Scottish Rite; Past Grand Master of the National Grand Lodge of Egypt, confirming the discovery beneath the foundations of a granite block, the upper part of which had been cut in the form of a mason's square. Embedded in the mortar were also a mason's trowel of iron or steel, and two granite blocks, one polished, the other unfinished, "the perfect and the rough ashlars of Masonry," representing the master craftsman and the apprentice, all laid out in the correct position to indicate emblems of Masonry—something the report assured could not be the work of chance.

The added discovery of an inscription in both Latin and Greek on one of the bronze astragals which had held up the obelisk indicated it had been erected by the architect

The crabs found in Alexandria with this inscription in Greek and Latin: "Placed by architect Pontius in the eighth year of Augustus Caesar with Barbarus prefect of Egypt."

339

According to Weisse and Gor-ringe, the decorations on the walls of the mystery chambers in the rock-excavated temple of Seti I and of his son Ramses II (discovered by Belzoni) repre-sent initiation to a Masonic de-gree. They believe that every-thing they saw in these structures "indicate the origin of modern Freemasonry for the atti-tudes, groups, rites, ceremonies, symbols, and signs, have a strik-ing similarity both with Medieval and Modern Freemasonry." Ac-cording to Weisse, the Isiac mysteries constituted the first Masonic degree among the Egyptians and the mysteries of Serapis, the second. "In the mysteries of Osiris the lesson of death and resurrection of Osiris was symbolically conveyed. The legend of the murder of Osiris was displayed to the affiliate in a scenic manner." All together Weisse and Gorringe describe nine different initiations through-out the thirteen highly ornament-ed mystery chambers of the tem-ple.

Chambers of the Tomb of Seti

Pontius during the eighth year of Augustus's reign, with Barbarus as prefect of Egypt; and this led the New York Masons to conclude that the obelisk had been raised in Alexandria at the time of the birth of Christ by a group of practicing Masons of whom Pontius was evidently one.

This amazing conclusion enabled Gorringe to launch into a campaign to prove that Masonry had flourished in Egypt at an even earlier period than had been believed. For evidence, he produced thirteen large colored illustrations showing in detail the carved stone panels of the rock-excavated Temple of Seti I (Osimandias) and Ramses II (Sesostris), painted *in situ* by Giovanni Belzoni in 1818. "No Mason," said Gorringe, "can look at the attitudes of this group of Grand Master, Guide, Candidate, and Assis-tant, without realizing that, if there are Masonic institutions now, there were similar, if not identical ones, about four thousand years ago, in the land of the Pharaohs, and that modern Freemasonry had its prototype in the Masonic Temple of Seti I and Ramses II, where applicants were initiated as Oriental and Occidental Masonic Orders initi-ate now."

This statement prompted an American Mason, John A. Weisse, to produce a book, *The Obelisk and Freemason-ry,* in which he set out to show, among other points, that Masonry had existed in America among so-called Ameri-

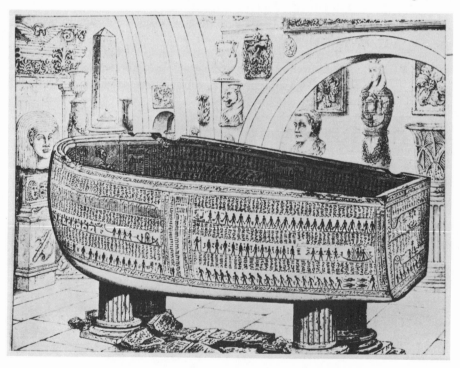

can Indians, long before the arrival of Columbus. Weisse quoted a letter from a William McAdams of Otterville, Illinois, dated April 25, 1880, to the effect that he had spent a considerable time exploring ancient mounds and earthworks, in which he was surprised to find well-known symbols of Masonry, such as circles, squares, and triangles; triangles with squares surrounded by circles; and a circle between parallel lines. "The triangle," wrote McAdams, "ever was and is now an important Masonic symbol. The equilateral triangle was adopted by most of the ancient nations as an emblem of the deity, and was regarded as the most perfect geometric figure. It occurs in Craft and Arch Masonry. In ancient and medieval magic it meant fire when the apex pointed upward, and water when the apex pointed downward."

Next Weisse told the story of a stele found in Iowa in 1877 which came to be known as the Davenport stele. Its history and its import were to make it as remarkable as Egypt's Rosetta Stone. On a cold day in January 1877, an amateur archeologist, the Reverend Jacob Gass, a German-speaking minister of the First Lutheran Zion Church of Davenport, was engaged in opening a small burial mound on what was known as Cook Farm. Aided by seven colleagues, several of whom were also clergymen, these "Sunday archeologists" dug through frozen ground for about 2½ feet, only to discover an intrusive Indian burial of obviously modern date. Later, as they descended into the mound, they uncovered the skeletons for which the mound had evidently been raised; two adults and a child. Beneath their bones the archeologists made an extraordinary find:

The Reverend Jacob Gass

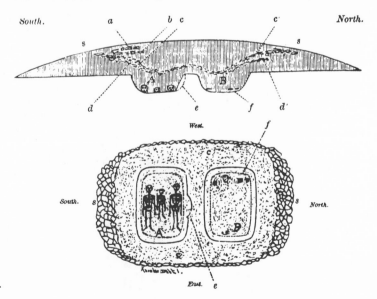

Plan of Cook Farm mound cavity . . .

341

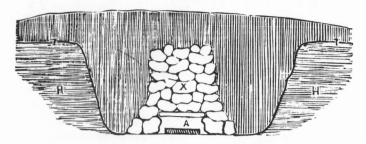

a bituminous shale tablet, about 13 inches square, engraved on both sides, as well as a smaller tablet engraved with what appeared to be a zodiac.

The large tablet showed several dancing figures in what was considered to be a "cremation scene." The opposite side showed Indians and animals around two obelisks pointing at an equilateral triangle. Strange signs, like lettering or glyphs, adorned the stele. Taken to the Davenport Academy of Natural Science (now the Putnam Museum), the tablets aroused great interest: they were believed to be the first discovered phonetic and astronomic monuments assignable to early inhabitants of America.

Charles E. Putnam, lawyer of the Davenport Academy, and later its president, was quickly committed to the validity of this rare archeological find, which he considered of worldwide interest. Encased in plaster casts, the tablets were sent to the Smithsonian Institution for appraisal, along with some background notes on the Reverend Gass, whom he described as of spotless character, "a good classical scholar, well grounded in Hebrew, with a scientific bend of mind." Also included were sworn affidavits from Gass's assistants confirming the manner in which the tablets had been found.

The Putnam Museum in Davenport, Iowa

The Smithsonian's first reaction was that the tablets were authentic and of great antiquity. But one of the institution's experts, a Dr. E. Foreman, on closer examination concluded that the so-called "cremation scene" depicted a disembodied Indian spirit going to "a place of probation before its final reception in the place of departed spirits," and that the works therefore "set forth the teaching of the missionary fathers of the Catholic Church, and must be of recent date." Ironically, he added that the Egyptians believed such an inquisitorial function was performed by Osiris, "but we are not apprised that the Indian mythology includes a functionary clothed with similar attributes."

The debate quickly degenerated into acrimony and was drawn out for several years in the columns of such prestigious magazines as *Science* and the *American Antiquarian,* climaxing in an official putdown from the governmental establishment when the Davenport Academy wished to exhibit the tablets at the Columbia Exposition in Chicago in 1894, "to give visitors from all parts of the world a chance to see something that has made a ripple in the scientific world and is only waiting, like the Rosetta Stone, for some Mariette to decipher the story hidden in its hitherto undecipherable hieroglyphs."

In a monograph in the annual report of the United States Bureau of Ethnology, Cyrus Thomas, its director of archeology, declared unequivocally: "A consideration of all the facts leads us, inevitably, to the conclusion that these

Calendar stone tablet

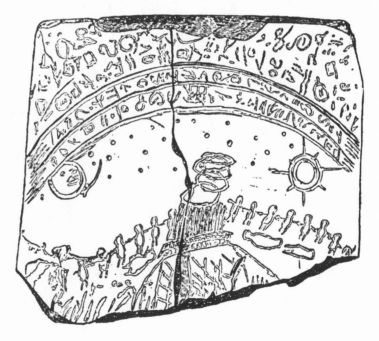

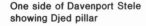
One side of Davenport Stele
showing Djed pillar

relics are frauds; that is, they are modern productions made to deceive." Thomas suggested the source of the hieroglyphic inscriptions was none other than the 1872 edition of Webster's *Unabridged Dictionary,* page 1,766, which illustrated various Old World alphabets.

Scholars who had previously taken a favorable position were quick to reverse themselves, and the tablets were labeled frauds. In 1930, when Dr. Henry C. Shetrone, director of the Ohio State Museum, reexamined the tablets, he reconfirmed their fraudulence. And as recently as 1970, Marshall Bassford McKusic, an Iowa archeologist, in a pamphlet titled *The Davenport Conspiracy,* published by the State Archeologist of Iowa City, declared that "by now the fraudulent nature of the tablets should have been accepted by everyone."

For evidence, to prove a conspiracy which he said resulted in "an almost unbelievable degradation of scientific research," McKusic brought out what he characterized as "one of the most detailed case studies of this period of American archeology, and of the history of science in this country."

In this opus, on careful reading, the new evidence turned out to be the drunken confession of a prominent Davenport attorney, Judge James Wills Bolliger, president of the Davenport Museum board, according to which the tablets had been taken from the roof of a whorehouse on the Mississippi River waterfront and then forged by himself and a gang of cronies who frequented the academy, in order to be placed in the mound for the Reverend Gass to discover. As the judge is reported to have told the story: "This group would go to the Academy and have a bull session because there wasn't any place else to go. They used to have a few drinks and just shoot the breeze.

Judge James Wills Bolliger

Shingle from the old state house
(courtesy of Marshall McKusic)

344

The janitor was in with us. We had two old almanacs, one German and one Hebrew and we copied out of them and inscribed the hieroglyphs on these slate tablets, and things. We just made up anything that would confuse them, especially Gass."

Ancient alphabets from *Webster's Dictionary* of 1872

ANCIENT ALPHABETS.
COMPARATIVE TABLE OF HIEROGLYPHIC AND ALPHABETIC CHARACTERS.

Chaldaic Letters	Conjectural Chaldaic Hieroglyphic Originals	Phœnician Letters	Conjectural Phœnician Hieroglyphic Originals	Egyptian Letters	Original Egyptian Hieroglyphics		Linearyl Hierogly phics	Hieratic Letters	Demotic	Coptic	Samaritan	Phœnician	Syriac	Arabic	Ancient Greek	Hebrew equiv.	

(table of comparative alphabets)

Professor Barry Fell

That this confession, and not the tablets, is fraudulent, is now clear at last, thanks to the brilliant scholarship of a Harvard epigrapher, though the shakiness of Judge Bolliger's evidence should have been clear from the fact that at the time he is supposed to have planted the tablet, the judge was only nine years old, and the building in which the academy was to be housed was only dedicated and occupied the following year.

Conclusive proof of the authenticity of the Davenport stele has been adduced by Barry Fell, professor emeritus at Harvard, and president of the Epigraphic Society which he founded. Far from being a forgery, the stele is one of

345

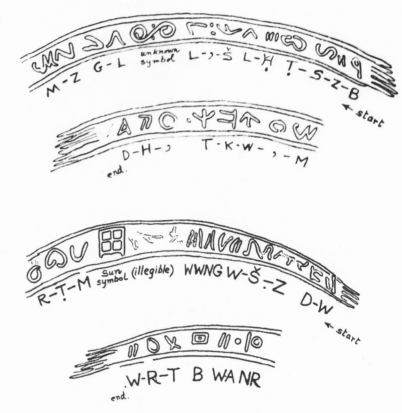

the most important ever found, amounting to an American Rosetta Stone, the only one so far on which occurs a trilingual text in the Egyptian, Iberic-Punic, and Libyan languages. As Fell points out, the Egyptian hieratic text could easily have been deciphered at the time of the tablet's discovery, but was evidently deliberately ignored.

Even more interesting is the content of the text, which elucidates the nature of the ceremony depicted. In the *Occasional Papers* of the Epigraphic Society, Fell gives a word-for-word translation of the Iberian and Libyan texts as they appear on the arched scrolls, each of which reports that the tablet carries a further inscription which will reveal the secret of how to regulate a calendar. This secret is contained in the Egyptian hieratic hieroglyphs, which Fell renders into English:

"To the pillar attach a mirror in such a manner that when the sun rises on New Year's Day it will cast a reflection onto the stone called 'The Watcher.' New Year's Day occurs when the sun is in conjunction with the zodiacal constellation Aries, in the House of Ram, the balance of night and day being about to reverse (the Spring Equinox). At this time hold the Festival of the New Year, and the religious rite of the New Year."

346

Identification by Fell of various Egyptian captions in the design of the stele

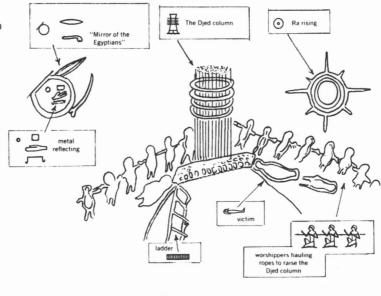

"Mirror of the Egyptians"

The Djed column

Ra rising

metal reflecting

victim

ladder

worshippers hauling ropes to raise the Djed column

Fell's translation of the Egyptian hieratic text on the upper part of the stele (to be read from top down)

1. To a pillar / attach / a mirror
2. so that
3. at the New / Year /
4. the sun being in conjunction with the Ram
5. at the tilting of the balance (i.e., of night and day, the equinox) in the Spring /
6. the Festival
7. / of celebration of the first New Year
8. / and religious rites of the New Year
9. are taking place
10. / [when] The Watcher /
11. / Stone /
12. / at sunrise /
13. / is illuminated /
14. / by /
15. / the sun /
16. [signed] Star-watcher /
17. Priest
18. / of Osiris
19. / of the Libyan region /

More extraordinary is the depiction referred to as "the cremation scene." With the help of a panel found in a tomb from the Eighteenth Dynasty in Thebes, deciphered by Adolf Erman, Fell shows the scene to represent the Djed Festival of Osiris, the Egyptian celebration of the New Year, which occurs on the morning of the March equinox, now corresponding to March 21, but which Fell says occurred later in March in ancient times.

347

In this festival, as Fell describes it, parties of worshipers pulling on ropes ceremonially erected a special New Year pillar, called the Djed Column, made of bundles of reeds encircled at the top by rings, representing the backbone of Osiris, in whose honor the column was re-raised each year on the day of the spring equinox. On the left side of the stele is the carving of a mirror, with, beside it, as deciphered by Fell, the Egyptian hieroglyphs for "Mirror of the Egyptians." On the mirror are hieroglyphs that read "reflecting metal." To the right is the rising sun, with the hieroglyph *Ra* (for "Sun god" or "Sun") on the disk of the sun. Stars seen in the morning are above.

On the Erman stele the Egyptian record tells that the ceremony occurred in Koiakh, a word meaning "the month of March." On the Davenport stele, the Egyptian text goes on to say that it is the work of Wnty ("star-watcher"), presumed by Fell to be a priest of Osiris in the Libyan region.

As to how the stele came to Iowa, Fell speculates that though the stone appears to be local, and engraved in America, it was perhaps copied by a Libyan or Iberian astronomer from an older model brought from Egypt, or more likely from Libya.

As to the genuineness of the stele, Fell points out that at the time Gass found the stone, neither the Libyan nor the Iberian scripts had been deciphered, which would have made it impossible for an impostor to produce texts consistent with the hieroglyphic text. Fell says the style of the Egyptian writing could be as old as 1400 B.C.; but he doubts that the stele itself celebrates a ceremony taking place in Iowa earlier than about 800 B.C., because "we do not know of Iberian or Libyan inscriptions earlier than that date."

What is clear, says Fell, is that Iberian and Punic speakers were living in Iowa in the ninth century B.C., making use of a stone calendar regulator whose Egyptian hieroglyphs they could read. These settlers, says Fell, had presumably sailed up the Mississippi River to colonize the Davenport area; he then hazards the guess that the colonists came in wooden ships commanded by a Libyan skipper of the Egyptian navy, sometime during the twenty-second Libyan Dynasty, the pharaohs of which were energetic men who favored overseas exploration. With them, he says, probably came an astronomer priest, and either he, or one of his successors, engraved the Davenport calendar stone.

On the reverse face of the Davenport tablet the scene depicted is the corresponding equinoctial Hunting Festival,

Hunting scene on the reverse side of the Davenport stele above and below two recumbent obelisks. Fell considers this the earliest known example of Micmac script. Unlike the Djed Festival, which is an Indian copy of an Egyptian original, this is the work of an Algonquin Indian dating back perhaps two thousand years. Fell roughly translates the text—which is replete with Egyptian features—as: "Hunting of beasts and their young, waterfowl and fishes." And: "The herds of the Lord (illegible) and their young, the beasts of the Lord."

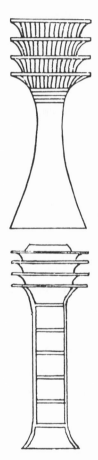

Egyptian Djed columns

held in September, six months after the Djed Festival, marking the second half of the Celtic year; based, evidently, on the Egyptian year. Fell sees this side of the tablet as being copied from an earlier original by Algonquin Indians about 500 B.C., though possibly as late as A.D. 100.

In the foreground a hunting scene deals with the September butchery and smoking of young wildstock, including waterfowl and fish. In the upper part of the picture are the portions of wildlife left unmolested, labeled in the text "Herds of the Lord." These scenes are explained in a double line of letters running down the center of two prostrate obelisks. The letters read from right to left, toward the center, with the animals facing the reading direction, as is usual with Egyptian glyphs. But why two huge prostrate obelisks should be depicted on a stele in

349

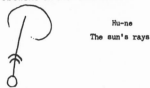

Geodetic functions of the two
obelisks on the Iowa stele

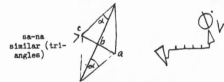

Hu-ne
The sun's rays

(text missing)

go-no ne

at varying angles (<u>or</u>, at various
latitudes)

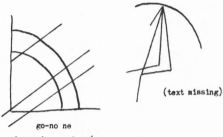

sa-na
similar (tri-
angles)

(text missing, but self-explanatory). If
an obelisk at a casts no shadow, when one
at b has a shadow bc subtending a zenith
angle α, by similar triangles, α must also
be the angle subtended at the center of the
Earth's curvature by the line ab, for, as
shown above, the sun's rays are parallel).

5. At Philae (⚳V), modern Aswan, the sun (☉)
can stand overhead, casting no shadow. From
Philae northward to the coast (▽) is a
distance of 5 thousand stades.

6. When the sun casts no shadow at Philae, the shadow
it casts at ▽ is ⚳ (angular 2/100ths), i.
subtends one fiftieth part of 360°.

Therefore the entire circumference of the earth
equals ((5000 divided by 2) times 100) stades

the middle of Iowa, and what was meant by the triangle at which they point, is left unsaid by Barry Fell. However, from another of his papers, dealing with Egyptian-Libyan hieroglyphs found on the wall of a cave in New Guinea, it is clear he understands that for the Egyptians the obelisk functioned geodetically as well as colendrically.

In 1937 an expedition from the Frobenius Institute of the Goethe University of Frankfurt am Main visited a series of limestone caverns on the coast of McCluer Bay, in northwest New Guinea. On the walls they found a number of inscriptions which they were able to establish as having been drawn between 235 and 225 B.C. The incriptions, as deciphered by Fell and his fellow epigraphers, are in ancient Maori, which Fell has shown to be based on ancient Libyan, with elements of Greek, Carthaginian, and occasional Egyptian hieroglyphs.

The writing indicates the author to have been a Captain Maui in the Egyptian navy acting as navigator and astronomer to the expedition's commander, a man named Rata. The expedition, though serving as a squadron of the Egyptian navy, was actually Libyan, says Fell, Libya then being a province of Egypt. As Rata and Maui correspond to the names of traditional leaders in Polynesian tales, the inscriptions also give an historical base to Maori legends. An eclipse, mentioned in the inscriptions as having taken place in November of the fifteenth year of the reigning pharoah, enabled Fell to identify the monarch in question as Ptolemy III, grandfather of the Ptolemy celebrated in the Rosetta Stone, in the fifteenth year of whose reign an eclipse occurred, on November 19, 232 B.C. From the fact that wives and children are indicated as being in the expedition, Fell infers that it was one of those sent out by Ptolemy III ''to seek new sources of gold for his enormous gold coinage emission,'' with a secondary aim of circumnavigating the world, a goal barred to the voyagers by the west coast of America.

The most extraordinary of these inscriptions directly refers to Eratosthenes—then professor of mathematics in charge of the great library of Alexandria—as being an acquaintance of Maui who personally demonstrated for him his method of computing the circumference of the earth by means of obelisks. The glyphs on the walls of the New Guinea cave explicitly show the use of the shadow of

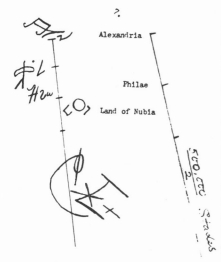

an obelisk in determining the angle of the sun's rays, and, by similar triangles, the latitude of the location. The text speaks of how this particular theorem of Eratosthenes, "an astronomer of the Delta country in Lower Egypt," was disclosed to Maui. The text specifies that because the sun's rays intercept the atmosphere at varying angles, and therefore latitudes, when the sun stands overhead at Philae (or Syene), it casts no shadow at the solstice. The text also states that from Philae northward to the coast is a distance of 5,000 stadia. Thus, it explains, when the sun casts no shadow at Philae, the shadow it casts at the coast, 5,000 stadia to the north, is 2/100ths of a full circle; that is to say, 1/50th of 360°, or 7.2°. Therefore, if 5,000 stadia equals 7.2°, the entire circumference of the earth must be 5,000 stadia times 50, or 250,000 stadia.

The first mention of this theorem by the Greek author Kleomedes, about a century after the dating of the inscription in New Guinea, states that Eratosthenes read in a book in the library at Alexandria that on the summer solstice a reflection of the sun can be seen in the water at the bottom of a well at Syene (or Philae) at midday. An additional epigraphic fragment in Maori from Sosorra, as translated by Fell, says textually: "It is a fact that whenever the sun's image is seen in the water at the well at Philae in Egypt, the obelisk erected at Alexandria at that instant is observed to have a shadow."

$$= 5000 \times 100/2$$
$$= \frac{500,000}{2}$$

Greek		Maori		
/E	=	)≣	=	5000
Φ	=	⊘	=	500
/Φ	=	⊘	=	500,000

Fell's translation of the Sosorra Rebus (with material of Joseph Roder and permission of the Frobenius Institut of Frankfurt am Main)

ntpw
it is a fact that

pwtrw
whenever

Rnwi nw
the sun's image is seen

nt hnmt
in the water of the well

Tmir
in Egypt

⊘ I ∧ E
at Philae

bn tkr
the obelisk erected

ALN (Greek letters)
at Alexandria

m
is with

nr
at that time

ZWT
shadow

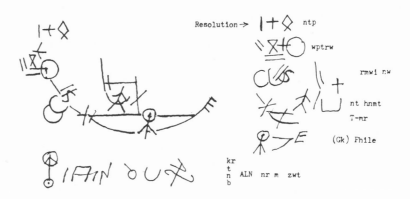

Fell notes that in this section of the calculation, vowels are omitted, with the interesting result that the sequences of residual consonants correspond almost exactly to standard Middle Egyptian forms—where the vowels are similarly omitted. Thus, if the Roman-letter equivalents are inserted in place of the Maori alphabetic signs, the text can be translated directly from the standard dictionary forms of Egyptian as given by Faulkner.

351

Kirchner related how the Arabs called Heliopolis Ainschems or "the eye of the sun," and that in the temple of the sun there was a marvelous mirror, constructed with great art to flash back the rays of the sun. And the Arab chronicler Maqrizi tells of two obelisks in Heliopolis, one of which was still standing in the fourteenth century, 50 cubits high, tipped with shining brass or electron, whose functions were to mark the extremes of the solar passage at the solstices. "The moment the sun enters the first minute of Capricorn, that is the shortest day of the year, it reaches the southernmost of two obelisks and culminates at its summit. When it reaches the first minute of Cancer, that is to say the longest day in the year, it reaches the northernmost obelisk and culminates at its summit."

The French professor André Pochan, in a bulletin of the *Royal Geographic Society of Egypt,* points out that in this arrangement at ancient Heliopolis the equinoxial line passed exactly between the two obelisks and that as the sun reached this line it gave rise to the Egyptian word Ⴔⴈ or Pâque which means "reaching or touching the rising sun at Passover." Furthermore, says Pochan, the Egyptians had similar observation devices at Tanis, Hermontis, Esne, Edfu and Thebes, and the glyph for the festival of the Spring equinox was △⊙△ or BaRa(m) —the sun in Ram between two obelisks, or Djed pillars. From this, says Pochan, the Moslems got Bairam or Ramadan.

Thus, according to the French professor, the Egyptian astronomers and geodesists established the equinox with a Djed pillar and a mirror. That they also did so with a well and an obelisk is equally clear. But you have to start on the Tropic of Cancer, or better still exactly at Syene where, at noon of the summer solstice, the sun will pass directly overhead, causing no shadow in a well. And any obelisk, in the same location, of whatever height, will also cast no shadow at noon of the solstice.

Why the Egyptians placed their sophisticated observatory at Syene at 24°06′ instead of at 23°51′, the actual line of the Tropic, is explained by the late Professor Livio C. Stecchini (in his appendix to *Secrets of the Great Pyramid*). By deciphering a common glyph of three short parallel lines which appears on virtually all the thrones of the pharaohs, Stecchini realized that the Egyptians calculated three different values for the tropic: 24° as a round figure for their mapping; 23°51′ for the actual path of the Tropic; and 24°06 for the actual point of observation at Syene. This, Stecchini explains, was because they knew that in order accurately to achieve the effect of the

According to Professor Pochan, the observation well used by the ancient Egyptians to establish the moment of solstice was not at Elephantine but at Philae, whose latitude was 24° 1′34″. He says that Elephantine was on the Tropic in 3200 B.C., but by the time of Eratosthenes, the Tropic had shifted to 23° 44′8″. The cubit used by Eratosthenes, says Pochan, was the Philae unit of .5275 meters, rather than the Elephantine cubit of .52367. The distance between Alexandria and Philae, which Eratosthenes computed as 7.2°, or 5,000 stadia, was marked by two obelisks at Philae, and was the exact halfway point on the meridian measured by the Egyptians from Alexandria all the way to Meroë, deep in southern Nubia. It shows, says Pochan, that the Egyptians knew the correct dimensions of the planet at least as early as 4800 B.C.

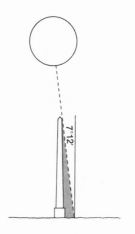

shadowless well, or shadowless obelisk, on one particular day of the year, they had to place their well or obelisk *half the diameter of the sun, or 15′,* north of the actual Tropic.

Once established that an obelisk casts no shadow at the Tropic at noon of the solstice, it matters not where the obelisk is raised; by knowing its height, and by measuring its shadow at noon of the solstice, the latitude can be established. To mark out a year's solar calendar, all that is needed is an obelisk; its shadow will automatically give the solstices, or longest and shortest days of the year, as well as the equinoxes and four intervening festivals, which can be marked out with horizon stones in a great circle as at Mystery Hill in Salem, New Hampshire, and elsewhere.

The Calendar Circle at Mystery Hill, New Hampshire, as drawn by Barry Fell and Osborne Stone, with the stone markers seen through a transit telescope from the observation platform marking the point of sunrise and sunset at the solstices and equinoxes

North   Stone

0°

N

303.5°   54.6°

June 22   June 22
Midsummer sunset   Midsummer sunrise

W   Observation   E
platform

236.5°   121.75°

S

December 22   (fallen stone)
Midwinter sunset   December 22
Midwinter sunrise

Berriman demonstrates how the circumference of the earth can be estimated by measuring a meridian length from *A* to *B* (between two obelisks several miles apart) and the length of the shadow at *B* when there is none at *A*. The same result is achieved by measuring the difference in angle of elevation of a star observed from two different points.

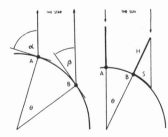

By measuring the distance between two obelisks on the same meridian and comparing their shadows as measured at solstice or equinox, it is simple, accurately, to extrapolate the circumference of the planet. Algernon Edward Berriman, in his *Historical Metrology,* shows that the same result can be obtained by measuring the difference in star angles between two obelisks at a known distance apart.

That the Egyptians used the Djed Column to establish the equinox and with it control their water clocks is clear

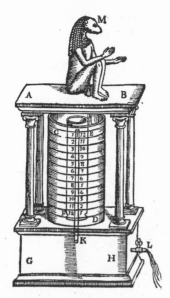

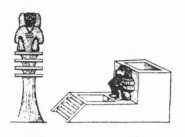

Urinating monkey with the twelve equinoctial hours of the day and night marked on the Egyptian clock, illustrated by Kircher in his *Oedipus Aegyticus*

The Kaf-ape, known as the clicking cynocephalus, because its clicks are believed to have preceded human speech, was used to represent the god who taught mankind speech and the hieroglyphs which led to alphabetic letters. By natives in Africa the dogheaded ape is still regarded with respect because it is believed to have an intelligence of the highest order, and can be more cunning than man.

from a carving on the ceiling of the Ramesseion in Thebes which shows a Djed Column surmounted by a cynocephalous monkey producing water from its penis. Horapollo explained the symbol: "To signify the two equinoxes they—the Egyptians—depict a sitting cynocephalus, for at the two equinoxes of the year it makes water twelve times in the day, once in each hour, and it does the same also during the two nights; wherefore not without reason do the Egyptians sculpture a sitting cynocephalus on their Hydrologia (or waterclocks); and they cause the water to run from its member, because the animal thus indicates the twelve hours of the equinox. And lest the contrivance, by which the water is discharged into the Horologium, should be too wide, by discharging the water quickly, does not accurately fulfill the measurement of the hour, neither the one that is too narrow, (for against both of these cautions must be taken, for one that is too wide, by discharging the water quickly, does not accurately fulfill the measurement of the hour, neither the one that is too narrow, since it lets forth the water little by little, and too slowly), they perforate an aperture to the extremity of the member, and according to its thickness, insert in it an iron." Furthermore, as was shown on the base of the Theban obelisk removed by LeBas, the male cynocephalous was used as a symbol of the priest, worshiping the sun at rising, with arms and phallus erect, for which, as Kenneth Grant shows in his *The Magical Revival*, "Horapollo preserved a talisman or gnostic gem in yellow jasper, on which was engraved a cynocephalus, crowned with baton erect, adoring the first appearance of the moon."

In ancient Egypt the passage of time was also registered in the temples by the periodic fluxes of the sacred baboon, the female cynocephalous, or dog-eared ape. As Grant points out, "She was the first Mother of Time in the pre-human phase of symbolism, and the prototype of the clepsydral horologue"—or waterclock.

Horapollo also gives a vivid description of how the ancient priests of Egypt used both male and female cynocephalous to establish the moment of eclipses: "At the exact instant of the conjunction of the moon with the sun, when the moon becomes illumined, then the male Cynocephalus neither sees, nor eats, but is bowed down to the ground with grief, as if lamenting the ravishment of the moon. The female also, in addition to its being unable to see, and being afflicted in the same manner as the male, emits blood from the genitals; hence even to this day Cynocephali are brought up in the temples, in order that from them may be ascertained the exact instant of

Mexican relief in Palenque with the equinoxial lions, recognized by Masons as replete with Masonic symbolism

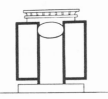

Equinoctial symbols identical in meaning with similar Mayan glyphs in Yucatán. The two lions represent Shu and Tefnut, guardians of the stability of the rising equinoctial sun.

the conjunction of the sun and the moon. And when they would denote the renovation of the moon, they again portray a Cynocephalus in the posture of standing upright and raising its hands to heaven with a diadem on its head. And for the renovation they depict this posture, into which the Cynocephalus throws itself, as if congratulating the goddess, if we may so express it, in that they have both recovered the light."

A clue to the depth and subtlety of the Egyptian use of symbols, and especially animal symbols, to denote philosophic and cosmic realities is given by Grant in his *Cults of the Shadow,* where he points out, with reference to the periodic emanations of the female cynocephalous, that "Time is the menstruum in which all material forms arise, transform and finally dissolve."

And so, at last, becomes clear the ancient purpose of the obelisk and Djed pillars in what could be called a precataclysmic era. Sometime far back in Egyptian history a geodetic view of the world and an astronomical view of the heavens were put together from a viewpoint that was located on the equator. Seen from this equatorial vantage, the earth was pictured falling off northward toward the North Pole and southward toward the South Pole, at each of which there appeared to be a fixed star for the heavens to revolve around. These poles were symbolized by two obelisks, one for Horus and one for Set, each of whom was considered to hold sway over half the globe, on either side of the equators. A similar division was made of the starry planisphere, from zenith to nadir, Horus charged with the northern half, Set with the southern, each equally responsible for twelve of the day's twenty-four hours—all of this, of course, long before any satanic, sinister, or evil character had been attributed to Set.

East and west, at the ends of the equatorial—and stably equinoctial—line, Shu and Tefnut, supporters of the sky, were pictured as the two lions of the "double-horizon," keepers of the balance between Horus and Set. This equatorial world—where there was obviously no solstice—was known as Apta.

The Jewish historian Josephus, who attributed to the children of Set(h) the invention of astronomy, preserved the tradition of two pillars erected in the land of Siriad, which Plato mentions in the *Timaeus,* but could not locate. According to John Greaves, who measured the Great Pyramid with Burattini in 1639, "these pillars of Seth were in the very same place where Manetho (the Egyptian historian priest of the third century B.C.) placed the pillars of Taht, called Seiread." Gerald Massey, in his two-

Zootypes of Set

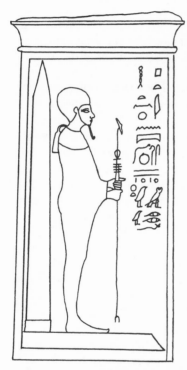

Ptah as the universe's djed pillar of stability. Ptah, "the father of fathers," was considered creator of the universe. Fashioned of his own body in his own image was Ra, the Disc of Heaven. In *The Book of the Dead*, Ptah is said to have raised up the gods from inertness, meaning that all the gods were merely other forms of Ptah himself. As master architect of the world, Ptah fashioned the bodies of men on earth and in the Tuat, or heaven. He is depicted as raised upon the level of Maat, or justice, bearing the menat, symbol of well-being and sexual intercourse, the ankh of life, and the djed pillar of stability.

volume *The Egyptians,* says *Seri* in Egyptian is a name for the south, and is also "the mount that is figured as the twofold rock," equivalent to "the pillars of the two horizons, south and north." And, as Massey points out, Seri is also the name of the giraffe—a zootype of Set.

Clearly something must have happened to upset this balanced equatorial view and forced it to be exchanged for one seen from much further to the north. Either the scanners of the sky moved north, or some agency caused a tilt in the planet. In either case, or both, it is clear that the domain of Set was seen to fall away into the underworld. Set's fixed star of the South Pole vanished. Fewer and fewer of the southern stars and constellations still rose above the horizon. And the north celestial pole, as it rose in the sky, became imaged as a dominating mountain, a summit for the gods. But as the ancient priests of Egypt, says Jean-Louis Bernard in his most original *Aux Origines d'Egypte,* were mythologers and astronomers as well as geographers, in their equation Horus came to symbolize the boreal constellation as the home of the gods, while Set, rather than being merely the geographical south, became the fire in the center of the globe. Thus Horus became the cold of the cosmos and Set the telluric heat of the earth.

The story of the two pillars, and the disappearance of the southern one, was kept alive in the Greek myth that tells of the temple of heaven being raised high by two brothers, Trophonios and Agamedes, followed by the sinking of Trophonios into a cave, corresponding to the engulfing of Set as the disappearance of the South Pole below the horizon. Travelers from the equator arriving in the valley of the Nile, 3,000 miles north, apparently continued the device of dividing their new land into two realms, a northern one for Horus, a southern one for Set, staked out by two obelisks.

Legend states that two pillars were reerected at Annu as symbols of the northern and southern poles. Massey says the original meaning of *Annu* or *On* appears to have been "the place of the pillar, or stone, that marked the foundation which preceded the ⊕ (equatorial) sign"; and, notes Massey, a relic of the two poles may be recognized in the two Egyptian cities of Annu—called by the Greeks Hermonthes and Heliopolis. The line between the two obelisks, as Pochan has demonstrated, marked the equinoctial Passover. Further legend relates that eventually the two pillars of Set and Horus were united into the Tat or Djed Column raised at the winter solstice. But here the legend becomes spiritual and eschatological, for it is said in the *Book of the Dead:* "When Osiris-Ptah had built his mansion in the double earth, the two horizons were united. Two pillars at the gateway to his house were Set and Horus." These pillars were portrayed as the double Tat or spiritual Djed stones of eternal stability in the making of Amenta, the Egyptian world of the dead.

Amenta as described by Massey "was the secret but solid earth of eternity opened up by Ptah when he and his followers, the seven Khnemmu, erected the Tat pillar that was founded in the winter solstice as the figure of a stability that was to be eternal." Some further clarity may be obtained in this apparent confusion if the mythological, astronomical, and eschatological views are kept separate, even though the characters and symbols appear and reappear in every scene. Whereas in the myths the Tat pillar represents the sun at the winter solstice, a sun which has the power of returning from the lowest depth and thus completing its eternal round, in the eschatology the Tat column is the god himself in the person of Ptah-Sekeri, or Osiris, the backbone and support of the universe.

Horus erecting the Tat in Sekhem (Sekhem being the glyph for potency or erectile force) was the raising of Osiris from the sepulcher; it was the father reerected as the son, or the typical resurrection and continuity of the human spirit in the afterlife.

The figure of Amsu-Horus resurrecting or "coming forth," with member erect, had two characters, one in the mythology, one in the eschatology. In the mythology he images the phallus of the sun and the generative force that fecundates Mother earth. In the eschatology the image of the erection is repeated as a symbol of resurrection; and in this phase the supposed phallic god, the figure of regenerative force, is typical of the resurrection or reerection of the mortal in spirit.

From this world, geodetic point of view, further clarity is obtained by postulating some real life cataclysmic event, or even a chain of such events, which affected the mythological characters in their astronomic settings, putting an end to what may have been the legendary and evidently equinoctial Golden Age of Saturn, in a land of "welling waters" where food came of itself and was perpetually renewed with little need for labor.

As the astronomer geodesists moved north, in a world whose axis may have tilted, they seem to have reproduced their former system with its former mythological, astronomical, and eschatological characters, but in a new geodetic and astronomic setting. Upper and lower Egypt

The figure of Amsu-Horus rising in the resurrection, or "coming forth" with member erect, has a dual character, says Massey: one in the mythology, one in the eschatology. In the mythology, he images the phallus of the sun and the generative force that fecundates Mother Earth. In the eschatology, the image of erection is repeated as a symbol of the resurrection; and in this phase, the supposed phallic god, the figure of regenerative force, is typical of the resurrection or reerection of the mortal in spirit.

were divided into seven nomes (each 1° of latitude) under the starry circle of the Great Bear, the goddess Apt, Taurt or Khept, symbolized by a big-titted female hippopotamus, mother of the cycles of time, with the *meanit,* or bull-roarer by her womb to represent the great generative source of life. Behind her stood a crocodile for the constellation Draco. No wonder the general picture as reconstructed from glyph, text and legend is not always pellucid, and often appears garbled, no doubt by the passage of several thousand years. But the central points remain.

The raising of the Djed, or Tat, Column, from a geodetic and astronomic point of view, was the restabilization of the axis of the world, and of the sky. As Livio Stecchini has pointed out, both poles, one for the earth's polar axis, and one for the sun's polar axis, were clearly known to the ancient Egyptians, who differentiated them in their designs, aware that the one formed a small circle around the other, causing the equinoctial point in the heavens, as observed from earth, to advance each year for the twenty-six-thousand-year cycle of the Precession of the Equinoxes.

In the myth in which Shu-Anhur lifts up the heaven from the earth, the Egyptians explain that the pillar of heaven was first erected. This pillar of heaven was envisaged as standing upon the earth; but when, in mythology, the earth was "hollowed out by Ptah," there was formed another earth below, in which the pillar had to be reerected. This pillar of "the double mount" was represented by the double Tat of Ptah as the backbone of that god, who later became Osiris. Eschatologically, when the sky was re-suspended by Ptah in the other world of Amenta, the act was symbolized by raising up the Tat type of stability and support. This not only sustained the sky of the nether world, it also imaged the divine backbone of the universe.

As Gerald Massey, who has the most scholarly, extensive, and intuitive approach to this view, points out in *The*

The ceiling zodiac removed from the Temple of Denderah, analyzed by R. A. Schwaller de Lubicz. It shows the circumpolar constellations spiraling rather than circling the pole of the ecliptic, indicating an understanding of the circular wobble made by the earth's north pole around the pole of the ecliptic, which causes the phenomenon of the precession of the equinoxes, whose ages are here identified on the zodiac by special markers on the perimeter.

Egyptians, "knowing as they did that the earth rotates on its axis, afloat in space, the two poles of the earth were signified by the two-fold tat-pillar of Ptah, doubled when Amenta was founded. . . . The two obelisks, then," he notes, "imaged the thrones of the two worlds, the double earth, or earth and heaven, and in Amenta the two pillars form the doorway from the one world to the other."

The power that sustains the universe is Ptah in one cult, Osiris in the other. God and cross are one. The deceased arises from the tomb as Tat for eternity in what is known as the mystery of Tattu.

When Queen Hatshepsut erected her two pillars, she said she had made two obelisks "for him who is the lord of the thrones of the two worlds—of earth and of heaven." The double obelisk, according to Massey, is a co-type of the twofold mount (of the poles) and the two pillars of Tattu, the place where it was shown that earth was fixed and heaven made stable forever on the two pillars of Set and Horus, which had once been the two poles in Equatoria.

The Tat, says Massey, was a figure of the pole, and the four corners, which united "five supports," the fivefold tree of the Egypto-gnostic mystery. Otherwise stated, it was a symbol of the power that sustained the heavens with the supporting pole and the arms of the four quarters. This power was personified in Ptah as well as figured in the Tat.

The tree was first of all a sign of sustenance when the sustainer was the Great Mother, Apt. On this, the type of Ptah was based as the Tat-image of a power that sustained the universe. Osiris-Tat then typified the power that sustained the human soul in death. This symbol Tat was buried with the mummy as a fetish in the coffin. Thus a cult of the cross was founded many thousands of years ago. And thus, says Massey, the genesis of the legend of the cross, like that of the Christ, can be traced in Egypt to the cult of Ptah at Memphis, where the religion of the cross originated; and to Annu or On where it was continued in the cult of Atum-Ra with Ie-em-hetep as the Egyptian Jesus.

Iu-em-hetep, says Massey, was the god Iusa, brought out of Egypt by the Jews—for thirteen thousand years the bringer of goodwill and peace and plenty to the world. "The Christian doctrine of the crucifixion, with the human victim raised aloft as the sin-offering for all the world, is but a ghastly simulacrum of the primitive meaning; a shadowy phantom of the original substance." Fundamentally, according to Massey, the cross was astronomical, a

359

The raising of Djed, or its "awakening," has been called the mystery of mysteries, or the secret of resurrection. The human body is described as an illusory solid, perishable, but what caused it was a real solid: the original djed, or "word" of Amon-Ra-Ptah. This djed "word," or pillar of Osiris, is described as the base of relative stability, and principle of whatever is durable in the fluctuating Osirian world of becoming and return. Man's job is to learn to make his own djet—or inborn word—secure against destruction. When awakened, man's djet becomes his incorruptible body. It is said to remain a prisoner of earth and Osiris unless Ra comes to deliver it by "untying the rope" or "undoing the knots." The two principles of Ra-Osiris are seen as the life-givers to the human djet, symbolized by the souls of Ra and Osiris shut up in the djed, or pillar. As such they are the two currents of universal life whose source is one, though they are two in nature. This duality is the cause of terrestrial continuity and the endless metamorphosis of the Osirian way. To escape from such slavery the soul of Ptah-Ra must absorb the Osirian: the universal must vanquish the particular.

figure of time, as is any clock. It is a measure of time made visible upon the scale and in the circle of the year instead of the hour. A cross with equal arms denotes the time of equal day and night, a figure of the equinox. Another cross, †, like the Christian cross, with one elongated stem, is a figure of the winter solstice. It is a modified form of the Tat of Ptah on which the four quarters are more obviously portrayed in the four arms. This elongated cross, or Tat, was reerected annually in the depths of the solstice when the darkness lasts some sixteen hours and daylight only eight.

The Tat cross is a type of the eternal Tattu. It was the figure, says Massey, of the all-sustaining, all-renewing, all-revivifying power that was reerected and religiously sought for hope, encouragement, and succor when the day was at its darkest and things were at their worst in physical nature—when the sun was apparently going out.

The Tat—for the time being—was overthrown. The deity suffered and was represented as dead. The god in matter was inert and breathless. Then they raised up the Tat, portraying the resurrecton of the god. "Let the mummy-type of the eternal be once more erected as the mainstay and divine support of all." It was thus, says Massey, that the power of salvation through Osiris-Tat was represented in the mysteries.

The work *Djed* in ancient Egypt meant "stable" or "durable." But it was used not only to represent a cosmic pillar, or sky support; it was also a symbol for revival and resurrection.

At their mystery festivals the Egyptians represented the passion of Osiris, the scandal of his death, and the miracle of his resurrection to a radiant immortality. As E. A. W. Budge points out, the Djed was in very primitive times the symbol of a god to which human sacrifices were offered, and the ground in front of it was "watered" with the blood of human beings, sometimes foreigners, sometimes warriors taken prisoner alive. The victims were slain before the Djed pillar, symbol of Osiris, and their blood was dug into the earth to make it fertile again. Osiris's death was commemorated by eating the body and drinking the blood—later the eucharist or mortuary meal at the Easter equinoctial festival of death and rebirth.

In the previous eon the Great Mother was sacrificed—comparatively young, says Massey, to preserve her from the effects of age, disease, and decrepitude. Her flesh was torn to pieces and her blood drunk to give life to her children. Salvation in this eschatology came from the virgin blood in which Horus was incarnate and made flesh.

360

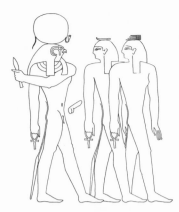

According to the Egyptian myths, the divine pair Hu Saa came into the world when Ra in his solitude cut off his sexual organs. The two deities arose from the blood of the sun god.

Later the ritual was performed symbolically with bread and wine in lieu of the body of Osiris-Horus; later still with Jesus. As Massey points out, the Egyptian Horus was continued by the various sects of gnostics under both the names of Horus and Jesus.

Egypt, says Massey, had anticipated Rome in attaining the "unbloody sacrifice" that was represented by the wafer, or loaf, of Horus as the bread of heaven, which took the place of flesh in the eucharistic meal, while retaining the beer or wine, as substitute for blood, representing the female element.

The earliest form of god-the-father who became a voluntary sacrifice in Egypt was Ptah in the character of Sekari, says Massey. As a solar god he went down into Amenta. There he died and rose again, and this became the resurrection, and the way into a future life as the founder of Egyptian eschatology. Atum, son of Ptah, likewise became a voluntary sacrifice as the source of life. The father who was blended with the mother in Atum, is portrayed as the creator of mankind by the shedding of his own blood. In cutting his member, Atum showed that he was the creator of the blood shed in a voluntary sacrifice. Later, this was ritually done to Attis, Adonis, Tammuz, Bacchus, Dionysus, all facsimiles of Osiris, all castrated on the tree of life, their testicles still glittering on today's Yuletide trees.

The agape was the way of celebrating the resurrection. But death came first. In the Nile Delta, at Busiris, known as "the city of the Djed Column," a great annual festival took place during the last month of the inundation of the Nile when the waters fell off—that is, in September, at the autumn equinox. The ceremony consisted in the dramatization of the death, vigil, and resurrection of Osiris. The final and most sacred act was the erection of the Djed Column, symbol of the backbone of Osiris. When raised upright it meant that Osiris had risen. But not, apparently, in the flesh; in the spirit.

As Rundle Clark, author of *Myth and Symbol in Ancient Egypt,* puts it: "The idea of the Djed Column is that it stands firmly upright—for to be upright is to be alive, to have overcome the inert forces of death and decay. When the Djed is upright it implies that life will go on." The greatest religious achievement of the Egyptians, says Clark, was to take this general fertility god and make him into the savior of the dead; or more exactly, the savior from death. "It was in the soul of Osiris the Egyptians believed they would live on." The rising of Osiris was the central fact in the structure of their universe; this they

361

There can be little doubt says E. A. Wallis Budge, "that the 𝔙 is a conventional representation of a part of the backbone of Osiris, namely the *sacrum* bone, which, on account of its proximity to the sperm bag, was regarded as the most important member of the body." Tet is the name of a very ancient god whose worship was merged with that of Osiris, and his symbol, says Budge, was the sacrum bone, 𝔦 , placed on a pedestal, which then took the form of the Djed pillar, "which was during the whole of the Dynastic period in Egypt regarded as the backbone of Osiris." The Djed, Tat, or Tet pillar was also the emblem of stability represented by Ptah, "the fourfold support of the universe."

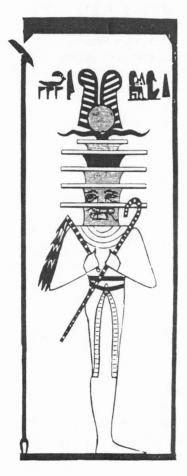

signified by the raising of the Djed, or stability, Column.

Osiris, Clark notes, did not rise up and leave the tomb or underworld. It was his soul that was set free into the life forces of the next year. He was the spirit of Life manifest in sprouting vegetation, in the seed of animal and man, the "orgone" of Wilhelm Reich.

Yet the raising of the column was not the final act of the drama. A loincloth was tied around the middle of the Djed Column, and feathers were stuck in its top. The resulting symbol was treated as a living god, so much so that in the later examples a pair of human eyes were painted onto the column to make the identification with Osiris more emphatic. Around the Djed was tied what Clark calls "a strange object known as a Tit, a knot of cloth or leather." This was the emblem of Isis, or the Mother Goddess. It is the symbol of the blood of Isis, when she gave birth to Horus.

Clark has trouble with this symbolism: "It is presumed that this combination of emblems denotes the Union of Isis and Osiris. . . . This union of male and female obviously has some meaning, but it is impossible to see how it links up with the rest of the symbolism."

Massey has less trouble. He explains the mysterious rag attached to the raised Tat: "It is the feminine garment, or apron, called the garment of shame because it was the garment of impurity to be trampled underfoot when the male and the female were to be made one in spirit, as spirit." And the same feminine garment, Massey points out, "is still worn without shame as the bishop's apron," an apron he traces back to the feminine loincloth first worn by that sex, for what he calls "the most primitive and pitiful of human needs at the time of puberty." The bishop in his apron, says Massey, "like the priest in his petticoat and the clergyman in his surplice, is a likeness of the biune being who united both sexes in one."

So the equinox came to be considered a symbol of equality, of all things being on a level. And promiscuity was a mode of making things fair and even in the sexual saturnalia. High and low, rich and poor, young and old commingled "on the mound, the hill, the high places." To symbolize this equality, a pair of scales was also erected at the equinox, "for with them the equilibrium of the universe was dependent on eternal equity."

The mystery of reproduction was enacted at the festival as a vicarious means of fecundating the Great Mother by the bountiful sowing of human seed. The ritual survived as the agape, or love feast, of the early Christian cult. The phallic festivals were then repeated at both equinoxes; at seed time and at harvest time. The desire was to produce an unlimited supply of food; and the rites of promiscuous sex were designed to help reproduce the fruits of earth and drive away inimical influences of drought and famine.

The women, being the begetters and regenerators, pleaded that their wombs might be replenished, as Isis and Nephthys had done with Osiris's corpse. Women are described by Elie Reclus in *Curious byways of anthropology; sexual, savage and esoteric customs of primitive peoples,* as losing all feeling of modesty, of becoming raging Bacchantes, wild with debauch. "At the Spring equinox," says Reclus "divinized Mother-earth had to be stirred from her winter sleep by lascivious spectacle to excite the spirit of fecundity represented by young women who danced and frolicked or lay down and scraped the ground with their heels . . . so many naked Danaes wooing the fertilizing sun . . . bursting out of all disguises, trappings, ties, and stays of civilization, running amok in all the nudity of nature."

Herodotus reports that in the Delta city of Bubastis 700,000 people assembled to celebrate the annual Festival of the Great Mother, Bast, goddess of strong drink and sexual passion, and that women exposed themselves on boats to watchers on the shores, signifying they were free to all comers, for that occasion only, in service of the goddess, the lioness of heat.

The phallic festival of promiscuous intercourse survived when the mysteries had become religious in Egypt, Greece, and Rome. In Rome the Saturnalia, which was intended to commemorate the carefree era of sexual promiscuity that had once obtained, was a mode of celebrating the fundamental equality of all at the equinoctial period, by means of various leveling customs, in which men and women exchanged their clothes to show the equality of the sexes.

All over the world tribes have reverted to utter promiscuity to celebrate the phallic festival, when "the only law was that of all for all." Reclus describes how with members of marital associations among the Eskimo, each wife must lawfully couple with the man to whom her husband would willingly lend her, and who would lend his own wife in return, holding that "all were made for all, and that sin was for a lawful wife to seek connubium with a bachelor."

In southern India, says Reclus, the Thodigars, at the Festival of Sowing Seed, improvised shelters by the roadside and stocked them with provisions for their wives, calling upon passersby to "procure the public good and ensure an abundance of bread."

Bast has been described as the gentle and fructifying heat of the sun, the very soul of Isis. Not only a pleasure-loving goddess who reveled in music and dance, Bast was protector of pregnant women and of men against disease and evil spirits. But the Hebrew prophet Ezekiel threatened that the joyous young participants of the rites of Bubastics would "fall by the sword and be carried into captivity for their worship of Bast."

363

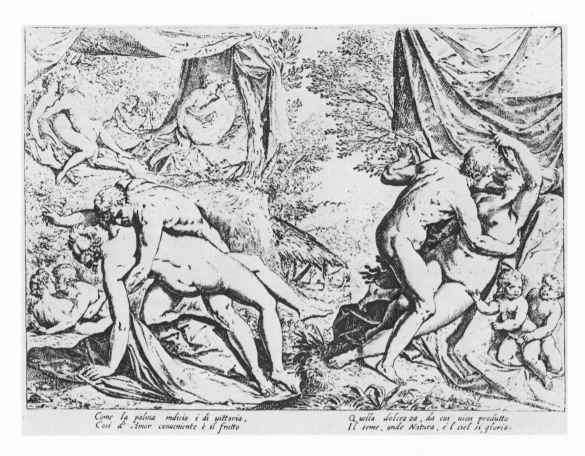

Come la palma indicio è di uittoria,
Così d' Amor conuemente è il frutto

Quella dolcezza, da cui uien produtto
Il seme, onde Natura, è l ciel si gloria.

In the world of totem, the raising of a pole served to announce the transformation of pubescent girls into the state of womanhood. The pole, raised high immediately after the ceremony or operation of introcision, was a signal for men from as far away as the pole could be seen to come and enjoy a festival of sexual promiscuity, one at which the freshened girls were "welcomed into communal connubium by the whole totemic group of grown-up males." On this occasion the girls were considered open and accessible to all the males of the group, each of whom had the right to ravish any or as many of the girls as he was able. As Massey explains it, the ritual was a revival of the ancient pretotemic days of totally permissive sexual freedom, free from all taboos.

What has been lost sight of by both the prurient admirer and puritan denigrator of these rites is their spiritual basis as practiced by the Egyptians. The agape, or phallic feast, with its sexual orgies, was a mode of celebrating not only the raising of Osiris, the return of sunshine and revival of vegetation, but the rerising of Horus, prince of Sekhem; Sekhem being the realm of the Akh or "bodies of

364

light," comparable to stars. Horus, erecting the Tat in Sekhem was raising Osiris from the sepulcher; it was the father, reerected as the son in the typical resurrection, and continuity of the human spirit in the afterlife.

The love feast at the equinox on earth symbolized, as Massey explains it, the triumph and regenesis of the soul in Tattu. And the enactment of the "holy kiss," or blending of the sexes in the feast of love, was a dramatic rendering of the union between human nature and the divine, of the original brother and sister, Shu and Tefnut. The "pair of souls" were blended in the Horus of the soul that was to live forever.

According to the mystery of Tattu, in blending back into one the two halves of a soul that was dualized in sex, and dualized in spirit and matter, there was a return to the type beyond sex, from which the soul had bifurcated in the human creation. Thus the two halves of the soul, male and female, Shu and Tefnut, were reunited forever in Tattu.

17. NEEDLING MOTHER EARTH

All over the world, amid all its peoples, in all known ages, obelisk, column, tower, steeple, and menhir have been understood to be phallic symbols, not just of the erect male member, but, as the nineteenth-century English Freemason Hargrave Jennings expresses it, of a "supersensual, superessential, divinely operative celestial 'fire'" —a force which makes things grow, harden, and rise against gravity, fecundating the universe, producing all beings and all life.

Among the Greeks, the most appropriate emblem for the power exercised by this "fire" was considered the dart or arrow—hence the word *obelos*. Every obelisk was a representative in stone of a ray or beam of "far-darting, operative, vivifying fire." It was likewise with the pagodas of China, the towers of India, the minarets of the Muslim, the cairns of Carnac in France, the biblical Jacob's stone, Saint Paul's Cathedral: all, says Jennings, symbolic of the power of creation. And the apex, whether it be the piercing pyramidion of the obelisk or the egg-shaped top of the minaret, represents the glans. The purpose of these phallic symbols, their justification for existence: to venerate the power behind generation, behind production and renovation.

In a 500 page opus on *Phallicism,* and in a 100-page booklet entitled *Obelisks,* Jennings chided his fellow Victorians for believing their science was more advanced than that of the Egyptians, and put forth his view that whereas obelisks, towers, and steeples were representations of the male principle, pyramids, circular forms, rhomboidal or undulating, and serpentine shapes, denoted the female power. Yet all alike, said Jennings, represent the natural motive power which causes and directs the world. Together, the male and female symbols represent the idea of swelling, rising, extending, to be consummated in what Jennings calls "the movement for that grand human act and holy sacrament which secures everything." The pudenda in both male and female he calls magnets, "and their natural, deliriously delightful presentment to each other is magic-magnetism." These phenomenal organs, Jennings observed, "superb and miraculous in their special address and use," are "positive-negative" in man,

and "negative-positive" in woman. "Yet both are corpore-
ally and sexually one, in complete coition, or double-tie, or
identification of 'two singles' into temporary, absolute 'one
single.' "

In these *avant garde* views, Jennings was apparently
strongly influenced by Richard Payne Knight's remarkable
volume *A Discourse on the Worship of Priapus,* published
at the time of the French Revolution, which set out to
show that the worldwide worship of generative powers
was neither obscene nor depraved. Designed to sell
privately, it caused such an uproar in Victorian England
that many copies had to be destroyed, so that for almost
a century it was hard to find, until recently reprinted. From
its sober scholarship Jennings became convinced of the
value of the pagan concept that sexuality is the fundamental power of life which animates the universe and brings
forth nature in all its beauty and wonder. He also got
inspiration from a contemporary, a colonial officer in India,
Edward Sellon, described by his Victorian compeers as a
"minor pornographer" and by modern commentators as an
"industrious lecher," whose booklet, *Annotations on the
Sacred Writings of the Hindus,* is, in fact, an equally sober
and scientific anthropological description of the mysteries
of Tantric sex as practiced in India. In it Sellon describes
the religion of the Hindus as being based on the deity
Bruhmatma, worshiped through an emblem, a black stone
in the shape of a phallus, or Linga, symbolizing the
procreative power of nature, which fructified the earth and
which manifested in three forms: as the creator Brahma,
the preserver Vishnu, and the destroyer Shiva. To create
the world, Brahma is described as making himself androgynous, the right half male, the left female.

A close analogy was found by Sellon between the
rituals of Hindus and those of the Egyptians. He equated
Shiva with Osiris, and Sacti with Isis, represented by the
same equilateral triangle with a dot in the center, the
same emblem of the generative power—two coexisting
principles of nature, active and passive, linga and yoni.

Sellon describes Hindu Tantric sexual rituals as being
performed with naked temple courtesans or *yoginis,* young
and beautiful, representing the goddess Sacti, or power,
reciting mantras, becoming sexually excited and inducing
promiscuous orgies among the votaries which he qualifies
as "very licentious" but constituting a mysterious initiation. He further describes Sacti as represented *in coitu*
sitting on Shiva's erect member, just as Isis "the goddess
who grants all desires" did with the dead Osiris. Similarly,
a statue of Minerva at Sais, who Sellon says was invoked

by the union of X and O, or phallus and kteis, he found bore a striking resemblance to Prakriti, the Hindu deity of generation.

In India temples were adorned with the most exquisite of couplings, and everywhere the phallus was worshiped publicly in the form of the linga, the vulva as the yoni. Twelve huge phalli are still objects of veneration today, regularly asperged and strewn with flowers. One, of basalt, at Benares, requires six men to encircle with their arms outstretched. In the villages there were once many small upright lingams as described by Dr. Thomas Inman in his *Ancient Pagan & Modern Christian Symbolism Exposed and Explained;* on these women lowered themselves "having first adjusted their dress so as to prevent interference with their perfect contact with the miniature obelisk." At the time of the Muslim invasion of India, the worship of the linga was still common all over the country, but many were destroyed by the reforming invaders. The most notable lingam, a polished black stone at Somnath in Guzerat, was demolished by Mahmud of Ghezni, but fragments of it ended up in the Kaaba in Mecca, an ancient pre-Islamic geodetic and holy spot.

King Solomon, said Jennings, devoted his energies and wealth to raising phallic or "fire" shrines over high places, and especially in front of the temple in Jerusalem. Though the temple was only 120 feet long, 40 broad, and 60 high, its portico was a large tower 240 feet high, which to Jennings represented an obelisk. On each side of this great spine, at the temple's entrance, were two more handsome phallic columns, over 50 feet high, capped with pomegranates, to represent the Queen of Heaven, or a gravid uterus. To the initiates of Eleusis, who, according to Arnobius, venerate the female yoni in their mysteries, the pomegranate was sacred to Demeter and Persephone, representing the hidden riches within divinized earth. The two columns outside the Temple of Solomon, called by Masons Jachin and Boaz, represent "the fundamental divine polarity which underlies all manifested nature, the two opposites whose union constitutes the symbolic great Work of Alchemy." And to Jennings these columns are the equivalent of the Buddhist pillars erected by their dagobas, or the pillars of Hercules beside Phoenician temples. In Syria the counterpart of these "pillars of Hiram" was the great phallus described by Lucian in *De dea Syria.* According to General J. G. R. Forlong, the image of gold set up by Nebuchadnezzar on the plain of Dura, in the province of Babylon, was also a phallic obelisk, 60 cubits high by 6 in diameter.

369

Irish round towers, and Osiris
swearing by his power

The round towers of Ireland, says O'Brien, author of a
book by that title, were all phalli, raised in adherence to
the ancient fire-worship of Persia, for the purpose of
worshiping the sun, or male principals in the universe, and
for studying the revolutions and properties of the planetary
orbs.

As for the worship of the lingam in Britain, according to
Forlong: ''The generality of our countrymen have no conception of the over-ruling prevalence of this faith and of
the number of lingam gods throughout our islands. We
have been hoodwinked by the unjustifiable term 'crosses'
applied to the ancient symbols which were always in the
form of obelisks or columns, erected on prominent
places.'' Forlong points out that the Nevern shaft at
Pembroke could pass for a Mahadeva lingam in any part
of India; the Cheddar shaft on the Mendip Hills and the
Chipping column of north Gloucestershire are clearly lingams such as the Assyrians revered. So are the large
obelisks of stone found in many parts of the north, such
as at Rudstone in Yorkshire, which Pliny says was sacred
to the sun. It is 24 feet long above ground and 6 feet
broad, weighing 40 tons.

Michael Harrison in *The Roots of Witchcraft* recounts
how in England just after World War II he was astonished
to discover a widespread cult of the lingam dating back to
medieval Britain revealed to him by Professor Geoffrey
Webb, formerly Slade Professor of Fine Arts at Cambridge
and then Secretary of the Royal Commission on Historical
Monuments. Commissioned to survey ancient churches for
aerial bomb damage, Professor Webb, an authority on
medieval church architecture, was amazed, while studying
the interior of an altar whose top slab of stone had been

Priapus, with an enormous erect member, was placed by Greeks and Romans in gardens as a magical aid to the growth of plants.

shifted by an explosion, to find in the interior, unmolested and possibly unseen since the eleventh or twelfth century, a large stone lingam. Later, Professor Webb found that ninety percent of all the churches he examined dating up to the middle of the fourteenth century contained a phallic symbol of the fertility cult concealed within the altar.

Jennings's fellow Freemason, Godfrey Higgins, author of *Anacalepsys,* considers Stonehenge phallic in its design, possibly a temple built during what he calls the post-Atlantian "First Dispersion." Its upright stone, known as the Friar's Heel, is a lingam or phallus, says Higgins, dedicated to Freia, the Friday lady, or Venus-Aphrodite. "And there to eastward of the holy pointer is the Os Yoni over whose apex the first ray of the rising god of the midsummer solstice shines into the center of the circle."

As a modern lady witch describes the scene at the summer solstice: "It is still thrilling as the sun rises above the phallic monolith, the Friar's Heel or Hell Stone: its rays strike into the feminine womb shape of the so-called 'horseshoe' of great trilithons, making a *hieros gamos,* or Sacred Marriage of heaven and earth."

Throughout Britain there are stones of Neolithic origin believed to possess the ability to promote fertility in barren women, who embraced them in the hope of having offspring. In Carnac childless couples would run naked around a special standing stone, though modern dowsers believe the power that once manifested in that region of trance has since shifted.

In the French Pyrenees, reverence for the phallus in the form of a menhir is still alive today; elsewhere in France, apart from the well-known bishop of Lyons, honored as Saint Foutin, patron of *foutre,* or frigging, there stood near Brest the chapel of Saint Guignole, whose phallus consisted of a long wooden peg traversing his statue and stretching out in front. With scrapings from this peg, votaries made infusions as an antidote to sterility. As the peg was worn down, a blow from behind with a mallet brought it to its pristine prominence.

In Italy, the phallus—also called the *fascinum* because it exercised such a power of fascination by sight alone that it drew all glances to itself—was everywhere in evidence, until the reformed Church. Thereafter a hundred thousand phalli were knocked from pagan statues and rural herms, and in architecture, as Jennings lamented, "the lingam of yore was thickened and wholly encased into a column, so veiled by ornate architecture that none but an awakened and practiced and educated eye could detect the old symbolism."

371

These naked females, representations of the great Fertility Goddess known as Sheila-na-Gigs, strikingly similar to the Yonis venerated by the Tantrics in India, indicate by their frequent appearance on Christian churches, that the old religion was still alive.

Elsewhere the phallus was reduced to a mere charm or amulet against the evil eye. To escape the attention of reformers, yet maintain the magic power of such an amulet, symbolizing coition of the sexual organs, it was tamely reduced to the least explicit of symbols: the hand.

Now modern authors have taken the whole subject of phallicism a step further to show that standing stones, both ancient and modern, are not only phallic symbols, but actual sources, or accumulators, of a power that is real—sexually and psychically stimulating, among its other varying qualities.

Guy Underwood, a dowser, and author of *The Pattern of the Past,* who has devoted a lifetime to unraveling the mystery of cosmic and telluric forces operating in and around the ancient temple sites of Britain, has demonstrated by means of various modern techniques of dowsing for water that the standing stones of the ancients are almost invariably positioned over important hidden sources of water, or "blind springs," as they are known to dowsers—a blind spring being the proper site upon which to sink a well. Not only upright menhirs, but flat supported dolmens, invariably mark blind springs of considerable telluric importance.

Brigadier General William Sitwell, author of *Stones of Northumberland,* describes the majority of standing liths

372

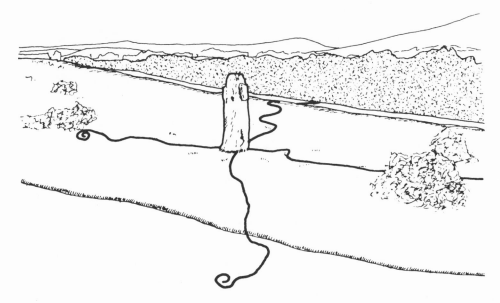

Waterlines crossing beneath a standing stone as depicted by Tom Graves in *Needles of Stone.* The Welsh water-diviner Bill Lewis has noted a force issuing from these stones which waxes and wanes. His work as an electrical engineer led him to conclude that water moving through a tunnel of earth, and particularly clay, creates a static electric field, and that two streams crossing, even at different levels, increase the field, and that a stone placed over the point of junction acts as an amplifier.

as "magnetic," by which he means that if one places a hand on them one receives the astonishing sensation that they vibrate. Other standing stones give off a tingling sensation of varying intensity, even amounting to an unpleasant shock which also seems to carry with it a shock to the psyche. Tom Graves, another professional dowser, author of *Needles of Stone,* has observed that some monoliths, if you lean against them, feel as if they were rocking slowly backward and forward; others seem to buzz.

Sitwell has observed that most of Carnac's standing stones have been raised with their smaller end buried in the ground. By measuring the flow of observed current with a sensitive dowsing instrument, Andrew Davidson, in his *Silbury Hill,* found that stones raised in a circle show a predominantly positive or negative current, each one oppositely charged to its neighbor. Davidson further discovered that the polarity changed with the phases of the moon. Dowsing by pendulum at the time of a polarity change, he found that the pendulum would slowly stop, then gain momentum in the opposite direction, the whole process regularly taking several minutes.

John G. Williams, another dowsing researcher, from Herefordshire, showed on TV the power emanating from the stones as a spiral-like force which builds up in the body with the effect of propelling the investigator away from the stone. He says that most standing stones, including the Stonehenge uprights, if properly tapped for their energy, can cause a person to be thrown from them.

373

Tom Graves illustrates the shock a man can receive from a standing stone. "The energy released," he says, "triggers off a violent reflex contraction of the back muscles, throwing him backward as much as ten or fifteen feet."

Graves makes an analogy between the change in a magnetic field caused by a soft-iron shield ring around a magnet and the effect produced by waterlines and overgrounds meeting a "shield ring" of stones. The ring, says Graves, allows the energy to bypass the area, isolating the outside world, as in a Faraday cage, from whatever may go on inside the circle.

Graves describes being knocked flat by a sudden burst of energy from a circle of stones at Rollright in Oxfordshire: "Some kind of energy, possibly derived from the blind spring, at the center of the circle, and implied by the concentric haloes round the center, spread outward from the center and was collected at the perimeter of the circle, to be stored there by 'spinning' the energy from stone to stone." Graves also tells of inserting a small amount of energy into one of what he calls the "gate-latch" stones—which released all the stored energy in one go. "That was what flattened us in its passing." The interesting point, adds Graves, "was that the pulse of energy, whatever it was, seemed to leave the circle at a tangent to the line of the stones, traveling in a dead straight line. I think it went about six miles to the southwest, to a stone called the Hawk stone, and then split off in two different directions from there—or that's what the dowsing results implied."

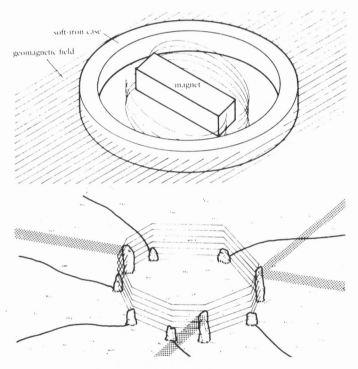

That megalithic man must have learned about such accumulations of energy at mounds, standing stones, and circles is clear to modern dowsers who believe these particular spots were used for spiritual benefit, to increase energy and fertility, and to heal—practices which were consciously or unconsciously followed by later builders of churches and cathedrals on the same spots.

Monument found at Nîmes in 1875

Louis Charpentier, in his *Les mystères de la cathédrale de Chartres,* expresses the opinion that the orientation of churches and cathedrals springs from the ancient knowledge of the mysterious forces of earth which he calls "telluric currents," symbolized by the earth serpent, or dragon *vouivre.* The cathedral stands on a large prehistoric mound over a buried chamber, the natural meeting place, says Charpentier, of several powerful streams of telluric current, once the site of a great Druid college. And Juan G. Atienza, in his *Los Supervivientes de Atlantida,* shows that the Templars who helped liberate the Iberian peninsula from the Moors did so on condition that they receive outright ownership from the kings of Spain and Portugal of *all* the major megalithic sites, specifically selected because of some mysterious quality known to the Templars but apparently not to their donors.

Druids, Templars, and witches were clearly aware that some sort of mysterious power emanated from these locations, and the direct physical use of this power appears to have been their secret specialty. As these holy centers were taken over by the Church, and the magic often reduced to superstitious rote, followers of the old religion took to the wilder parts of the country, there to carry on their vivifying rituals.

Modern dowsers claim they can actually see the effect of nighttime dancing around standing stones. Graves describes how the pillars pick up the energy generated by the dancers. "They all glow with the same blue fire. The energy created by the ritual spreads the blue, the color of healing, throughout the countryside, that surrounds these

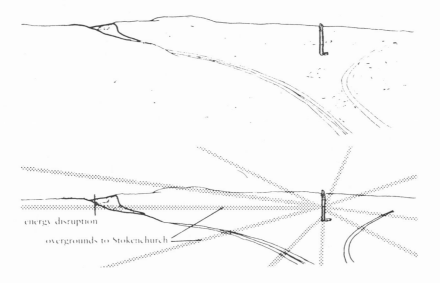

energy disruption

overgrounds to Stokenchurch

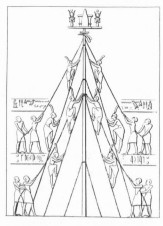

The central axis of the world, symbolized by the maypole, came to be regarded as a tree with the circumpolar stars—or souls—perched on its branches. Next, it was imaged as a pole with guidelines. "The great god lives fixed in the middle of the sky upon his support, as the universe, symbolized by the guide ropes, revolves around it."

ageless sacred sites." But not all the energies created by the ritual, he says, are necessarily physical. "They can be made physical by the way in which they affect people's attitudes, and thus their actions."

In a report on the perdurance of fertility rituals in Elizabethan England, the Puritan propagandist Philip Stubbs wrote: "Against May, Whitsonday, or other time, all the young men and maides, olde men and wives, run gadding to the woods, grooves, hills and mountains, where they spend all the night in pleasant pastimes," adding that he had heard it credibly reported "that of fortie, three-score, or a hundred maids going to the wood over night, there have scaresly the third part of them returned home again undefiled."

The maypole, as a phallic fertility symbol, used to stand in every village square in England until savagely torn down by sex-hating Puritans. In villages throughout Germany it is still at the ready. The energy produced by dancing around a maypole—a living needle of wood—has to be primed, says Graves, to work toward fertilizing the area. He notes that it is primed and directed by the state of mind of those participating in the dancing: "and what better way of framing a 'fertility' state of mind than spending the night in the woods, engaged in 'pleasant pastimes'?"

The sacred centers, by their accumulation of what Wilhelm Reich called orgone, may have helped to produce mass orgasms, therapeutic, in Reichian terms, to the whole person, as well as the whole countryside. And the suppression by the various churches of these pagan fertility rites may have stunted not only the natural sexuality of those who could no longer enjoy the ritual, but stunted great parts of the land. As Graves puts it: "The enforcement of a 'civilized' life has resulted in the destruction of the countryside and produced the meaninglessness of the life we suffer today."

Paul Screeton, an Englishman from Hastlepool who has written widely on the ancient wisdom, suggests that in prehistoric times the land may have been much more fertile, producing several crops a year, fertilized through fertility rituals. And modern witches, such as Doreen Valiente, author of several books on witchcraft, believe that a certain magical current commences at the equinox or solstice, reaches its peak at the following sabbat, and then declines, until the next station of the sun, when a new magical tide commences, and so on. Thus the tide set in motion at the spring equinox peaks at the witches' May Eve, then slowly ebbs until the summer solstice, when a new impulse commences.

376

Screeton, in his delightful *Quicksilver Heritage,* points out that the earth's magnetic field is estimated to have been 50 percent stronger in A.D. 500, and could have been even greater in megalithic times. Other observers believe that in earlier times man had a less dense body, more easily attuned to natural sources of power. And megalithic builders may have known how to draw extra energy from the sun—by the use of stone machines. Screeton suggests that prehistoric man, with his megalithic sites, gained control of terrestrial currents through manipulation of solar power, thereby producing a better environment. As the sun passed over the natural centers, it could cause an extra surge of energy, especially at noon, with differing effects at zenith, equinox, and solstice—the main festivals of Bards, Ovates, and Druids along with intervening festivals of Candlemas, Beltane, Lammas, and All Hallows.

John Michell, an avantguardist viewer of this magical world of antiquity, is poetic in his re-creation of the ancient magic: "At certain seasons of the year the dragon passed overhead down a straight line of country, drawing in his wake the fertilizing powers of life. Astronomers observed its passage, astrologers predicted the moment of its appearance, geomancers marked its course with alignment of mounds and stones."

Modern occultists such as Geoffrey Hodson suggest that "etheric rays" from the sun may have helped raise the level of consciousness of participants in rituals, helped cure disease, healed wounds both physical and emotional. Merlin is quoted as saying to Aurelius: "Laugh not so lightly, King. . . . For in these stones is a mystery and a healing virtue against many ailments."

Iris Campbell, a remarkable English psychometrist, believes that in megalithic times the distribution of the colors of the sun was different, with less violet and more blue rays, blue being the color attributed to the etheric or orgone energy. She suggests that in ancient healing centers the monoliths must have been carefully positioned in accord with the solar rays in order to bring about an accurate influx of solar force to the body, not too strong to overwhelm it. Did megalithic man harness cosmic rays, asks Screeton? Were they concentrated, stored, and channeled at stone circles?

The megalithic builders' great interest in eclipses may have been connected with the fact that the sun, in addition to altering the atmosphere's properties, alters the nature of the earth's magnetic currents. An eclipse of the moon has no apparent physical influence on the earth other than the effect it produces on the level of terrestria magnetism.

377

Jean-Louis Bernard in *Aux Origines de l'Egypte* makes a very good argument that the ancients had learned to capture from outer space and make use of what he calls a "green ray," a ray too intense for humanity to use directly, which needed the science of Toth to be assimilated by man—which could, of course, mean by reflection from the moon! The assimilation was apparently done with megaliths and ultrasonics. The repercussion by stones of the ultrasonic waves caused a vibration in the cerebro-spinal column, says Bernard, and especially at the nape of the neck, which made it very easy to go into trance. The ray was best captured, apparently, on mountain tops or on top of stepped pyramids or ziggurats.

Bernard also finds evidence for a race of giants who opposed the green ray with a telluric force derived from the center of the earth. Coming up through the soles of the feet it affected their legs and their pelvis, rising like static electricity up the cerebro-spinal column. With this telluric force the giants are said to have had the power of paralyzing their adversaries, as a snake does a bird. The result, says Bernard, was a cosmo-telluric war that hastened the biological decline of the giants, ending their stay on earth sometime about 10,000 B.C. coincident with a series of cataclysms which changed the inclination of the earth's axis, shifted the poles, caused the glaciers to withdraw and brought an end to the civilization of the Atlantean archipelago.

All the evidence from the remote past, says John Michell, points to the inescapable conclusion that the earth's natural magnetism was not only known to men

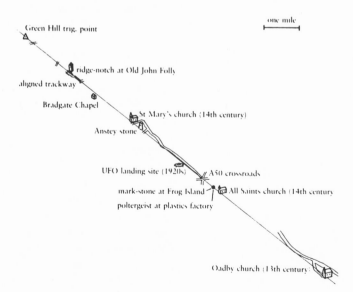

Forty dowsing and electronic experts recently organized the Dragon Project to make a scientific study of the phenomena of the ancient leys in England.

some thousands of years ago, but that it provided them with a source of energy and inspiration to which their whole civilization was tuned. In his words: "From the rocks, mountains and headlands a mysterious current once flowed down avenues of standing stones over mounds and earthworks towards some central hill dedicated to Mercury, the terrestrial spirit. Below the hill an instrument of solar generation produced the spark by which the current became animated and recoiled in a wave of fertility through the hidden veins of the land, urged on by the music and clamor of the rejoicing people."

Much research has recently been done, especially in England, by dowsers and "ley hunters" who claim to have established the existence of power channels linking one megalithic site to another in vast networks of what they call "ley" lines, which they differentiate from the track line, the water line, and the acquastat. Ley lines are straight, point-to-point lines which ley hunters have traced all across Britain, set out with what they describe as the accuracy of a modern surveyor, with alignments precise between standing stones. The existence of leys, they insist, is as obvious as that of electricity, and can be felt by anyone who can feel electricity. Screeton says that leys bear a geometrical relation to each other, either in parallel, or forming isosceles or equilateral triangles, with regularly recurring angles of intersection and standard distances between points. He explains the leys as avenues of "etheric" energy, made visible by trees with spiraled or double trunks, by the flow of what Kipling called "the mysterious earth currents which thrill the clay of our bodies."

A comparison between etheric energies and orgone energy, says Screeton, shows such great similarities it would be surprising if they were not identical. Both are everywhere, and both can be accumulated. Orgone energy as described by Wilhelm Reich is an energy which operates most noticeably on the emotions, but with physical and physiological effects—a sort of basic life force. In constant flow, he said, it provides the medium through which magnetic and gravitational forces manifest their influence. To Michell there is no doubt that the natural flow of force related to the earth's magnetic field is the orgone energy rediscovered by Reich, present everywhere in the universe, mass free, and consequently hard to isolate, except that it appears to be susceptible to being channeled and accumulated.

By placing standing stones on ley lines and their crossing points, Screeton believes, the ancients managed

Herms were raised in the ancient world on every highway and at the corners of any property.

Barrows were discovered to be almost invariably built up of layers of organic and inorganic material—a storehouse, as Graves points out, for the energy known as od, odyle, prana, or Reich's orgone.

to channel, increase, and control the current. Underwood, in his *The Pattern of the Past,* says old walls, hedges, and roads are aligned on track lines which made it possible to divide the land into parcels of convenient size, with precise, unalterable limits, apparently easily divinable and redivinable by priests, as in Egypt after the flooding of the Nile. Since the greatest antiquity, these geodetic lines and patterns have been clearly assigned topographical markings, making them distinguishable to persons initiated into the code. Throughout the Roman empire the limits of lots were identified by standing "herms" mostly with phallus erect.

Screeton notes that where ley lines cross are centers of power associated with magic, the life forces, fertility, "getting high" or tripping, and the appearance of phantoms. Though some of the lines appear to be on a more refined plane than is easily perceived by our basic senses, animals seem to have sensory organs which enable them to perceive such energies.

Other ancient structures associated with standing stones and blind springs are mounds of earth in circular or elongated shapes, known as barrows, believed by archeologists to be mere tombs, but which, in fact, may be "enliveners"—initiatory chambers designed, as is reputed of the Great Pyramid, to awaken the spirit from its hypnotic trance within the body. Whether or not they contain a sepulcher, barrows are built of alternating layers of organic and inorganic matter. Varying from 15 to 150 feet in diameter, there are more than twenty thousand round barrows in Britain alone, though many have been destroyed by farming. On the crest of the hills surrounding Avebury there were once fourteen such round barrows. In the Americas there may have been a hundred thousand.

Long barrows in Britain are dated by archeologists from Neolithic times. About two hundred survive. They are mounds of earth and chalk, 4 to 20 feet high, mostly from 100 to 300 feet long and 30 to 100 feet wide. Set over one or more blind springs, they are mostly oriented east and west, to face the rising and setting sun at the equinox.

Michell believes that chambers in these barrows, made of alternating organic and inorganic material, which is the requirement for a Reichian orgone accumulator, once served that purpose and were used for healing and for expanding consciousness. He and others have noted that these ancient sites are linked in a network that covers all of Britain in a multidimensional ramification of forces—mercurial, or quicksilver lines, as they are called, the domain since antiquity, of Toth, Hermes, Mercury, or Saint Michael.

American mounds are, or were, wonders comparable to the pyramids of Egypt, their origin almost as mysterious today as when they were first discovered by immigrants traveling west. Atlantean experts such as Egerton Sykes and Henrietta Mertz are convinced that at least the eastern United States was once part of the Atlantean Empire and that the extraordinary artifacts found in American barrows were the product of descendants of refugees from sunken Atlantis—a notion as quickly derided by conservative archeologists as has been the incontrovertible evidence produced by Barry Fell and his fellow epigraphers of the presence in "Lost America" of Phoenicians, Libyans, Egyptians, Celtiberians, Hittites, and a whole chain of European and Mediterranean followers. Silbury Hill, the largest such mound in England, which, like the Pyramid of Cheops, served, among other purposes, to mark the equinoxes and solstices, is estimated by Richard Atkinson to have required the carefully directed work of 500 men for fifteen years—"a fraction of the gross national product at least as great as that devoted by the United States of America to the whole of its space program."

Graves has also noted a distinct correlation between megalithic sites and weather patterns—particularly of rainfall and thunderstorm activity, as noted from the weather distribution maps of Britain. He says that he has observed during a thunderstorm that standing stones and church spires gain a visible nimbus, becoming actual glowing points in the landscape. He believes this happens because they collect charge from the springs and streams below them. He says that standing stones have a thunderstorm-control ability similar to lightning conductors. He even plays with the notion that the energy of thunderstorms may somehow be stored in barrows, as energy reservoirs. This may clarify why witches were traditionally credited with the ability to control the weather, and particularly to raise storms.

Graves goes further, believing that standing stones and circles not only controlled thunderstorms in the past; they still do. Megalithic sites, he says, are in the right places, and their shapes and semiconductor properties are such as to help the production of an "electric wind." Dowsers have certainly found that lightning usually strikes directly above the intersection of two or more water lines. Dowsers say that a conductor, placed directly over or even close to a water line, or, better, at an intersection of water lines, should be able to collect charge from the whole area underlying the stream. The effect of a lightning conductor connected to water lines would be to change a potentially violent thunderstorm into an ordinary rainstorm.

The Washington Monument attracting a bolt of lightning

Graves illustrates two ways in which thunderstorms may be controlled by the stone-and-barrow system. In the upper drawing a stone collecting negative charge from an underground stream attracts the positively charged cloud, which is neutralized by releasing its rain. In the lower illustration the subterranean stream draws charge from the cloud and stores it in the barrow, which either leaks it back slowly into the sky through the stone or collects a neutralizing charge from the water flow.

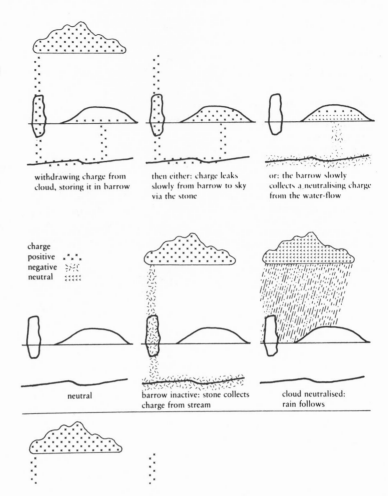

withdrawing charge from cloud, storing it in barrow

then either: charge leaks slowly from barrow to sky via the stone

or: the barrow slowly collects a neutralising charge from the water-flow

charge
positive
negative
neutral

neutral

barrow inactive: stone collects charge from stream

cloud neutralised: rain follows

All of which was incontrovertibly demonstrated in real life in modern times by Wilhelm Reich, who showed the relation between lightning and vivifying orgone. In the most scientific manner he accumulated and dispelled great clouds, at will, producing rain where it was wanted; and in the quantities required, or turning the sky back to blue.

In the course of the these experiments, Reich discovered that the orgone energy assumed two forms, "orgone radiation," or OR, and "deadly orgone radiation," or DOR. The former, the healthy manifestation, can be sensed according to Reich as a feeling of "life" and brightness in the atmosphere, visible as bright fast-moving dots of light, or a haze of blue. DOR, on the other hand, is responsible for "dullness" and bleakness in the atmosphere, of the sort that builds up on days before a big storm.

In Chinese geomancy, or *feng shui,* energy flows along the earth's meridians in an interplay of the two prime

This adaptation from Wilhelm Reich's *Selected Writings*, (Noonday Press, 1960) shows the cloud-buster system he developed at Orgonon, Maine, where he accumulated and discharged rain from a cloud by pointing directly at it 10-foot hollow steel tubes mounted on the back of an old anti-aircraft gun carriage, grounding the received energy into a running stream. If the tubes were aimed near, but not at the cloud, they would cause it to expand and hold more moisture. It was Reich's premise that a hollow tube will push or pull "orgone" energy, which can then be carried away by running water.

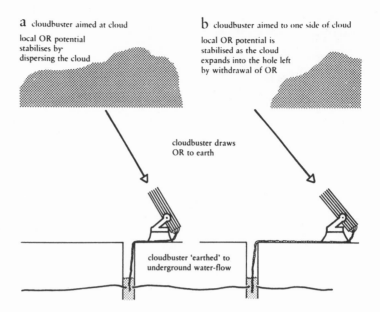

a cloudbuster aimed at cloud

local OR potential stabilises by dispersing the cloud

b cloudbuster aimed to one side of cloud

local OR potential is stabilised as the cloud expands into the hole left by withdrawal of OR

cloudbuster draws OR to earth

cloudbuster 'earthed' to underground water-flow

forces of yin and yang; the product is know as either *ch'i* or *sha*. The former occurs when yin and yang fuse together in harmony. The latter occurs where they are out of balance, where the primal energies are separated and stagnant. What is this but Reich's chief cause of neurotic ailments in humans—sexual stasis—applied to Mother Earth?

A clear parallel between the British system of standing stones and ley lines and a combination of Chinese *feng-shui* and acupuncture, is drawn by British dowsers. To Graves, Britain's geomancy has every indication of having been a system of earth acupuncture with sacred sites as acupuncture points on energy channels, both sinuous and straight, with standing stones as massive needles, designed to promote a healthy, sexy, fertile earth.

Michell, again, is poetically specific: "These upright stones were essential to the great work of alchemy, which

charge neutralised

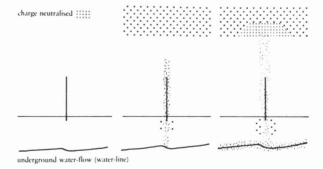

Graves demonstrates how a lightning conductor placed over a waterline can collect charge from an underground water flow and "literally spray charge up into the sky," causing the same Saint Elmo's fire which so distressed the sailors on the *Cleopatra*.

underground water-flow (water-line)

383

Tantric tradition describes over 300,000 nadis, or channels of vital force permeating the physical form through which solar and lunar energies ebb and flow to animate the subtler body. Connected to these nadis, the seven chakras are seen as receivers and distributors of the negative lunar and positive solar energies which spiral around the spinal cord, along the path used to raise the kundalini.

formed the climax of all prehistoric ritual, the introduction of solar or atmospheric energy into the terrestrial life current. It is well known that flashes of lightning have an effect on the nitrates of the earth, through which they can be absorbed by plants, thus ensuring the seasonal return of fertility. This process, regarded in the past as the act of union between the earth and the heavens, is indeed necessary for the continuation of life; for if there is no lightning, the earth becomes barren. In order that plants should grow, it is necessary to fuse the electrical current of the atmosphere with the streams of terrestrial energy." In man, energy permeates the body by flowing along the twelve meridians of the acupuncturist from one to the next in a set sequence, making a complete cycle in twenty-four hours, controlled by the sun whose rays are reflected by the moon.

Because the landscape has no obvious organs, no arms, legs, or head, dowsers assume there must be even more meridians or energy lines on the body of earth than on the human body, and that they would be laid out in a far less obvious way than in human acupuncture. In such a system of earth acupuncture, what, asks Graves, could be a more obvious "needle" than a standing stone? Noting that it could be dangerous to use stone needles to heal the land without a suitable and safe means of disposing and dispersing the collected *sha* or DOR drawn up through an earth stake, Graves suggests that the barrow-and-stone weather-control systems were, in fact, designed for just such a dispersal.

But the employment of needles is only part of acupuncture, which also uses moxibustion, or controlled fire. Our civilization, says Graves, has completely concealed the ancient magical use of fire—the beacon fires on Old Beacon Hills. Graves tells of having been with a ley-hunter team at the Dunstable bonfire festival where he enjoyed an extraordinary sense of unity, of nonverbal communication—"so rare in our civilization"—which he and the others felt as each bonfire was lit and linked with the others. Michell describes the scene: "From hilltop to hilltop, the light struck straight across the country, reflected in ponds and moats, transmitted by flashing mirrors, celebrated with music and singing, the whole line illuminated by the flames and by the heavenly light."

As in acupuncture, most of the problems in our modern landscape, says Graves, stem from blockages and disturbances of energy flows, arising from insensitive man-made causes: motorways, high-voltage lines, mining and quarrying. Modern organization has the noxious effect of blocking a natural flow in the energy matrix. Electric pylons appear to have an especially deleterious effect on the fertility of the land.

Another function of the standing stones may have been to communicate from point to point. Analyzing the forces at play on a standing stone, Graves notes that as well as the flow of orgone to and from a needle, underground water flows can produce a regular mechanical vibration in a stone, which can be used to carry a signal.

Screeton visualizes the ancients as transmitting messages on standing stones by tapping. He says that in order to pick up the modulated currents, they would use the palm of their hands against the stone, retransmitting the signals by their nervous system to the pineal gland. In other words, they would transmit the message to the mental receptive consciousness and then to the spiritual consciousness.

A number of correspondents, says Graves, have told him that the transmission of complete mental images, or telepathy, is much easier between sacred sites than elsewhere. Graves describes how the King Stone at Rollright was linked to more than a dozen other stones and believes that, if all the minor and irregular links are included, as many as a hundred more could have been linked into Rollright, creating a vast telephone exchange of stone circles and standing stones; from which it would appear that telepathic communication in the present, and clairvoyant communication with the future or the past may be effected through the same occult medium.

The presence of certain types of quartz in standing stones, and most especially in the granite obelisks of Egypt, leads Graves to postulate the possibility of their acting as a sort of stone maser or, as he puns, "leyser." Quartz, in its smallest unit, consists of three molecules of silicon dioxide, arranged in a spiral or screw form, either right- or left-handed. It has the power of rotating in either direction the plane of polarization of light.

Graves finds a parallel between the quartz "seeds" in limestone and the chrome atoms in a ruby, from which a laser can be fashioned. He suggests that it might be possible for the mechanical vibration from the stream of water below a standing stone, or the spiraling energy flow around the stone ("and note," he adds, "the analogy with the old laser spiral flash-tube"), or both, to provide energy to be stored in the quartz "seeds." As with a ruby laser, says Graves, this energy storage should reach a critical or supercritical state, at which time a suitable stimulus could set the whole thing off. He considers a

Graves describes seven energy bands as appearing on standing stones as well as on buttresses. In the illustration (a) is a "Christianized" stone near Postbridge in Devon; (b) is at Rollright; and (c) is the northeast buttress of nearby Knowlton Church. All are drawn to scale, and all, says Graves, are tapping points into a spiral release of some sort of energy. He describes the narrow bands as a "double strength geomagnetic field running horizontally across the stone at various heights." The bands are said to move up and down, following what appears to be a lunar cycle. Two of the bands are usually below ground level; the top one is very close to the peak of the stone.

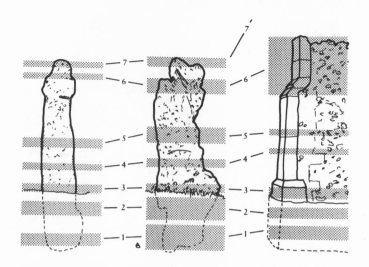

suitable stimulus to be a gravitational alignment of sun, moon, or planets, which could result in a massive pulse of energy traveling in a straight line—just such a pulse as he accidentally released at Rollright, and which appeared to travel away at right angles to the standing stone.

A German dowsing magazine, quoted by Graves, warns that it is important to beware of quartz in buildings when dealing with "earth engines," for they "change the plane of the radiations from the vertical to the horizontal." Thus, says Graves, if quartz can turn its own "radiations" from the vertical to the horizontal, we would appear to have our "leyser."

The frequency of a crystal's resonance depends on its size, shape, and cut. Were the Egyptian obelisks, which are largely quartz, deliberately cut and shaped like a wireless crystal to vibrate synchronously with another transmitter, the vibrations transmitted through earth like a system of telegraphy? Or were they wireless, going from point to point on ground leyser beams pulsing from quartz?

Such a system would explain how the ancient Egyptians could have used a row of obelisks stretching from the delta to the cataracts—if not to the equator—to transmit instant information of great help in geodetic and astronomical observation. Used east and west, they would resolve the mystery of how the ancients plotted longitude with such extraordinary accuracy, as is evident from a whole series of mysterious prehistoric maps.

Other dowsers describe overgrounds and waterlines as able to carry a code or modulated signal. There are several dimensions in which water can carry a coding, the most obvious being with physical substances, either in solution or suspension. The key, says Graves, is the bent structure of the water molecule. Water that has been blessed or affected by a psychic (such as was demonstrated by the healer Olga Worrall when she changed the molecular structure of water by irradiating it with her hands) is recognizably different, and at some level may be a carrier of nonphysical or metaphysical messages.

Carlos Castaneda describes what he calls his personality traveling along water courses, apparently for hundreds of miles; which suggests to Graves that water lines as well as overground leys could be used to assist astral traveling. A modern magician told Graves that astral traveling, or projection of the inner personality, is made easier by hitching a ride on the energy that passes along "ley lines" and "overgrounds." And the *feng-shui* concept of "spirit paths," or clearly marked pathways on which the spirits of the dead may travel, suggests, as the Egyptian *Book of the Dead* elaborates, that astral traveling is as much for the dead as for the living.

Did the witches astrally ride the ley lines to their midnight sabbaths at megalithic sites?

18. DIANA AND THE HORNED GOD

The large phallic stone at Rollright stands on a lonely Cotswold hill by a prehistoric yonic circle 20 miles from the villages of Long Compton and Chipping Norton. In a nearby field, as a witness, stands a cromlech of large stones called by the natives Whispering Knights, silent now except in a high wind. For centuries, if not millennia, Rollright has been a gathering site for witches. On a recent night of full moon, with the soft scent of summer, a coven of witches was dancing around the standing stones to celebrate their sabbath—it was May 12, 1949. Eyewitnesses tell of men and women chanting and dancing under the direction of a leader wearing a goat-bearded mask. An even more recent ceremony at Rollright was described with pictures in *Life International* of May 1964.

The Rollright Stones

Witches performing at Rollright from an article in *Life International* of May 1964

Such ceremonies were possible, after almost half a millennium of witch-burning, because in England, on January 3, 1951, the law against witchcraft was stricken from the books. It had been a long, painful siege since that December 5, 1484, when the appointee of the butcher, Torquemeda, issued a bull, as Innocent VIII, in which he deplored the prevalence of witches and empowered two Dominican monks, Heinrich Kraemer and Jacob Sprenger,

389

Innocent VIII (1484–1492) issued the papal bull *Summis desiderantes effectibus,* which served as justification for pitiless persecution. The bull was prefixed to the Inquisitors' textbook, *Malleus maleficarum,* and called on the wrath of God Almighty against all who did not comply. In his last months, Innocent was kept alive by sucking milk from a young woman's breast, and an attempt to rejuvenate him by blood transfusions resulted in the death of three boys. Contemporary Catholic chroniclers note that he kept a mistress by whom he had two children—a boy who married into the Medicis, and a girl whom he married to his papal treasurer.

to launch a holy war against "this satanic sect." Kraemer and Sprenger were ordered to be given every assistance by bishop, priest, and lay authority. As guidelines for the monstrous pogrom of witches that was to ensue, the two holy brothers produced a primer, the *Malleus maleficorum,* which went into details as gruesome as possible to enable dutiful Inquisitors to force confessions from a tortured body. It became the standard manual for witch-hunting and witch extermination. Michael Harrison, in *The Roots of Witchcraft,* adds the cynical note that the two Dominicans, unable to obtain for so horrid a script approval from the Cologne University censors charged by the Pope with vetting it, resorted to the same device used for the Donation of Constantine: "Nothing daunted, this precious pair of rascals proceeded to forge a document which purported to show the approbation of the Cologne faculty."

As an incentive to the Inquisitors to ferret out their heretical bunnies, it was decreed that the property of a condemned witch was to be divided, after the costs of the trial had been deducted, between Inquisitors and State, with a bonus for informers. And not all witches were poor. The first one condemned in England, Dame Alice Kyteler of Kilkenny, was of considerable means. For the rest, there was that depraved compulsion, described by Wilhelm Reich as the "emotional plague," whereby a pox of sexually malfunctioning "armored" individuals, unable to enjoy the pleasure of natural lovemaking, set about relieving their pent-up sexuality through ripping, tearing, and burning the very flesh they could neither kiss, caress, nor inflame with pleasure.

The *Malleus* gave detailed instructions for the selection of suspected witches who could then be tortured until they confessed. If a prisoner muttered, looked at the ground, or did not shed tears, he or she was suspect. As most of the witches were shes, the administration of torture to their frail bodies was both easier and more rewarding.

According to the Church, somewhere on the body of a female witch, the "devil" left his mark, the most obvious of which was a supernumerary nipple—sure sign of dedication to the many-breasted goddess Diana, queen of the witches. And, as the modern medical profession estimates that three out of a hundred women have such vestiges, the chances of netting a witch were considerable. When nothing like a mole or birthmark came readily to finger, it was argued that the mark must have been applied in a subtler manner which required the investigator to indulge in closer scrutiny by totally stripping the suspect naked and subjecting her to a minute inspection, often in front of

390

a crowd of pruriently curious onlookers, ostensibly impelled to the scene by their religious duty.

To increase the number of hits, the subtle notion was concocted that the devil's mark left a spot insensible to pain, only discernible by an inspector probing with a sharp prick. Thus was raised a whole guild of "witch-prickers," paid only when they discovered a witch, which led to the foolproof system of using an auxiliary retractable prick. The pricker, having painfully, and visibly, drawn blood from several spots on a naked victim, would painlessly plunge the substitute bodkin to the hilt, astounding the crowd, and ensuring his fee for a witch delivered to trial.

Diana's supernumerary nipples were also frowned upon by the majority of moralists because the goddess, with her unbounded generative and nurturing power, could indiscriminately suckle one and all.

Kraemer and Sprenger in *The Hammer of Witches* based their authority for burning witches partly on the teachings of Thomas Aquinas, who maintained there were servants of the devil "more subtle and more dangerous than the heretics"—the witches; and partly on a totally specious reading of Chapter 15 of the Gospel according to Saint John: "If a man abide not in me, he is cast forth as a branch, and is withered; and men gather them, and cast them into the fire, and they are burned."

Any blemish on a woman's body—wart, mole, scar, or birthmark—could be used by the Inquisitor as a mark of the devil, sufficient to charge her with witchcraft.

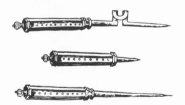

Regular and retractable prickers

The Devil's mark

Placed in the hands of the actual Inquisitors, the women were scrutinized even further by having the hair of their pudenda shaved and the folds minutely inspected on the excuse that therein was likely to be hidden a small parchment with a magic sigil to use as a talisman against feeling the forthcoming pain of torture. Immediate and sadistic rape of the victim became so common that bishops had to pronounce against the practice. "The victims," report the chronicles, "were so barbarously used that modesty forbids to mention it."

And the chronicles are truly amazing. In 1599 at Dôle, in France, a woman named Antide Collas, found with an

391

Matthew Hopkins, an unsuccessful attorney, with a pretended commission from Cromwell's Parliament naming him Witch-Finder General, spent two years running down women whose pets might incarnate witches' familiars. In England he revived round-the-clock torture and the medieval ordeal of tossing women into rivers to see if they would drown or if the devil would save them to be burned. He was responsible for several hundred executions before being brought to account for illegal profiteering.

abnormality in her sexual conformation that was regarded as explicable only by her having had shameful intercourse with Satan, was repeatedly stripped and scrutinized by doctors and judges, until her disability was officially described as *"un trou qu'elle avait au dessous de sa parti gorrière."* Repeatedly put to torture, the poor woman confessed to having received the deformity from the penis of Satan, and was therefore ritually burned at the stake.

In those rare countries where the torture of witches was illegal, as in England, confessions could still be obtained by the more modern methods of binding the suspect naked to a stool without food or sleep for as many hours or days as it took to break her will; or by walking the victim up and down for days until her feet blistered and

If a victim refused to confess, he or she was subjected to three grades of torture: by cord, by water, and by fire—all in the name of Most Merciful Christ. Torture by cord meant being raised and lowered in jerks to dislocate arms. If this failed to elicit a confession, the victim was flogged and then stretched on the rack till all his members were disjointed. The water cure consisted of having a silk ribbon stuffed down the throat and as many as thirty pints of water forced along it into the body, causing pain beyond description. As an alternative, a cloth was laid over the face so that water poured onto it virtually drowned the victim. Torture by fire meant having one's feet placed in stocks with the soles well greased, so that a blazing brazier could blister and fry them. More painful but less fatal than racking, this torture was in vogue for females, and for a child required to testify against its parents.

Torture was supposed to be administered only once, and be limited to one hour, but if the torturers stopped just short of the hour they could renew the torment indefinitely, varying the fare by inserting red-hot needles under finger and toenails, ripping out the nails with tongs, crushing thumbs in thumbscrews, or reducing the victim's foot to pulp in a leg crusher. Other subtleties were being broken on the wheel and being pierced by an Iron Maiden. To determine how long a victim could be tortured without risk of dying, a physician was present, usually a barber whose sole knowledge of healing was to let blood, apply leeches, or amputate a limb. If the victim confessed under the first bout of torture, he was allowed to be tortured again to ascertain his motives for confessing, and again to induce him to betray his accomplices or sympathizers, accusations which were in turn sufficient to convict a friend or stranger, irrespective of guilt or innocence.

her mind wandered. But of all the systems, the simplest— heads I win, tails you lose—was to bind the witch's thumbs to her big toes and throw her into deep water. If she floated—on the grounds that having rejected the water of baptism, the water now rejected her—she was considered a witch. If she sank, she drowned.

On the Continent, an accused witch could be given two hundred lashes on her bare back before being sent to torture. Teen-age girls were regularly stripped by notaries and scourged until they confessed or agreed to bear testimony against others, including their mothers.

What most interested the Inquisitors was a female victim's description of intercourse with an incubus—a male demon—which they believed to be of extraordinary voluptuous pleasure to the witch. The authors of *Malleus,* declaring such demons to be visible only to the witch, described how a bystander might yet be able to enjoy the sight: "The witches have often been seen lying on their backs in the fields or woods, naked up to the navel, and it has been apparent from the disposition of their limbs and members which pertain to the venereal act and orgasm, as also from the agitation of their legs and thighs, that, all

393

invisible to the bystanders, they have been copulating with
Incubus devils; yet sometimes, howbeit this is rare, at the
end of the act, a very black vapour, of about the stature
of a man, rises up into the air from the witch.''

As a result of the *Malleus*'s system of questioning,
thousands of confessions were extracted from women,
young and old, in exact conformity with the blueprint
questions predetermined by the holy brothers Kraemer
and Sprenger. All the judges required was that the victims,
under agonizing torture, confirm what they were reported
to have done. With no hope of surviving, they would
confess, knowing that if they did so, they stood a chance
of avoiding having their tongues cut out on the way to the
stake, or their mouths scored with a red-hot poker; they
might even be mercifully strangled as the fires were lit,
instead of being burned alive—no small consolation when
it took a minimum half hour to die from smoke and
blistering—an ordeal which could be stretched to as long
as a day by the application of slow-burning charcoal.

In Munich, of eleven victims on the way to the stake, six had their flesh torn with red-hot pincers, five had their limbs broken on the wheel, one woman had her breasts sliced off, and one man was impaled through the anus with a lance. At Chamonix, in 1462, a woman found guilty of prostituting herself to demons was made to sit naked on a red-hot iron for three minutes before being tied to the stake for burning. All of which was officially done *ad majorem dei gloriam;* and after the burnings, public dinners were held to celebrate "an act pleasing to God."

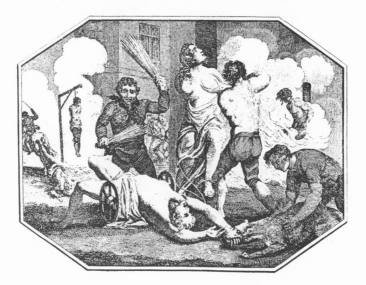

395

Various historians specializing in witchcraft, such as the Swiss authority Dr. Guido Bader, estimate that a hundred thousand witches were burned in Germany alone between the fourteenth and eighteenth centuries; the number of victims throughout Europe may be comparable to the millions of Jews far more charitably disposed of by Hitler.

From a Catholic point of view, this gruesome carnage was considered essential, since witchcraft was an overt manifestation of the old pagan religion, which threatened, if it were allowed to flourish, to sweep away the religion of Rome. For the truly believing Inquisitor to destroy a human body with fire was essentially an act of mercy if it meant saving a soul from the torment of eternal fire. To the Catholic, death of the soul through "sin" was worse than death of the body through fire, and sexuality, other than for strict procreation, preferably without pleasure, was the cardinal sin, whetted by all manner of life's desirable experiences, such as feasting, wining, dancing, singing, and being free and naked together. All of which were afforded by the witch's sabbat, a ritual which, when compared with the self-accusatory, misery-ridden worship

To historian Margaret Murray witchcraft was a highly organized "Old Religion" practiced and protected by French and English royalty (as late as under Henry VIII) and by many clergymen who secretly joined in the rites worshiping the horned god and the Mother goddess, even engaging in ritual intercourse and the indiscriminate copulation practiced by the ancient Egyptians and Gnostics, whose rites were precursors of the witches' sabbath.

of the Catholic symbols of pain and death on the cross, was welcomed by the older religionists as beautiful and exciting. Why else would so many witches have risked torture and an agonizing death to attend the sabbat? It was a spiritual, other-dimensional experience as well as a physical pleasure.

There were two kinds of sabbat: one with real bodies, which took place by moonlight in some desolate spot; and the other, to which the witch could travel out-of-body, usually thanks to some psychedelic drug, in what came to be known as the "astral plane," there to cavort with the goddess Diana and her playmates.

That the witches used a special salve to teletransport themselves to this second kind of sabbat has been known since 1600, when Giovanni Battista Porta, in his *Magiae*

The Roman initiate Lucius Apuleius, in his pre-Christian romance of witchcraft, *The Golden Ass,* described seducing Pamphile's maid Fotis to allow him to watch her naked mistress anoint herself with a magic unguent. That he got turned into an ass and had to eat the roses of Isis to be redeemed only adds to the Rosicrucian flavor of the allegory.

397

naturalis, gave the recipe which contained herbane, belladonna, and mandrake. The resulting ointment, known as "lifting balm," was said to be viscous, with a repulsive green-black color, and an offensive odor. Porta, founder of the Academy of Secrets in Rome, whose meetings were interdicted by the same Clement VIII who burned Bruno, was a teacher of science and inventor of the *camera obscura,* and is credited by John Weisse with being an Italian representative of the Rosicrucians.

Reginald Scot, in his *Discoverie of Witchcraft,* published in 1584, describes naked witches rubbing "all parts of their bodies exceedingly, till they look red, and be very hot, so as the pores may be opened and their flesh soluble and loose. . . ." Scot describes how, on a moonlit night, witches "believe themselves to be carried in the air to feasting, singing, dancing, kissing, culling and other acts of venery with such youths as they love and desire."

More specific are descriptions of witches applying the salve to their labia minora by means of an anointed

An ancient recipe for transvecting ointments is given in *Witchcraft and the Mysteries:* "Grind together into a paste of sufficient quantity to anoint the entire body of the following: *Acarum vulgare,* the blood of a bat, parsley cinquefoil, aconite, yellow watercress, belladonna, sweet flag and pure olive oil in equal parts of half a palm. When this ointment has been kneaded into the consistency of a viscous, light oil, massage it into the naked body covering all parts. Rub vigorously until the skin 'look red and be very hot, so the pores will be open and the flesh loose and pliable.' Finally, face an open window (or door, or lie flat upon a hearth in front of a chimney that is not obstructed to the top) and rub the limbs with pure olive oil, which will seal . . . the skin, that the force of the ointment may rather pierce inwardly, and so be more effectual."
Ancient Druids, like modern shamans, claim to be able to accomplish magical flights out of the body. Following the dictates of Hermes Trismegistus, the witches sought to separate from their physical selves and travel

398

on the astral plane in what theosophists call their "Body of Light." To project the finer body and acquire the faculty of functioning in it, as well as to educate it to fulfill one's wishes was, and is, a fundamental practice of magic. But Israel Regardie, a Reichian therapist and adept of magic, points out that to leave the physical body bereft of its guiding intelligence "is tantamount to extending an open invitation to whatever astral entity, malignant or otherwise, is in the vicinity to take possession." The return to the body, says Regardie, must be attended to with care and precaution. "Upon entering the physical frame a few deep breaths should be deliberately undertaken in order to ensure the close conjoining of the two organisms." John Michell goes further and suggests that Druids and shamans appear to have been able to accomplish magical flights *within* their physical bodies, "often from those very mounds and hilltops where the great heroes of mythology achieved their apotheosis." He adds that there may be something about such places "which attracts those forces capable of modifying the normal influences of gravity, or which, alternately, reacts upon an intensified field of human magnetism to produce circumstances conductive to levitation." Michell then describes how the Druids may have flown. "On the eve of the day when the line, on which stood a chambered mound, became animated by the rising sun, they would enter the mound, seal the entrance and spend the night in accumulating a degree of energy by which the animal magnetism of their bodies became raised to an active pitch. The appearance of the morning sun, stimulating a current of terrestrial magnetism all down the line to the mound, would act on the body charged with energy, enabling it to levitate and to move along paths of a certain level of magnetic intensity." To which Michell soberly adds that as the suggestion has not been proved by experiment, it obviously still leaves a great deal unexplained.

"broomstick." Albert Barrere and Charles Godfrey Leland in their 1899 *A Dictionary of Slang, Jargon and Cant,* equate the term broom handle with the word *dildo,* and the word *broom,* or *plantaginesta,* with the female pudenda.

From various accounts it appears that the broom head was often carved in the shape of a phallus complete with a glans, discreetly disguised by the addition of the broom—a symbol and an artifact in one.

Discussing the greasing of the broomstick and the "nakedness of the rider" Michael Harrison suggests that the word *ride* in this context is but a euphemism for "sexual congress." He further suggests that such phrases as *between witches' legs* are also euphemisms for "inserted" between or within. "Here we have, in the fourteenth and seventeenth centuries," says Harrison, "one of the most ancient ritual objects to be found in religious celebrations, the "ὄλιδβος, olisbos, of boiled or moulded leather, that the sexually excited woman bore in the Bacchic processions; the less 'religious' but more personal surrogate—penis against whose use the German bishops thundered during the thirteenth and fourteenth centuries and, indeed, the artificial penis worn and used by the 'Devil' of the Sabbats."

By placing the anointed broom handle between her lips and prancing around, the witch may clearly have induced a psychedelic trance during which she believed she flew with Diana "to keep a tryst with the Incarnate God." Better to be affected by the salve, the witches appear to have rigorously fasted and abstained from sex for several days before a sabbat. The fifteenth-century author known as Abraham the Jew, writing in *The Book of Sacred Magic,* describes how he watched a witch anoint herself. He says she fell to the ground and lay there for three hours as if dead, and that on regaining consciousness, told him she had flown.

To establish the scientific veracity of this phenomenon, Dr. Erich-Will Peuckert of the University of Göttingen, in Germany, recently mixed up a potion of the salve as directed, with herbane, deadly nightshade, wild celery, and hog's lard, in order to perform an exhaustive experiment. He and a colleague—deliberately kept uninformed as to what might be expected—anointed their bodies with Porta's ingredients, and each fell into a deep sleep which lasted twenty-four hours. When they awoke, each separately wrote his report. To their mutual amazement, each found that he had enjoyed virtually the same erotic dream of flying to a mountaintop and participating in wild orgiastic rites with "demons."

The devil, or Satan, a Judeo-Christian idea, possibly borrowed from the Mesopotamians, was taken and turned by the Dominicans into a useful PR prop for their distorted propaganda. Onto the horned god of the pagan ritual—happy, sexy, wining and dancing and fluting—they foisted a harsh, evil, vindictive, scatological damning-with-hellfire monster—a reflection of their own tormented souls. As Reich has so remarkably documented, obscenity is all in the eye of the beholder, and unwilling or enforced sexual abstinence, far from leading to a Freudian sublimation, is more liable to turn into a self-castrating, voyeuristic compulsion to control, imprison, torture, and execute, the last at last affording the executioner the relief of a dispersal of energy in the form of a black "orgasm."

Occultists explain the experience of these *terre à terre* scientists sharing a similar dream by saying they "traveled" on the inner, or "astral," plane, a more rarefied world, whose substance is described as responsive to both thought and emotion, where one exists during sleep, trance, or after death, in what is known as the body of "desire," the ka of the Egyptian, the kama rupa of the Hindu.

Occultists see the universe as multidimensional interpenetrating worlds, vibrating at different frequencies, with what we call the physical only a restricted part of the spectrum. The energy in the astral world, they consider to vibrate at a higher rate than the physical; but once the adept, using his astral body, learns to handle the bodies of the astral world, they too become solid to the touch.

The secret astral world to which the witch flies in her astral body, by means of an ecstasy-producing unguent—while her physical body lies asleep or in a trance—is described as being divided into seven layers, the highest of which is said to be of extreme beauty, whereas the lowest is frequented by debased souls. Travelers are inclined to exist on the level to which they belong spiritually, like attracting like. It is a world filled by the occultist with many orders of spirits, some of a caliber lower than humans, others much higher. And it is the world

400

Kenneth Grant gives a simple formula for evoking a succubus: Sleep should be preceded by some form of *karezza* (or sexual intercourse continued without reaching orgasm), during which a sigil symbolizing the desired object is visualized. "In this manner libido is baulked of its natural fantasies and seeks satisfaction in the dream world." Grant adds that when the knack has been acquired the dream can be extremely intense and dominated by a succube, or shadow woman, with whom sexual intercourse occurs spontaneously. The modern expert on witchery, Doreen Valiente, tells of a girl she knows who was loath to have an incubus exorcised because it gave her such sexual pleasure and thrills as she had never experienced from a man. Osman Austin Spare, whose early drawing shows a psychic sexual transport, was said to be able to materialize atavisms from his subconscious and clothe them fleetingly in the sexual ectoplasm (or astral semen) of his "atmospheric copulations." Grant says that occasionally these entities could actually achieve a degree of density sufficient to make them visible and even palpable to other people. Spare called these apparitions "elemental automata" or "intrusive familiars," and says they "frequently copulated among themselves, engendering offspring simultaneously." With them he describes attending sabbaths. But the danger of such acts becoming obsessive or compulsive is indicated by Grant, who says that "such was his hunger that in one night he copulated with eighteen women, calling these outbursts: Dionysiac spasms of pansexualism in which he had visions of all things fornicating all the time." Even so, such transport may be less spiritually degrading than the burning of a witch or the torture of a wise one.

of elementals, both "authentic" and "artificial," the latter being described as formed by thought or desire from the tenuous material of the astral plane, beautiful or hideous, protective or menacing, depending on the thought or emotion which has given them life. This they explain as the world of the witch's elementals, of the incubus and the succubus, created by desire, and rendered more or less sexy by the degree of the dreamer's desire. It is a world quite as real to psychologists as it is to occultists. Jean Marquès-Rivière, in his *Tantric Yoga,* says that through Prayoga, "it is possible to visualise and animate certain female entities who are called *succubes.*" And Arthur Avalon, in *The Serpent Power,* corroborates that through Prayoga "commerce is had with female spirits."

Modern adepts of Tantric or sexual magic suggest that witches can indeed have "offspring" from their intercourse with incubi, but that these creatures are produced on the astral plane, where any discharge of energy from the physical plane invariably has an effect. Adepts claim that ejaculated semen, whether lodged in the womb or not, still manages to contribute to the creation of forms of a subtler nature. The flow produced by masturbation, sodomy, or fellatio is said by occultists to be taken up by astral entities to reinforce weak organisms already preexisting on the subtler plane. Thus are created the homunculi of the medievalist.

The actual live-bodied sabbat would have had as one of its purposes the initiation of a witch into the art of spiriting herself out of her physical body into the astral world of Diana and Pan. Having learned the ropes, she could apply the unguent at home and astrally meet with her playmates anytime she chose, freed from the miserable bondage of life in a Church-dominated Europe.

Goya's witches

With all this wonderland at the end of a broomstick, it is clear why the witch risked practicing the craft, and *knowing* herself to be, at heart, a spiritual creature with a whole world of similar playmates, she might have come to care less what the executioner did with her mortal body. She might even have learned the mysteries of becoming stable enough out of the body to rise to a level of power at which she could watch, as if self-hypnotized, her body being burned without feeling the pain, as is said to have been the case with some of the Anglican martyrs burned by Bloody Mary, who, wise to their tormenters' folly, could smile and bless their claybound executioners.

Of the actual flesh-and-blood sabbats, rather than the purely "tripping" routines—though there were presumably astral features in both—the most convincing historical analysis is to be found in the two twentieth-century classics of Margaret Alice Murray, *The God of the Witches* and *The Witch Cult in Western Europe.* Discredited by her academic colleagues because she supported James Frazer's *Golden Bough* theories of the sacrificed king, and because she was an Egyptologist rather than strictly a historian of their limited disciplines, Murray nevertheless admirably develops the notion of the sabbat as a ceremony of the Old Religion of the horned God, worshiped for thousands of years, going back to the Egyptian Khoum. She describes how, for camouflage, on the way to the sabbat, the witches, male and female, wore the familiar black-hooded cloaks, so as not to have their features easily recognized.

The sabbat proper, in which any number of covens of witches might participate, was the main ceremony of the craft, celebrated eight times a year on the same days as the Druid festivals of Candlemas (or Walpurgisnacht), Lammas, Halloween, and, of course, the perennial astral stations of the solar orb, the solstices and equinoxes. A lesser festival, the Esbat—from the French to "frolic," or "leave one's worries at home"—was generally celebrated by no more than a single coven of thirteen witches, at the full moon, thirteen times a year.

For further security, the more intimate Esbat might take place in a spooky, lunar spot such as a graveyard, whereas the larger sabbats, more numerously attended, were likely to be held in remote and desolate spots such as Rolling Rock, with its megalithic remains. Many sites in England still carry the names of the former rituals performed at them, such as the Seven Sisters and Dancing Maidens.

403

Witches perform their rites in the nude within a circle prepared with a consecrated knife, or athane, by high priest or priestess of the coven. By the athane, means of the "astral light" and its denizens can be dispelled or dispersed, and by molding the "astral," or orgone, field within the circle, a protective and power-charged cone can be raised, visible and directable by the will of the coven. Within this circle usually stands an altar with the Tarot symbols of Pentacle for earth, Wand for air, Sword for fire, and Chalice for water. There are also candles, salt, a censer, a bell, and a scourge—the latter not less likely a means of mild control than—as discovered by Reich—a means for liberating sexual energy, so pent-up by enforced restriction that it can no longer find its natural genital outlet. Witches were initiated into three degrees of the craft, with rites similar to those of the Templars, requiring "the fivefold kiss" on feet, knees, groin, breast and lips.

The object of the initiations was spiritual and psychic development of each individual, teaching them how to reach other levels of consciousness and a heightened awareness of reality.

To keep away evil spirits, a circle was invariably drawn around the site of the ritual. W. G. Gray, in his *The Rollright Ritual,* claims he could distinctly sense a magnetic ring a mile in diameter as he approached the magical site. In smaller circles, the witches would raise by their magical powers a cone of energy, visible to the clairvoyant, almost palpable. It is this engendered power which is still used by the craft today for therapy, prophecy, and sexual magic. By concentrating the will on a wish at the moment of orgasm the witch believed her will would be done.

The rule was for all to go naked at the sabbat to allow the magnetic current to flow more freely. For wintery nights, the anointed unguents served the double purpose of insulating the skin and drugging against the cold. And then, there was always the bonfire, the ashes of which were later spread in the fields for fertility.

With their cast-off clothes, the covens were wont to cast off their worldly cares, the distinction of class being lost in the nude as all became one with each other and nature. It was this freedom and beauty, says Doreen Valiente, witch, and informed writer on the craft, which constituted an important ingredient of the religious ecstasy of the pagan ritual. One of the great appeals of the sabbat to women was the freedom it afforded, not only sexually, but as creatures in their own right, rather than the slaves to which they had been reduced by Judeo-Christianity, silenced in church, with few legal rights, unclean since Moses, because of their sex.

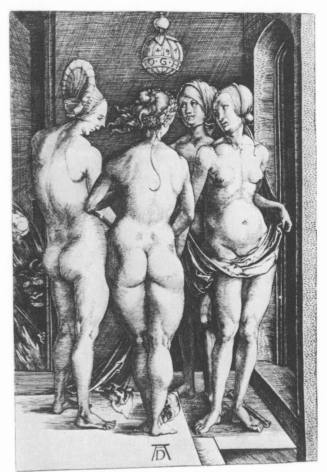

At first sight nothing but four lovely ladies, discreetly avoiding any frontal exposure, Dürer's witches actually convey a Hermetic message in that their various hairstyles betray the fact that women of totally different social strata could happily meet as equals during the sabbath.

At the sabbat, they could revert to the matriarchal roles of the pagan world, tending the fire, stewing the pot, collecting the herbs—healers, soothsayers, interpreters of dreams and casters of lots. Among the various rituals of the sabbat was scrying in crystals or in the smoke of the bonfire, to become aware of past lives, and to foretell the future.

Diana, queen of the night, bade her followers feast and drink, sing and dance, to show that they were truly free, both men and women, as naked in their rites as they were naked in their souls, as ecstatic in their loving intercourse as was their stunning goddess of fertility with her phallused mate, the Hornéd God. Hence the feasting, wining, dancing into Bacchic, Dionysian frenzy, chanting to the cosmic goddess to engender that mysterious *élan vital* or "astral light," awaken the secret serpent power that could raise the participants to that universal ecstasy of Bruno, or the Sufi saint Al Hallaj, or any of the other frenzied martyrs of the God of love.

405

That men and women, pairing off for a deliberately promiscuous intercourse as practiced by the early Gnostics, might have been indulging in an intentionally Christian act of sharing designed to cement the brotherhood of man, was overlooked by the Inquisition, as was the conceit that the ritual might be designed to destroy that most fiendish and bloodthirsty of human devils, the green-eyed jealousy engendered by a compulsion to possess, which—as Wilhelm Reich laid down his life to show—leads only to sadism, servitude, and senseless slaughter. What rational spirit would choose the torment and disaster of war and Inquisition over the ecstatic fertilizing ritual intercourse of the sabbat, in which the greatest pain and damage might be the tearing of a hymen.

Although the early accounts of these sexual orgies tell of their being of the most voluptuous and satisfying kind, enjoyed by women *maxima cum voluptate,* victims of the witch trials were brought to confess to the Inquisitors that the "devil's" member was always cold, hard, and often hurt them.

All of which, by the sexually deviant Inquisitor, was reduced from a symbolic *hierosgamos,* or marriage between heaven and earth, from the world of eros and agape, to an analytic if not pornographic probing for the dimension and consistency of the penis of the Devil.

Gradually, as the persecution intensified, and the covens were thinned out by execution, the craft was forced more and more underground, and security had to be increased to keep out inquisitive spies. Hence the obligation of members to spit or piss on the cross, the most effective measure for identifying a spy who, as a believing Christian, would cringe in fear of hell for urinating on an otherwise harmless symbol. As the repression continued, the craft became the repository of more inverted religious rites and symbols, so that the witches' commitment, as Kenneth Grant puts it succinctly, was not so much to an anti-Christian faith as to the ante-Christian one.

It is also not difficult to see how the image of the sexy, beautiful witch could become distorted into that of the wicked witch of Halloween. At the peak of the persecu-

The esbat, with its full moon, provided a monthly flood tide of astral and psychic power, affecting not only the menstrual flood of women, but the formation of sperm in men. And the witches' ceremonial imbibition of the seminal fluid has found its *raison d'être* in modern science, which has discovered that young virgins need the imbibition because the hormones in sperm set their cycles going.

tion, any old widow, without relief, forced to subsist in rags on the edge of a moor, might be inclined to use what magical powers she could muster against a pharisaiacal Church. Hence the stereotype witch of black magic: old, gaunt, loathsome, toothless, squatting in tombs, feeding on corpses, forcing the dead to reveal the future, "taking a recent corpse and pouring into its breast a mixture of warm menstrual blood, the guts of a lynx, a hyena's hump, the froth of a mad dog."

And the black mass, according to the French expert on witchcraft Jules Michelet, came as a revolt against the false Christianity of harsh and narrow-minded Puritans, of the gross injustice and cruelty of Catholic Inquisitor with his butchering secular arm.

As Harrison points out, the extirpation of the Old Religion launched by Kraemer and Sprenger succeeded not only in almost totally destroying the simple fertility cult as it had survived into the fifteenth century, but of substituting for it the false sabbat, or black mass, with its Satan, a totally spurious and totally Christian affair which required that a Host be desecrated only by a consecrated Catholic priest inserting it into the vulva of a naked female which he then asperged with semen. Such a performance conducted with a small piece of bread could only be laughable to a non-Christian.

Yet nobles of the court of Louis XIV hired as many as fifty or sixty authentic Catholic priests to conduct special black masses on the belly of a nude girl stretched across an altar. Madame de Montespan herself lay naked on such an altar in the hope thereby of retaining the favor of the king.

Sade in *Justine* describes such a black mass, during which a young girl is stripped and made to lie belly-down on a large table, with a statue of Jesus between her legs so that the mass can be celebrated on her buttocks. Part of the host, says Sade, was pushed into her "obscene entrance" while the priest "ignominiously crushed it under the repeated lunges of his monstrous tool, shouting blasphemies and emitting foul surges of the torrent of his lubricity over the very body of his Saviour."

Hardly the spiritual ethics and aesthetics of Diana. And no wonder the witches ran from the horrors of the established society to the refuge of a Rollright circle to learn to master the magic of the astral world and the more spiritual realms stretching beyond, presumably *ad infinitum.*

The religions of the world

19. MAGICIANS OF THE GOLDEN DAWN

The nineteenth century's most renowned magician and expert on the "astral plane" began his career as a Catholic abbot, but soon found himself wondering whether the priests of his chosen religion in fact believed in God. In Paris, his religious schooling—"like a prison where one learns ignorance slowly and with difficulty"—convinced Alphonse-Louis Constant that from a scientific point of view the ancients had been libeled by "the infinite historical ignorance" of the professors of his day.

His fellow seminarians he found "stiff, oily-skinned, greasy-haired, with revolting *soutanes,* their natural mistrust and extreme reserve revealing a mortal coldness."

For warmth—though he had already vowed perpetual chastity—the young subdeacon fell into the arms of a pretty Parisienne and never looked back on the priesthood. Yet it did not diminish his religious ideals or his zeal. As a radical writer, and a prolific one, Constant wished to regenerate and universalize religion by a synthesis and rational explanation of its symbols, constituting what he hoped would be "the true Catholic Church," a universal association of all men—and women. An early supporter of women's rights, Constant maintained that "honest" women, to avoid selling their bodies, should be admitted by law to any job they could do as well as a man.

Such notions from a religious progressive earned him frequent and unpleasant sojourns in jail. His writings on magic, which he produced under the pen name of Eliphas Lévi, were, on the other hand, better received, especially in England, where he was welcomed by Hargrave Jennings and Bulwer Lytton both as a friend and as an Hermetic brother who believed, as they did, that the material universe constituted only part of a greater reality whose planes of existence could be explored through other modes of consciousness.

Asked to demonstrate the expertise of his magic in an English country house, Lévi invoked the spirit of Apollonius of Tyre, whom he described as appearing wrapped from head to foot in a gray shroud, "lean, melancholy, and beardless."

Too frightened to pose the questions he had prepared,

Lévi identified Mesmer's animal magnetism with "astral light," which he described as a universal medium analogous to the all-pervading ether, "a subtle matter of admirable virtue, for it attracts all that is near it." He called it a unity compounded of opposites which, like a magnet, had opposite poles, and said it responded to the human will, whose "astral body" was made of it. He also called it "the fluidic and living gold of alchemy," avowing that to control it was to master all things. At the same time Lévi warned that astral light "could be an instrument in subservience to fallen spirits," that it was "the terrestrial Mercury to whom sacrifices were ordained by diviners, the fluidic genius of the earth, fatal for those who arouse it without knowing how to direct it; for it is the focus of physical life and the magnetized receptacle of death."

Lévi swooned away. Nor could he explain the physical laws by which he claimed to have seen and touched such a phantom. Yet he insisted, "I did see and I did touch. I saw clearly and distinctly, apart from dreaming." And that, the French magus maintained, was sufficient to establish for him the real efficacy of magical ceremonies.

To explain apparitions, he posited, or fell back on, a universal agent called "astral light," a plastic medium upon which thoughts and images can be imprinted, serving as a matrix for all forms, a mirror for the imagination and dreams, a medium which can take up any form evoked by thought, causing it to become manifest even to touch. Through this astral light, Lévi concluded, healing could be accomplished, the weather affected, and such apparent miracles as the raising of Lazarus performed.

The basic function of magic, according to Lévi, is to enable the magician to direct his will more effectively, so as to be master of the "astral light," not affected by it.

Astral light, Lévi explained, consists of two opposing or complementary currents, masculine and feminine, which the magician must balance—a balance symbolized by the androgynous Baphomet of the Templars, with its woman's breasts and male phallus, or by the cabalists' Tree of Life, with its masculine and feminine currents around a mediating column.

Though ostensibly still a Catholic, Lévi became a Free Mason in 1861, initiated into a Parisian Lodge called the Rose of Perfect Silence. The same year he was visited by a young English occultist, Kenneth R. H. Mackenzie, a Master Mason, author of the *Cyclopedia of Masonry,* who claimed to have been initiated into a Continental Rosicrucian fraternity by an Austrian count named Apponyi.

In a detailed report on his visit, Mackenzie told his English brethren how Lévi had shown him the photographic copy of an inestimably rare book containing a prophecy by Paracelsus, illustrated with symbolic figures, predicting the French Revolution, the rise of Napoleon, the downfall of the papacy, the restoration of the Kingdom of Italy, the abrogation of the power of the pope, the downfall of the clergy, and, as a means of restoring general harmony in society, the ultimate ascendancy of the occult sciences. Lévi had also produced for his guest a "cabalistic plate" which he said he had bought on one of the quays along the Seine, and which was the source of a curious story. In a manuscript attributed to Cagliostro—then owned by a Count Braszynsky—the prediction was made that in the nineteenth century, a certain person by the name of Alphonse would clearly understand the meaning of the plate.

"I," said Lévi, "am that Alphonse." He then spent the rest of the interview filling in Mackenzie on the arcane mysteries of magic.

Back in London, Mackenzie shared with his fellow Freemason Hargrave Jennings all he had learned from the French magus. Jennings had meanwhile acquired from the estate of a deceased French occultist, J. B. Ragon, certain rare manuscripts which purported to give details of authentic Rosicrucian degrees and rituals. To perpetuate this wisdom, Jennings and Mackenzie got together with some other enthusiastic occultists such as Robert Wentworth Little to form the Societas Rosicruciana in Anglia, of which Eliphas Lévi was made a Master. Any other Mason with a master's degree interested in the "discovery of the secrets of nature through the symbolism of the art and literature of the past" was welcomed into the society, which began publication of its own organ, *The Rosicrucian*, naming as its Honorary Grand Patron the former British minister to Egypt, author of the Rosicrucian novel *Zanoni*, now Lord Lytton.

Among the first to join was Master Mason W. J. Hughan, and he and Jennings became pupils of an extraordinary character, said to be the greatest wizard in England since Merlin, George Pickinghill, who promised to show them how to master various elementals. It was one of their main endeavors to find the proof that the Masonic craft and the rites of the Rosicrucians were descendants of the old religion of the horned god of the Egyptians.

In a five-hundred-page opus, *The Rosicrucians, Their Rites and Mysteries,* Jennings hinted as strongly as he could that these rites and mysteries were of a fundamentally sexual nature, though to make his point in Victorian England he was obliged to resort to some involved and often poetically purple prose. Dancing around the theme of Tantric sex as the basis of the Rosicrucian philosophy, Jennings was almost specific when he pointed out that just as the Masonic seal of Solomon symbolizes the intertwined triangles of male and female, which in conjunction represent life, so the obelisk always indicates the male power derived from the sun, whereas "the pyramid indicates the female corresponding tumefactive or rising power—not submissive, but answeringly suggestive, synchronized in the anatomical clitoris (Greek from sunflower turning to the sun, that eccentric minute object, meaning everything in the Rosicrucian anatomy.)"

Ignored by his contemporaries and pilloried by later critics, Jennings nevertheless went on to produce *The Indian Religion, or Results of the Mysteries of Buddhism,*

The man and woman reaching for each other across the inverted triangles of creative sexuality (appearing in the Rosicrucian *Anthology of Christian Rosenkreutz*) are less obscure in their meaning than the Hermetic Latin surrounding a medieval alchemist, and the captions from Proverbs: "The full soul loatheth the honeycomb; but to the hungry soul every bitter thing is sweet." And "A scorner seeketh wisdom and findeth it not: but knowledge is easy unto him that understandeth."

413

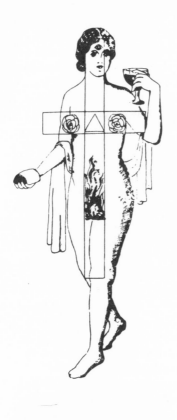

in which, though maintaining as did the Theosophists that the human soul was a spark of fire taken from the eternal ocean of light, he argued that divine and supernatural illumination was the only means of arriving at the truth.

Jennings went on to explain that the Fire-Philosophers, the Rosicrucians, and the Illuminati all taught that knowable things both of soul and body were all evolved out of "fire" and finally resolve into it again, but that "this fire is not our vulgar, gross fire, but an occult, mysterious or inner supernatural fire."

The Rosicrucians, said Jennings, "claimed not to be bound by the limits of the present world, but to be able to pass into the next world (inaccessible only in appearance) and to be able to work in it, and to come back safe (and self-same) out of it, bringing their trophies with them. . . ." To this he added that they were merely following in the footsteps of the ancient Egyptians, who, "acquainted with the wonders of magnetism, built a bridge."

To achieve this passage, said Jennings, was the point and purpose of Egyptian, Rosicrucian, and Masonic initiation. Like Saint-Germain he believed that man had not originally been created susceptible to death. "The Rosicrucians contend that diseases are not necessarily incidental to the body . . ."

To drive home the point, Jennings translated from the Latin into English, Robert Fludd's opus on Rosicrucian philosophy, his *Apologia comendiaria fraternitatis de rosea cruce,* originally printed in Leyden in 1616. It hardly caused a ripple.

For several years the Societas Rosicruciana in Anglia progressed without undue notice until a member of its high council, William Wynn Westcott, decided to form an even more secret society. A supreme magus in the order, Westcott was also a London coroner, who, in the course of a lifetime may have conducted as many as ten thousand inquests, a calling which provokes the rumor that his penchant for autopsies involved a greater interest in corpses than in spirits.

Westcott had also acquired a mysterious manuscript, this one in cipher, to which he had managed to find the key—not too difficult a task, as it was the same cipher devised by the Abbot Trithenius and used by alchemists of the fifteenth century, which John Dee had spent ten solid days translating, and examples of which were at hand in the British Museum. The key made possible the transcription of five mystical rituals which Westcott claimed to be Masonic, drawn from the ancient Egyptian texts, but which later exegesists, from their inner content, believed to have

William Wynn Wescott (1848–1925), Supreme Magus of the Societas Rosicruciana in Anglia and Worshipful Master of the Masonic research lodge Quator Coronati, translated Eliphas Lévi's work on the Tarot, and originated a groundbreaking work on the Isiac tablet of Cardinal Bembo. He died in South Africa.

been concocted some time after Champollion had deciphered the glyphs, perhaps as late as 1870.

Westcott further claimed that the document opened the way to higher degrees of Rosicrucian initiation, to which had been given the high-sounding Latin titles of zelator, theoricus, praticus, and philosophus, used in the eighteenth century by the German rite of The Golden and Rosy Cross. Westcott also maintained that a letter found with the manuscript enabled him to get in touch, through an initiate in Germany, with the actual "Secret Chiefs" of the ancient order, originally introduced into Strict Observance Masonry by Baron von Hund, and that they had granted him permission to form a lodge in England, the Isis-Urania Temple of the Hermetic Order of the Golden Dawn.

This was considered an exciting breakthrough into the realms of higher magic; but as Westcott was no great magician, the real power in the new lodge fell into the eager hands of a character with the given name of Samuel Liddle Mathers, who, because of a Jacobite ancestor ennobled by Louis XV, was pleased to assume the title of McGreggor, comte de Glenstrae, and was not unwilling to have people believe him to be, in reality, James IV of Scotland, not killed at the Battle of Flodden, an adept who had learned, like the comte de Saint-Germain, to become immortal.

A Master Mason, then in his thirties, Mather had acquired a profound knowledge of Egyptology by reading every book he could find in the British Museum on magic, alchemy, symbolism, and the religious mores of ancient Egypt. To an acquaintance who spotted his gaunt, resolute figure in the reading room, he confided: "I have clothed myself with hieroglyphs as with a garment."

Further to explore the various astral planes, Mathers also taught the use of Dr. John Dee's Enochian magic. From the jumbled mass of Dee's papers and diaries, preserved in the British Museum and the Ashmolean Library at Oxford, Mathers managed with some effort to produce a coherent system of Enochian magic which seems to have helped initiates of the Golden Dawn explore the superphysical world of Dee's thirty "aethyrs."

Mathers also partially translated from the German Knorr von Rosenroth's seventeenth-century *Kabalah denudata,* which enabled him to equate the ten sephiroth of the Jewish cabalist's *Tree of Life* with the inner planes of the astral world, "reaching up to a limitless light beyond which nothing more can be known."

To secure his grasp on the Order, and to impose on it obedience, Mathers claimed to have forged a personal

Samuel Liddell MacGregor Mathers in a rare photograph. The picture drawn of him by biographers is of a mother-fixated, sexually impotent male who avoided women and whose real passions were magic and the theory of war, and who was eventually converted to the Church of Rome. With no money, he sold inside information on the stock market to would-be investors. Kept alive by a lady adherent of the Golden Dawn, Anne Horriman, Mathers wrote and translated several important hermetic and occult works, including a lost book on Egyptian symbolism based on his exhaustive study of the Egyptian collection in the Louvre. Crowley accused him (in fiction) of sending his pretty wife out on the boulevards to make money, and of compelling her to undergo an abortion. He is credited by Ithel Colquhoun with being the mastermind behind the Golden Dawn before it was taken over by Crowley.

415

Florence Farr (1866–1917)—
Mrs. Edward Emery—mistress of
the poet W. B. Yeats and of
Bernard Shaw, was a leading
member of the Golden Dawn,
who specialized in "Scrying the
Spirit-Visions." Left by Mathers
in charge of the society, she
wrote plays dealing with the
Egyptian magical tradition. She
also ran an avant-garde gallery
where the paintings of D. H. Law-
rence were seized as shocking.

Moina Mathers, lovely, delicate
sister of Henri Bergson, was a
clairvoyant who could bring to
earth material from the "inner
planes." But the sex act was
reported to have "filled her with
revulsion" and her marriage appeared to have been sexless, at
least with her husband.

link with Westcott's "Secret Chiefs," about whom he could say nothing other than that they conveyed to him arcane knowledge, either clairvoyantly, on the astral plane, through automatic writing, or by means of a sort of ouija board, the use of which he said required great skill and attention to avoid interference by opposing "demonic" forces.

Mathers admitted he seldom had seen the "Chiefs" in the flesh, nor did he know their earthly names, but they appeared to him to be human with superhuman powers which were manifested as "transcendent health and vigor, as if they possessed the Elixir of Life." To be close to them, said Mathers, was like being close to a lightning flash during a violent storm.

The grades of initiation in the Golden Dawn were divided into three main levels, the first corresponding to the material world, the second to the astral, the third to the transcendental. Among the more prominent of the hundred-odd members some, like the wife of Oscar Wilde, were determined to practice magic. Others, such as Florence Farr, the actress, and mistress of G. B. Shaw, claimed to be controlled by "a certain Egyptian astral form first contacted through a piece of mummy case." W. B. Yeats, the Irish poet, more interested in inspiration, was intro-duced by Mathers to the world of symbolic "archetypes," where "images well up before the mind's eye from a deeper source than consciousness or subconscious mem-ory." Yeats described visions which recalled "the planetary images of Ficino and Bruno," and, by concentrating, said he could even transfer symbols to someone else's mind.

In Paris, where he had moved for financial reasons, Mathers found in the Bibliothèque de l'Arsenal another magical system spelled out in a sixteenth-century manu-script, which he translated into English as *The Book of the Sacred Magic of Abra-Melin the Mage.* He claimed it enabled his fellows of the Golden Dawn to attain, through another ancient Egyptian ritual, "knowledge of, and conversation with, their own Holy Guardian Angel."

For some years Mathers continued to run the Golden Dawn from France with the financial help of one of its lady members, who, somewhat neurotic, accused Mathers and his wife, Moira Bergson, sister of the French philosopher, of dabbling in sexual magic. Both denied the charge of having made pacts with qliphotic or demonic forces, but their financial support was rescinded. Worse troubles, as lucidly described by Ellic Howe in his *The Magicians of the Golden Dawn,* were to follow. First Mathers failed to convince his fellow Golden Dawners of the actual exis-

Edward Alexander Crowley in his twenties

Rose Kelley Crowley

tence of his "Hidden Chiefs"; then he admitted he had known all along that the original letters from Germany accrediting the Order had been forged, presumably by Westcott. Quarrels between members of the Golden Dawn accelerated its day toward a sunset. It only remained for the youngest and most energetic of its aspirant magi, Aleister Crowley, to ease Mathers into a personal *daemmerung,* by first taking his side, and then taking his place.

Edward Alexander Crowley, better known by the first name of Aleister, was twenty-three and just down from Cambridge when he was initiated, in London's Mark Mason's Hall, into the Golden Dawn as Frater Perdurabo ("I will endure"). Two years later, he was a thirty-third-degree Mason. Within the minimal time he had worked his way up to the top of the complex order of Hermetic degrees concocted by Mathers. This he accomplished with the help of a senior magus, Allan Bennett (Frater Jehi Aour), who broke his oath to supply Crowley with the required secret data, later abandoning the Golden Dawn to become a Buddhist monk.

The next step, the contacting of his own guardian angel through the magic of Abramelin the Mage, Crowley could not speed up because it required a concentrated six-month effort which could only take place precisely between the vernal and autumnal equinoxes. To find the right atmosphere of privacy for this magical exercise, Crowley spent £2,000 of his father's inheritance to acquire a pink-washed, one-story lodge called Boleskine, overlooking the murky waters of Loch Ness between Foyers and the Enochian-sounding village of Inverfarigaig.

Exhausted by several months of apparently unsuccessful endeavors, Crowley suddenly reverted to his penchant for exploring exotic corners of the planet and set off for Mexico and the Far East, returning via Ceylon, India, Burma, Baltistan, and Egypt, having tackled and nearly mastered two of the highest unclimbed peaks in Asia. To Egypt he returned with a young bride, Rose Kelley, sister of Gerald Kelley, later Sir Gerald, president of the Royal Academy.

Masquerading through Cairo as a Persian prince called Chio Khan (Hebrew for "the beast"), dressed in flowing golden robes and a jewel-encrusted turban—so that runners would clear a path for him through the crowded streets—Crowley took his bride to honeymoon in the King's Chamber of the Great Pyramid, where he said he demonstrated to her his magical powers by causing the entire chamber to glow a pale lilac with "astral light."

Back in Cairo in an attempt to convince Rose of the

A page from Crowley's handwritten *Book of the Law*. The author, says Crowley, claimed to be a messenger—like Mohammed and others—of the Lord of the Universe, and therefore to speak with absolute authority. The book is said to be a statement of transcendental truth, and to have overcome the difficulty of expressing such truth in human language by what amounts to the invention of a new method of communicating thought. This Crowley describes as not merely a new language but a new type of language. "A literal and numerical cipher involving the Greek and Hebrew Cabbalas, the highest mathematics, etc." The book, says Crowley, ". . . claims to be the utterance of an illuminated mind coextensive with the ultimate ideas of which the universe is composed . . . an intelligence both alien and superior to myself, yet acquainted with my inmost secrets, a discarnate intelligence." Kenneth Grant says of the *Book of the Law* that anyone possessing any capacity for understanding the language of symbolism "will be staggered by the adequacy and accuracy of the summary of the spirit of the Aeon. . . ." It gives the basic law of the new aeon as: "There is no law beyond 'Do what thou wilt' and 'Thou hast no right but to do thy will.' " The theory being that every man and woman each has definite attributes whose tendency, considered in the relation to environment, indicate a proper course in each case. To pursue this course of action, says Grant, is to do one's true will. Hence: "The word of Sin is Restriction."

existence of elementals by invoking sylphs, or spirits of the air, Crowley merely managed to put his bride into a mild trance in which she informed him that the Egyptian god Horus awaited him with instructions to sit at his desk at noon on April 8, 1904, to receive a message.

At the appointed hour, Rose—whom Crowley now called by the pretty Arabic equivalent of Ouarda—suddenly spoke over his shoulder in a rich baritone in an English "uncannily perfect and free of ascertainable accent, native or foreign," which identified its owner as Aiwaz, Egyptian minister to the Lord of Silence, Hoor-Paar-Kraat.

On three consecutive days, the deep timbre of the voice "poured forth slowly, steadily, solemn, voluptuous, tender, fierce, in harmony with the message delivered," while Crowley with his Swan fountain pen scribbled and scribbled. Result: a twenty-one-page prose-poem known as the *Book of the Law,* which was to revolutionize Crowley's life, and would, he believed, greatly affect the future of mankind. It announced the advent of a new eon in which Crowley was to become the priest-prince of a new religion, the Age of Horus. He was to formulate a link between humanity and the "solar-spiritual force, during which the god Horus would preside for the next two thousand years over the evolution of consciousness on this planet." The technique used by Crowley to commune with Horus was "to seal the plasma of his astral body in the mentally formed image of a golden hawk—a vehicle of Horus—and in that form explore the subtle aethyrs of the universe, angelic or non-terrestrial dimensions of consciousness not usually experienced."

The message from Aiwaz, whom Crowley understood to be his own guardian angel, convinced him that his mission in life was to give the *coup de grace* to the Age of Osiris with its moribund appendage, the Christian faith, and build on the ruins a new religion based on the law of Thelema— Greek for "will." The theme of this new dispensation Crowley summed up in the dictum "Every man and woman is a star. Do as thou wilt shall be the whole of the law." To which he added the further and even more important proviso of "Love is the law, love under will." But love and affection under the law of Thelema was not to be confused with the possessive kind that breeds pain, jealousy, and hatred. It was to be a Charter of Universal Freedom for every man and woman in the world, each individual considered as the center of his own universe, his essential nature determining his relations with similar beings, and his proper course of action. Crowley's law of Thelema, as an ideal Freemasonry, saw each member of the

Crowley's diploma as a 33° Mason, issued in London, October 1910

The Grand Secretary General of the Supreme Council 33° in London declared Crowley and Yarker to have been expelled from the brotherhood of Masons.

human race as unique, sovereign, and responsible only to himself. "In this way," says Crowley, "it is the logical climax of the idea of democracy. Yet at the same time it is the climax of aristocracy by asserting each individual equally to be the center of the universe." The conclusion from these premises was that the sole and whole duty of each human being was to discover the purpose for which he or she is fitted and devote every energy to its accomplishment. The *Book of the Law,* said Crowley, opened a path of progress to mankind which would eventually enable the race to strike off the fetters of mortality and transcend the limitations of its entanglement with earth. He also called it "a veritable Golden Bough," an absolute passport through the Amenta of the Egyptians.

By his adepts, the *Book of the Law* was described as containing occult formulae of cosmic scope, "some openly expressed, some veiled in the most complex web of qabalistic ciphers ever woven into a single text." Nor was it just a piece of "automatic writing," said Crowley, but a clearcut message from an intelligence of superhuman power and knowledge, some extraterrestrial transcendental source, "one of the real hidden masters who would thereafter manifest to him."

Crowley describes Aiwaz as appearing to him later in the form of a tall, dark man in his thirties, "well-knit, active and strong, with the face of a savage king, and the eyes veiled lest their gaze should destroy what they saw." The apparition's dress, says Crowley, was not Arab, but suggested Assyrian or Persian, only very vaguely, because "at first I took little note of him as he was like an angel, such as I had often seen in visions, a being purely astral."

Later still Crowley was inclined to believe that Aiwaz was not only "the God or Devil once held holy in Sumer, and mine own Holy Guardian Angel, but also a man as I am, insofar as he uses a human body to make his magical link with mankind, whom he loves, and that he is thus an Ipsissimus, the highest spiritual achievement possible to man, literally his own very self, the head of the Great White Brotherhood."

By this Crowley did not necessarily mean that Aiwaz was a member of the human race, but that he could apparently form for himself a human body, as circumstances indicated, from the appropriate elements and then dissolve it. "I saw him again often in different human guises all equally material."

Acting upon the authority of Aiwaz, Crowley was happy to supplant Mathers and his Golden Dawn by forming a

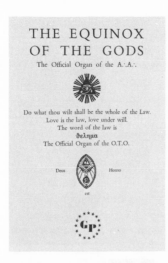

The poet Victor Neuburg

By some experts, Dee's Enochian language is suspected of being Ur-Semitic, the source of later Semitic tongues. To others it is "the language that lies behind Sanskrit," or even the language of the Atlanteans. It was, in any case, a hieratic tongue to be used in ritual, its vocabulary related to a transcendental world, a sacred alphabet of letters and numbers, in which the letters were also sigils, or glyphs.

new order called Astrum Argentum, or Silver Star, named after Set, or Sirius, of which he claimed our sun was but a reflection, or son. The order, which Crowley considered the truly occult representative of the Great White Brotherhood, was designed to bring out into the open the secret knowledge so painstakingly preserved by initiates. The rituals of the A: A:, as it was glyphed, were to be simpler, including yogic practices Crowley had learned in the East. Their purpose: to prepare humanity for the next stage of its progress—initiation into the solar consciousness of Horus. At first there were few recruits to the A: A:, other than a sycophantic young admirer down from Oxford, the poet Victor Neuburg; but Crowley pressed on. With what was left of the money inherited from his father, he decided to launch a twice-yearly publication, *The Equinox*. The first issue, beautifully bound in white and gold, appeared in March 1909. Crowley described it as the first serious attempt to put before the public the facts of occult science "since Blavatsky's unscholarly hotch-potch of fact and fable, *Isis Unveiled*." He considered his to be the first attempt in history to treat the subject with scholarship and from the standpoint of science. It contained the technique for assuming a god-form, of ritually evoking and banishing astral, elemental, and planetary entities. In the second issue, in October, true to his promise to reveal the initiatory secrets, Crowley published the neophyte ritual of the Golden Dawn with fifty-four diagrams to illustrate the mysteries. The cat was out; and once he and Neuburg had seen that it was well received, they took off for the North African desert of Algeria to embark on a more ambitious experiment in magic: further exploration of Dee's astral levels with the use of a large topaz as a shew-stone which Crowley would scry while Neuburg scribed.

Crowley says that eventually he learned not to travel in his astral body because he realized that space was not a thing in itself, but merely a convenience enabling one to distinguish objects from each other. When in one of Dee's Aethers or Aires he says he found himself simply in a state characteristic of its nature, his senses receiving its subtle impressions. Thus he claims to have become as cognizant of the phenomena of Dee's worlds as ordinary man is of his. But unable to break into the fourteenth Aire, Crowley had the sudden impulse to use sex to advance his magic. "We accordingly took loose rocks," says Crowley, "and built a great circle, inscribed with the words of power; and in the midst we erected an altar and there I sacrificed myself."

Crowley claimed he was obliged to write his more

According to Kenneth Grant, the barbarous names of evocation and invocation, whether Enochian, Goetic, Gnostic, or Tantric, are peculiarly adapted to unsealing the subconscious, their potency lying chiefly in their being unintelligible to the conscious mind. Crowley says: "The long strings of formidable words which roar and moan through so many conjurations have a real effect in exalting the consciousness of the magician to the proper pitch." He quotes Dee as voicing: "ZODACARE, ECA, OD ZODOMERANU! ODO KIKALE QAA! ZODOREJE, LAPE ZODIREPO NOCO MADA, HOATHATE IAIDA"; or: "Move, therefore, and show yourselves! Open the mysteries of your creation! Be friendly unto me, for I am the servant of the same your God: the true worshipper of the Highest!"

specific explanation in hieroglyphs because it had to do with matters "of which it is unlawful to speak openly under penalty of the most dreadful punishment: but I may say that the essence of the matter was that I had hitherto clung to certain conceptions of conduct which, while perfectly proper from the standpoint of my human nature, were impertinent to initiation. I could not cross the Abyss till I had torn them out of my heart."

Crowley the magician

Francis King, in *The Magical World of Aleister Crowley*, is more specific when he writes that the magus "sacrificed himself in a way which consumed every particle of his ego . . . he deliberately humiliated himself by being Neuburg's passive partner in an act of buggery."

The result, at the moment of joint orgasm, appears to have been a stunning entry into Dee's fourteenth Aire, where Crowley learned "to allow my ego to be totally destroyed so as to unite my spirit with the ocean of infinity."

From then on, said Crowley, sexual acts, which he had indulged in "with casual abandon," became for him a sacrament, a rite to be performed deliberately for the glory of the gods. Buggery, Crowley avowed, other than for religious purposes, was abominable; and to differentiate his magick from the nonsexual variety, he added to the word a *k,* symbol for kteis, Greek for the female genitals.

One of the demons conjured up by man from his own created storehouse

Crowley used *key* and *aethyr* for Dee's *call* and *aire*. A gramophone record of Crowley exists in which he recites the first forty-eight Enochian "calls." It was a language, says Ithell Colquhoun, that had to be vibrated like a mantra, and she suggests that Enochian magic is a Western equivalent to Hindu mantra yoga, and that vocalizing the sound gave access to an Atlantean world, "a superstructure unimaginably attentuated and jewel-clear, which the Egyptian *Book of the Dead* symbolizes as 'the lily of green felspar.'" She believes the Enochian Tables conceal a musical system, a record of frequencies on which the calls should be sent out, and "may even suggest the construction of an instrument." Crowley called the language "very much more sonorous, stately and impressive than Greek or Sanskrit, and the English translations, though in places difficult to understand, contain passages of a sustained sublimity that Shakespeare, Milton and the Bible do not surpass."

Reaching the tenth Aire—which had to be approached backwards, since it had been taken down by Dee for fear of unleashing demonic forces—Crowley realized he must consciously cross what he called the "Abyss," or great psychological barrier separating ordinary men from the "Secret Chiefs," a barrier guarded by the mightiest devil of all, the demon of spiritual chaos, the same Chorozon encountered by Dee. It now became clear to Crowley "that one must look inward and face one's own demons, for they may be the same as those one evokes."

There was a flash of lightning followed by a rumble of thunder, and a voice intoned: "I am the master of Form and from me all forms proceed."

Chorozon, Crowley later explained, represented all the suppressed fears and hostilities which had flourished in his subconscious. By materializing them, and by integrating them openly into his psyche, he says he disposed of their power; as a result of which ordeal he claimed to have earned a higher occult degree than Mathers, becoming a Magister Templi.

Mathers, in London, afraid that all his powers would now be lost by publication in *The Equinox* of the most secret rituals of the Golden Dawn, filed a restraining order against the third issue; and though at first he succeeded with the help of a judge renowned as a Freemason, the judgment was reversed on appeal and the second issue of *The Equinox* appeared intact.

Mathers, who admitted at the trial, under oath, "to raising devils, making himself invisible, transforming men into animals, making gold, making rain, and all the other fabled arts of sorcery," managed to further annoy several occultists by claiming to be *the* chief of the Rosicrucian order. Another such chief, a German, Theodor Reuss, reputed agent of the German secret service, employed to spy on British Marxists, was equally annoyed. As head of the Ordo Templi Orientis, Reuss considered his occult order to be the successor to the Knights Templar, and to be the true successor of the Rosicrucian fraternity, just as his earlier order, the Grand Lodge of Memphis and Misraim, had been the successor to both Cagliostro's Egyptian rite, and to Adam Weishaupt's Order of the Illuminati (OTO).

Reuss had inherited leadership of the OTO a few years earlier from a wealthy Austrian iron founder and high Mason, Karl Kellner, who had died in mysterious circumstances after changing the order's name from the Hermetic Brotherhood of Light to the Order of the Temple of the East, on the grounds that the East was the locus and source

First Matter of Hermetic Philosophy, or the Font of Miracles. The text that goes with this illustration from the Rudolph Steiner Christian Rosenkreutz Anthology reads: "I am the mixture which preserves everything in nature and makes it alive. I pass from the upper to the lower planes. I am the heavenly dew and the fat of the land. I am the fiery water and the watery fire. Nothing may live without me in time. I am close to all things; in and through all things; nevertheless, unknown." The caption alongside the hermetic drawing reads: "This moisture must be caught, lest it should change into vapor or fume. The two vapors or fumes are the roots of the art."

of the illumination symbolized by the solar-phallic energy.

Reuss called on Crowley in London to accuse him of having revealed the innermost secrets of the ninth degree of the Ordo Templi Orientis. Surprised, Crowley replied he could hardly have done so as he had not been admitted to that degree and could therefore not know its secrets.

Reuss reached for a copy of Crowley's *Book of Lies* and pointed on page forty-six to the Ritual of the Star Sapphire. Crowley was thunderstruck. In his own work—in which he claimed to have surprised the supreme secret of all practical magick by pure chance while lying with a whore—he recognized a reference to sexual magic disguised beneath the symbols of the "rood" for phallus and the "mystic rose" for vagina. The scales fell from his eyes. At last, said he, his suspicion was confirmed that "behind the frivolities and convivialities of Freemasonry lay in truth a secret ineffable and miraculous, potent to control the forces of nature, and not only to make men brethren, but to make them divine."

Reuss was quite categoric: the OTO was a body of initiates in whose hands was concentrated the secret knowledge of *all* oriental orders and of all existing Masonic degrees. Its chiefs were initiates of the highest rank, but not in conflict with the grand lodge of England. It was all clearly stated, said Reuss, in the organ of his Grand Lodge of Memphis and Misraim, a magazine called *Oriflamme,* which spelled out that the order had "rediscovered the great secret of the Knights Templar, the magic of sex, not only the key to the ancient Egyptian and hermetic tradition, but to all the secrets of nature, all the symbolism of Freemasonry, and all systems of religion."

In the secret code of the order, Crowley found *Athanor* to be the name for penis; *blood of the red lion* for semen; *curcubite* or *retort* for vagina. Vaginal liquids were known as the *menstruum of the gluten,* and when mixed with semen, they became *first matter;* further impregnated with magic, they equaled the *Elixir of Life.*

Karl Kellner, the OTO's founder, said Reuss, claimed to have rediscovered the "secret doctrine" during his travels in India, where he had been initiated into Tantrism and the use of the sexual current by a notorious Arab magician, Soliman Ben Aifa, practitioner of an unorthodox form of Sufism, and by two Indian Tantrics, Bhima Sen Pratap and Shri Mahatma Agamya Paramahamsa, initiates of the *vama marg,* or left-hand path, the magical use of sexual energies accomplished with the help of a female companion, or *shakti.*

The OTO, said Reuss, had been founded in the 1890s

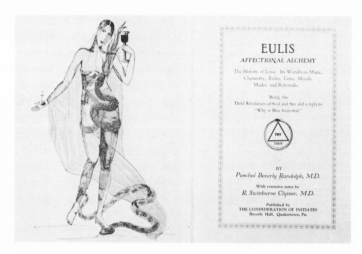

Crowley became convinced that his job was to cure the whole world of sexual repression, a plague that was paralyzing spiritual progress. He wanted sexual expression to be not a legal or a financial or an endured performance but a "magnetic phenomenon"; he wanted love to be a gift to be treasured without shame or hypocrisy. And he saw his mission not merely to illuminate the few, but "to set in motion occult forces which would result in the illumination of all by 2000 A.D." To achieve his goal he determined to study every detail of sexual behavior and bring every sexual impulse up to the region of rational consciousness. To this end he experimented with altered states of consciousness, including hashish, cocaine, and opium. To push his consciousness to its limits, to reach a transcendent state, he used orgiastic practices, believing that in a deathlike trance of the body, the spirit was free to unite with an invoked "god." But he warned: "Sex is, directly or indirectly, the most powerful weapon in the armory of the magician, and precisely because there is no moral guide, it is indescribably dangerous. I have given a great many hints, especially in *Magick* and the *Book of Toth*—some of the cards are almost blatantly revealing; so I have been slapped rather severely over the knuckles for giving children matches for playthings. My excuse has been that they have already got the matches, that my explanations have been directed to add conscious precautions to the existing automatic safeguards."

by an amalgamation of the original order of Bavarian Illuminati and the Hermetic Brotherhood of Light, an order formed by the American Paschal Beverly Randolph, natural son of a rich Virginian and a mulatto woman said to be of royal Malagasy blood. As a friend of Lincoln's, he is said to have encouraged the president in his aid to Negroes. According to Serge Hutin, Randolph became involved with Freemasonry and the Fraternitas Rosae Crucis, and thanks to his extensive travels in the East had met Tantric initiates who enabled him to produce his main work, *Magia sexualis*.

So the chain linked Reuss and Kellner and Paschal Beverly Randolph back to Hargrave Jennings and the early members of Rosa Crucis in Anglia who had been obliged to keep so secret the fact that they too practiced the secret rituals of Tantric sex which Edward Sellon had described in his book. Suddenly all of Jennings's Hermetic phrases, teetering on the verge of revelation, became easier to comprehend.

Furthermore, says Manley Hall, it is possible that Jean Marie Ragon and Alexandre Lenoir could have been pupils of Saint-Germain when he practiced masonic and rosicrucian rituals in the palace of Prince Karl of Hesse at Eckernforde in 1780–85.

Delighted by Crowley's grasp of Tantric yoga, Reuss offered to initiate him into the highest degree of the OTO, suggesting that his new adept head a British section to be known as Mysteria Mystica Maxima, wherein initiates could be given hints in the lower grades of the whole truth of the power of sexual magic, which would be revealed during the higher degrees.

The first six degrees of the OTO Crowley found to be simply Masonic. In the seventh the initiate was given a

424

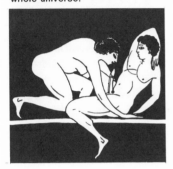

glimpse of sexual magic. In the eighth he or she was taught to practice autosexual magic through masturbation. According to Henri Bertreux in *Aux pays du Dragon,* astral energy can be released by a form of massage, or magical masturbation, which stabilizes the astral field of a person, making his or her magnetic force more harmonious. It can then be used as a form of protection against sexual vampirism performed by sexual entities operating in another dimension. "A wall of light," said Crowley, "can be made to encircle the magician charged with solar-phallic power drawn from the sun. . . . Sexual vampires seeing the radiant wall of light are drawn precipitately towards it and dashed to pieces, electrocuted on impact."

In the ninth degree of OTO heterosexual magic was performed involving sexual congress, the essential goal of which was the same as in witchcraft: concentration of the will at the moment of orgasm in order to obtain a wish. As with the witches, Crowley said he performed this magic on the astral plane in his so-called body of light. His imagination, powered by sexual energy, was set to function on an astral level, and, according to Crowley, at the moment of orgasm the sexual organ actually "shines" astrally. The ability to function on the inner, or astral, planes, to travel freely in the realms of light, or inner space, are derived, as Crowley explained it, from a purification and condensation of "vital force," which he described in its densest form as being identical with sexual energy. "The emanations of the 'Body of Desire' of the material being whom one visits," he said, "are, if the visit be agreeable, so potent that one spontaneously gains substance in the embrace."

He explained that in order to transform sexual energy into magical energy, the dormant fire-snake at the base of the spine is awakened. And the function of semen in the ritual is to build up the body of light, or astral body. "As the vital fluid accumulates in the testicles it is consumed by the heat of the roused Fire Snake radiating waves of astral energy whose subtle fumes go to strengthen the inner body."

Curious to discover whether a magician could produce the phenomenon at will through *any* practice of sexual magick, Crowley went with Victor Neuberg to Paris, where they enlisted the help of the correspondent of the *New York Times,* Walter Duranty. Beginning in January 1914 they performed twenty-four rituals of sexual magick in forty-three days, designed to invoke several disembodied entities ranging from Hermes to Jupiter. Crowley kept a diary describing these events, which he wrote up as *Rex*

425

According to Horapollo, the Egyptians used the falcon as a symbol of the god Horus because of its long life, its piercing sight, its ability to climb straight up and to drink the blood of a victim while flying upside down; also because the female was said to accept the male thirty times a day.

Crowley describes his method for assuming a god form. "By concentrated imagination of oneself in the symbolic shape of any god, one should be able to identify oneself with the idea which he represents." Crowley describes invoking a god form with Neuburg in a locked temple: "On one occasion, the god came to us in human form and remained with us, perfectly perceptible to all our senses, for the best part of an hour, only vanishing when we were physically exhausted by the ecstasy of intimate contact with his divine person, and sank into a sublime stupor; when we came to ourselves he was gone." At other times, Crowley continued the evocation of elemental forces "to visible appearance," and to make various talismans charged with spiritual energy, by means of meditation. He also continued to build up "my (so-called) astral body until it was sufficiently material to be perceptible to the ordinary physical senses of people I should visit in this shape."

de arte regia, listing every sexual act of any form in any possible combination, with the goal to be achieved at the moment of orgasm. Occasionally Duranty would substitute for Neuburg as a partner and "magician joined to magician," they would make the invocation: "Hermes, King of the Rod, appear, bringing the ineffable word!"

To impersonate an Egyptian god-form, mental concentration on the form of the god was required throughout intercourse; one had to imagine the god to have a life of its own. At the moment of climax, a transference of consciousness to that of the image was necessary, "blending the personality of the initiate with that of the god." Crowley still insisted that the practice of buggery was "an abomination" except in magick, and Serge Hutin says Crowley could not have been a homosexual or he would not have been admitted by the Hindu Tantric masters to their secret rites of the "left hand" because homosexuals are excluded—not for moral reasons—but because the normal polarity is reversed, and the magic will not function. Not satisfied with these extraordinary results, Crowley was to develop two more grades of sexual magick for the OTO, based on homosexual ritual.

It was clear to Crowley that the accusations against the original Templars of practicing sodomy and orgies with women had been grounded, but not as understood by their detractors. The Templars were evidently practicing rites they had picked up in the East. G. Legman, in *The Guilt of the Templars,* a composite work by five distinguished English academicians, says the Templars did not practice homosexuality *faute de mieux* but as a formal dedication, betrayed by the ritual nudity required at their secret initiation, and by the scatalogical kisses on mouth, penis and arse, which "clearly could or did end with the fellation or pedication of the recruit by the Templar receiving him." Legman suggests that the whole secret ritual implied or symbolized "a complete erotic itinerary of the recruit's bare body under the guise of ritual kisses." This was followed by the admonition that if at any time he felt the "stirrings of the flesh" (which Legman says could certainly be observed if it occurred while he was kissing the recruit's penis) it was permissible to "unite himself carnally with any of the brethren, and that he was to submit himself passively to them if asked." The neophyte was also told that it was better to satisfy each other than give a bad name to the order by going after the women pilgrims they were charged with protecting. Though it appears, says Legman, that the rich and powerful Templars had all the women they wanted "very handsome and elegant."

That there was more to the Templar ritual than a banal satisfaction of the senses is indicated by the nature of its kiss on the mouth—a hermetic means of transmitting a subtler spiritual breath from initiate to novice.

The Templars appear to have realized long before Wilhelm Reich that society could not be reformed into a peaceful brotherhood so long as repressed sexuality could be distorted into neurosis and aggression, and that any sexual discharge of pent-up vital energy was better than having it turn noxious, as with the torturers and warmongers.

What actual Tantric practices the Templars may have indulged in, whether masturbatory, homosexual, or heterosexual, is not easy to determine; for the brothers were understandably reticent in exposing the fabulous secret of their Order.

Crowley, in his *The Secret Garden,* adds a curious footnote to the Western Christian laws against homosexuality illustrative of the folly of man's misconception in matters of religion: "When the power of the Crescent menaced that of the Cross, sodomy was put down with Draconian rigour because the Turks believed that the Messiah (a reincarnation of Jesus) would be born of the love between two men. Sodomy was thus a religious duty with the Turk; at any moment his passion might be used to bring about the Millenium; so with the Christian it became heresy, and was punished as such!"

The Tantrism of the left-hand path, revived in the West by Kellner, was based on the Hindu mystic concept of a mindless universal energy, personified by the goddess Shakti, locked in embrace with the god Shiva, from whose eternal orgasm every factor in the universe is derived.

Practiced by individuals, heterosexually, it is similar to Pico, Ficino, and Bruno's means of slipping through the mesh of sensitive illusion, a sort of magical ascent beyond the world of appearances, during which the participants, in a paroxysm of orgiastic ecstasy, burst forth from the limits of the body to explore the more rarefied regions of the cosmos, to experience directly, as two gods embraced, the consciousness of Shakti and Shiva—at One.

That these secret Tantric practices had flourished in widely scattered cultures from China to Africa, from India to the Middle East, and that they may have come to America and Africa from lost Atlantis was claimed by Gerald Massey; and it was through him that Crowley was able to track sexual magick back to its Egyptian prime, developed from an African source—the same source which took it to Haiti as voodoo.

Crowley synthesized his message: "I say to each man and woman: You are unique and sovereign, the center of the universe. However right I may be in thinking as I do, you may be equally right in thinking otherwise. You can only accomplish your object in life by complete disregard for the opinions of other people. . . . My mission is, in short, to bring everyone to the realization and enjoyment of his own kingship, and my apparent interference with him amounts to no more than advice to him not to suffer interference." This, said Crowley, in no way diminishes the advantages of "joint action directed to the attainment of a common purpose."

427

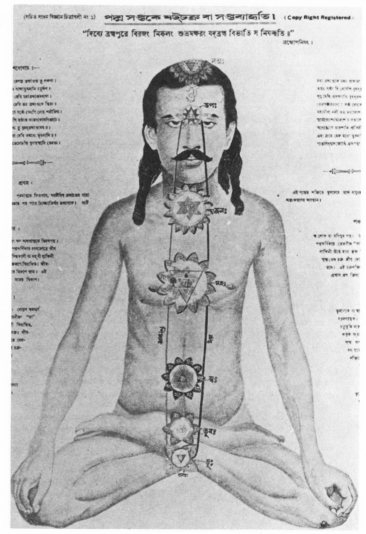

The essence of Tantric lovemaking is to postpone orgasm by various postures, meditations, incantations, and prayers so as to raise the kundalini.

The liquid known as amrit (ambrosia of the gods), or the elixir of life, is said to flow from the genital outlet of the priestess chosen to represent the goddess. In man the fluid is said to be charged only when the Fire Snake—controlled by a form of yoga involving the anal sphincter—flashes back and forth between the prostate region and the brain. Once the kundalini was raised the human organism was to be used as a condenser to draw in stellar or transmundane energy by tapping the appropriate chakra once it was animated and magnetized. The OTO aimed at using the subtle energies of the Fire Snake for establishing a door into space through which extraterrestrial cosmic rays might enter and manifest on earth, enabling humans to have intercourse with extraterrestrials more evolved than man.

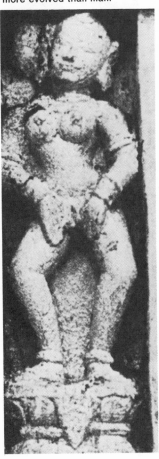

In all Tantric magic, the essential requirement—whether in the ecstasy of couples or the solo rituals of a priestess—involved the raising of the energy known as the serpent of fire, or kundalini. This mysterious energy, described as lying dormant in the lowest of the seven chakras, can be aroused by two distinct methods, called, traditionally, the right- and the left-hand path. The right hand allots supremacy to the male principle, the left to the feminine. As the serpent power is aroused, according to clairvoyants, it climbs up the backbone of the adept, energizing each chakra, till it emerges from the skull—symbolically as a snake's head like those so clearly depicted in Egyptian statuary. The excited chakras are seen clairvoyantly as whirls of multicolored lights, glowing and pulsing along the spinal column, with lesser lights "pulsating like stars throughout the ganglionic network of nerves which constitute the subtle anatomy of man." The aroused chakras are described as petaled lotuses, tuned as receivers of powerful cosmic rays to link the microscopic body to the macroscopic universe.

As adepts describe the rising serpent, it unites with the "many-petalled lotus of the cerebral region" to bring about illumination—or the highest form of initiation—as the current "climbs back from duality to unity by reversing the path it originally took down the chakras to procreate humanity."

Details of the OTO's initiation into Hindu and Tibetan Tantra, including ceremonies involving the use of "exudations" from specially trained priestesses, were brought to a wider public by Crowley's follower Kenneth Grant. Sacred courtesans, experts in ritual eroticism, known in India as *nautch* girls, *manjaris, suvasinis,* or *devadasis,* were exceptionally honored, says Grant, and given advanced education in music, dance, painting, literature, and philosophy. Their magic exudations, known as kalas, from the goddess Kali, have, for centuries if not millennia, been taken by adepts of Tantra as a medicinal elixir, quite possibly the "elixir of life."

David Farren, an ex-Jesuit professor of philosophy who married a witch, says in *Sex and Magic,* it was the Chinese Taoists who dared to use human sexuality in an effort to produce a substance that would provide physical immortality. According to the Taoists, if a man could provoke a woman into producing vaginal secretions while he kept himself from ejaculating, he could then assimilate her own life-force, or yin, while not losing any of his yang. A man who could take ten women in a night was considered well on his way to being one of the legendary immortals.

Adepts of the left-hand path use the kalas, or vaginal essences, by invoking the goddess at the Muladhara chakra, by the female genital outlet. Grant says the Elixir of Eternal Life manifests in the high priestess at the climax of the sacred rite. "The invisible seed (bindu) at the heart of the central yoni represents the 16th Kala." Grant calls the kalas essences, or "rays of time," and suggests that as the earth's aura continues to be impregnated by rays from the stars, new and subtle kalas penetrate human consciousness. The stars, he says, represent, magically speaking, astral consciousness concentrated in the subtle essences of the kalas, or vaginal vibrations. The sixteenth kala, or ray of the moon, which he calls the most secret of all, is "the essence where time stands still, where time is NOT, i.e. NUIT."

To arouse sexuality in the priestess, and to build up her libido, various methods were employed in different cultures. Whereas the Chinese Tantric Taoists are reported to have used infraliminal vibrations from large gongs reverberating just beneath the threshold of normal audile receptivity, the Egyptians, from extant depictions, used what are described as "manipulative techniques of sexo-somniferous magnetization." And whereas the Atlanteans, to arouse the fire-snake, are believed to have applied magnetized metal instruments to the chakras of a priestess, one of Crowley's more eccentric fellows, a Royal Navy commander G. M. Marston, experimenting with the rhythm of tomtoms, was able to lead demure English women to "shameless masturbation and indecent advances."

The goddess Kali was, in any case, invoked at the region of the Muladhara chakra, seat of the kundalini, the zone whose gate is the female genital organ. As the kundalini rises in the temple priestess, Crowleyans describe it vitalizing not only the chakras but a series of secret erogenous zones known as marmas, imbuing them, in the poetic language of Tantra, with nectar, or vibrant energy, causing each sacred lotus to generate subtle effluvia, or kalas, of great potency, considered by Crowley the "Magick Light," the Hadit, or Set of the *Book of the Law,* the Aub or Ob of the voodoo.

The science of the marmas, says Kenneth Grant, is highly complex, and only communicated under cover of secrecy during an initiation. According to Havelock Ellis, only fourteen of the seventeen bodily secretions known to Tantrics have been recognized by Western science. The fifteenth and sixteenth, which are known to orientals, only manifest, says Grant, in the vaginal emanations of the fully trained and developed suvasini. Crowley and his fellow adepts found that the kalas differ in chemical composition according to the phases of the feminine cycle, the age and condition of the woman, the phases of the moon, the relative location of the stars—which, if nothing else, indicates that the Paracelsian notions of the effect of planets and stars on humans contained greater wisdom than his contemporaries were able to accept, a notion more fully developed by the clairvoyant scientist Rudolf Steiner.

In the world of Tantra, the sixteenth kala is represented by the invisible seed, or "bindu," the catalyst that makes the "virgin" glow and emanate the nectar, or amrit, which contains in its fragrance the ultimate essence—the elixir of life. Bindu, or semen, is represented by a point or dot at

Crowley said the ancients did not obtain their ductless-gland extracts from brainless dead cats, dogs, or pigs, but from living humans, where the substance was of greater value. "The urine of a healthy young female which contains the internal secretions from various organs of therapeutic value and health-giving importance is used as the medium for the imbibition of tonics.

the heart of a triangle, or yoni. Shades of the Davenport stele!

An essential part of the Tantric ritual is the vibration of mantras, or magical sounds. Whereas the creative mantra of the fire-snake is the familiar Masonic and voodooistic Om or Aum, the mantra that effects the gradual release of the sixteenth kala, as described by Grant, is one of the most guarded secrets of the left-hand path, consisting of sixteen syllables each vibrated for one kala.

In the *vama marg* ritual the resulting elixir, or "secret seed of the stars," is caught on a leaf and is absorbed orally by the magician without contact with the priestess, whose supersensitivity aroused by sexuality could be short-circuited by a touch.

Imbibition of the kalas, charged with the upward-directed kundalini current, is said by Crowleyans to transform human consciousness and make possible communication with transcendental entities: the sport of Apollonius, de Molay, Ficino, Pico, Dee, Cagliostro, Lévi, and their followers.

Conversely, Grant warns, the intake of the downward-directed venom brings man into contact with the demonic world of the lower elementals, where only a powerful adept may venture with impunity. The sixteenth kala is also said to bisexualize those who absorb it in the prescribed manner; hence the representation of Shakti gods as androgynous, like the Baphomet of the Templars.

Thus the source of the vital elixir sought by the alchemist and adept of yore was exuded from a human female flower. Crowley adds that the secretions of the endocrine, or ductless, glands from a healthy young female are much finer and much better for human imbibi-

431

tion than those used by modern medics and extracted from the dead glands of animals which lack the essences of humans.

Understanding the ritual of the *vama marg,* says Grant, gives meaning to the Hermetic opening of Crowley's *Book of the Law,* where in the first stanzas, it proclaims, "Behold! it is revealed by Aiwass [spelled differently at different times by Crowley for numerological reasons] the minister of Hoor-paar-kraat. The Khabs is in the Khu, not the Khu in the Khabs." Incomprehensible, until it is realized that *khabs* in Egyptian means "star," and *khu* is the female essence, or magical power. Interpreted thus, it is the starlight which resides in the magical power of the female generative essence. Stars, rays, flowers, essences, perfumes, oils, unguents, times, cycles, emanations—all, as Grant points out, are concentrated in the black goddess Kali, the flower, the living symbol of time.

In his *The Magical Revival,* Grant goes on to show how Crowley's use of sex as a means of gaining access to the invisible worlds, and other planes of dimension, was a return to the rituals of predynastic times in Egypt, where the great mother goddess Tuart was worshiped through sexual rites which were then exported to India and the East, and later perpetuated in a more or less decadent form in the *orgia* of the Greco-Roman mysteries. The Egyptian predynastic tradition, known as Draconian, or Typhonian, is traced by Grant from an earlier African mystery system, similar to voodoo, possibly derived from Atlantis. According to his analysis of the Crowleyan data, the Draconian cult in Egypt was the cult of the fire-snake, based on "magnetism, intercourse with spirits, and elemental manifestations seen clairvoyantly. The astral body was an observed fact, and indicated spiritual survival after death."

The contention is clearly that the "mysteries" moved from ancient Egypt to Sumer, India, Tibet, and China, where they flowered into the Taoist Tantras. That the oriental systems were based upon the Draconian-Typhonian cults of ancient Egypt is deduced by Grant from the many Egyptian terms in the texts of the Tantras, particularly those of India. Shakti, or power, the central concept of the Tantras, he equates with the Egyptian Sekht, or Sekmet, consort of the gods, typified by the heat of the southern sun, or the sexual heat of the lioness. Khart in Egypt is Horus, child of the god; in India the son of the sun god is Kartikeia. The Egyptian sun god On is the Vedic Ong or Om. Sesheta, which typifies the female period, is Sesha in Hindi.

Budge describes Tuart as the wife of Set, or Typhon, also known as Apt. Her common title was "mistress of the gods" and "bearer of the gods." One of her forefeet rests upon the symbol of magical power, which, says Budge, probably represents a part of her organs of generation. To de Lubicz, she is the womb, considered as volume, one that embodies and materializes substance. She is the sky when considered as three-dimensional space that engenders all volumes. She is a *mammal* because she symbolizes the function of nourishing or quantitative multiplication brought about by selective affinity.

The predynastic Egyptians worshiped the feminine principle, the great mother goddess represented by the seven stars of Ursa Major and her child Sirius the dog star, or Set. Sirius was also represented by the same symbol as his mother, whom he is supposed to have fecundated. Those Draconians or Typhonians, says Grant, oblivious of the role of the male in the biological mysteries of creation, worshiped the "whore and her bastard," later typified as Virgin and Child. And so, back to the mother goddess of the witches and the old religion.

To the ancient Egyptians, Ursa Major was Ta-Urt, goddess of the mysteries of time and cycles, from whose name Crowley derived the Tarot's use for divining past and future. Ta-Urt was also known as Serk, to whom the dog-star Sirius, or Set, was sacred. During the Draconian migration from Egypt to Sumer, says Grant, Set became Shaitan, and then Aiwaz in Babylonian Akkad.

One of the names for Set was an upright stone or pillar, and Grant points out that the gemantic number for IHVH, the name that cannot be uttered by Jews, was twenty-six, which he equates with the middle pillar, or phallus, twenty-six being also the gemantic formula for the phallus in function, or extended in action.

The Sabean form of Set, which was Sevekh, later became Sebek-Ab-Ra, meaning "lamb of Ra," or "lamb of the sun." This Grant equates with the solar-phallic energy perpetuated by the gnostics as Abrahadabra, Had being Chaldean for Set.

The Sabean cult of the stars was followed first by a cult of the moon with the moon god Thoth, lord of the double light, who replaced Set; though Grant points out that Thoth's symbol, the dog-headed cynocephalous ape, is a continuation of the dog symbol of Set. The moon cult was in turn superseded by the solar cult of the Osirian, or Ammonite, supporters of male supremacy, with its deleterious effects down to the present.

Conflict between the Draconian-Typhonian worship of the feminine principle and the solar masculine cult, says Grant, split Egypt for centuries, yet the Draconian tradition "lingered on into the dark dynasties whose monuments were gradually laid waste by the solar cultists who abhorred all reminders of the Sabean origins of their theology." It was a conflict, says Grant, which lasted from the predynastic eras to the final fall of the Draconian cult, around the time of the Seventeenth Dynasty (variously estimated by Egyptologists as between 1650 and 1570 B.C.).

An effort to revive the Draconian cult of Sabek-Ra, or

In *Across the Gulf*, volume six of the *Equinox*, Crowley described in opalescent language his re-construction of what he called his own life as a priest in the Twenty-sixth Dynasty, "when I was ANKH-F-N-KHONSU and brought about the Aeon of Osiris to replace that of Isis." The name, he said, means "his life in Khonsu"—Khonsu being the moon god of Thebes. Crowley regarded the recovery of "past lives" through overcoming the obstacle of past deaths as es-sential to "understanding the general object of existence." Grant adds that the Ankh, or sandal strap, the glyph of Venus, symbolizes the ultimate tran-scendence of individual con-sciousness.

Those who do not read Crow-ley's work with care, says Grant, miss the deeper implications; yet, properly understood, it pre-sents the most precise and aus-tere code of conduct ever enun-ciated. But because it implies the total freeing of sex from the shackles of the convential, "it creates an immediate resistance in the mind unprepared for New Aeon attitudes." Spiritual attain-ment, said Crowley, was "incom-patible with bourgeois morality," and he opined that the social and moral inhibitions and restric-tions of his day were a crime against nature for which a se-vere toll would be exacted. The

Set, was made by a Theban priest of the Twenty-sixth Dynasty, Ankh-af-na-Khonsu, in the seventh century B.C. And the effort of this Theban priest of the Saite Period throws light on Crowley's hypnotic involvement with Set and Aiwaz. Crowley maintains that *he* was that Theban priest. "Tradition asserts that we forget our previous incarnations, because the shock of death erects a barrier; wihout assenting to this theory, I will say that having trained myself to face the fact of Death without mental disturbance, I found myself able to recall my last death."

Crowley recalled not one, but many past lives; very few of which, says Grant, "were outstanding in a worldly sense." Some, as described by Crowley, were "of almost uncompensated wretchedness, anguish and humiliation," voluntarily undertaken, he says, so he might resume his work "unhampered by spiritual creditors."

Crowley says he found it difficult to remember his "magical mistakes," and was "barred from remembering details of a tremendous magical catastrophy in the remote past." Its effect he describes as being hurled from a series of incarnations in which he was a high initiate, "to climb painfully once more to my present state." There was thus a large gap in his magical memory, "a shape of shame and horror which I have not yet found courage to unveil." In volume one, part ten of the *Equinox,* Crowley gives details of the life of Ankh-af-na-Khonsu, and of his failure to reinstate the worship of Set.

As a result of this failure, says Grant, the faint echoes of the ancient cult died down, and in their stead came "the flood of grotesque occult lore and debased sorcery that was to wash away the last vestiges of Egypt's glory." The remaining few dynasties saw merely an acceleration of this process of degeneration. "It was not till many centuries had elapsed that the Draconian Current re-awakened, not in Africa but in Asia in the guise of the Tantras of the Left Hand Path."

Crowley's memories of a life as a Roman named Marius Aquila and those of a Cretan priestess called Aia are relatively banal, but those of a disciple of Lao-Tse, and author of the *King Khang King,* give meaning to the art of clearing the blocks which veil man's memory of the past.

John Blofeld, in his *The Wheel of Life,* refers to adepts of Taoist Tantra in China who, controlling their conscious-ness, were able to achieve what he calls "a relative immortality," with no need to preserve a physical body in order not to "die" in one body and be reborn without losing the train of their identity; although, says Blofeld, the alternate aim was "total absorption in the Goddess,

mere mention of sex, he said, "draws man into a blind spasm of lust, either exploding into priapism or camouflaged into shocked indignation." Only when people can contemplate any given sexual idea without emotion of any kind will they be on their way to freedom. Crowley saw as his object to release their minds from bondage—or, better, themselves from the bondage of their minds. In the end, says Grant, Crowley left a loose-knit network of occult groups using the Ophidian current (kundalini) to prepare human consciousness for intercourse with the denizens of other dimensions.

accomplished through Tantric sexual union with the priestess who embodies her." To the Taoist, the purpose of raising the kundalini appears to have been the creation of an astral body that would survive both death and the dissolution of consciousness.

In his *Confessions,* Crowley gives a brief view of a life shortly before Mohammed when his goal was "to bring Oriental wisdom to Europe and restore paganism in a purer form." He describes being present at a "council of Masters" in which various illumined ones were appointed to undertake different adventures. "Mohammed, Luther, Adam Weishaupt, the man we knew as Christian Rosenkreutz, and many servants of science were chosen. Some of the movements have succeeded more or less, some have failed entirely. . . ." Crowley, adds Grant, would not have referred to Weishaupt as a master unless he knew him to be far advanced upon the path in a magical or mystical sense.

In *Heart of the Matter,* which Crowley wrote under the pseudonym of Khaled Khan, or "Sword of God," he claimed to have been a reincarnation of the warrior who delivered the Arabs from the stranglehold of Christianity at the Battle of Damascus—in 1126. Crowley's next encounter with Tantra may have been in an incarnation in which he switched sides—a game often played by disembodied spirits. "I was involved," he said, "in the catastrophe which overtook the Order of the Temple."

This was followed by a less noble life as Pope Alexander VI, the Borgia menace, of which Crowley, in a masterpiece of understatement, reflected that "I failed in my task of crowning the Renaissance through not being wholly purified in my personal character," adding by way of exculpation: "An appropriate trivial spiritual error may externalize as the most appalling crimes."

Crowley's next three lives, in terms of the magic of obelisks, are more to the point. As Sir Edward Kelley, the Tantric adept and scryer friend of Dr. John Dee, Crowley maintained he misunderstood certain messages that referred to the New Aeon of Horus announced by Aiwaz. But as to the genuineness of the Keys Crowley submits that the best guarantee is "the fact that anyone with the smallest capacity for Magick finds that they work."

Grant suggests that Crowley, using Dee and Kelley's system of scrying with Enochian language, was able to go far beyond what they had managed to acquire at the beginning of the seventeenth century, and that by systematically exploring Dee's Aethyrs, he was able to "penetrate unknown dimensions of consciousness outside space

435

If it is of any consolation to those who believe that Crowley the heretic deserved the same flames that devoured Bruno, or the same jail that asphyxiated Cagliostro and Reich, he or she may rest assured that armored society did its very damnedest, decade after decade, to vilify Crowley in every possible way, publicly calling for the execution of "the wickedest man in the world" or longing to put him in jail forever; and had it not been that throughout his life he never committed the smallest infraction of the law, they might have succeeded. The press in Britain launched a campaign of libel comparable to if not worse than that provided by Morande, achieving for London the honor of producing the very worst as well as the very best of periodic pressings. Stevenson has provided a limpid analysis of how grossly and deadly unjust a press attack such as Beaverbrook's can be against a man unsupported by the vast sums it takes to bring suit. And once in a newspaper's morgue a libel lives forever. Whatever else Crowley may have achieved in his life, historian Robert Amadon says of him "This man is the greatest, and perhaps the only magician of the twentieth century in the West." Approaching death, Crowley asked fellow Mason Gerald Yorke to have him embalmed in the Egyptian manner; then he reconsidered, saying: "Since I already look like a mummy, I want to be cremated." Yorke admitted he was beginning to believe that AIWAZ could more

and time," and thus obtain solutions to many cosmic problems.

But the surprising chain is by no means over. Next, Crowley says he was born into the body of none other than Count Alessandro Cagliostro. This time his remembrances of events differ somewhat from those given by most Cagliostro biographers, though they make as much sense, and may be every bit as "historical." As Cagliostro, said Crowley, "I was born in a brothel, kept by my mother's mother. My mother was half Arab, my father presumably some rich traveller." There was, Crowley added, "a profound horror and gloom antecedent to this birth."

The mystery of Cagliostro's marvelous pomade, so good for ladies' skin, may at last have been revealed by Crowley in his most recent incarnation. Like the so-called Sicilian Magus, Crowley kept himself in revenue for a while in London by selling, for 2 guineas a jar, an effective pomade for ladies' complexions, whose prime ingredient was his own semen.

And the elixir of life promoted by Cagliostro may well have been Tantric kalas obtained from Serafina. Serge Hutin, the French professor who has written on every known occult subject, and especially on both Tantra and Cagliostro, suggests that the magus and Serafina may well have been a natural Tantric couple, and that the highest level of the Egyptian rite corresponded to an act of ritual sacred marriage, or *hierosgamos.*

Hutin further suggests that Mozart, privy to this secret, deliberately cast Papageno and his simple bride Papagena as symbols of common marriage, whereas in Tamino and Pamina, he represented a couple initiated into the world of Tantric love by none other than the Egyptian magus Sarastro-Cagliostro.

To cap this train of quite fantastic coincidences, Crowley next described his most recent death: "I found myself able to recall my last death and so pick up many memories of my previous life as Eliphas Lévi."

In his *Magick in Theory and Practice,* Crowley pointed out that Lévi's death occurred about six months before his own birth in 1875. Crowley thus found the explanation for his immediate pleasure and incomprehensible familiarity with a certain district in Paris's fifth arrondissement, by the rue de l'Ancienne Comédie. Lévi had lived in that neighborhood for several happy years.

Taken in series, these lives form a linkage. In Crowley's incarnation as Crowley he "expressly and unequivocally describes his work as the rediscovery of the Sumerian

436

accurately be named Eyewash, and that Crowley was a pseudo-messiah, not a prophet, yet he did not doubt "that this extraordinary man was a genius and a gifted teacher of the highest mystical illumination." In the end Crowley admitted that he might have "failed at everything" but that he nonetheless stood by his life's work and message: "I have not failed at love for the only abiding love affair of my life is the one I have with God! Oh my beautiful God! I swim in thy heart like a trout in the mountain torrent. I leap from pool to pool in my joy. . . ." Whether Crowley's was the God of all, or only of Crowley, at his funeral Louis Wilkinson read aloud the magus's "Hymn to Pan": "Thrill with lissome host of the light. / O man My man! / Come careening out of the night / Of Pan! Io Pan, / And I rave; and I rape and I rip and I rend / Everlasting, world without end, / Manikin, maiden, maenad, man / In the might of Pan. / Io Pan! Io Pan Pan! Pan! Io Pan." Crowley's god, whose manifestation occurs at high noon, *en marquant midi,* he equated with Hadit and conceived that at the precise moment that man becomes Pan his point of view is dissolved into Nuit—pure nothingness: "for all is naught." To paraphrase Crowley, when a man, growing in consciousness by repeated acts of love under will, expands his consciousness to embrace all other consciousness, he becomes Pan: i.e., one with all. Omne, Aum, Amen, Amoun.

Tradition of Set"—precisely what he was supposed to have been doing as Ankh-af-na-Khonsu in the Twenty-sixth Dynasty. In the past, says Grant, several adepts attempted the rehabilitation of the worship of Set, among them Adam Weishaupt, Cagliostro, Eliphas Lévi, and Helena Blavatsky; but all failed. Only Crowley, he notes, succeeded, "because he had received initiation of a higher order." Using the hermetic numeration of the Golden Dawn degrees, Grant classes Cagliostro and Mathers as 7°=4,□ Blavatsky and Levi as 8°=3,□ and Weishaupt as possibly 9°=2.□ Whereas Crowley, according to his own verdict, reached the highest grade of 10°=1□ or Ipsissimus.

In this rarefied air Crowley found himself "free from all limitations whatsoever, including good and evil." Across the abyss, says Crowley, the words of the Enochian Key "thrilled me with a meaning I had never suspected, each curse concealing a blessing . . . I understood that sorrow had no substance; that only my ignorance and lack of intelligence had made me imagine the existence of evil."

Grant considers that Crowley's crossing of the abyss, thanks to the power of the *Book of the Law,* which he calls "the utterance of an illumined mind co-extensive with the ultimate ideas of which the universe is composed," enabled him to "unite his consciousness with the universal cause, shift the center of gravity from himself to God," and so "proclaim his word (Thelema) as Allah and Buddha proclaimed theirs." But Grant's co-editor of *The Confessions of Aleister Crowley,* John Simonds, less partial to the self-proclaimed Ipsissimus, says that this is where Crowley made a false step, suggesting that "he illegally assumed this most exalted grade, and that it choked him." Prophets being seldom honored in their own country, the truth, as Bacon declared on the cover of his New Atlantis, remains to be known: *Tempora patet occulta veritas.*

But whereas Crowleyans claim it to be the imperative duty of the theurgist to thoroughly investigate in his "Iridescent Body of Light" the upper levels of Astral Light before transcending to a higher plain, Gopi Krishna, author of several works on Kundalini yoga, wisely says that almost all great spiritual teachers have pointed out the danger of succumbing to the lure of psychic power or visionary experiences on the Astral or mental plain, "For these constitute entanglements for the soul as confusing and as hard to shake off as the entanglements of earth." To perform surprising feats with invisible psychic or other cosmic forces, says Gopi Krishna, is descending again to the plain of earth.

437

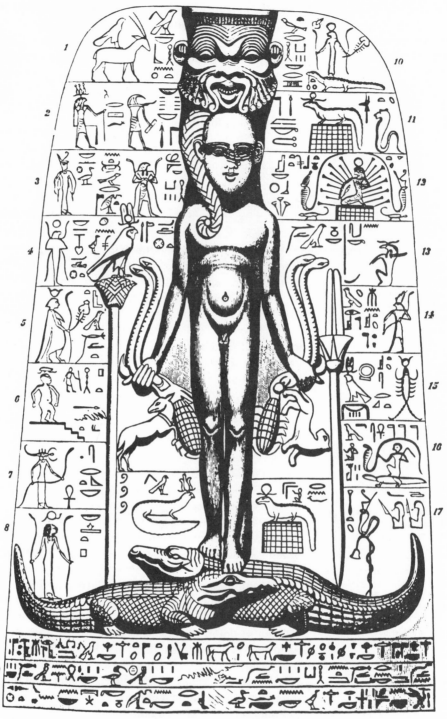

Cippus representing Horus on the Crocodiles, with the head of Bes.

1. Horus. 2. Thoth and Har-shef. 3. Hek and Neith. 4. Khnum. 5. Ast.t. 6. Ptah. 7. Serq, or Selk. 8. Nebhotep. 9. Commencement of long inscription continued on back. 10. Urhek. 11. 'Great god in Kat, and snake User.' 12. Isis. 13. Sebak. 14. Horus. 15. Golden hawk, Isis, Selk. 16. Horus. 17. Buto, Hu, and Sa.

20. RETURN OF THE PHOENIX

Horus the younger dominating the reptilian symbols of attachment to earth. Crowley maintained that hidden within the young Horus were two poles of energy, which he called HOOR-PAAR-KRAAT (or Harpocrates, the Greek god of silence or withdrawal) and RA-HOOR-KHUIT (KRU-MACHIS or HERAHATY), Lord of the Balance, or Double Horizon—i.e. of the two equinoxes. This left for Set the two solstices, with the sun at zenith and nadir. Two birthdays were assigned to Jesus by the Christian Fathers, one at the winter solstice, the other at the vernal equinox. This system, says Massey, was based on the birthdays of the double Horus, the dual form of the solar god in Egypt, child first, adult at the vernal equinox. In Egypt, Massey points out, the year began with the summer solstice, when the sun descended from its midsummer height, lost its force, and lessened in size. This represented Osiris born of the Virgin Mother as the child Horus, the diminished infantile sun of autumn, who descended into hades, where he was transformed into the virile Horus and rose again at Easter, the sun of the resurrection, Horus of the two horizons. To the Egyptians, Osiris, as the child Horus, comes to earth to enter matter and becomes mortal. His father is Seb, the earth, whose consort is Nu, the bearer, one of whose names is MERI, the Lady of Heaven.

A Journal of Scientific Illuminism was the subtitle given by Crowley to *The Equinox,* and Kenneth Grant has no doubt that Crowley took the term *illuminism* from Weishaupt, adopting with it his glyph of the point in the circle as a secret cipher for the order, a glyph which is preternaturally sexual and Tantric. It represents, says Grant, the yin and the yang of China, the Chockmah and Binah of the Cabala, the Odnada and Obatala of Africa, the Kamakala and Tribindu of India, the caduceus of Mercury, the Nuit and Hadit of Egypt. In Hadit, Crowley saw the emblem of consciousness: a ray of light projected in the dark of night. Nuit, in Crowley's cosmology, was nothing that can be thought of or in any way formulated by the mind of man, "the infinite and eternal void or inner space, the undying darkness, symbolized by the yoni." Yet Crowley saw it as the hidden source of light, for Nuit can be stirred into being by Hadit, symbolized by the point, the male coefficient, typified by the phallus. In Crowley's words, "the infinitely great Nuit and the infinitely small Hadit unite in explosive rapture and the ensuing holocaust generates the event." In union the poles of Nuit and Hadit produce the objective universe.

In the macrocosm the immortal principle is represented by the sun, in the microcosm by the phallus. As the sun drenches the earth with its creative rays, the phallus drenches the womb with its seed. Yet the symbolism, note Crowley and Grant, is imperfect, for neither the sun nor the phallus in itself has power beyond that which flows through it from another source. In the case of the sun, they say, this power is refracted through Sirius, the star of Set. Set to them represents the light of initiation, "the opener of man's consciousness to the rays of the Undying God who is typified by Sirius, the Sun in the South."

To Crowleyans, in the new Aeon of Horus, Isis will rediscover the immortal principle in Osiris, and man, consciously using the formula of Love Under Will, will advance his spiritual development.

The old Aeon of Isis, according to Crowley, glorified matter, the mother, the body. The old Aeon of Osiris, denying the body, glorified the spirit in the afterlife; with its appendage, the Christian Era, it was characterized by blood and agony, Osiris, the god of the Dead, exemplifying the Christian cult with its emphasis on death, suffering, and sorrow. Yet Isis, copulating with the dead Osiris, brought forth the child Horus, or unified cosmic consciousness, to produce, as Grant expresses it, the balance of these extremes in the realization of the identity of matter and spirit of male and female—a realization that comes through the union of opposites.

In Crowley's new aeon, man is no longer "to die to his body" in order to experience everlasting life; he will know, says Grant, that he never was a body, and realizing that he was never born, and therefore never died, that the body is a mere play of spirit undergoing ceaseless transformations, he will know that the spirit endures forever, triumphant, changeless, yet ever new. "Subject and object will be realized as one. Death, as understood, or rather misunderstood, by earlier cults will be finally and experientially transcended, abolished, nullified."

Grant further elaborates on Crowley by explaining that in the Aeon of Horus the dualistic approach to religion will be transcended through the abolition of the present notion of a God external to oneself. The two will be united. "Man will no longer worship God as an external factor, as in Paganism, or as an internal state of consciousness, as in Christianity, but will realize his identity with god." The new Aeon of Horus, based on the union of male and female polarities, will involve the magical use of semen and ecstasy, culminating in an apotheosis of matter—"in the realization that the old Gnostic notion that matter is not dual but one with the Spirit"—symbolized by the androgynous Baphomet of the Templars and the Illuminati.

Robert Anton Wilson, in his *Cosmic Trigger: The Final Secret of the Illuminati,* a more factual sequel to his fictional *The Illuminatus Trilogy,* came to the striking conclusion that at last he understood the secret of the Illuminati to be sexual. "They are not the fantasy of right-wing paranoids. The Illuminati was one of the names of an underground mystical movement using sexual yoga in the Western World." Wilson explains that "the veils of obscurity and mystery around such figures as Giordano Bruno, John Dee, Cagliostro, the original Rosicrucians, and Crowley himself, as well as various other key figures in the conspiracy, had nothing to do with politics or plots to take over the world. It was a screen to protect them from persecution by the Holy Inquisition in earlier centuries and from puritanical policemen in our time."

Wilson says that when he remarked to Timothy Leary—then in Vacarilla Prison for having experimented with hallucinogenics—that Giordano Bruno, "the first philosopher in history to suggest that there were Higher Intelligences in this galaxy," used Tantric sex, Leary replied: "It was obvious from Bruno's own writings. Sex-magic is *always* the first of the secrets."

Dr. Walter Huston Clark, in his *Chemical Ecstasy,* claims that most human beings normally only perceive less than .5 percent of known pulsations in the universe, but that people who take the metaprogramming substances soon assert contact with higher intelligences.

Wilson postulates that the "angels" who spoke to John Dee were extraterrestrials, but that Dee, unable to comprehend them in those terms, considered them, as have other shamans and mystics, to be "messengers from God." Wilson further adduces Gurdjieff's allegory in support of the notion that a group of interstellar intelligences already evolved to stages less mammalian than ours, are watching us all the time, and, occasionally, intervening to accelerate our evolution toward their level. He then quotes Leary and Dr. Jack Sarfatti to the effect that the mysterious entities—whether angels or extraterrestrials—reported by visionaries, rather than being members of races already evolved to this level, "may be ourselves in the future!"

In *The Sirius Mystery,* Robert K. Temple devotes much space to demonstrating that to the ancient initiates Isis was a symbol of Sirius, and Osiris a symbol of the dark companion of Sirius. But, as Wilson points out, Temple was unaware of Crowley and Eliphas Lévi's insistence that the traditional secret revealed in the Eleusinian mysteries was that "Osiris was a black God." As Wilson reports,

Hassan-Ibn-Sabbah, mystic philosopher initiated into the sect of Ismaili and known as the Old Man of the Mountain, formed his own sect to practice the ecstasy of the Sufis. Surrounded by a vast library in his Castle of Alamut, the biggest outside of Baghdad, he found a way of mixing hashish with henbane so that a man could gain inflexible determination. Magre says that Persians, Indians, and Chinese all used hashish and opium and other plants to promote the emergence of the astral "double" and attain early degrees of ecstasy.

Horus, said Isha Schwaller de Lubicz, is the key to Egyptian theology. "In the beginning and throughout time the universal Horus is the axis of the animating soul of the world. . . . He is the animator of preternatural Adamic Man before his fall into dualization. . . . The fall into matter creates his antagonist Seth, who through his constant opposition manifests the latent powers of Horus in nature." Seth is everything that tends to contrast and fix spirit in matter, a situation he seeks to perpetuate. Horus strives for the triumph of spirit in matter, light in darkness. His struggle with Seth makes history. In the eschatology, Horus the victorious becomes in the human being the supernatural Horus who reunites the divided complements and resolves all opposition. The Christian revelation introduces the god-man, Christ-Horus, incarnate in the human being. But after victory Horus returns to the black whence he came to start a new battle. He never rests. Massey points out that the Gnostic Jesus is the Egyptian Horus, and in the gnostic iconography of the Roman catacombs, child Horus reappears as the mummy-babe who wears the solar disc. "Royal Horus is represented in the cloak of royalty, and the phallic emblem found there witnesses to Jesus being Horus of the resurrection." Massey lists among the numerous types of Horus repeated in Rome as symbols of an alleged historic Jesus. Horus as Ichtus, the fish; Horus as the bennu, or phoenix; Horus as the dove; Horus as the *bambino;* and Horus as the reversed triangle.

George H. Williamson, in *Other Tongues, Other Flesh,* claims that a secret order on earth has been in contact with Sirius for thousands of years and that its emblem is the Eye of Horus. Williamson, an early "contactee" of the 1950s, also claims to have met flying saucerites from Sirius and prints huge chunks of their language. Among these, Wilson found a few of the words that were almost identical with the "angelic language used by Dr. John Dee, Aleister Crowley and other magi of the Illuminati tradition."

As Grant describes the new aeon, a race will be propagated of magically generated beings able to probe extraterrestrial dimension. And the next stage in the advancement of evolution on the planet "will be achieved by a willed congress with extra-terrestrial entities of which, in a sense, Aiwaz is the immediate messenger to humanity."

When Theodor Reuss died in 1922 he nominated Crowley as his successor, and the German OTO lodges accepted him as chief. Reuss had also granted other charters outside Germany, and Gerald Encausse, the great French occultist, known as Papus, was chief of the OTO in France as well as of the French rite of Memphis and Misraim. In Berlin, Rudolph Steiner, who had broken away from the Theosophical Society to found the Anthroposophical Society, better to fulfill his Rosicrucian ideals, formed, as deputy Grand Master of the OTO, a chapter of its grand council known as Mysteria Mystica Aeterna.

Since childhood Steiner had been aware of spirit beings and their workings, and had found a whole universe permeated through and through by spirit activity. To Steiner, matter was spirit manifesting in material form: both man and the physical world were of a spiritual origin, and both had a spiritual destiny. The real ego, said Steiner, is spirit, and lives in a world of spirits. To Steiner this supersensible reality behind physical reality was directly perceptible, and he claimed that the knack, once a normal human faculty, could be reacquired, universally. Through his own clairvoyance Steiner was already able to give contemporary scientists answers to puzzling problems in physics.

To his own science, based on his understanding of the supersensible world and its relation to ordinarily perceived phenomena, Steiner gave the name Anthroposophy, *sophia* being "wisdom" and *anthropos* "man," the latter, with the former, capable of understanding the secrets of the universe by attaining ever higher levels of consciousness. And Steiner described in detail how man can shift

Ba, depicted as a bird with a human head, represents the human soul that goes back and forth between heaven and earth. It can be seen ranging about a tomb hoping the shade will emerge free from its bonds to the earth. Ba is the life-giving power in nature, the breath whose departure causes death. Pure, formless spirit, immeasurable, indivisible, unfractionable, free, and mobile, it needs an objective means if it is to manifest but it cannot be confined in a body. From Ba derives everything that constitutes the world and its final perfection. Ba, in its divine nature, is man's kinship with the creator, realizable through consciousness.
Ka assimilates Ba and generates a new being. Ka individualizes and binds the spirit. Ka is the attractive force that causes and fixes Ptah's incarnation in matter. Ka is the carrier of all powers of manifestation and the activator of cosmic functions. The original Ka is the creator of all Kas of nature: mineral, vegetable, animal. Man's individual Ka comprises his inherited and his personal character and defines his destiny. But Ka is not the slave of fate, because it is not part of nature. The soul is not subject to the stars: it is free and can alter its course. Man's higher Ka, the highest part of his spiritual being, the consciousness of the heart, is in touch with his lower Ka, or the aspects of Ptah imprisoned, which the consciousness of spiritual Ka alone can liberate, with the help of Ba.

his consciousness, as if tuning a radio, to different points of view from which he is aware of operating subtler bodies than the physical, etheric, astral, spiritual; and that man's life, on its various levels, is related to the universe of stars, sun, planets; that out of the physical body, or between death and birth, man lives in the spirit world of the stars in endless relationship with the divine spiritual beings of the star world.

All of which was evidently perfectly understood by the ancient Egyptians, who gave different names, such as Ka, Ba, Khaibit, Shout, Khu, and Sekhem to the various bodies, all equally real, but operating in different dimensions. To the Egyptian there were three basic worlds: the most immediate being this earthly one of everyday consciousness. Then came Amenta, the realm of the mummified Osiris, a sort of purgatory in which spirits of the dead made up for their earthly errors. Then came Tuat, or heaven.

Crowley's personal secretary and follower, Israel Regardie, who became a Reichian psychologist, describes Amenta and Tuat as two aspects, inferior and superior, of the astral plane of the occultist, every yard of which had been mapped out for the Egyptian theurgist, and its qualities noted, together with the names of the guardian watchers of the pylons through which the defunct soul had to pass in order to gain admission to some other of the halls of the kingdom of Osiris. Only on what it already understood of the strange "astral" world into which, reawakening from the defunct body, it suddenly found itself in the shape of an astral body, could the spirit get through Amenta to Tuat. If previously initiated into the mysteries of this strange world, while still alive, it could better cope, says Regardie, progressing on its mastery of the magic words contained in the *Book of the Dead,* described as "the most ancient yet detailed grimoire for those who will come forth in the light of full consciousness." As Gerald Massey puts it: "The object of the words of power, the magical invocations, the funeral ceremonies, the purgatorial trials, is the resurrection of the spirit to life everlasting." And he sums up the ordeal: "Learn the *Book of the Dead* in life and it becomes the Book of Life in death."

The spirit in Amenta pleads that his "mouth be opened," that his memory return so that he may utter the words of power required to handle the shifting world of astral forms. And memory, Massey explains, is restored to the deceased through the words of power stored up in life, to be remembered in death. Practice for this occasion

could be achieved in life during trance, when the spirit,
leaving the body, could assume any form, at will, traveling
anywhere under any guise.

In Amenta, the object is to avoid what is known as "the
second death," which awaited those beyond purgation
who once more lost consciousness; all of which makes of
the gamut of earth, heaven and hades, but various states
of consciousness, from the most illumined to the blacked-
out, of which, in the end, the conscience of man is the
only true judge, being both the knower and the known.

How is it that all this wisdom, sensed by gnostic,
Templar, Rosicrucian, and Mason, was lost and only
surfaced intelligibly with modern clairvoyants such as
Crowley and Steiner? Michel Vladimirovitch Skariatine, an
émigré Russian, who spent his life studying the ancient
wisdom and wrote about it under the pen name of Enel,
recognized in the Hebrew Cabala a mixture of Egyptian
and Chaldean teachings, but found them often improperly
put together, full of obscurities and even contradictions.
So he went to the source: the sacred glyphs of the
Egyptians. Puzzled by a language with so many homonyms
and homophones, often with meanings diametrically opposed, Enel concluded that Champollion's phonetic decipherment, though it made possible pronunciation of the
glyphs, concealed a further symbolic meaning, sensed by
Champollion, but almost unanimously denied by succeeding Egyptologists until the Second World War.

The brilliance of the Egyptian form of writing, says Enel
in his *La langue sacré,* is the fact that it can contain more
than one meaning, conveying an overt, and often banal
phonetic significance, available to anyone, plus a Hermetic
meaning available only to the initiate. The texts containing
the overt credo of the Egyptian people, the funerary
prayers, and the representations of life beyond the tomb,
which needed to be available to all, were written phonetically. Yet they also contained the esoteric teaching of the
initiates, designed only for adepts. The structure of the
hieroglyphs made it possible to form a word with one
direct meaning, read phonetically, and a recondite, mysterious meaning, symbolically.

The purely magical texts, written solely for the adept,
says Enel, were not even given a phonetic sense, and
were therefore untranslatable by Egyptologists, who concentrated solely on the phonetic approach, without pursu-
ing the symbolic sense, the only one which could reveal
the religious and philosophic doctrines of ancient Egypt.
As Enel puts it: "Able to describe the body of Egyptian
glyphs they ignored the soul which gave it life."

the fundamental character of the created universe. "This duality is the principle of sexuality. At the same time, duality implies a comparison within a succession of phenomena which produces the cerebral consciousness." Spirit, or formless substance, is passive, the feminine principle in the cosmos, but becomes generative when acted upon by the "verb." And all, de Lubicz felt, is manifest by its opposite. There would be no dark without light; nor any way to know light except by shadow. And just as a corporeal obstacle creates touch, so a liquid environment creates taste, and terrestrial or corporeal emanations create odor. In the course of "evolution" the energies within the different states of matter have developed the senses. As the river creates its bed, so light creates the eye, and sound creates the ear. The causal energy becomes mineral, the mineral becomes plant, the plant becomes animal, the animal becomes man, and man becomes Cosmic Man, the Saint, Buddha, Jesus (Jehoshuah). But Nature, said de Lubicz, only shows us the closed, Osirian cycle, which renews itself spirally in its progression towards the liberation of consciousness. Here the essential theme is reincarnation, with its karmic consequences, which forms a "wheel of elimination" moving toward liberation. It is the law *for all*. Punishment is reincarnation; but reincarnation is also a divine mercy that allows one to be redeemed. This is true justice, without cruelty, without threat, a justice everyone can accept. But it was only for the masses that ancient Egypt maintained the Osirian cult of renewal and reincarnation. To the temple elite it taught the Horian principle: Horus the Redeemer. The redeemer—the Unction of the Divine Verb—was the Christ within, but only for the man who realized it within himself. Throughout historical Egypt, said de Lubicz, the common people lived in the Osirian faith, which is a teaching of renewal, evolution through reincarnation of the living soul. Man lived then under the sky, under the ordinances of the heavens.

Neither through Coptic, nor through Greek, according to Enel, is it possible to understand the symbolic meaning of the hieroglyphs: the only route is via the Hebrew Cabala, offspring of the ancient Egyptian tradition. The object of the hidden symbols, he realized, was also to conserve for eternity the ancient knowledge of the mechanics of the solar system and the measurements of time and space accessible to human comprehension—a fact amply demonstrated by the extraordinary data encoded into the Great Pyramid of Cheops.

Enel believes the conquerors who brought this wisdom to Egypt were refugees from Atlantis, who came to found a colonial reflection of their powerful civilization with its sophisticated religion. Certainly the wisdom and science of ancient Egypt appears along the banks of the Nile already in flower, developed in some previous location, presumably the equinoctial land of the Golden Age of Saturn.

The twenty-six phonetic signs of the Egyptian alphabet, says Enel, also serve to describe the principles of creation, spelling it out in bold strokes as the ancients envisaged it. The glyph ⌡ , *B* symbolizes a perpendicular raised on a plain, such as the raising of an obelisk. As Enel deciphers its cosmic meaning, cosmic forces agitating inert matter attack the surface with the involutive spiraling force of ⌡ , *Bn;* and by means of an evolutive spiraling force raise it to ⌢⌡ , *Nb.*

The action of these forces creates combinations of the four elements—fire, water, air, and earth—all of which derive from the same *MW,* ≋ , the basic mother, or *mater.* Unformed mass △ , which is *q,* is transformed into organized matter ▢ , *p.* The glyph for the current which descends and ascends through twisted interlacings to manifest spirit on the material plane is ৪ . ৪⌡⌈ is to envelope in matter. And ৪⊙৪ is eternity, or the body of Ra which was and which will be. The creative verb ⌣ , Ra, by its action produces the realization of the declared verb *Nou,* or protomatter, father of all the gods, and of all manifestation in the universe.

From the primordial waters of Nou came into being the self-engendered Atum rising up as a primeval hill, the symbol for which came to be the temple hill of the sun at Heliopolis, dwelling place of this high god manifesting as light and symbolized as an obelisk. The mount was now the image of mother earth, the great bringer forth, and "the pillar of heaven", or obelisk, was the symbol of fatherhood, "the rock that begot." "Oh Atum! When you came into being you rose up as a High Hill. You shone as

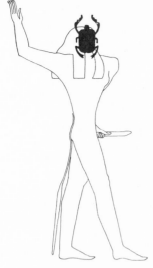

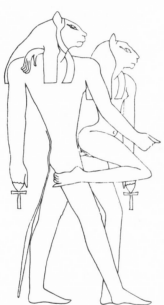

The symbolism of Nut, Geb, and Shu is based on the legend that originally earth and sky were together in total sexual union. Thus when the sky descends ritually upon the earth, Nut is impregnated by Geb. But Nut's father, Shu, so loved her, he separated her from her mate Geb, and, as air, held her aloft with his arms. Nut then gave birth to the stars and allowed them to sail across her belly.

the Benben stone (or obelisk) in the Temple of the Phoenix at Heliopolis.'' The phoenix, or bennu bird, was, of course, the symbol of both Ra and Osiris. ''For the Heliopolitan,'' says R. T. Rundle Clark in *Symbol and Myth in Ancient Egypt,* ''morning was marked by the shining light on an erect pillar or pyramidion on a support or shaft which could reflect the rays of the rising sun. At the beginning, a light bird, the Phoenix, had alighted on the sacred stone, an obelisk, known as the Benben, to initiate the great age of the visible God.''

When Atum, the aboriginal deity and ultimate but hidden godhead, at first alone in the universe, came into being, symbolized by the primeval serpent in the dark waters of the abyss, his act was symbolized as autoerotic. ''In one sense,'' says Rundle Clark, ''he is the Atum figure of Heliopolis performing creation by masturbation.'' Noting that masturbation was the most popular creation motif throughout Egyptian history, Clark quotes a pyramid text to the effect that Atum proceeded to masturbate himself in Heliopolis: ''he put his penis in his hand that he might obtain the pleasure of emission thereby; and there were born brother and sister, Shu and Tefnut.''

And so all of creation came into being. Shu, the elemental force representative of air, breath, the wind, was, in Africa, most especially the breeze of dawn and evening, the very breath of life, imaged by the Egyptians as a panting lion crouched upon the horizon, lifter-up of the darkness of the night sky. Tefnut, the other supporter

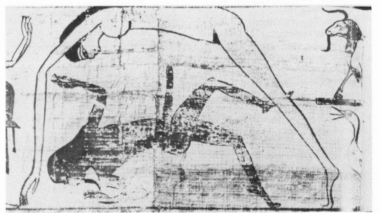

This annunciation scene on the walls of the Temple of Luxor, says Massey, shows Thoth, the divine word, or *logos,* hailing the virgin queen, announcing she is to give birth to the coming son or sun. In the next scene the god Kneph (in conjunction with Hathor) gives life to the queen. Kneph, says Massey, is the Holy Ghost, or spirit that causes conception. Impregnation is apparent from the virgin's fuller form. Next, the mother is seated on the midwife's stool, the child in the hands of a nurse. In the scene of adoration (*below*) the child is enthroned, receiving homage from the gods and gifts from three wise men. The child announced, incarnate, born, and worshiped, says Massey, was the representative of the Aten-sun, the child-Christ of the Aten cult, the miraculous conception of the ever-virgin mother in the sky.

of the atmosphere, and eventually of world order, was moisture. Together Shu and Tefnut produced Seb (or Geb) the earth god, a phallic fellow, father of food, symbolized by the goose of plenty, and Nut, the sky goddess, who were kept apart by the atmosphere of Shu until Thoth, the god of wisdom, took pity on them and allowed them to unite to produce Osiris, Horus the Elder, Set, Isis, and Nephthys, all, in this guise, members of the solar system. And much of what actually occurred in the cataclysmic past of our system may be explained by the myth of the castration, death, and resurrection of Osiris as Horus the Younger, the returning sun, weakened after the tilt of the pole. Immanuel Velikovski, when asked which of the heavenly bodies in our sky suffered castration, replied laconically: Saturn, or Osiris. A remark about which a whole book might be written.

Gerald Massey complains that the wisdom of the Egyptians, hidden in their hieroglyphic language—at once their knowledge of both the physical and spiritual cosmos, obtainable in trance—was never really understood by Semite, Greek, or Roman. But Africans and American Indians could still summon spirits and commune with them, and even make them appear for others to see, or could travel to them in a trance. Among the Christians, says Massey, only the sects of gnostics, and such individual gnostics as Saint Paul, could detach from their bodily condition.

Tracing the texts of the Gospels of the Christian canon to their sources in ancient Egypt, Massey found that "from beginning to end they contain the Drama of the Mysteries of the Luni-Solar God, narrated as human history." The gnostics, he says, understood them to be mythical; the Christians took them for fact.

From the texts it is clear to Massey that the doctrine of the incarnation had been evolved and established in the Osirian religion at least four thousand years and possibly ten thousand years before it was "purloined and perverted in Christianity." It is so ancient that the source and origin had been forgotten and the direct means of proof lost sight of or obliterated except among the gnostics, who sacredly preserved their fragments of the ancient wisdom, "with here and there a copy of the *Book of the Dead,* done into Greek or Aramaic."

Massey claims sufficient warrant to affirm that Christ-the-anointed was a mystical figure which originated as the Egyptian mummy in the twofold character of Osiris in his death and Osiris in his resurrection; that is, as mortal

447

Horus, the Karast, and as Horus divinized as the anointed son. "Say what you will, or believe what you may, there is no other origin for Christ-the-anointed than Horus the Karast, anointed son of god the father."

Furthermore, says Massey, none of those initiated in the esoteric wisdom ever looked upon the Kamite Iusa, or gnostic Horus, Jesus, Tammuz, Krishna, Buddha, Witoba, or any other of the many saviors as historic personalities. A gnostic arose in another life as a spirit, not as a human being. Egypt had no doctrine of the physical resurrection of the dead. All of these notions Massey considers a perversion of the original wisdom.

The creation of evil Massey considers a miscreation traceable to the Akkadian, Babylonian, Assyrian, and Hebrew theologies. Hebrews and Babylonians, he says, confused the Uraeus-serpent of life with the serpent of death. The tree of life was changed by the Babylonians into the tree of death. The serpent that offered fruit for food as Rannut, representing Mother Earth, was transformed into the evil serpent that "brought death into the world." The same types which represented evil in the Babylonian mythology represented good in the Egyptian. A god of eternal torment is a Christian ideal not an Egyptian one. "Theirs was the all-parental god, Father and Mother in one, whose heart was thought to bleed in every wound of suffering humanity, and whose son was represented in the character of the comforter." The Great Mother, no matter how hideously portrayed, was not originally evil, but the bringer-forth and renewer of life in earth and water. Nor, says Massey, were the elemental offspring evil; though imaged as monsters or zootypes, they were not wicked spirits as made out to be by the Euphrateans—the devils of Western theology.

The Egyptians, says Massey, "had no fall of man to encounter in the fallacious Christian sense. Consequently they had no need of a redeemer from the effects of that which had never occurred." There was indeed a fall, he says, but it was "from the foothold first attained by the Egyptians to the dismal swamp of the Assyrian and Hebrew legends."

Nor did the Egyptians rejoice over the death of their suffering savior "because his agony and shame and bloody sweat were falsely supposed to rescue them from the consequences of broken laws; on the contrary, they taught that everyone created his own Karma here, and that the past deeds made the future fate."

In Massey's reading of the Egyptian texts, Horus did what he did for the glory of his father, not to save the

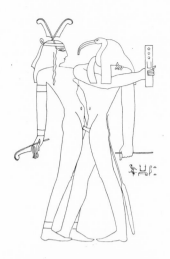

The Egyptian myths couple Maat, the protectoress of Truth and the Ibis-god Thoth, patron of Wisdom.

Maat, the female counterpart of Thoth, daughter of Ra, helped Ptah and Khnemu carry out the orderly creation ordered by Thoth. Goddess of the unalterable laws of heaven, she is "straight," "just," "true," "genuine," and "steadfast," and her emblem is the feather. All feminine neters, said Isha de Lubicz, are only revelation and manifestation of the great universal mother, for whom Maat is the divine wisdom that links the "divine" and the "natural" through consciousness. "Maat is universal consciousness, the consciousness of all consciousnesses."

souls of men from having to do the same. There was no vicarious salvation in the Egyptian view. Horus symbolized the justification of the righteous, not of the wicked. He did not come to save sinners from taking the trouble to save themselves. "He was an exemplar," notes Massey, "a model of the divine sonship; and his followers were to conform to his example."

For the Egyptian, eternal life was the ultimate reality. His god was just and righteous. The Egyptian did not pray for mercy, nor seek sentimental forgiveness for his sins. He knew his conduct now would count for the life hereafter. He must speak and act the truth. The standard of law was set up as Maat, the eternal rule of right. The Egyptian's creed was to fulfill Maat. Judgment with justice. The wickedness of the soul, said Hermes, is ignorance. Virtue is knowledge.

That the quest in Egypt was for the Christ within, the Christ of the Essene and the Gnostic, was at last driven home after World War II by an Alsatian archeologist with a Baltic title, R. A. Schwaller de Lubicz, who demonstrated that the sophisticated system of physics and metaphysics developed by the ancient Egyptians to account for the mechanics and purpose of the cosmos. With de Lubicz, Egyptology gained a true adept, not one of the ditchdigger or grave robber type of the nineteenth century, nor one of those of the twentieth who used the Rosetta Stone in a quest not for the Rose on the Cross, but for the acquisition of the rosette of the Legion of Honor.

Like Rosenkreutz, Cagliostro, and Crowley, de Lubicz arrived in Egypt already an initiate, having worked his way through the disciplines of theosophy, anthroposophy, yoga, alchemy—for which he had a special laboratory— and the wisdom of the East. He too studied with Moslem and Sufi masters in North Africa. And his wife Isha, who was to put the initiatory wisdom of Egypt into the form of two novels, *Her-Bak Chick-Pea,* and *Her-Bak, Egyptian Initiate,* arrived in Egypt with six years of strict classical

Knowledge, wrote de Lubicz, can only be synthetic, so it can only be intelligibly transcribed by an architectural monument; that is to say, by a *simultaneity of plane and volume,* accompanied in Egypt by the symbolism of writing, of image, and of statuary. "To this is added an entire architectural *grammar,* represented by the form of the stone blocks, their joints, overlappings, by their 'transparencies' and 'transpositions' on the walls. There is also a subtle grammar where the finishing of an engraving or its rough aspect, the absence of essential parts—such as the eye, or the navel—the introversion of the right with the left, etc., come to play the role of accents, declinations, conjugations, or conjunctions."

The ancients had an accurate knowledge of the centers of life and intelligence, said de Lubicz, and knew all about the brain. In the temple, each vital center of the human body is clearly marked. "The glands and the vital relationships between the organs are figured by the scenes showing their correspondences with the *Neters* who control them; this throws a great light on the true sense of the pharaonic pantheon and on pantheism in general."

Isha pointed out that the advantage of the Egyptian teaching is that the authentic texts are in the very place where they were inscribed, unaltered by successive transcribers. The number, key, and symbol of the texts allows direct access to the esoteric meaning hidden beneath the apparent meaning. If you take note of anomalies in the texts, said Isha, the various arrangements of letters in each word, the different forms used for the same letter, the color of the signs, you will decipher the riddles. The *secret message* is in the fundamental metaphysical significance of the individual letters and their syllabic arrangement *irrespective* of the overt text, which may be perfectly banal. "All traditional teachings," said Isha de Lubicz, "considered the fire in the spinal column as the evolutionary element in man.

Egyptology, through which she had acquired a key to the secret reading of the hieroglyphs. In the miasmic underworld of modern Egyptological exegesis, the analytical commentaries appended to her fiction threw the clearest light onto the complex system of Egyptian symbology enshrouding its cosmological theology.

In the same Temple of Ramses II at Luxor where Champollion spent five months and Lebas fifteen, de Lubicz and his wife spent fifteen years. With the help of her daughter, Lucie Lamy, they devoted the years between 1937 and 1952 to measuring and reproducing with extraordinary finesse and accuracy the entire stonework, including every glyph, every stele, every joint. As a team they were able to find what Bruno and Kircher and Cagliostro had all intuited, the key to the Hermetic philosophy and religion secreted in the ancient glyphs. The Temple of Luxor they found to be a vast stonework symbol incorporating the totality of Egyptian wisdom: science, mathematics, geodesy, geography, geometry, medicine, astronomy, astrology, magic, myth, art, and symbolism. To de Lubicz this vast library, containing the totality of knowledge pertaining to universal creative power, embodied in the building itself, constituted the greatest achievement of New Kingdom Egypt.

Not that the team could have made their discoveries any sooner. As late as 1881, when Gorringe researched the obelisks of Thebes, the temple was still covered by several meters of dirt and windblown sand. Only its southernmost part was accessible to view. In 1885 Gaston Maspero, director of antiquities for the Egyptian government, made the first serious attempt at excavating the area, revealing footings of walls, pylons, and columns buried beneath millennial layers of detritus. Thereafter the

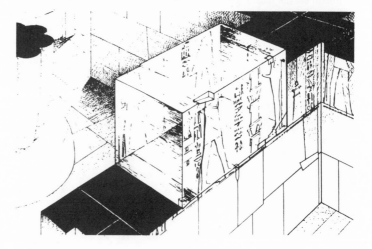

The awakening of this fire, asleep at the base of the sacrum, and its passage through the different centers of the body, were part of the practical initiation into the acquisition of human mastery." To this she added: "The energy *ner,* active fire of the world, is specialized in man's marrow as *sa,* his vitality. A man who succeeds in becoming conscious of it can augment and use it at will. This controlled power is *wscr.* A man who has mastered it, is *ser."* Isha explained: "The Sethian power of the testicles of Seth is mastered and sublimated into superhuman power." And she was explicit about the method: "It is through renenutet that the djed, the pillar of Osiris, is raised in nature and man, and it is she who when man has reawakened the fire of life in his djed leads it to the summit, the frontal ureaus that is the third eye of Horus. . . . This eye of fire masters the neters "or 'gods' and rules their blind powers."

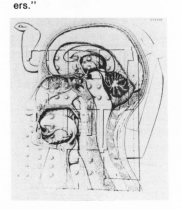

backbreaking work was continued under the supervision of a series of archeologists down to the recent author of *The Obelisks of Egypt,* Labib Habachi.

As collaborators at Luxor, de Lubicz added to his team the expertise of a French Egyptologist, Alexandre Varille, who had worked ten years for the Luxor Archeological Institute, and an archeologist-architect, Clement Robichon, who had been digging in north Karnak for the French Institute of Oriental Archeology. And during the whole of their long stay in Luxor, Lucie Lamy copied, with minute care, the plans, bas-reliefs, and inscriptions on the walls of the Temple of Luxor, which enabled de Lubicz, when back in France, to compose over the next ten years his monumental work *Le temple de l'homme,* in which he was able to spell out that the Luxor temple symbolically represented man, cosmic man, in whom all the laws ordering the universe are inscribed.

With this notion de Lubicz caused as great a shock to staid Egyptologists as had Champollion a century earlier. Yet R. T. Rundle Clark was to admit, at last, that "in recent years it has come to be realized that Egyptian art is nearly all symbolism. The architectural arrangements and decoration were a kind of mythical landscape. This was worked out down to the last detail of the furnishing; everything had a meaning or could be made to have one. Columns, capitals, walls, window-lattices, drainage outlets, gateways, screens and shrines all had significant traditional schemes. An Egyptian temple simultaneously appealed to the eye and the imagination."

De Lubicz discovered that it was by means of the harmonic relations in its design as a whole, and by the endlessly varied parts of its structure, that the temple, together with the mythological vignettes intaglioed in high or low relief, became a library in stone, one which told in bold lines the story of the creation of man, indicating his development stage by stage: a temple which recreated in artistic form man's relationship to the universe.

The proportions which de Lubicz found in the temple were those of pre-Adamic man, man before the Fall, and of perfected man, who, through his own efforts, regains his cosmic consciousness. Man, says de Lubicz, if he understands himself perfectly, understands the universe. "Man is not an image, a condensation of the Universe; man *is* the Universe."

The same theme is echoed by Kenneth Grant. "As man goes on unveiling and understanding the powers of his own constitution, he realizes that the macrocosm is contained within him, not *vice versa,* for Man—being the

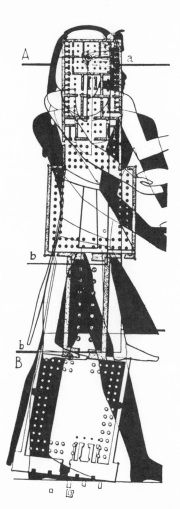

only complete Microcosm—he alone of all orders of
existence has a link with, or possesses within himself, the
potential of the entire gamut of manifestation."

De Lubicz formulated the axiom in what he calls his
doctrine of athropocosm: We have nothing to discover
outside of ourselves. The universe is neither an "imagination" nor a "will," but a projection of human consciousness. The reason for life, says de Lubicz, is to become
conscious of self. The goal of life is cosmic consciousness, beyond all transient, mortal contingencies. The
universe, he says, presents only an evolution of consciousness, from beginning to end, which is the return to
its Cause. Thus the aim of every initiatory religion is to
teach the way that leads to this ultimate merging.

Yet the ancient Egyptians distinguished two types of
consciousness: an intelligence which *knows* this universe
without having to reason it, and a cerebral intelligence,
which de Lubicz qualifies as that of "fallen" Adamic man.
Cerebral consciousness, peculiar to the animal kingdom
and the human animal, requires the faculty of registering
notions that are only acts of comparison, and this faculty
the Egyptians located in the cerebral cortex and the
double cerebral lobes.

Cerebral man, says de Lubicz, is not a creator; his or
her free will only allows for a decomposition of what is
there, and the choice among the pieces with which to
reconstruct an artificial whole. Cerebral man distinguishes
what creates from what is created, and tries to separate
the giver from the receiver, as if futilely hoping to sever
the north from the south pole of a magnet.

But the Temple of Luxor does not deal with cerebral
man, rather with the spiritual being which inhabits a human
body. To de Lubicz the temple served to guide the
civilization of the Nile Valley toward the gestation of divine
humanity out of the transitory human form. "The goal of
the Temple was to elevate our being towards the Being
which animates all." All of the temples extending along
the length of the Nile represent together a global teaching, each temple consecrated to a divine principle, developing a particular theme, inseparable from the whole, just
as the entire pantheon of Egyptian gods represent facets
of a single supreme being.

In Egypt the temple was the expression of a self-
perpetuating group of initiates responsible for keeping
intact a wisdom, based on a precise knowledge of universal laws, throughout Egypt's long history, a sacred science passed on through myth, ritual, and music, based on

number and measure, incorporated into structures and built into tombs and temples.

It was the same knowledge passed on to the builders of the great medieval cathedrals—a profound understanding of universal harmonic, rhythmic, and proportional laws, and a precise knowledge of the manner in which to employ these laws to create a desired effect. And the dimensions of the temple, like those of the Great Pyramid of Cheops, resolve themselves into fractions of terrestrial and cosmic measure. What stunning simplicity to build into the base of the Great Pyramid the foot to measure seconds of arc, 1.296 billion of which make the circumference of the earth, and a foot and a half, or cubit, to measure seconds of time *and* arc, $\frac{1,296,000,000}{1\frac{1}{2}}$ being the number of seconds of time *and* cubits in one revolution of the planet, or 864,000,000.

An analysis of number had already been published by de Lubicz in 1917. There he explained that "properly to understand the real successive steps of creation one must first know the development of abstract number: how the many are derived from the one. Because it is evident," he wrote, "that the first Unity, or uncaused cause is indivisible. As a prime unity it is purely qualitative and without quantity."

Through an endless symphony of measures one slips with de Lubicz past Alice's looking glass into the world of Parmenides and Zeno, where everything is always one no matter how you slice it. Numbers are but names applied to the functions and principles upon which the universe is maintained. The interplay of numbers causes the phenomena of the physical world. Frequency oscillating between two poles produces the form apprehensible to the senses. The body, the earth, the stars, are but complex vibratory systems with harmonic overtones. To be, is to be in harmony with the universe. Man and the universe are linked harmonically. This is the message of the Sufi saints.

In Egypt the de Lubicz family found themselves dealing not with the remains of a corpse, but with "a witness to an active presence." For the ancient Egyptians the entire temple had to live. Its intricate alignments, its multiple asymmetries, made the whole temple oscillate about its several axes. The secret of its life, as discovered by de Lubicz, was the harmonic play of number, proportion, measure, and orientation. "We must once and for all conceive of the pharaonic temple," says de Lubicz, "as a seed in the process of bearing its fruit."

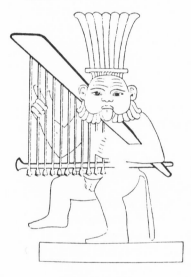

The Neter Bes, Egyptian god of music

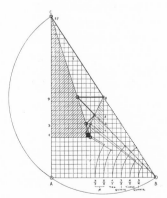

453

An exhaustive study of a single wall of a room within the covered temple, said de Lubicz, would require a book in itself. The orientation axes linking the temple to cosmic influences, the stone joints pointing to the physiological functions of the human body, the geometrical functions covering the numerical relations appropriate to the locations of the temple, the dimensions of the figures, the offerings, the attributes, the situation of the hieroglyphs in relation to the images and their ritual meaning—all must be taken into account. Each stone of the walls of the temple, he said, is cut according to preestablished measures; similarly, the stone beds were chosen according to an exact knowledge of the scene which was to be drawn there; the joints are situated in such a way as to cut, with intention, the head, feet, hands, attributes, etc. of the figures to be drawn. All of this concerns the hieroglyphic writing. The epigraphy alone never reveals the secret teaching of the sages. It is necessary to learn to *read the images*.

The Temple of Luxor is called Apet or Ipet of the Land of the South. The very name, says de Lubicz, is cabalistic. Ipet is the ancient Egyptian name of the female hippopotamus, symbol of the gestating womb. *Ipet,* he points out, derives from the root *ip,* which means "to count" or "to enumerate." Consequently gestation is identified with the act of counting, or multiplication. Phi, or the Golden Section, plays a dominant role in de Lubicz's identification of the Temple with man. He shows how the Golden Section, in no way a dead number, lies at the heart of what he calls the "primordial scission" of the One, engendering a universe that is both asymmetric and cyclical. Phi is the symbol of generation, of procreation, of growth in all directions; "it is the fire of life, the male action of sperm, the *logos* of the gospel of St. John," a symbol to which all of nature subscribes, from molluscs to giant redwoods, from the structure of bones to the ages of growth in man.

The discrete phases of growth as marked and carved into the temple stand in harmonious relationship to earlier and later stages. The various sections of the human body stand in complex but always harmonious relationship to each other. The entire temple explains the secret functions of the human organs and nerve centers. Every vital center is indicated. But these edifices, as Kircher was intuitively aware, speak a language addressed to spiritual man. And the architecture of the ancients was a living language. Only with the invention of printing, as Bruno lamented, was architectural teaching dethroned, the spirit eliminated, leaving the empty letter.

Like Enel, Schwaller de Lubicz saw the hieroglyphs not as overt phonetic signs, but as deeper Hermetic symbols conveying the subtle metaphysical realities of what he calls the "sacred science of the pharaohs." He saw in the glyphs a means of communicating the intuitively understood essence of life, one which slips through the net of language, something that can be glimpsed, like an aura, by not being viewed directly. The Egyptian symbols, says de Lubicz, were used as a deliberate means of evoking a deeper, spiritual understanding, as opposed to merely conveying information. They were pictorial devices to evoke an idea or a concept entirely, a complete hierarchy of meaning, bypassing intellect, moving straight to "the intelligence of the heart." They were magical symbols to evoke the form bound in the spell of matter. To be grasped, the symbol demanded a shift in consciousness, the same sort of shift which occurs when the print on the page of a novel is transformed into images of life.

This relief appears on the west side of the south wall of the hypostyle hall in Karnak, part of a scene called "Hunting Birds." In an adjoining relief, the figures of Thoth and Sechat were sculpted in relief by Seti I then intaglioed under Ramses II. In the hunting scene a net is filled with birds in a thicket of papyrus reeds surmounted by seven birds in flight separated in groups of three and four by a phoenix, or bennu bird. The horizontal rope is pulled by Horus with his falcon head, watched by the young pharaoh, while in the next panel, the horned Khnoum looks toward Thoth, master of numbers and measure, with his arms outstretched, indicating a fathom of 6 feet or 4 cubits. His proportion, said de Lubicz, indicates the essential numbers for a hexagon, the division of a cycle by six, and the means of translating curved into linear measure. This is no banal hunting scene, de Lubicz observed, but a symbolic one, tied to mythology. This is the location where Set was caught in a net by Horus. Sechat, standing by Toth, is described as the one who will conceive and raise the royal child, who, as Ra, will mount the throne of Horus. Here, said Schwaller, is a cabalistic scene which indicates the capture of an abstraction. He then proceeded to analyze the meaning of each single symbolic thread in the net.

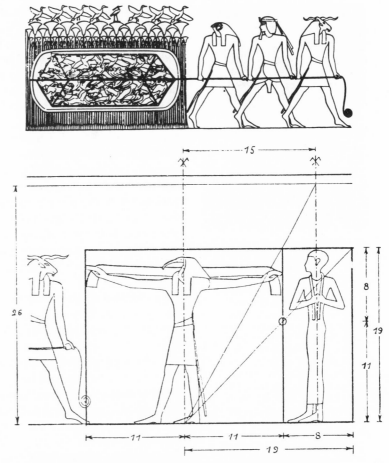

The advantage of the system of symbols over the phonetic, says de Lubicz, is that the meaning of symbols lasts indefinitely, from lifetime to lifetime; and the fundamental purpose of the initiatory texts is to convey the truth of resurrection and reincarnation. To anyone unconvinced of this truth, the glyphs, says he, will remain a dead letter. And not only did the glyphs have a cosmic meaning, they were further amplified by the sound attributed to them, which, when reverberated, could magically key in the past. The technique was rediscovered by L. Ron Hubbard in Dianetics, where the mere repetition of a key word can bring into focus in full three-dimensional color and sound a whole scene from the past, no matter how remote. The whole of history, the whole of the "akashik record," is available to man merely by tuning his consciousness, perhaps by reciting a mantra. For cerebral man is but a shadow of the cosmic creature—whether aboriginal or umbilically tied to the darkness of Nuit—whose will, under love, can make the universe magically manifest.

The mythology of ancient Egypt abounds in sexual tales. Rundle Clark says "it shows that the Egyptians lived much closer to the dark Powers of the unconscious than we realize." During a truce between Horus and Seth, they go off to rest. In the night Seth violates Horus. Horus runs to his mother, Isis, with Seth's seed in his hand. Isis cuts off her son's "contaminated" hand and throws it into the water. In revenge Isis obtains some of her son's semen and sprinkles it on a lettuce in Seth's garden. Seth (who eats nothing but lettuce) becomes pregnant with the seed of Horus. Before the judges Seth claims that Horus is unworthy of the royal office because he allowed Seth to bugger him. Anthony S. Mercatante has another version: "During the night Seth had an erection and thrust his penis between Horus's legs in an attempt to rape him. But Horus put his hands between his thighs, catching Seth's semen."

Horus avenges his father's death by stealing the seed of Set's testicles.

The gods of the Egyptians, called *neters,* phonetically related to nature, represented the powers of the cosmos—gravity, levity, magnetism, and light. They were concealed behind animal masks because, along the road of evolution, animals come to symbolize certain states of nature. And following the stages of life, as the principals took on different aspects, so did their names. Ptah, Sekhmet, and Nefertoum became Amon, Mut, and Khonsu in the human genesis. Ptah, says de Lubicz, a pure fire fallen to earth to be solidified as an obelisk in Memphis, became, in Amon, a water of lunar or solar fire. That which has been in Sekhmet a venusian water, becomes Mut, a lunar water, the former warm, the latter cold. It is necessary, says de Lubicz, to see in Amon a liquid coagulation substance, like the masculine sperm, and in Mut a substance liquid as well but susceptible of being coagulated by Amon.

Aor is the Egyptian word for "magic light," or electricity. It was the name de Lubicz received in the course of his own initiatory development. Aud or Od, also magic light, is the vibration of Set. Set and Horus, sometimes called Neter-wy, are "the two *neters,*" aspects of the universal light, one dark, material, fixed, contracted, satanic—Set; the other radiant, spiritual, penetrating, open—Horus. The paternal, constricting, styptic power of sperm, contracting, causes spirit to materialize. But spirit, says de Lubicz, fights to free itself by a counterreaction which is movement.

The biblical cabala speaks of a fallen archangel who brings with him the remembrance of the divine light, the chaos composed of Set, the mephitic Satan, and it speaks of Horus-Lucifer, who carries the light and causes it to reappear. This, says de Lubicz, is the same story which the pharaonic cabala describes as the struggle between Set and Horus—builders of the temple which is man. It is the eternal conflict in every creature who undergoes the contradictory attraction of the two powers: the horian, immutable light, and the sethian—atavisms attached to terrestrial form.

And Set and Horus are gravity and levity, aspects of the same fundamental energy. In Mesoamerica, Quetzalcoatl and Tezcatlipoca are depicted Januslike; one aspect dilates, the other contracts, and all of life is in the cyclical pulse between the two. This pulsation, this gravitational, levitational swing of the pendulum the Egyptians knew to be the heart of the matter, as their glyphs clearly show:

Among the unpublished papers of de Lubicz, written just before his death, is a monograph in which he shows how

Time

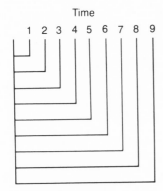

Side = time
Surface = the distance covered
These surfaces superimposed
one on the other form a stepped
pyramid. As the distance covered
increases by the square of the
time it does so at a constant
acceleration.

(from de Lubicz's notes)

Lucy Lamy's notes deciphering
the Egyptian understanding of
the fundamentals of physical science symbolized by the heart,
plumate, and obelisk

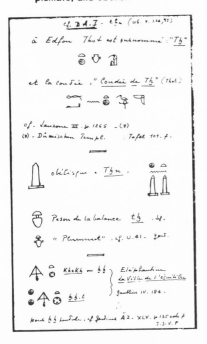

the Egyptian obelisk incorporates the formula for gravity, with a geometric acceleration which grows by squares. This was an idea already formulated in *The Lost Solar System Discovered,* a remarkable mathematical opus produced in the middle of the nineteenth century by an obscure but brilliant researcher, John Wilson, who pointed out that the sectional axis of the obelisk may be regarded as symbolic of time, velocity, and distance, or the generator of lines, areas, and solids. With his equations Wilson endeavored to establish that obelisks represent the laws of motion when a body falls near the surface of the earth, or when a planet revolves in orbit. By his analysis of the pyramidal and hyperbolic temples of the past, he interpreted the ancient theory of the laws of gravitation as the key to understanding the mechanics of celestial motion.

The obelisk, according to Wilson, was called "the finger of God" because it indicates the laws by which the universe is governed. ⊤ , said Wilson, is the symbol of time and distance as a body descends to earth. ⊥ is the symbol for velocity and distance. The *crux ansata,* or sacred Tau, ☦ , symbol of the divinity of Osiris, he interpreted as symbolic of time, velocity, and distance of a falling body which cannot descend beyond the surface of the attracting orb or sphere. "But this sacred type of the eternal laws," he said, "appears to have become more and more obscure as the days of science declined, till ultimately it ceased to be intelligible; when, instead of this spiritual symbol, a physical one, palpable to the senses and adapted to the capacity of the unlearned, was substituted, and so the Phallic worship became embodied and revered in the religious rites of Egypt, India, Greece and Rome."

That the pull of gravity is the same for all falling bodies, and that only the mass of a body varies according to its distance from the center of the earth, depending on latitude and height above sea level, was known to the Egyptians millennia before Galileo. And they also knew that the force of gravity for any locality can be obtained by the number of oscillations in a plumb bob within a certain time—the number of swings in a pendulum being the same no matter what its weight. What varies the effect is the length of the string.

Sir William Flinders Petrie, founder of the British School of Archaeology in Egypt, and promulgator of scientific archaeology, showed how the double remen, a diagonal of one of the many Egyptian cubits, that of 29.161 inches, is virtually the natural length of a pendulum which swings 100,000 times in twenty-four hours at the latitude on which

457

Memphis lies. "There would have been no difficulty to the Egyptians," says Petrie, "in developing the use of his familiar plumb-bob to find this result."

And Livio C. Stecchini, perhaps the greatest scholar of the science of measure, that primary discipline without which there can be no physics, suggested, before his death, that the size of the base of each obelisk may have been deliberately designed to indicate the height above sea level at which the obelisk was raised.

To ferret out the truth, more research is needed into pylon, pyramid, and obelisk; but these two great pioneers in Egyptological physics and metaphysics, de Lubicz and Stecchini, have indeed left their mark. In his unfinished book on the canonical Jesus, Stecchini points out that whereas Hebrew justice was based on the strictest law of giving fair measure, when the spirited Nazarene suggested giving back five in return for three or not rewarding the fellow who buried his talent, they quickly nailed him to a cross.

Isha de Lubicz described her husband's final moments on earth as his features became illumined by an ecstatic smile. "Reality," he said, "is not at all what one imagines. . . . One must look in silence, without wishing to see . . . and accept pure nothingness . . . for what man calls nothing, *that* is Real: Oh, we are so blind! Isha, I will show you. The worst impediment to illumination has been my mental being. I see its game now. It has been my enemy all my life. I did not believe it could be so fierce! I sensed it was an obstacle, but I did not recognize all its ruses, all the forms it could take to mislead me. It is terrifying, Isha. I wish you too could see it, so as to help others free themselves from fear; for it is the mental which creates fear and doubt. . . . What is real is outside time and beyond 'good and evil.' It is not what appears to the senses."

POSTSCRIPT

Just as I forewent a final caption to the phoenix, a young friend appeared on my doorstep fresh from Egypt, unaware of the content of this book, and, unsolicited, began to recount adventures in the Saqqara region with a clairaudient lady. For some time my friend has been studying Egyptian glyphs, hoping to reconstitute the original sounds of the ancient language.

It was the full moon of the vernal equinox. In a Saqqara tomb he found that his clairaudient friend could chant without understanding them the invocations to the Neters, or gods, appearing on the walls while my friend ad-libbed a translation. To their surprise they both felt a presence; forthwith the lady began to chant a stream of messages from what purported to be the ancient gods of Egypt, invoked by the sound of her voice. And what did they say? According to my friend, nothing more phenomenal than to express their pleasure that human beings had once more found the means of communicating with them for the welfare of the planet, and a preoccupied warning that we have become so out of touch with mother earth she may be on the point of spewing out the toxins with which we have poxed her body.

I did not press my friend, for he and the lady intend to publish the entire story of their contact, with all that was said and done. But it made me wonder about Dee and Crowley and company, and I thought again of Isha de Lubicz's statement that "to know a thing's real name is to know its power. And to pronounce it exactly is to free its

Was Crowley on the track? To some extent, without question. Though he may or may not have garbled the answer. Isha de Lubicz is more crystalline when she has her aspirant initiate Her-bak ask about the meaning of three Egyptian words: "I am looking for the relation between *za,* magic power, *sa,* back, and *saa,* Sage." To which his master answers: "The power *za* has nothing to do with the projection of thought or will, unless in a popular reading and by extension. This word gives the active power of the fire whose channel is the vertebral column . . . there are various centres of residence and radiation in our body. It may be Sethian fire, consuming, destructive, when it is constrained or switched to sex or brain. That is why the back is said to belong to Seth. But when this fire is subtilised it is vivifying, quickening. This is the true magic fire, triple in its nature, giver of life or death."

459

"Is it a power to be feared then!" exclaims Her-bak. "Is it in all men?"

"It is latent in them," answers his guru, "but few know how to make use of it wisely, very few how to master it. It reaches its perfection in him when a man, being quickened, radiates it without effort of his own, life a life-giving sun. Such a man is *saa*, a wise man, in whom the Horus-fire masters the Seth-fire and subjects it to his service. The same fire as yet unevolved gives the characteristics and signature of the personality *sa* or *za* and in its spermatic capacity it transmits paternal characters to the son *sa* or *za*."

Another modern guru, Gopi Kirshna, wants to put modern men of science onto the trail of kundalini, which he calls "the greatest mystery of creation still lying unsolved and even unattended before us . . . a force present in the human body that is drawing humankind toward a sublime state of consciousness inconceivable for even the most intelligent mind that has not experienced it." Gopi Krishna is convinced that man is evolving toward a state of awareness in which the reality behind the universe can become perceptible, if only the activity of the reproductive mechanism can be made to stream inward and upward. "This reversal," he says, "true for both men and women, causes an amazing transformation in the cerebro-spinal system, leading to an explosion of consciousness. . . . On the arousal of kundalini, the nectarean substance flows into the head [as radiant, living energy] and then circulates in the body."

As he describes the phenomenon, the reproductive system is employed as a transfer center, where the life-energies are transformed into an ever more volatile and radiant energy that streams upward into the brain. This transformation, he explains, is built on the copiously produced "ambrosia" of the reproductive mechanism, working day and night. "The ambrosia is the nectarlike reproductive secretion which, at the highest point of ecstasy, pours into the brain with such an intensely pleasurable sensation that even the sexual orgasm pales into insignificance before it. This unbelievably rapturous sensation—pervading the whole of the spinal cord, the organs of generation and the brain—is nature's incentive to the effort directed at self-transcendance, as the orgasm is the incentive to the reproductive act." Like Bruno, Gopi Krishna asks: "Is the creator, or God, of such limited intelligence that he should build man in such a way that the sexual urge is the most awful impulse in him, attended with such an intense pleasure, and then rule that he is not to touch it?" Of course not: the object of the process is to release the self-conscious mind of man more and more from "the thraldom of the subconscious, to enable it to touch levels of cognition which, in its present fettered condition, it can never reach."

During the course of a genuine mystical experience, says Gopi Krishna, a higher dimension of consciousness intervenes, eclipsing the normal individuality, partially or wholly, for a period. "It then seems as if a new world, a new order of existence, or superhuman being has descended into view. There is an unmistakable enhanced perception of lights, color, beauty, goodness, virtue, and harmony which lend to superworldly appearance to the whole experience."

How the transformation of the genes is effected through a rejuvenative activity of the reproductive system, or the arousal of the Serpent Power, how the seminal fluid in men is sent in a cascading stream of radiant energy to the brain, and in women in the form of hormones and secretions—a secret so closely guarded by adepts of the past—Gopi Krishna promises to reveal in detail as a solution the problems of mankind. Certainly the arbitrary imposition of intolerable dogma enforced by torture cannot but be the very last form of rational brotherly or loving government. Yet it is what we have had for two thousand years. As the Founding Fathers of this republic fully understood, the only way for humans of different religious persuasions to live peaceably together is to live under the common law and refuse to fight or impose in matters or religion. This is what the obelisk stands for on the mall in Washington, D.C.

And the self-appointed arbiters of morality may learn the difference between erotic, livening, enamoring, and generative sex on the one hand and the world of porno, which can only exist under restriction, for who would deliberately look upon the corrupt if, all around, the woods and fields were full of young Dianas and their hornéd lovers.

Crowley suggested that nine-tenths of social misery not due to poverty arises from the hallucination of personal jealousy and ill-regulated passion. "There shall be no property in human flesh," says Aiwaz in *The Book of the Law*. "Nobody has the right to say what anyone else shall or shall not do with his or her body." Establish this principle of absolute respect for others, says Crowley, and the whole nightmare of sex is dispelled. "Blackmail and prostitution automatically lose their *raison d'être*."

As for contraception, abortion, sexual stasis, overpopulation, and the wars that ensue, for some millennia the

461

Chinese Taoist and the Hindu Tantric have solved these problems by the practice of highly satisfactory sexual intercourse without ejaculation, not the gross Roman notion of *coitus interruptus* but the more salubrious *coitus ad infinitum,* satisfying sexually and emotionally to both men and women, leading to a mystic fusion of the two in one.

So let us be loving and free, and intrepid, and let us stop arming and killing. For Augustine warned, karma imposes that every sword thrust pierces its wielder. Let us return to the gospel of the canonical Jesus, let us gently turn Roma back into Amor.

BIBLIOGRAPHICAL NOTE

In the filed bibliography for this opus there are over a thousand titles, far too many to list, yet each of value in its way; and I must have consulted thrice that many. The masters on the subject of obelisks, Michele Mercati, Anathasius Kircher, Georg Zoega, Cesare d'Onofrio, and above all, Erik Iversen, are credited in the text wherever possible. Some authors, such as Serge Hutin, have written a score of books every one of which touches on some facet of the subject. Books on or about Aleister Crowley fill several shelves. To have listed every volume on every subject dealt with would be tedious to all but the rare scholar who could not find them for himself. Rather than burden publisher and reader with an endless list, I am, through the publisher, available at any time to answer any bibliographical question and indicate the whereabouts of any publication hard to find.

INDEX

"Then this most holy land, the seat of palaces consecrated to divinity, and of temples, shall be full of sepulchres and dead bodies. O, Egypt, Egypt, fables alone shall remain of thy religion, and these, such as will be incredible to posterity, and words alone shall be left engraved in stones, narrating thy pious deeds."—Hermes Trismegistus